FileMaker® Pro Business Applications

Arthur W. Evans

Wordware Publishing, Inc.

Library of Congress Cataloging-in-Publication Data

Evans, Arthur W.
   FileMaker Pro business applications / by Arthur W. Evans.
   p. cm.
   Includes index.
   ISBN-13: 978-1-59822-014-8
   ISBN-10: 1-59822-014-4 (pbk.)
   1. Business--Data processing. 2. FileMaker (Computer file).
   3. Business--Computer programs. 4. Database management. I. Title.
   HF5548.2.E82 2006
   005.75'65--dc22   2006011041

ISBN-13: 978-1-59822-014-8
ISBN-10: 1-59822-014-4

10 9 8 7 6 5 4 3 2 1
0607

Dedication

To Jo, Thomas, and Owen.

Contents

Contents

Contents

Preface

The Road Less Traveled — Are You Ready to Start Writing Your Own Business Applications with FileMaker?

People who have previously published a book tell me that getting it written is like a road journey. If this is true, then the road in question is the M6 motorway that runs between London with the English Lake District and a meeting I had with Jeremy Hall some 15 years ago.

Jeremy's father, Peter, was a Kiwi Spitfire pilot based in Britain during the Second World War*. After the war, Peter set up a joinery business to offer handcrafted custom furniture and restore antiques. Peter Hall and Son soon gained a reputation for quality furniture that would become heirlooms for any buyer. The British National Trust, a charity that looks after historic houses across the UK, heard of Peter Hall and Son's reputation and over recent years has entrusted the restoration of irreplaceable pieces of historic furniture to the firm. I will never forget arriving at Jeremy's workshop one morning to be presented with a steaming mug of coffee. I asked tentatively where I should put the coffee down so as to avoid leaving a ring stain on any items of valuable furniture. Jeremy pointed out that it might be best not to put a hot mug on the item immediately in front of me, as it was Wordsworth's writing desk!

Jeremy and the team at Peter Hall and Son are trusted by the nation's custodians to repair priceless furniture and by customers who commission pieces that will be treasured and enjoyed for generations. The firm, in turn, trusts FileMaker Pro to manage its enquiries, customers, quotations, orders, timesheets, and invoices. Like thousands of business owners across the globe, Jeremy has had little or no formal software programming training. Despite this, he has taught himself to use FileMaker Pro and build a database solution that matches the exact needs of his company. Business managers rarely do this for the challenge alone of mastering a new software application. It is simply the case that an "off-the-shelf" software application will so rarely fit the specific criteria or "wish list" that a business owner requires. This book is designed to help you, as a business owner or workgroup manager, customize FileMaker to help you manage and report on your information.

I would like to thank Jeremy and dozens of other business owners whom I have had the pleasure to work with over the years for reminding me that nobody knows your business better than you do, and that FileMaker is in a class of its own for helping you run it. This book is designed to give you some guidance and pointers for writing business applications with FileMaker Pro and to get you started. You may find yourself bitten by the FileMaker bug. There are a lot of FileMaker users and professional developers out there who are nothing short of evangelists about what you can do with FileMaker. Appendix B includes some useful information about getting more advice on FileMaker and joining the FileMaker Solutions Alliance.

* Did you know that most of the reflective gun sights used in Spitfires during the Battle of Britain were manufactured in…Austria? The British Air Ministry's principal supplier went bust in 1938 and a firm in Austria was proud to win the contract. A good client and orders database can help you highlight the business you do want, and sometimes the business you don't!

Acknowledgments

There are many people who have both inspired and actively encouraged me to write this book. I would like to thank the many colleagues and clients with whom I have had the opportunity to work on FileMaker projects over the past 16 years. I am especially grateful to Jeremy Hall, Richard Nissen, and Anthony Nissen.

Keith Harris, vice president of FileMaker, and his European team have done a terrific job of making FileMaker a global software brand. Tony Speakman, Neil Wright, Jim Kinloch, Tim Poole, Wendy Channing, and all in the UK office provide a great service to FileMaker Solutions Alliance members. No other software developer association enjoys such a productive and beneficial relationship with the product's manufacturer.

At the FileMaker head office, Delfina Daves, Kevin Mallon, Jay Welshofer, and Rick Kalman have been extremely helpful over the past few months in keeping me up to date with FileMaker product developments and the launch of FileMaker Pro 8, to help me tie in this book to the latest version of the application.

I am indebted to Tim McEvoy, Wes Beckwith, Martha McCuller, and the team at Wordware Publishing for giving me the opportunity to write this book. I would also like to thank Beth Kohler and her editorial colleagues for all their help and guidance.

Finally, my family deserves a special thank you for enabling me to take the time to work on this project.

Introduction

If you run your own business or manage a workgroup, welcome to a FileMaker book with a difference. This one has been written for you!

Most FileMaker textbooks are written for established or aspiring software professionals with the primary purpose of improving the reader's technical knowledge of FileMaker. Many do an excellent job of teaching the reader to become a more professional developer.

This book aims to be different. It is designed to demystify FileMaker Pro, enabling you to customize your own software for your specific requirements. The end result will be a custom database solution, written in FileMaker, that addresses 100% of your data management needs.

Is This Book for You?

A key element for businesses to thrive or simply survive in an increasingly competitive market is the initial capture, querying, and reporting of information, and the management of this data. Ever heard of "knowledge management" or "data mining" in the course of your work? Surprisingly perhaps, and contrary to popular opinion, knowledge isn't power. However, the ability to make a good business decision with that knowledge can be.

How do you manage your information? Do you find yourself repeatedly writing out a customer or supplier name and address at the top of invoices or purchase orders? Are you unable to rapidly retrieve the last price charged by a supplier for a particular product or service in order to get the best price for a repeat order? Do you know your gross profit on your last job, or your most and least profitable business activities? Do you know how many hours your team really spent on a particular project, in order to quote realistically for the work next time around? If you are unable to get answers to questions like these and you think this information would be useful to improve the management of your business, then read on.

How can the owner of a small business, often with a limited budget and resources, add value to critical business information? Traditionally, the high cost of developing, testing, installing, training, and fixing customized software has restricted the implementation of custom business systems to the realm of large government departments or corporations. Cost aside, the small business owner may be further turned off by the idea of custom software because of frequent media stories of how yet another major government IT project has failed to deliver on expectations, often despite exceeding budgets and timescales.

Nobody knows your business better than you!

Imagine yourself sitting down with a professional software developer in your office or place of work. Your task is to explain your business model and how you would like a software package to complement your workflow and add value to your business. You may have previously done this, or you may have direct experience of using commissioned software, by preference or unwittingly, that resulted from such an initial meeting.

The success of such a meeting would be linked to the skill of the IT developer in picking up the specific nuances of your business workflow, coupled with your own skill in explaining what is unique about your business and your specific requirements. Could you be sure the project specification brief matches your actual needs?

You might be a business start-up or have many years of experience behind you. Either way, when it comes to introducing custom software into your business, you already understand your business needs. In which case, you have already done the hard bit!

This book will show you how FileMaker can be adapted for your specific database requirements.

Why FileMaker Pro?

Do you already have a software application installed on your computer that enables you to construct a database? On the Windows platform, Microsoft Office Professional 2003 includes the Access database application. However, many professional developers have commented that a FileMaker Pro solution can be developed within a third of the time needed for a comparable Access database. In contrast to Access, which expects you to know a lot more about the theory of database design, FileMaker lets you design powerful databases with no prior programming experience.

FileMaker is estimated to have over 85% of the Macintosh database market. If you work in a mixed platform office, with colleagues using Windows and Macintosh computers (commonly the case in design and media sector offices), a database written in FileMaker can be shared across both platforms.

At the time of publication, more than 10 million units of FileMaker have been sold to customers worldwide. Nearly half of all FileMaker users are based in companies with a head count of 10 or less. But don't assume FileMaker is simply a product for small business! More than 70 of the Fortune 100 companies in the U.S. use FileMaker, as do many nonprofit organizations and government departments. Impressively, more than 4,000 government agencies and institutions in the U.S. alone use FileMaker to manage their information.

Databases written with FileMaker can be deployed with FileMaker Server, enabling as many as 250 colleagues to work with the same records, or, with FileMaker Server Advanced, publish the database to the web. Do you need to manage information out of the office? FileMaker Mobile is a companion version of FileMaker designed specifically for Palm OS and Pocket PC handhelds. The FileMaker product family is described in more detail in Chapter 2.

Why FileMaker Is Right for Your Business

The use of a database to add value to business information is still a new concept to many managers. There can be few business decision makers left who are not familiar with the concept of a spreadsheet, with a series of columns containing the titles of items and several rows going down the page containing values for those items. The first thing that most of us learn to do with a spreadsheet is add up a row of numbers to get a total, whether it is for items on an invoice, total timesheet entries for a task, or (for anyone who manages sales staff) expense items.

So how do you replicate the complex flow of information within a business in a spreadsheet? Many small businesses want to keep track of prospects or targets, clients and customers who have bought goods and services, invoices, and purchase orders for goods and services. A well-designed database will be able to answer a manager's questions. These questions might include justifying the cost of an advertisement in terms of new business leads generated, the time it takes to convert a prospect to a successful sale, or the gross profit generated on an invoice line item. FileMaker Pro is an ideal application to capture, store, and report on these types of business activities.

FileMaker Pro may be new to you, or you may have come across a previous version of the product in the past. The application is now over 20 years old. This book assumes no prior knowledge of FileMaker Pro or database design. FileMaker is designed to make you productive and add value to your business information in a remarkably short time period.

Custom Software — Why Do It Yourself?

I am frequently asked by FileMaker end users why, for an application that is so easy to adapt and customize, there is such a thriving and successful worldwide commercial developer community that charges fees to customize the product.

You should expect a skilled professional FileMaker developer, particularly those who are members of the FileMaker Solutions Alliance (see

Appendix B, "FileMaker Resources"), to be able to customize FileMaker to meet your exact business requirements. The ingenuity of top FileMaker developers with many years of experience is amazing, and a phrase often heard at the annual FileMaker Developer Conference is, "If you can't do it in FileMaker, it's not worth doing."

However, these developers are using the same copy of FileMaker Pro that is available to you in most computer stores. The many shortcuts and workarounds in a professional developer's toolkit are only worth knowing if they can make the job of managing your business information easier. The developer may be able to apply the tips and tricks learned from many previous projects to solve a commissioning client's software "wish list." However, with your inherent knowledge of your business issues, you should be able to build a FileMaker database that is just as effective in addressing your needs.

Do you still think that the concept of writing your own custom software is a daunting one? Are you considering seeking professional development or training from a certified FileMaker professional? If this is the case, this book should still be of benefit to you in understanding the methods employed to build a FileMaker solution and help you "speak the same language" as a professional developer.

Remember, most professional developers will have speed and rapid development to offer. You have the advantage of knowing your business operation. This book will show you how to customize FileMaker so that your data flow can match your workflow.

The improved information management benefits of introducing FileMaker into your business is, for many managers, only the first step. I would advise anyone who implements FileMaker Pro in their workplace to consider joining the FileMaker Solutions Alliance (see Appendix B) to keep their FileMaker skills up to date and share ideas and good database practices among an enthusiastic peer group.

How This Book Is Organized

This book is divided into three parts. Part I provides an introduction to the FileMaker range of products, the nature of a relational database, and how FileMaker is used to construct a customized software solution. Part II demonstrates applied FileMaker projects for a wide variety of businesses. You might like to start with a case study that is close to your own data management requirements. Each project case study uses different features available in FileMaker Pro 8, and hopefully you will find many of the techniques useful in planning your own database solution. Once you have built your own business management database, read the chapters in Part III, which discuss how you can best deploy FileMaker in your workplace for colleagues to use. Other ways of sharing business data, by publishing your database to the web and exchanging information with other software applications, are detailed.

While, with the possible exception of some franchise operations, no two businesses are the same, the methods by which successful firms manage critical business information do have certain common themes. The furniture craftsman restoring Wordsworth's writing desk for the National Trust will want to compare the price of the wood and labor costs. The same calculation is performed by the kitchen cabinetmaker. I am grateful for the experience of working with many business owners to deploy FileMaker in a variety of commercial sectors, and have grouped the most successful methods by which FileMaker is deployed in business into distinct project areas in Part II of this book, "FileMaker Project Case Studies."

Good ideas in business usually spread and, for most database deployments, a frequent request is for more colleagues to have access to information across a network. In Part III, "Deploying Your Business Solution," examples demonstrate how a FileMaker file can be shared across a network or with other common business software applications, and published to the web.

The three parts are described in more detail below.

Part I — Getting Started with FileMaker Pro

This part of the book introduces the FileMaker Pro application and develops the concept of good database design for business. A set of FileMaker templates, which are included with FileMaker Pro 8, are copied into the FileMaker folder with the default product installation. Some examples of these templates are described in outline and used as a starting point to demonstrate how a relational database is put together in FileMaker. The standard templates are then used as a launching point to present how FileMaker can be customized to match specific business database requirements. Key to building a successful solution for your own business is an understanding of FileMaker's calculation fields, ScriptMaker steps, and relational database structures. These powerful FileMaker features are introduced as a framework to assist you in planning and building your own database.

Part II — FileMaker Project Case Studies

The FileMaker techniques presented in Part I are then applied to build a series of distinct database projects that have common themes for many business practices. Contact and communication management is central to most business managers. The steps needed to build a comprehensive customer relationship management (CRM) solution are presented. The project template can be further adapted by the reader to address specific CRM requirements, in preference to an off-the-shelf CRM package that rarely meets all the user's requirements.

Most businesses have to account for staff time. A timesheet solution is presented that reports on the time spent by staff on client-specific projects and tasks.

With its cross-platform capabilities and ability to match workflow forms for data input layouts, FileMaker enjoys a huge customer base in the creative and news media business sectors. Three job and workflow management case studies are presented that address broadcast or advertisement scheduling, print and production, and quotation management for small businesses.

For manufacturing businesses with production procedures, a dynamic stock control solution is presented that can be easily customized. FileMaker's ability to update information in related files is used to show how stock item levels change with new purchase inputs and sales outputs.

FileMaker is an excellent resource for training record management. FileMaker's capability for managing education and commercial events is discussed in a case study. While no two events or delegates are the same, a relational database can be used to manage bookings and invoices.

An asset and facilities management system is developed to indicate how FileMaker can tackle a huge variety of scales in reporting on building costs and equipment management.

Many publishing houses and magazine offices use FileMaker to manage subscriptions and distribution. A subscription management example database is introduced in one of the case studies.

The database needs of a professional practice are described with examples of patient management for physicians and for vets. A private health clinic practice is built, using standard codes for procedures, treatment, and billing. A veterinary practice management system is developed to show how an invoicing system with multiple sales tax rates is handled by FileMaker.

Part III — Deploying Your Business Solution

The FileMaker design techniques developed in Part II should help you to design a database for your own business. Once a solution has been successfully built, colleagues will wish to make use of the system over the local network, using mobile devices, and via the web. The methods by which the FileMaker product family can accommodate all these user requirements is detailed.

FileMaker is an excellent companion product to most common business software, and examples are given for exchanging information with other business applications and enterprise-level database systems.

Appendices

Finally, the appendices include a list of FileMaker resources along with a description of a FileMaker Pro 8.5 feature that can be used to enhance your database. The Web Viewer control enables you to add a dynamic Web Viewer window within a FileMaker layout.

If you haven't done so already, now would be a great time to install FileMaker Pro on your computer! Let's get started.

Getting Started with FileMaker Pro

Chapter 1

An Introduction to Database Software

In this chapter:

- What Is a Database?
- FileMaker and Database Terminology
- FileMaker and Other Types of Databases

What Is a Database?

The word "database" is often used in business but rarely defined. For the purposes of this book, a *database* is considered to be a collection of data that is stored in an orderly manner to assist the user with recording, finding, and reporting on information. An orderly manner is considered to be a consistent pattern. If you wish to record and store customer records, you would expect to put names and telephone numbers in the same place for each record. If you were planning a sales trip to California, a database that holds business card information in a standard format would make it easy for you to find and retrieve prospects and customers in San Francisco or Los Angeles, or with any address that contains a California zip code. The need for consistency in how business contacts are stored is the same for a paper-based system, where business contacts might be transferred to a card index system or, as will be explored in this book, in a computer database.

We can make a distinction at the outset between database applications, such as FileMaker, Access, Goldmine, or ACT, which are software packages used to store, retrieve, and manipulate data, and the database itself, which is the collection of data.

In business we use, and are used (or misused) by, databases daily. When you use a business telephone directory or call operator assistance you are querying a database, or asking an operator to query it for you, to find a specific product or service provider.

The trade directories in which you might list your business or the web search engine hits on your website are examples of how others will use a database to find you.

The supermarket giants have spent millions commissioning heavyweight database projects to find out more about us and our consumer habits. A club card or loyalty points system is simply a great way of finding out where we shop, at what time, and what we buy when our card is swiped at the checkout.

With an easy-to-use database like FileMaker, a custom database designed to target prospects, identify sales patterns, calculate the gross profit on an order, or a hundred other useful ways of adding value to your business data is no longer the preserve of big companies. You can build your own business databases. The purpose of this book is to show you how.

FileMaker and Database Terminology

A brief overview of common database terminology is useful to help describe a database in more detail.

To begin creating databases with FileMaker Pro, you need to install the application on your computer. When you create a database with FileMaker Pro, you create a new file, in just the same way that you create a new file in Microsoft Word or Excel. In order to store and retrieve data in a FileMaker file we need to create a *table*. A table is made up of a set of named *fields* that hold data. Each individual or item in a set can be added to the database as a single *record*. A spreadsheet provides a good analogy for each of these terms. We can think of each worksheet in a spreadsheet file as being equivalent to a table. Each column is equivalent to a field. If the column has a title cell at the top of the worksheet, that is exactly the same as the field name. Each row in a worksheet is equivalent to an individual record. You can import data directly from an Excel worksheet into FileMaker, and records are created in exactly this format. Column headings are turned into field names, and each row becomes a new record in the selected destination table.

Professional database designers may use the words *entity* to describe an item that has its own table, such as a contact, and *attribute* to describe any field in that table, such as "surname."

A big departure from earlier versions of FileMaker, since the introduction of FileMaker Pro 7 and now 8, is the ability to add more than one table to a FileMaker Pro file. This means that fields and record sets are associated with a specific table within a database file. It is relatively straightforward to link, or join, records in one table with records in another, if both sets of records have at least one field in common with the same value. This is how *relationships* between tables can be created, converting a *flat file* solitary table into a *relational database*.

Records for each table are displayed by FileMaker in a *layout*. The database designer can decide what fields should be displayed in a layout. FileMaker includes a Status area to assist the user in determining what records from which table are currently being viewed on the screen.

With all these analogies to Microsoft Excel, you might be wondering what the benefit of adding business data into a FileMaker file is in the first place. Why not stick with a spreadsheet?

Business data held in a spreadsheet can often seem cluttered, where all fields that describe an individual record are usually on display in a worksheet as columns, and all records in a set are always visible as rows. With FileMaker, to improve the clarity of displaying records, layouts can be easily customized to avoid clutter and only show selected fields for a record. While FileMaker's built-in Status area clearly indicates the number of records that fit a search criteria as a found set, the total set of records in a table is always visible.

FileMaker is a database application that enables you to easily search records by their field contents. A particular record or group of records in a database can be found by switching from Browse mode to Find mode. This can be done using the same layout that is used to type records into the database, so the records and the way in which they are queried on screen will look reassuringly familiar to new or inexperienced users of FileMaker. Novice database users can carry out advanced searches of records in a table without the need to build or learn a complex query form to interrogate the data, unlike other Windows or Mac database applications.

FileMaker and Other Types of Databases

We have already mentioned how easily FileMaker can import records from Excel. It is also possible to export records from FileMaker into several common database formats. You may be considering purchasing commercial prospect database lists such as Standard and Poor in the U.S. or Dunn and Bradstreet in the UK. Importing these lists can easily be done if you have the correct fields already defined in your tables to capture the data. If you are planning on publishing information to the web or to an InDesign or Quark document, or providing information to an external fulfillment house, this is all possible using FileMaker's built-in Export Records feature. Incidentally, FileMaker works seamlessly with Microsoft Office for creating customer mail merge letters in Word or sales charts in Excel.

FileMaker Pro 8 can work with enterprise-level database systems such as Structured Query Language (SQL). FileMaker also supports Open Database Connectivity (ODBC), which means it can query other data systems and respond to queries from them.

FileMaker can serve as a back-end database to a website and exchange information with XML web services. You can use FileMaker's built-in Instant Web Publishing features to share database records via the web.

With its built-in data exchange features, if you are running a growing small business or managing a workgroup with increasing data management requirements, FileMaker has the capacity to grow with you.

Chapter 2

The FileMaker Product Family

In this chapter:

- The FileMaker Pro 8 Product Lineup
  - FileMaker Pro 8
  - FileMaker Pro 8 Advanced
  - FileMaker Server 8
  - FileMaker Server 8 Advanced
  - FileMaker Mobile 8
- FileMaker Product Limitations
- Need a Copy of FileMaker to Work with This Book?

The FileMaker Pro 8 Product Lineup

With over 10 million units shipped worldwide at the time of publication, FileMaker Pro is the world's best-selling easy-to-use database. FileMaker Pro 8 is not simply a single product; the database application actually consists of five different products that are designed for specific purposes.

FileMaker Pro 8

FileMaker Pro 8 is the standard application version of FileMaker. FileMaker Pro 8 can be used to design new database files. It can be used to open a file and act as the host for this file, which can be shared by up to four other networked client users (each with their own installed copy of FileMaker). FileMaker Pro 8 can also open and work with database files that are remote, or hosted on other computers, acting as a client user. FileMaker can also publish up to ten database files for five simultaneous users to a web page using the Instant Web Publishing feature. FileMaker Pro 8 enables you to easily export records as PDF documents or Excel files.

FileMaker Pro 8 Advanced

In addition to all of the features and functionality available in FileMaker Pro 8, FileMaker Advanced includes several development and customization tools. With FileMaker Advanced you can customize menus and add tooltips to your databases, which can assist users. Database scripts can be debugged, and complex reports on a file can be generated using the built-in Database Design report. A set of utilities is included that allow you to create a run-time database solution with FileMaker that can be opened by a single user without needing a copy of FileMaker Pro. Custom functions can also be added to a database file.

While this book concentrates on the features of FileMaker Pro 8 for building business applications, if you "get the bug" for developing solutions in FileMaker and find yourself writing ever more complex databases, there are some great benefits to purchasing a copy of FileMaker Pro 8 Advanced.

FileMaker Server 8

FileMaker Server is a specialized application specifically designed to host up to 125 FileMaker Pro database files for a maximum of 250 simultaneous client connections. The Server software can automate backup schedules for database files, provide a log file of client usage, disconnect idle users if required to maximize the number of clients for a file, and manage application plug-in updates.

FileMaker Server 8 makes shared databases run faster by increasing the performance of operations and taking advantage of server hardware and software components.

These include performing searches and calculations on the server instead of the client, making use of high-performance hard disk storage or multiple CPU servers, and exploiting available server RAM using sophisticated memory caching.

FileMaker Server 8 Advanced

FileMaker Server 8 Advanced has all the features of Server, and can also host Structured Query Language (SQL) Open Database Connectivity/Java Database Connectivity (ODBC/JDBC) connections to files and web client connections, up to an additional maximum of 100 clients. Server 8 Advanced also supports Extensible Markup Language (XML) to provide Custom Web Publishing solutions for a FileMaker database. The methods for publishing FileMaker databases to the web using Custom Web Publishing are not covered in this book, but it is worth noting that FileMaker software is scalable to do this when the need arises.

If you use FileMaker Server and find yourself needing the enhanced connectivity features of FileMaker Server 8 Advanced for your database deployment, you can purchase an option pack that can enhance your existing FileMaker Server 8 installation to Server 8 Advanced. The cost of purchasing Server 8 and later adding the option pack is equivalent to the cost of FileMaker Server 8 Advanced.

FileMaker Mobile 8

FileMaker Mobile is a stripped-down version of the application that is designed to run on Palm and Pocket PC personal digital assistants (PDAs). FileMaker Mobile can extract records from a FileMaker database for reference or for editing and updating on a PDA, and the modified set of records can be synchronized with the record set in the original database file. With FileMaker Mobile you can view, search, sort, add, edit, and delete information on your handheld in an intuitive interface. You can also edit existing records or create new records in FileMaker Mobile using a barcode wand linked to the PDA.

FileMaker Product Limitations

FileMaker as a product has evolved significantly since it was first made available on the Windows operating platform in 1992. Back then, the size limitation of a FileMaker Pro 2 database was 32 MB of data. Images and QuickTime movies had to be stored within container fields, as opposed to storing a reference to the file, so any multimedia work with FileMaker was limited. Storage of a national data set, such as the U.S. Zip Code file or the Postcode Address file for the UK, was previously beyond FileMaker's record storage capabilities.

Since FileMaker Pro 8 now has an 8 terabyte file size limit, restrictions on database record numbers is likely to be imposed by the available computer storage and memory capacity before FileMaker reaches its application limits.

The design limitations of a FileMaker Pro 8 database and FileMaker Server 8 are detailed in Table 2.1.

Table 2.1: FileMaker Pro 8 database and Server limitations

Feature	Limitation
Number of tables per file	1,000,000
Maximum file size	8 terabytes
Maximum amount of data in a text field	2 gigabytes
Maximum amount of data in a number field	Up to 800 digits, or other characters, and the negative values of the same range. Index is based on the first 400 significant digits. Number fields can also contain Boolean values, to indicate true, false, yes, and no. Number fields cannot contain carriage returns.
Maximum number of files that can be opened by a client	Limited by computer memory
Maximum records in a file	64 quadrillion over the lifetime of the file
Maximum amount of data in a container field	4 gigabytes
Maximum number of fields in a table	256 million over the lifetime of the file
Number of FileMaker clients supported by FileMaker Server	250
Number of web clients supported by FileMaker Server Advanced	100

Need a Copy of FileMaker to Work with This Book?

The case studies explored in this book can all be opened with FileMaker Pro 8 and FileMaker Pro 8 Advanced. If you have not yet purchased a copy of FileMaker and you would like to see if the case studies described in this book could help your business, download an evaluation version of FileMaker Pro 8 from the company's website at www.filemaker.com. If you register your company details with FileMaker, you will be able to download a full copy of FileMaker that will work for 30 days from the installation date. In addition to English, trial copies of FileMaker Pro 8 are available in French, German, Italian, Spanish, Dutch, and Swedish.

Chapter 3

Using FileMaker Pro 8

In this chapter:

- Installing FileMaker Pro 8
- The FileMaker Pro Contact Management Template
- FileMaker's Application Interface
- FileMaker's Four Modes
- Browsing Database Records
- Adding Records to the Database
- Finding Database Records
- Customizing Views in Layout Mode
- Checking Printouts and Reports with Preview Mode
- Using Sort to Change the Order in which Records Appear in a File
- The Next Step

Installing FileMaker Pro 8

FileMaker Pro has its own distinctive user interface which, although intuitive and easy to use, can be unfamiliar to both users of previous database applications and new users.

The best way to get to know how FileMaker manages a database on screen is to open and work with one of the standard database starter solutions that ship with FileMaker Pro 8. This book is designed to give you the skills to start designing your own business database applications; however, the database templates that come with FileMaker Pro and are installed in the FileMaker application folder as part of a standard software installation are a great source for design ideas and techniques.

If you have not already done so, you need to install FileMaker Pro 8 on your computer. If you choose a standard installation of FileMaker, a set of FileMaker starter solutions will be installed within the subdirectory C:\Program Files\FileMaker\FileMaker Pro 8\English Extras\Templates.

The minimum hardware and operating system requirements to run FileMaker are shown in Table 3.1.

Table 3.1: System requirements for FileMaker Pro 8

Operating System	Requirements
Macintosh	Macintosh computer with a PowerPC G3, G4, or G5 processor 256 MB of RAM CD-ROM drive and hard disk drive Mac OS X 10.3.9 or 10.4
Windows	Pentium III 500 MHz or higher 256 MB of RAM CD-ROM drive and hard disk drive SVGA (800 x 600) or higher resolution video adapter and display Windows 2000 (Service Pack 4) or Windows XP (Service Pack 2)

The FileMaker Pro Contact Management Template

To become familiar with how a simple FileMaker database looks on screen, we are going to start by working with one of the FileMaker starter solutions. We first need to create our own copy of the Contact Management starter solution that ships with FileMaker Pro 8.

With a standard installation, FileMaker includes a list of database templates that are referenced in a drop-down list within the New Database dialog box. This is shown in Figure 3.1.

Figure 3.1:
The New Database dialog box contains a drop-down list of database templates categorized into Business, Education, and Home categories.

If you don't see this dialog box after you have launched FileMaker Pro from the Start menu or by clicking on a shortcut icon, you need to change a preference setting in FileMaker. If you see the dialog box titled Open New or Existing File, as shown in Figure 3.2, when you first launch FileMaker or when you choose the menu option File>New Database, you need to make a change in FileMaker's Preferences dialog box.

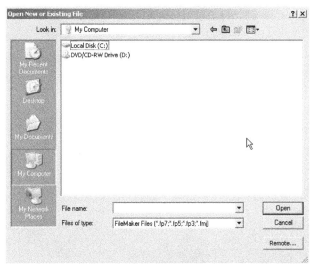

Figure 3.2:
The Open New or Existing File dialog box.

1. Click the **Cancel** button and select the menu option **Edit>Preferences**.

2. Click the **Show templates in New Database dialog box** check box, as shown in Figure 3.3.

Figure 3.3:
Setting FileMaker's preferences to "Show templates in New Database dialog box."

3.   Click the **OK** button and now, when you select the **File>New Database** menu option, the New Database dialog box should appear, as shown in Figure 3.1.

4.   Select the **Business - People & Assets** category from the drop-down list. A sub-category list should appear that includes a database called Contact Management.

5.   Highlight **Contact Management** and click **OK**. The Create a copy named dialog box will appear, as shown in Figure 3.4.

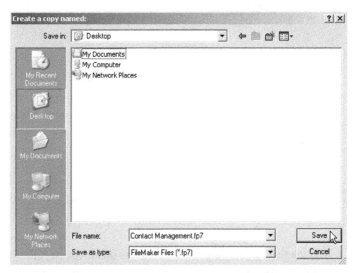

Figure 3.4: Choosing where to save a new FileMaker file in the Create a copy named dialog box.

You need to decide where to save the new FileMaker file on your computer. The database file is about to be saved to the desktop in the example shown in Figure 3.4.

6.   Click the **Save** button, and the Contact Management file should appear as shown in Figure 3.5.

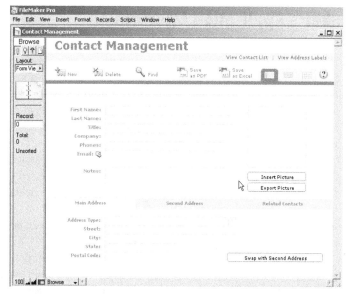

Figure 3.5: The Contact Management starter solution waiting to have records added to it.

When you start to create your own FileMaker database files, the application will automatically create the new first record for you. This is not the case for copies of the starter solutions. This can be the source of some confusion initially, as the dialog box shown in Figure 3.6 will appear if you click within the active FileMaker window.

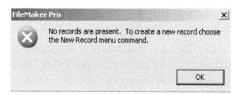

Figure 3.6:
A dialog box will prompt the user if no records are present in a FileMaker file.

To prevent this dialog box from reappearing, we can create a new blank record at the outset.

7.   Click once on the **New** icon (with a green cross), and a new record will be created in the file and a flashing cursor will appear in the First Name field.

FileMaker has created a new blank record and is now waiting for us to start typing in contact information, starting with the first name. Now is a good time to introduce FileMaker's unique application interface.

FileMaker's Application Interface

Database files created with FileMaker contain not only information in the form of records and fields to describe those records, but also a visual method for displaying those records, adding new records or modifying existing data, and creating reports on records. This is all done by using layouts, which form the basis of how records are displayed on screen and printed on reports, labels, letters, or PDF documents.

A FileMaker file combines record information with a series of layouts that are used to display a chosen set of records, with a selected group of fields, in a particular design. The three levels of options — what records to select, what fields within those selected records to display on screen, and how the screen should look based on the underlying layout — can be easily determined by you, wearing your database developer hat.

Let's start by examining how the Contact Management database file is presented on screen in the FileMaker window. A gray border can be seen running down the left side of the screen; this is known as the Status area. A Book icon can be seen in the Status area. The rest of the screen to the right of the Status area is used to display a single contact record, which of course is blank at this stage. The look of this screen has been determined by the design of the underlying layout. We will be discussing layout design shortly.

FileMaker's Four Modes

We work with a FileMaker file by switching between four modes: Browse, Find, Layout, and Preview. Provided that we are authorized to do so by the database designer (database security and access privileges will be discussed in Chapter 24), we can toggle between any of the four modes using the Mode icons at the top of the Status area, as shown in Figure 3.7. The yellow pencil identifies the Browse mode button, the magnifying glass is the Find mode button, the T-square is the Layout mode button, and the folded page is the Preview mode button.

Browse mode is used to display information held in fields for each record in the database. We need to be in Browse mode to view and edit the contents of fields, add new records, or delete existing records in a file. Find mode is used to carry out searches for a single entry or set of records held in a file, based on the search criteria used. Layout mode is used to determine how record information will appear on the screen or when printed. Preview mode is similar to Print Preview for Word and Excel, and is used to view how the printed record set would look, based on the selected printer settings.

Figure 3.7:
The four mode buttons in the FileMaker Status area.

When you are working with a FileMaker file, you can switch between modes by clicking the mode buttons, by selecting any of the first four menu options in the View menu, as shown in Figure 3.8, or by using the Mode pop-up menu at the bottom-left of the application window, as shown in Figure 3.9.

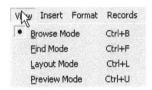

Figure 3.8:
Modes can be selected from the View menu.

Figure 3.9:
You can also switch between modes using the pop-up menu at the bottom of the application window.

Browsing Database Records

Figure 3.10:
FileMaker's Status area in Browse mode.

FileMaker Pro defaults to Browse mode when a file is first opened. In Browse mode, the Status area shows the title of the layout that is on the screen. In Figure 3.10, the Book icon indicates that we are currently viewing the first record in a set since the left arrow on the left-hand page of the book is ghosted. The arrow on the right-hand page of the book is solid, indicating that we can click on this page to view the next record. We can also click and drag the button on the slider below the Book icon to move between records. Below the slider, the currently viewed record and the total number of records in the underlying database table are also displayed. We can type a specific record number in the Record box, immediately below the Book icon, and when the Enter key is pressed on the keyboard, we will jump to the selected record. The word Unsorted displayed in the Status area signifies that the records have not been sorted by FileMaker based on the contents of any fields.

We are currently viewing records on the screen using the Form view layout. You can switch between layouts by using the Layout pop-up menu, which is above the Book icon in the Status area. If you click on the right arrow button, a list of available layouts in the file appears, as shown in Figure 3.11. Note that it is possible to hide layouts and prevent them from appearing in this list, which will be discussed when we begin to design our own layouts in Chapter 6. The check mark, as shown in Figure 3.11, indicates the current layout that is being used to view records in the file.

✔ Form View
  List View
  Table View
  Information Layout
  List Report
  Avery 5160

Figure 3.11:
The Layout
pop-up menu.

In Browse mode we can move between records using the Book icon and view information in different ways by moving between layouts using the Layout pop-up menu.

We can navigate within a record on screen by using the mouse to click into a field. It is often easier to use the Tab key on the keyboard to move one field forward, and use Shift+Tab to move back to the previous field. The database designer can decide whether to allow a user to access a field in either Browse or Find mode.

Adding Records to the Database

Before we get into searching and printing records, now would be a good time to type in some business contact records into the Contact Management database. Type in your own business card information, as well as information for one or two colleagues, or you can add some records for your clients or suppliers. Remember to click on the button marked New to add a new record each time, or you can use the keyboard shortcut Ctrl+N or select the menu option Records>New Record.

As you type in contact details, you will notice that the cursor changes to a flashing I-beam at the start of each field rectangle, ready for you to type in information. When you tab to the first address field, which is labeled Address Type, you may notice an arrow at the right-hand side of the field, which signifies that the field has a drop-down list, as shown in Figure 3.12. The database designer has created a list of possible address types along with the option to add additional types or change the values with the Edit... option. FileMaker has four methods for displaying value lists in a field to assist the user in accurate data entry: a drop-down list, a pop-up menu, a check box set, and a radio button set. Each of these will be examined in Chapter 6, when we describe layout design in detail.

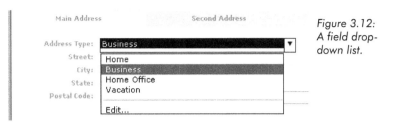

Figure 3.12:
A field drop-
down list.

When you have typed in a few records, you may want to see how the records
are displayed in other layouts, such as List view or Table view, by selecting
these layouts from the pop-up Layout menu. You may also notice that the layouts include tab buttons at the top of the screen, as shown in Figure 3.13, to
assist you in switching between Form, List, and Table views.

Figure 3.13:
Tab buttons can be used to
switch between layout views.

You may also have noticed three tab controls in the address area of the Form
view layout, titled Main Address, Second Address, and Related Contacts. Tab
controls, which are new to FileMaker Pro 8, can be used to add additional
fields to the same layout without overcrowding the record display in Browse
mode.

FileMaker automatically saves the new records that we have added to the
Contact Management file.

We are now ready to examine how FileMaker helps us to search for
records in a database.

Finding Database Records

Any FileMaker database is a collection of records. While often you will want
to browse through all the records on screen at the same time, FileMaker
makes it very easy to find a specific record or a subset of records. This is
done by finding records based on what information is included or excluded in
particular fields. Once you have found a set of records that match your search
criteria, you can sort them into a particular order based on the field contents.
Record sorting is described later in this chapter.

Let's start by trying to find our own record in the Contact Management
database. For the Contact Management example, there are five ways to
switch to Find mode. We can click the Find button in the Status area, select
Find from the Mode pop-up menu at the bottom of the FileMaker window,
select the menu option View>Find Mode, use the keyboard shortcut Ctrl+F,

or add a custom button to a layout that when clicked is defined to enter Find mode.

1. Switch to Find mode.

Note: If you did not add your name and contact information to the database, please do that now so that you can perform this Find procedure.

In Find mode, the Status area changes to display a large button labeled Find, as shown in Figure 3.14, and the Mode pop-up menu displays the word Find. The FileMaker Find mode looks very similar to the Browse mode. Fields and buttons are all in the same places on the screen, but the records we created are no longer visible. FileMaker is waiting for us to type in information by which to search the database. We need to decide what to search for and, very importantly, what fields to type the search criteria into.

2. In Find mode, type your own name into the Last Name field.

3. Now click once on the **Find** button in the Status area to submit the find request (you can also press Enter on the keyboard to submit your find request).

Figure 3.14: The Status area in Find mode.

When a find request is submitted, FileMaker displays any records that match the search criteria and automatically switches to Browse mode to display the found set of records. If no records were found that match the search criteria, a dialog box appears stating that "no records match this request," as shown in Figure 3.15. The dialog box offers the choice of modifying the previous search criteria and submitting another find request, or canceling the search. If you select the Cancel button, FileMaker reverts to Browse mode, displays the previous found set of records and, if the records were previously sorted, preserves this sort order.

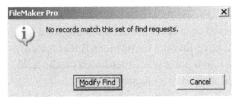

Figure 3.15: The dialog box that appears when no records match the find request.

You have by now hopefully retrieved your own record by submitting your find request. Notice that the Status area in Browse mode now displays the number of found records above the total number of records in the set. Only the single found record, or a subset of records, can now be browsed using the left and right pages of the Book icon or the slider below it. To make all records available for browsing again, you need to choose the menu option Records>Show all Records or press the keyboard shortcut Ctrl+J. (Notice that FileMaker displays keyboard shortcuts alongside the corresponding menu option.)

FileMaker can perform quite powerful searches on a record set. It is possible to search on the contents of more than one field in a single search request, or submit multiple search requests. You can also ask FileMaker to omit records that match the search criteria by checking the Omit box that appears in the Status area in Find mode.

To create a single find request and search records based on the contents of more than one field, you first switch to Find mode and type the values in each field that you wish to search for. For example, you can search for someone with the last name Davidson based in London. If you want to search for someone with the last name Davidson who is based in London or Newcastle, you need to create a second find request, as the City field is being used for two search criteria. In this case, you would need to switch to Find mode, type in the surname and first city of interest, then select the menu option Requests>Add New Request. The surname and second city of interest can now be entered in and the Find button clicked to submit the search.

You may have noticed that the Status area displays the number of requests created, which looks similar to a record count, and the Records menu switches to the Requests menu when in Find mode. If the majority of field contents do not differ between multiple find requests, you can choose Requests>Duplicate Request to avoid having to type the same field contents with each new find request.

The Omit box is a powerful tool in find requests. For example, you could create a find request for anyone with the last name Davidson, and then create a new request using London in the City field and clicking the Omit box in the Status area. This find request will display all records with a last name of Davidson but not include anyone named Davidson based in London.

A useful pop-up menu of symbols is available in the Status area when in Find mode to assist you in creating complex search criteria. The Symbols menu is shown in Figure 3.16.

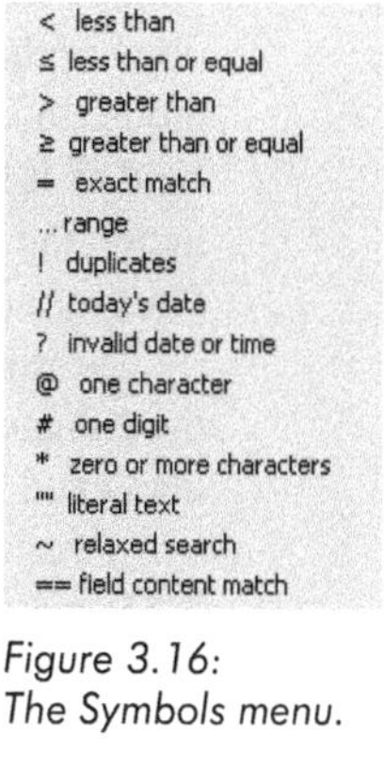

These symbols can also be typed into a field in Find mode using the keyboard. The $<$, $\leq$, $>$, and $\geq$ mathematical symbols can be used to prefix a number value in a field to find records that are less than, less than or equal, greater than, or greater than or equal to the subsequent numeric value. The $=$ symbol can be used to prefix a value in a field to search for an exact match of the subsequent text or number value.

<	less than
≤	less than or equal
>	greater than
≥	greater than or equal
=	exact match
...	range
!	duplicates
//	today's date
?	invalid date or time
@	one character
#	one digit
*	zero or more characters
""	literal text
~	relaxed search
==	field content match

Figure 3.16:
The Symbols menu.

The ... (range) symbol is used between two values to search for records with a field value in a specified range. For example, searching for 60...70 in a test score field would display all records where the test score was in this inclusive range.

A new feature of FileMaker Pro 8 lets you instantly find matching records based on the contents of a field while you are in Browse mode. If you were clicking through records in the Contact Management database, you might wish to see if details are held for any other personnel at the same company as the currently viewed record. To do this, click into the Company field, right-click the mouse and choose Find Matching Records, and FileMaker will present you with a subset of records that have the same Company field contents.

Customizing Views in Layout Mode

Layouts are used to display record information. A database designer has complete control over what fields should be displayed on a layout and in what order they should appear. While a layout exists within a database file, it is totally separate from the data and records held in that file. You can add, modify, or delete layouts without affecting the records held in a database file.

You can switch to Layout mode by clicking the Layout mode button, choosing the menu option View>Layout Mode, or selecting Layout in the pop-up list at the bottom of the FileMaker window. You will notice that the Status area now shows a series of tool buttons (see Figure 3.17). The function of each of these layout tools will be described in Chapter 6. The relative positions of the Contact Management fields are the same as when in Browse mode. In Layout mode, the underlying name of each field is visible within the field as it is displayed. A field's label can be any text and does not have to match the field name, as can be seen for the label Phones alongside the fields Phone 1 and Phone 2.

At this stage, you might like to take a look at some of the other layouts in the Contact Management database and see how they affect how records are displayed in Browse mode.

Between the Status area and the Form view layout, as shown in Figure 3.17, is a gray vertical rectangle titled Body. This indicates the vertical extent of the body part of the layout. All FileMaker layouts are made up of at least one part. A part is a vertical section of a layout that is used to organize how a single record, a list of records, or a summary of record data is displayed. The body part is used to display fields that describe an individual record. A header part is included above the body in the List view and Table view layouts. If a header part is included in a layout, it always appears above the body and can be used to display buttons, graphic images, company logos, or information that is applicable to the displayed records, such as field titles in a list report (similar to column headings in a spreadsheet).

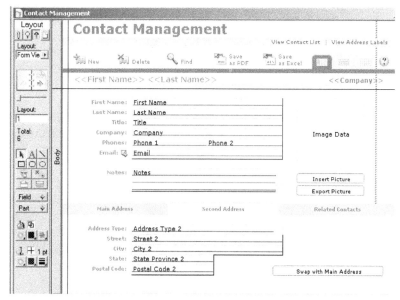

Figure 3.17: The Form view layout in Layout mode.

The List view layout is shown with its header and body parts in Figure 3.18.

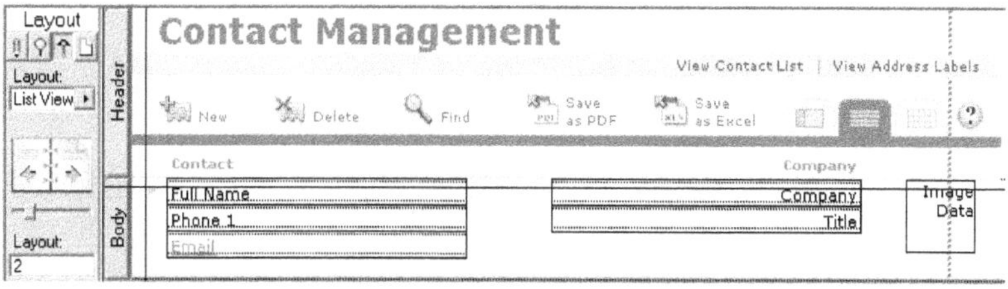

Figure 3.18: This List view layout is made up of a Header and a Body.

To ensure that field contents, field labels, and any graphic objects that are placed on a layout are displayed correctly in Browse mode or when printed, care should be taken not to let any layout object straddle the boundary between two parts. The types of parts and when to use them in a layout are discussed in Chapter 6.

If you take a moment to toggle between Browse mode and Layout mode, while switching in turn between the Form view, List view, and Table view layouts, you may notice that while the first two layouts look similar in their format regardless of whether you are in Browse or Layout mode, the Table view layout looks very different in either mode. This is because it is possible to specify up to three different views for any FileMaker layout: Form, List, and Table.

Form view displays records individually on the screen. To move to the next or previous record, you need to use the Book icon or the slider in the Status area. List view presents records in a list, with the positions of fields and field titles being influenced by their positions in the underlying layout. You can move through the list of records by using the Status area or the vertical scroll bar, or by clicking on any of the records displayed. Table view displays records in a spreadsheet-like format. Each row displays a record, and each column displays a field. The relative order of the columns is linked with the order in which fields appear in the underlying layout, and the way in which records are displayed in Table view differs greatly from the underlying table.

The available views for any layout can be set when in Layout mode by selecting the menu option Layouts>Layout Setup. The Layout Setup dialog box contains three tabs. If the Views tab is selected, you can choose at least one and up to three of the views to be available for a database user when in Browse or Find mode, as shown in Figure 3.19. More detailed options for Table view can be selected by clicking the Properties button.

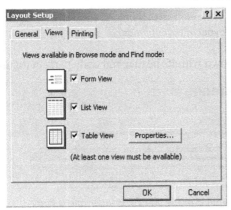

Figure 3.19:
The Layout Setup
dialog box.

If the OK button is clicked and you switch to Browse mode, you can see how any of the available views can be selected by choosing the menu option View>View as Form, View as List, or View as Table.

In our Contact Management example, the Table view layout only has the View as Table option checked. This is why the way in which the records are displayed in Browse or Find mode differs considerably from the format of the underlying layout.

Checking Printouts and Reports with Preview Mode

FileMaker's Preview mode provides the user with a way of viewing how an individual record or set of records will appear on the printed page, based on the current Print Setup parameters. You cannot edit or enter information in fields while in Preview mode. If a FileMaker layout includes summary parts or has been formatted to print in more than one column on a page, Preview mode will display these reports correctly.

In Preview mode, the Status area is modified so that the Book icon now displays the number of pages for a report and the current page being viewed. The user can jump to the next or previous page by clicking on the left or right Book icon page. If you are planning to print records in FileMaker onto special paper, envelopes, or label sheets, the total page value in the Status area tells you how many pages or envelopes you need to insert into your printer tray. The Status area in Preview mode is shown in Figure 3.20.

Figure 3.20: The Status area in Preview mode.

It is also possible to select any object on a layout and tell FileMaker not to print it, which can be invaluable for making sure that a field containing confidential notes on a colleague, client, or supplier is never printed. To demonstrate this, switch to the Form view layout and select Layout mode. Highlight the Notes field and choose the menu option Format>Set Sliding/ Printing. In the Set Sliding/Printing dialog box, check the box labeled "Do not print the selected objects," as shown in Figure 3.21. Now do the same with the Notes label.

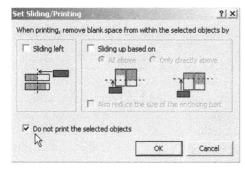

Figure 3.21: The Set Sliding/ Printing dialog box is used to change the relative position of layout objects by sliding, and to also hide an object in Preview mode or on a printed page.

If you now switch to Preview mode, you should see a gap on the screen where the Notes label and field were previously.

If you wish to print from FileMaker after viewing how a record or group of records looks on screen using Preview mode, it is important to select whether you want to print all records in a report or list, or only the current record. This print choice can be found in a drop-down list within the Print dialog box, as shown in Figure 3.22. A third option is available to print a blank record that only shows the position of fields on a layout. This option is usually only used by database or report designers.

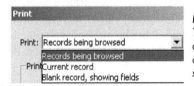

Figure 3.22:
The Print dialog box drop-down list lets you choose to print records being browsed, the current record only, or a blank record that shows the field positions.

We will discuss in Chapter 9 how we can tell FileMaker to remember our preferences for whether we wish to print the current record or all records being browsed. From experience, most FileMaker developers will tell you that when viewing 3,000 or more contact records in FileMaker, it is better to accidentally print out a single address label for the current record and then have to change the Print dialog setting than to unwittingly start printing a letter to all contacts when you only meant to select the current record. (And the environmentalists will thank you too!)

Using Sort to Change the Order in Which Records Appear in a File

You can sort records to change their relative order in a file based on the contents of one or more fields in Preview mode as well as Browse mode. This is a good thing, as the order by which a set of records is sorted is critical to a sub-summary layout part working correctly. Records can be sorted by choosing the menu option Records>Sort Records. The Sort Records dialog box is shown in Figure 3.23.

To change the sort order for all or a found set of records in a file, you need to choose the fields by which to sort the records by highlighting one field at a time from the field list in the left-hand side of the dialog box. Double-click on the highlighted field or click the Move button to place the field in the Sort Order list on the right-hand side of the dialog box. A series of radio buttons lets you choose to sort the selected field contents by ascending order (a to z), descending order (z to a), or a custom order based on a value list (e.g., Prof., Doctor, etc., in a title value list). Any number of fields can be included in the sort order. You are not limited to fields used in the current layout. Other fields can be selected from the database by clicking on the top-left drop-down list arrow. In Figure 3.23, the contact records are to be sorted by the company name, an individual's last name, and by first name, all in ascending order.

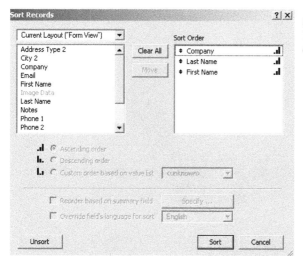

Figure 3.23:
The Sort Records
dialog box.

To sort the records in Browse or Preview mode, click the Sort button.
Records can also be sorted in Browse mode by right-clicking in a field and
choosing the desired menu option (Sort Ascending, Sort Descending, or Sort
by Value List), or simply by using the keyboard shortcut Ctrl+S, which will
open the Sort Records dialog box shown in Figure 3.23. Any field can now
be selected on the left side and included in the sort order by highlighting the
field in the list, clicking the Move button, and specifying the desired sort
order.

The Next Step

It is hoped that this chapter has gone some way to introduce you to the
FileMaker Pro 8 application interface by using the Contact Management template that ships with FileMaker. In the next chapter we will use FileMaker to
build our own database file.

Chapter 4

Getting Started with FileMaker — Your First FileMaker Database

In this chapter:

Introduction

The best way to start getting to know FileMaker and how it manages business data is to build a simple database with it. One of the most popular uses for FileMaker is to manage business contact information, and in Chapter 11, we will build a customer relationship management (CRM) application in some detail.

For the present, let's start by building a simple database to capture business contact details. The object is to put together a FileMaker file that can hold supplier prospect and customer business card information. It might be a great opportunity to transfer some of the business cards in your desk drawer into an easily searchable database.

For reference, a copy of the Contacts database that is described in the following section is available for download from the book's website at www.wordware.com/files/fmapps or from the author's website at www.aweconsultancy.com.

Building a Contacts Database

1. If it is not already open, launch FileMaker Pro 8 by clicking on the **FileMaker Pro** icon or by selecting **FileMaker Pro** from the Windows Start menu. If your FileMaker preferences are set to Show templates in the New Database dialog box, your computer will display a screen simi-lar to Figure 4.1.

    This is the default setting when FileMaker is first installed. (You can pre-vent this dialog box from appearing the next time you open FileMaker by choosing the menu option Edit>Preferences and unchecking the "Show templates in New Database dialog box" option, or by clicking in the "No longer show this dialog" check box.)

Figure 4.1:
The New Database
dialog box.

2. Click the **Create a new empty file** radio button in the New Database dialog box and click the **OK** button.

    A second dialog box will then appear, as shown in Figure 4.2, which enables you to type in a name for your new file and choose where to save it on your computer.

3. Name the new file **Contacts** and click **Save** to save it to your computer's desktop. On the Windows platform, FileMaker will automatically give the new file an .fp7 file suffix.

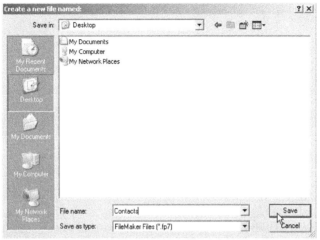

Figure 4.2:
The Create
a new file
named
dialog box.

Adding Fields to the Database

When you click the Save button, FileMaker automatically opens the new file and switches to the Define Database dialog box. The Define Database dialog box is central to any database file written in FileMaker. It is in this dialog box that any tables required for your solution are created, any fields used to describe records are added to a selected table, and finally, any relational links between tables are created using the relationships graph.

At this stage, our new Contacts file consists of a single table called, unsurprisingly, Contacts. We will investigate how relationships are built between tables and their benefit for database design in Chapter 7.

As with any database project, it is a good idea to plan what information you want to capture as individual records and what fields you want to create to describe each record. Your database design plans do not have to be comprehensive and fixed; FileMaker is an incredibly flexible application that lets you add new fields to your database at any later stage.

A FileMaker file consists of one or more tables. When we create new fields in a database, we need to tell FileMaker to what table our new field should be added. The currently selected table is displayed in a drop-down list in the top left of the Define Database dialog box, as shown in Figure 4.3.

FileMaker will always create a new table with the same name as the database file. This table can be renamed at any stage by clicking on the Tables tab of the Define Database dialog box.

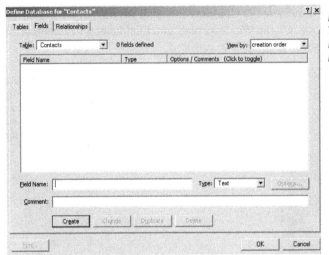

Figure 4.3:
The Define
Database dialog
box.

We need to add fields to the Contacts table to describe our business contacts.

1. Type the field name **Title** into the Field Name area.

2. Select **Text** as the field type from the Type drop-down list, and click on the **Create** button to add the Title field to the fields list.

3. Continue adding the field names shown in Figure 4.4.

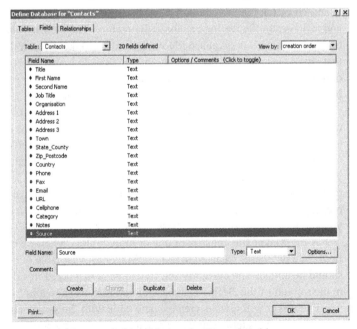

Figure 4.4: New text fields added to the Contacts table.

In addition to text fields, a FileMaker table can include number, date, time, timestamp, container, calculation, and summary fields. These eight field types and their uses are described in detail in Chapter 5. You can add additional fields and tables to an existing FileMaker database by selecting the menu option File>Define>Database or by pressing Ctrl+Shift+D on the keyboard.

We have added a series of text fields that describe business contacts to the Contacts table. We are now ready to start adding contact records to our database.

4. Click the **OK** button and FileMaker will close the Define Database dialog box and switch to a data entry layout with the same default name as the table (Contacts).

If we added more tables to our database and include at least one field in each table, FileMaker will add a new layout with the same name as the table to our database. FileMaker has also switched to Browse mode, ready for us to populate our new Contacts database.

Our default layout looks fairly sparse at this stage, with a white background and plain text fields left aligned vertically with right-aligned field labels. The basic Contacts layout is shown in Figure 4.5.

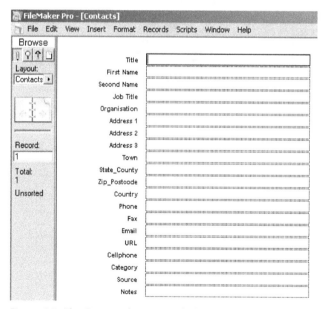

Figure 4.5: The Contacts layout, ready for adding new records.

FileMaker has automatically added a new blank record to the Contacts table. Notice that the cursor is already in the first field in our layout, Title, ready for us to start typing in some contact records.

Adding Records to the Database

Information for each record is typed into fields just as if you are using a word processor. You can move to the next field by using the Tab key or return to the previous field using the Shift+Tab keys. While FileMaker is capable of manipulating the format of text in fields at a later stage, using calculation text and text style functions, it is a good idea to type the text correctly at the time of data entry. If you want to use a contact's name and address fields to create form letters or mailing labels, it can save time later if you use title case formatting at the time of data entry.

When you are ready to add a new record to your database, you can use the menu option Records>New Record or the key combination Ctrl+N. If you have selected to display the Standard toolbar from the View>Toolbars menu, a series of buttons is available that let you add, duplicate, or delete a record. You may notice that the record count in the Status area automatically increases as you add records to the database, and a solid arrow appears on the left and right pages of the Book icon to assist you in navigating through your record set. A sample record is shown in Figure 4.6.

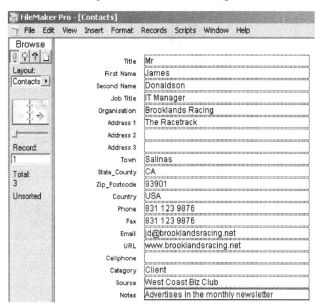

Figure 4.6: A new record added to the Contacts database.

Assisting with Data Entry

FileMaker can help you to type records quickly and accurately. Value lists can be used to select an existing value for a field without retyping it each time. You can also decide whether or not to make FileMaker require that a new value in a field be part of an existing value list by using the Options for field dialog box.

In our Contacts file, we might like to make a drop-down list of name pre-fixes appear when we select the Title field.

1. Define a new value list for a file while in any of the four FileMaker modes by selecting the menu option **File>Define>Value Lists** to open the Field/Control Setup dialog box. In Layout mode you can also right-click on a field and select the menu option **Field/Control>Setup**.

   The Field/Control Setup dialog box, shown in Figure 4.7, lets you choose a control style for the selected field; in this case, a drop-down list.

2. Click on the **Display values from** drop-down arrow to tell FileMaker how to populate the new value list.

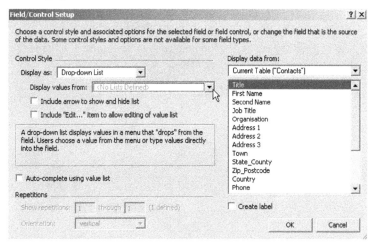

Figure 4.7: The Field/Control Setup dialog box.

3. Select the **Define Value Lists** option in the drop-down list, and the Define Value Lists dialog box will appear.

4. Click the **New** button and another dialog box will then appear, with which you can name the new list and decide how to populate it. The Edit Value List dialog box is shown in Figure 4.8.

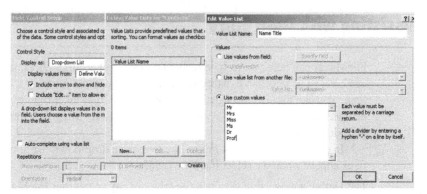

Figure 4.8: The Edit Value List dialog box provides three methods for populating the value list.

In the example shown in Figure 4.9, a list of name prefixes, including Mr, Mrs, and Miss, has been typed into the custom values list. Each entry in the list should appear on a new line. It is also possible to populate a value list using values from a record set's field content in this or another file. You can choose whether to use the field contents of all records in a file or only related records. A third method to populate the list is to reuse a predefined value list from another FileMaker file.

5.   Type the custom value items shown in Figure 4.9, name the value list **Name Title**, and click **OK**.

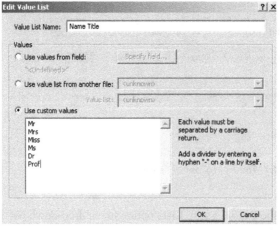

Figure 4.9: Creating a new custom value list called Name Title in the Edit Value List dialog box.

If you now return to Browse mode and click in the Title field, a drop-down list of preset values will appear. A value can be selected from the list and added to the field by clicking on it. If you want to avoid having the list appear every time the field is selected, you can choose FileMaker Pro 8's new feature in the Field/Control Setup dialog box titled "Include arrow to show and hide list." When a drop-down list is chosen as the display type, this option makes a drop-down arrow appear on the right side of the field when it is selected, as shown in Figure 4.10. The drop-down list will only appear after the arrow is clicked.

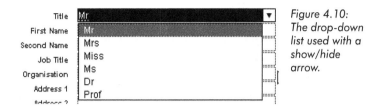

Figure 4.10: The drop-down list used with a show/hide arrow.

You may want to substitute a drop-down list for a pop-up menu, a check box, or a radio button set in the Field/Control Setup dialog box, and see how the value list is displayed back in Browse mode.

In addition to value lists, FileMaker has other tools to help speed up accurate data entry. The Field Control/Setup dialog box also has a check box labeled "Auto-complete using previously enter values." The auto-complete field control will make previously entered values in that field appear as the user starts to type a new entry. The Auto-complete check box option is shown selected in Figure 4.11.

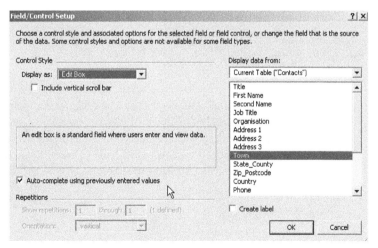

Figure 4.11: The "Auto-complete using previously entered values" option.

In Figure 4.12, the name Salinas has appeared in the Town field as soon as the letter S was typed into the field. The user can select an auto-completed value by clicking the field or by pressing the Enter key.

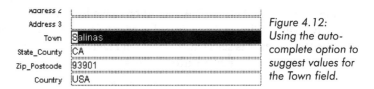

Figure 4.12:
Using the auto-
complete option to
suggest values for
the Town field.

FileMaker's Three Views for a Layout

FileMaker provides three different views for a layout: Form, List, and Table. Form view is the default setting for the first layout in any new database. In Form view, a single record is displayed on the screen. The vertical scroll bar can be used to display the full length of a Form view layout, but it will not be able to scroll to the next record. In List view, one or more records can be seen on the screen at the same time and the vertical scroll bar can be used to view other records if they are in the current set of records. In Table view, all fields on a layout are displayed as columns in a format similar to a spreadsheet.

In our initial default layout that FileMaker has created to display contact records, we can toggle between any of the three modes. Notice how the record display changes when you select View as List, View as Table, or View as Form in the View menu. In Figure 4.13, all three view options are displayed in the View menu.

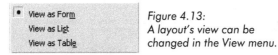

Figure 4.13:
A layout's view can be
changed in the View menu.

You may decide at a later date to restrict the choices for how a record set is displayed. For any layout, you can decide which layout views are available in Browse and Find modes. In the layout of interest, switch to Layout mode and select the menu option Layouts>Layout Setup, click on the Views tab, and decide which views you want to make available to users. As shown in Figure 4.14, you must keep at least one view available.

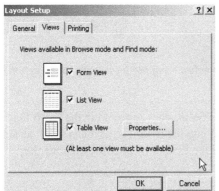

Figure 4.14:
Selecting which
views to make
available for a
layout in the
Layout Setup
dialog box.

To assist colleagues who may be using your Contacts database for the first time, it may be best to offer the choice of selecting any of the three views to display records.

Since novice users of FileMaker may not be familiar with the menu comands, after we create two new layouts in the Contacts file, we will add a set of buttons to jump between the layouts.

Adding a List Layout to the Contacts Database

Most FileMaker databases enable you to view a set of records one at a time on screen or as a list.

1. Add a List view layout to the Contacts file by switching to Layout mode and selecting the menu option **Layouts>New Layout/Report**. Notice that the available menu choices change depending on which mode is active. In Layout mode, pressing Ctrl+N will open the New Layout dialog box, while in Browse mode the same key combination will create a new record.

   The New Layout/Report dialog box is shown in Figure 4.15. A FileMaker layout needs to know from what table to display records. In this case we only have one table, Contacts, in our file, and this is selected in the Show records from box.

2. Select **Columnar list/report** in the layout type box.

   The use of some of the other layout types is described in Chapter 6.

   Next, we will choose a suitable title for the new layout and decide whether we want to include it in the Status area's Layout drop-down list. FileMaker developers often choose to hide control or administration layouts from general users by unchecking this option.

3. Type **Contacts List** for the layout name and click the **Include in layout menus** option.

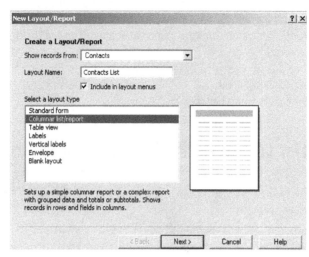

Figure 4.15:
The New
Layout/Report
dialog box
with a list type
selected.

4. Click the **Next** button to move on to the next stage of creating a new layout.

    If you have chosen to create a columnar list/report layout, FileMaker will now ask you to specify either a simple columnar list layout or a more complex report layout with grouped data. If several fields are used in a list layout, FileMaker also gives us the option to extend those fields to the right beyond the page margin or to wrap the fields into a new line and keep all the fields within the page boundaries. For this example, leave the "Constrain to page width" option unchecked, as shown in Figure 4.16.

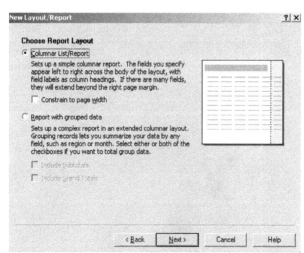

Figure 4.16:
For list/report
layouts, the
dialog box
gives you the
choice of
creating a
simple list or a
complex group
report using
summary
values.

5. Click **Next** to move on to the next stage of the layout assistant, where we can specify the fields to include in our new layout. A list of available fields from the current table, or other tables in this or other FileMaker files, can be seen in the left-hand side of the dialog box. Fields can be added to the layout by double-clicking on them or by highlighting each field and clicking the Move button. You can add or remove all fields from the layout, and you can change the order of the layout fields by clicking on the vertical pair of arrows to the left of the field name and pulling the field up or down in the field order. Choose the **Move All** option to add all fields to the new list layout, as shown in Figure 4.17.

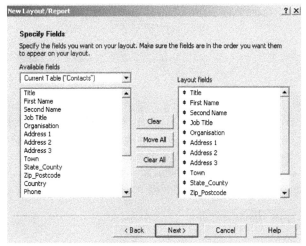

Figure 4.17: The Specify Fields page of the layout assistant.

6. Click **Next** again. The dialog box now gives us the option to choose which fields to sort and the order by which records appear in our new list layout. In this case, contact records are to be sorted by second name, first name, and organization.

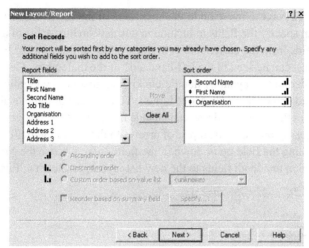

Figure 4.18:
The Sort
Records page
of the layout
assistant.

7. Click **Next** again. This dialog now gives us the option to choose a theme
    for the new list layout. Themes vary the color of layout parts and the for-
    mat of fields and field labels in the layout. Themes can be used to add
    graphic appeal to the way in which records are displayed and printed.
    Choose the **Aqua screen** theme, as shown in Figure 4.19, and a theme
    sample is displayed in the dialog box.

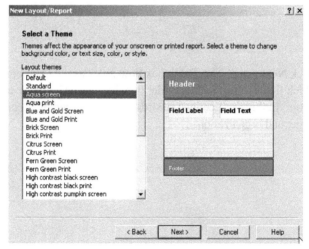

Figure 4.19:
The Select a
Theme page of
the layout
assistant.

8. Click **Next**. The final page of the layout assistant gives you the option of
    adding header and footer layout objects to the new layout, as shown in
    Figure 4.20. You can choose to add layout objects such as the page num-
    ber or current date symbols, the layout name, a report title, or a company
    logo. Note that if you do not choose to add information to a part, the part

will not be included in the new layout. Layout parts can also be added at a later stage by switching to Layout mode and using the Part button in the Status area.

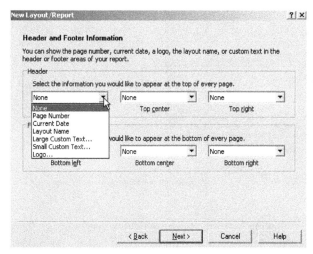

Figure 4.20: The Header and Footer Information page of the layout assistant.

9. When **Next** is clicked, the new list layout will appear on the screen with the record set displayed, as shown in Figure 4.21.

Figure 4.21: The newly created Contacts List layout.

Adding a Table Layout to the Contacts Database

The layout assistant can also be used to create a Table view layout for our contact records.

1. Switch back to Layout mode and select the menu option **Layouts>New Layout/Report**.

2. Select to show records from the **Contacts** table, type in a suitable name for the layout (**Table View**), and select **Table view** as the layout type, as shown in Figure 4.22.

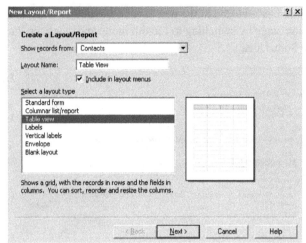

Figure 4.22: Adding a new Table view layout to the Contacts file.

3. After clicking **Next**, the Specify Fields screen appears. The order in which the fields are placed on the layout dictates the order in which the fields appear as columns in Table view. In the example shown in Figure 4.23, all fields will be visible in Table view because the **Move All** button has been clicked. The maximum number of fields you can display as columns in Table view is limited by the total width of all the columns. FileMaker has a layout limit of around 8,000 pixels. This is enough room to display the full list of fields for most tables.

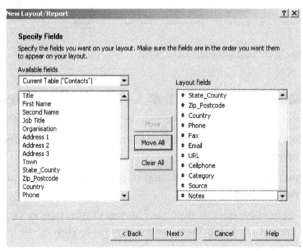

Figure 4.23: Specifying fields and their order for the Table view layout.

4. Click **Next** again, and the dialog gives the option to select a theme for our Table view layout. Choose the **Aqua screen** theme, as shown in Figure 4.24, and click **Next**.

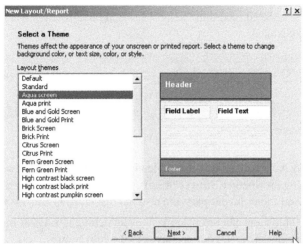

Figure 4.24:
Selecting a
theme for the
Table view
layout.

5. Finally, we can choose whether to view our new table layout in Browse or Layout mode. Choose **View in Browse mode**, as shown in Figure 4.25, and click **Finish**.

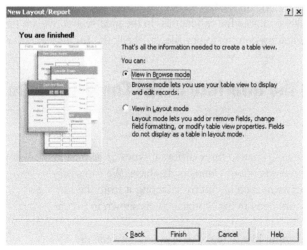

Figure 4.25:
Choosing to
view the new
table layout in
Browse or
Layout mode.

Once we return to Browse mode, we can see our record set displayed in the newly created Table view, as shown in Figure 4.26.

There are advantages in being able to view a record set in Table view. It is easy to visually scan the information held in records. We can click and drag on column headings to change the relative order in which fields appear in the table, or click and drag the edge of a column heading to change its width. If you click on a column heading once, you can sort the record set by the contents of the selected field. You can alternate between ascending and descending sort order by clicking the column heading again. Note that the currently selected record in the table list will remain active when the sort order is changed.

Browse	Title	First Name	Second Name	Job Title	Organisation	Address 1
Layout:	Mr	James	Donaldson	IT Manager	Brooklands Racing	The Racetrack
Table Vie ▶	Ms	Susan	Osbourne	Travel Advisor	Euro Travel	211 Piccadilly

Figure 4.26: The Table view layout.

You may have noticed that the Table view layout looks completely different depending on whether Browse or Layout mode is selected. By default, the header and footer layout parts are also not displayed in Browse mode.

1. A Table view can be customized by switching to **Layout mode** and selecting the menu option **Layouts>Layout Setup**.

2. Click on the **Views** tab and you will notice a button labeled Properties next to the Table View check box. Click the **Properties** button and the Table View Properties dialog box appears, with the option to include a header and footer part in our Table layout.

3. We use this dialog box to decide what Table view features we want to make available for colleagues. In the next section we are going to add navigation buttons to our file, so check the **Include Header Part** option.

Improving the Interface of the Contacts File to Assist Users

We have now created three different types of layouts to display records in our Contacts database. We can easily move between each layout by selecting it from the Layout pop-up menu in the Status area, as shown in Figure 4.27.

We might like to make navigation between the layouts in our file a little easier for colleagues by adding some buttons to switch between layouts.

1. Return to the Contacts layout and switch to **Layout mode** so we can add three buttons to the layout header that switch to each of the layouts

Figure 4.27: The Layout pop-up menu.

when selected. Click on the **Button** tool in the Status area. The Button tool has a hand pointing to a button on it.

2. Now let go of the mouse button and move the mouse to the top left of the layout within the header part. You should notice that the cursor has changed to a crosshair. Click and drag the crosshair pointer diagonally until the new button is the size you want, and then release the mouse button. This will automatically open the Button Setup dialog.

You can also choose the menu option Insert>Button to add a new button to a layout. The Button Setup dialog box will appear, as shown in Figure 4.28.

3. Select the **Go To Layout** command in the Navigation section, and in the Specify drop-down list to the right, select the target layout.

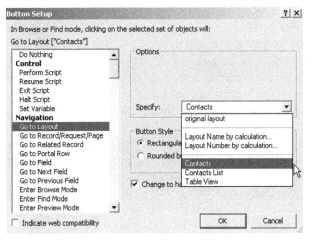

Figure 4.28: Defining a button to switch to the Contacts layout.

When you click OK, the new button will appear on screen with the flashing I-beam pointer in it so that you can type in a suitable text label for the button.

4. We need to repeat this process twice to add buttons for switching to the Contacts List and the Table view layouts.

To keep all three buttons the same size, you might want to highlight the original button and either choose the menu option Edit>Duplicate or press Ctrl+D. You can move the duplicated button with the mouse or with the keyboard arrow keys. You will need to rename each duplicated button by clicking on the Text tool in the Status area (marked with an A) and clicking on the button with the I-beam pointer. You will also need to change the command for each duplicated button to switch to a different layout. To change a button's command, select the Pointer tool from the Status area, if it is not already selected, and double-click on a button. The

Button Setup dialog box should then appear. You can also highlight a button and select the menu option Format>Button Setup. Choose the target layout from the drop-down list shown in Figure 4.28.

The set of three layout navigation buttons should look like the example shown in Figure 4.29.

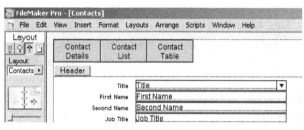

Figure 4.29: The navigation buttons designed to assist users in changing how records are displayed on screen.

The strip of buttons can be made to look like a floating menu in FileMaker by copying all three buttons and pasting them into the same header position in the List and Table layouts. To give the illusion of a floating menu palette, it is important that the relative positions of the buttons remain static on all layouts. You can use the keyboard arrow keys to nudge layout objects into their correct position. You may find that switching FileMaker's Object Grid on or off is helpful in adjusting the exact position of a layout object. The Object Grid is selected from the Arrange menu. Objects on layouts can also be aligned using the View>T-Squares menu option while in Layout mode. When T-Squares is selected, horizontal and vertical alignment lines appear on the active layout. The relative positions of these two lines remain constant across all layouts in a file. As it is dragged across a layout, an object's left, right, top, or bottom boundary, or center point "snaps" to the T-square line.

Now that you have started adding your own buttons to the Contacts database, let's include another button to assist colleagues in adding new records to the database.

5.   Use the same steps used for the previous buttons to add a button labeled **New Record**. If the New Record button is placed too close to the others, it may be clicked on by accident and blank records will begin to appear in the table. In Figure 4.30, a New Record button has been positioned to the right of the layout navigation buttons.

You might also consider adding the New Record button to the List and Table layouts; however, a button can only be defined to carry out a single command. You may not want new records typed into the Table or List views as not all fields may be included in those layouts. At this point, FileMaker's built-in ScriptMaker feature would be needed. ScriptMaker lets us join several commands together in a permanent script that we can assign to a button or select from the Scripts menu. In this case, we would need to define a script to switch to the Contacts layout before adding a new blank record to the file for data entry. ScriptMaker is a great ally in designing business applications with FileMaker; it is discussed in detail in Chapter 9.

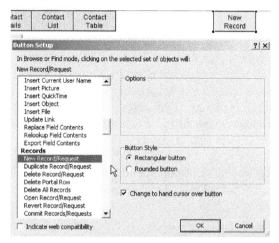

Figure 4.30:
A New Record button added to the Contacts layout.

Our original Contacts layout still lacks the color of the List and Table layouts. We can easily add color to the layout by selecting each of the layout parts and giving them a fill color.

Layout parts are selected by clicking on the part label. With the part label highlighted, choose a color for the part from the Fill Color palette in the Status area. In Figure 4.31, the header, body, and footer parts have all been given the same fill color.

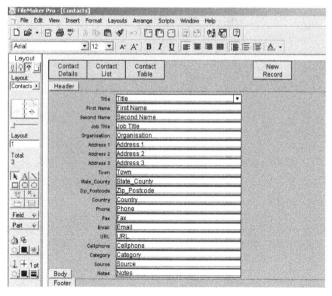

Figure 4.31:
Adding a fill color to the Contacts layout parts.

It is worth bearing in mind that part fill colors are also printed when the current record or records being browsed in FileMaker are printed.

A method for adding color to a layout and avoiding having a background color behind printed records is to use the Rectangle tool in the Status area to draw a background rectangle with a fill color, but to choose not to print the background rectangle.

When you have drawn a rectangle on your layout, make sure that you select the menu option Arrange>Send to Back. This will ensure that the rectangle does not obscure any layout objects in Browse mode. You may find that the background rectangle keeps being selected by accident when you try to highlight other layout objects. If this happens, you can lock the rectangle by highlighting it and choosing the menu option Arrange>Lock. Before you lock the rectangle object, it is a good idea to tell FileMaker not to print it. For any layout objects that you don't want to include in a FileMaker printout, highlight them and select the menu option Format>Set Sliding/Printing, then make sure that the "Do not print the selected objects" option is checked, as shown in Figure 4.32.

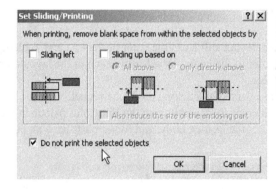

Figure 4.32:
You can choose not to print any object in a layout.

You are now ready to use your Contacts database and share it with colleagues.

Deploying the Contacts Database on Your Office Network

While we will discuss FileMaker deployment options in more detail in Chapter 22, you may have colleagues who want to access your new Contacts database right away. You need to make sure that your Contacts database is correctly set for network sharing.

1. With the Contacts file open, select the menu option **Edit>Sharing> FileMaker Network**. The FileMaker Network Settings dialog box will appear, as shown in Figure 4.33.

2. Any open FileMaker files on your computer will appear in the Currently open files area, and the Contacts file should already be highlighted.

3. Click the **On** radio button next to Network Sharing, and select the **All users** radio button under Network access to file.

   We will be addressing the issue of network security in Chapter 24, but for the moment we can deploy the file with full access for all users.

4. Click **OK** to accept the settings.

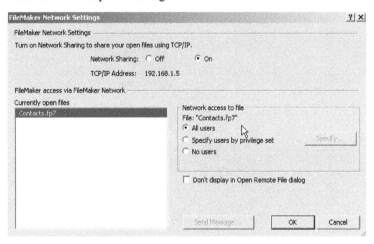

Figure 4.33: The FileMaker Network Settings dialog box.

5. Provided that your colleagues have a copy of FileMaker Pro 8 installed on their computer and are attached to the same network as our computer, they should be able to locate and open the Contacts file from within the Open Remote File dialog box by using the menu option **File>Open Remote**.

You may want to add additional buttons to the Contacts layout to enable colleagues to enter Find mode, sort records, or show all records. You may also want to add new layouts to create mailing labels or form letters for records in the Contacts file.

You may also think of additional fields to add to the Contacts file and include additional field types in the field list. We will be adding other field types to the Contacts file in the next chapter.

The Next Step

We have now created our own FileMaker database to manage business contact records and created a set of layouts to display the record set.

The techniques that we have used in this chapter will be applied to add features to our FileMaker business solutions and start to link FileMaker tables together to create relational database solutions.

Chapter 5

Field Types and When to Use Them

Introduction

Fields are the fundamental building blocks of a FileMaker Pro database. For this reason, any new FileMaker file you create begins by opening the Define Database dialog box, with the Fields tab selected. Data is entered into a record using fields. It is your job, as the database designer, to plan what fields are needed in a table to manage business data with FileMaker. New fields are added to a FileMaker file by giving each field a unique name within a table and selecting a set of options that determine how a field enters, validates, calculates, stores, and displays data.

In this chapter the various FileMaker field types are introduced and practical examples of each are added to the Contacts file that we created in the previous chapter. For reference, a copy of the Contacts file with additional fields added is available to download at the book's website at www.wordware.com/files/fmapps or the author's website at www.aweconsultancy.com.

Naming Fields in FileMaker

Each field in a FileMaker file table must have a unique name. A field name can contain up to 100 characters and, since FileMaker field names can be referenced in calculation field formulas, this means that you cannot use certain characters, symbols, or words in a field name. There are other characters that you should avoid in a field name if you plan to publish a FileMaker database on the web or exchange information with other data sources such as SQL.

To avoid problems, do not use any of the following symbols or words in the field name:

- , (comma), +, –, *, /, ^, &, =, ¹, >, <, ( ), [ ], { }, ", ; (semicolon), : (colon), :: (relational indicator), $ (variable indicator)

- AND, OR, NOT, XOR, TRUE, FALSE, or the name of any FileMaker Pro function

In addition, don't begin a field name to be used in a calculation formula with a space, period (.), or number.

Use _ (underscore) in place of a space to avoid restrictions in ODBC, exporting, web publishing, and other operations.

If you're exchanging data with another application, check the field naming restrictions in the file formats supported by that application.

If you're using ODBC or JDBC to share FileMaker Pro data, avoid using SQL keywords in field names.

FileMaker provides a helpful prompt, which is shown in Figure 5.1, to let you know that you have used a field name that might cause problems.

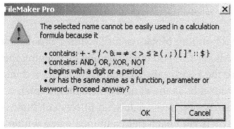

Figure 5.1:
FileMaker will prompt you if the field name is likely to cause problems later for database development.

You can ignore FileMaker's advice and keep the original field name, or you can remove the problem characters by overwriting them in the Field name box and clicking the Change button in the Define Database dialog box.

Field Types

A FileMaker table can include any of the following field types (it is also possible to leave a table blank with no fields added).

Text Fields

For a single FileMaker database record, a text field can, in theory, hold up to 2 GB of data (about a billion characters) in any form of letters, symbols, and numbers. The exact storage limit is likely to be restricted by a computer's available RAM and hard disk capacity. FileMaker can index a text field based on the first 100 characters of each word or value. Text fields may contain carriage returns and tab symbols.

Number Fields

A number field can support values up to 800 numeric digits or other characters, and the negative values of the same range. An index is based on the first 400 significant digits, ignoring non-numeric characters. Number fields can contain text and Boolean values (to indicate, for example, true or false), with a zero or null value being false. Number fields can't contain carriage returns.

When you sort a FileMaker database by the contents of a number field, the record set will be sorted numerically, such as 1, 2, 3, 10, 20, 30. The sort order for a text field containing the same data will be sorted by the number characters, such as 1, 10, 2, 20, 3, 30.

Date Fields

Date fields can only accept the entry of date formatted data, in the form of the Gregorian calendar with a range of 1/1/0001…12/31/4000. The month, day, and year order is based on system settings when the file is created. Dates in a FileMaker file are internally stored as the number of elapsed days since 01/01/0001. This can be useful when creating a calculation field that references date field values. When you type in a date value, you can separate the month, day, and year value with a period (.) or backslash (/) symbol. In Browse or Find mode, to insert today's date in a date field, click in the field and press Ctrl+– (minus).

Time Fields

A time field can contain times values only, in the form HH:MM:SS (and, if required, a two-digit fraction of seconds). A time field can contain the hours, minutes, and seconds portion of a time. Times in a FileMaker file are internally stored as the number of seconds since 12:00:00 (midnight) of the previous day. This can be of assistance when creating calculation fields that may compare values in two or more time fields. In Browse or Find mode, to insert the current time in a time field, click in the field and press Ctrl+: (colon).

Timestamp Fields

The timestamp field combines date and time information. It contains a date and time, separated with a space, in the form 06/06/2005 15:15:48. A timestamp field in a FileMaker file is stored as the count of seconds from 1/1/0001 00:00:00. Timestamps are common in other database and accounting packages such as Sage Accounts software, where they are used to log and audit record modifications over time.

Container Fields

Container fields can contain a picture; an Excel, Word or PDF file; a QuickTime movie; or an OLE object (Windows) of up to 4 GB per field. You can reference container fields in calculation and summary fields. You can't find or sort records based on container fields, but you can create calculation fields to test if they are empty. You can choose whether to store a file within a container field, which can increase the size of a FileMaker file considerably, or only store the path reference to a file. If you double-click on a container field containing a referenced file, provided you have the relevant application installed on your computer, the file will open automatically. This can be extremely powerful if you want to store asset information within a record, such as a personnel record linked to a staff CV written in Word or an architect project record linked to a CAD file.

Calculation Fields

Calculation fields are used to create formulas that manipulate data in a FileMaker file. A calculation formula references field values from tables within the current record or related records. The result can be one of these types of data: text, number, date, time, timestamp, or container. A calculation field's formula may include mathematical operators and functions that are recognized by FileMaker and are available in a drop-down list and button tools within the Specify Calculation dialog box.

Calculation fields, along with scripts, are central to FileMaker automation. Both subjects warrant their own chapters later in this book.

Summary Fields

The value in a summary field is produced by summarizing field values from one or more records in a table. Summary fields cannot be indexed. Summary fields can evaluate the total, average, count, minimum, maximum, standard deviation, or fraction of total of a set of field values.

The use of these fields in a FileMaker database will now be discussed in more detail.

Field Options

When a new calculation or summary field is added to a FileMaker table, either the Specify Calculation dialog box or the Options for Summary dialog box appears automatically. For all the other field types, the database designer can decide what field options to employ for a new field. Field options are managed by clicking the Options button when a new field is created and selecting from a range of options to automatically enter values, validate the information submitted, or store the contents of the field.

You may want to record certain information when a record is created or modified. Many database projects include a set of four fields to record the date a record was created, the name of the creator, the most recent date the record was modified, and the name of the modifier.

This is easily done by adding two date fields and two text fields to the Contacts database we created in the last chapter.

1. Add the four fields shown in Figure 5.2 to the Contacts database, changing the field type each time.

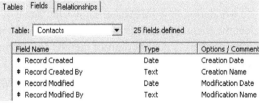

Figure 5.2: Add fields to track when a record was created and modified and by whom.

2. Click on the **Options** button to open the Options for Field dialog, then choose the **Creation** and **Modification** check boxes under "Automatically enter the following data into this field" as appropriate for each field.

To make FileMaker automatically enter a date or name value, you click the Options button and select the Auto-Enter tab. As shown in Figure 5.3, the values in the Creation drop-down list will vary depending on the chosen field type.

3. For the new fields, select **Date** in the Creation drop-down list for the Record Created field and **Name** in the Creation drop-down list for the Record Created By field.

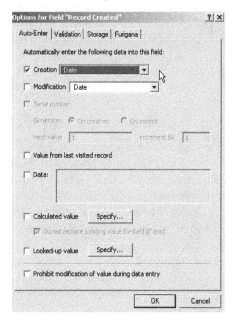

Figure 5.3:
The Auto-Enter tab
of the Options for
Field dialog box.

By using the Modification drop-down list, if any of the field contents of a record are changed, today's date and the name of the database user can be automatically inserted into the Record Modified and Record Modified By fields.

You may be wondering how FileMaker knows the name of the database user. If you select the Menu option Edit>Preferences, you will notice a field box for the user name. This is not a foolproof method for logging who last modified a record in a file, however. In Chapter 24 we will explore the use of account names to control access to a file and limit record changes.

Adding a Unique Serial Number Field to a Table

We can add a new number field to the Contacts database and use it to auto-enter a unique serial number for each record in the table. In doing so, we will introduce the most important field concept in this book for writing business databases: the use of a key field.

1. In the Contacts database, create a new number field called **Contact Serial Number**.

2. Click the **Options** button while the field is still highlighted and check the **Serial number** box in the Auto-Enter tab, as shown in Figure 5.4.

3. To prevent a user from accidentally deleting or modifying the serial number value in a field, click the "Prohibit modification of value during data entry" check box at the bottom of the Options for Field dialog box.

The use of a unique serial number in a record is crucial for the design of key fields and creating a relationship between one or more FileMaker tables. This method is examined in more detail in Chapter 7.

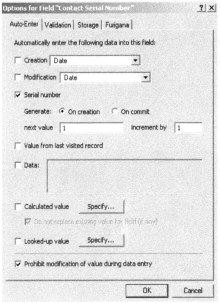

Figure 5.4:
Using the Auto-Enter tab of the Options for Field dialog to add an incrementing serial number to each new record in a table.

The Next Step

Deciding what fields are needed to describe records in a table does require some planning. Fortunately, in FileMaker, additional fields can be added to a table and existing fields can be modified very easily.

While calculation fields are described in more detail in Chapter 8, the applied use of each of the various field types is discussed in the project case studies later in this book.

Chapter 6

Designing Layouts

In this chapter:

- Introduction
- Layout Types
  - The Standard Form Layout
  - The Columnar List/Report Layout
  - Table View Layouts
  - Label Layouts
  - Envelope Layouts
  - Blank Layouts
- Adding Parts to a Layout
- Printing with Layouts
- Working with Fields in a Layout

Introduction

Layouts are used to display information held in a FileMaker database. A layout displays field information, and the settings in the layout determine how field data is displayed on screen or printed and whether a field in a layout can be clicked in for editing or for record searching.

Information in a database is stored in fields. Fields can be added to or removed from a layout without affecting the underlying data held in a file. When the contents of a field are edited or deleted, the change can be seen in any layout that includes the same field for the same record.

FileMaker has a set of layout types, each of which can be useful for displaying and reporting record data in a particular way, such as for a contacts telephone list or as address labels. A layout may consist of more than one layout part, depending on how the database designer wishes to present information from a single record or a record set. There are, in addition, three views that can be used in conjunction with any layout to determine how records are displayed: the Form, List, and Table views.

While layouts were introduced as part of the steps needed to create a new FileMaker database in Chapter 4, layout design is discussed in more detail here.

This chapter presents each of the layout types, discusses the options available for working with layouts in a database solution, and describes how layouts can be used for editing, searching, and reporting on business data.

Before designing a new layout for a FileMaker database, it is important to consider the information that is to be displayed and whether the layout is to be used for data capture, searching, or reporting.

Layout Types

A good way to introduce FileMaker's family of layout types is to first create, and later customize, a set of layouts for a simple database.

When a database file is created, FileMaker includes a new standard default layout for each table in the file. This default table is seen in Browse mode as soon as the OK button is pressed in the Define Database dialog box. The layout is based on the default or first table created for the file and includes all the table's fields.

A basic contact database can be used to become familiar with FileMaker's default layouts and how custom layouts can be created and modified.

1. Launch FileMaker and create a new database called **Business Cards** with the text fields shown in Figure 6.1.

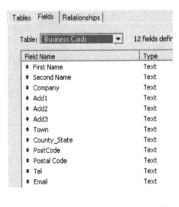

Figure 6.1: The Business Cards database fields.

2. Click the **OK** button. The Define Database dialog box closes and the database opens in Browse mode, ready for data entry, with a new blank record displayed using a standard form layout. This layout will have the same name as the initial table that was created for the file.

To work with layouts in FileMaker you need to be in Layout mode. You can alternate between FileMaker modes using the View menu, selecting the Mode pop-up menu, which always displays the current mode at the bottom left of the FileMaker window, or using the keyboard shortcuts Ctrl+B, Ctrl+F, Ctrl+L, and Ctrl+U, for Browse, Find, Layout, and Preview mode, respectively.

3. Switch to Layout mode and notice that the Business Cards layout consists of three parts, labeled Header, Body, and Footer. These are shown in Figure 6.2.

FileMaker has added all the table's fields to the body part of the layout. The body layout part should always be used to display record-specific information. A header or footer can be used to display information that a set of records has in common. This does not always have to be information from a field, but could also include a report title in a header or a page number in the footer.

Figure 6.2:
The default
standard form
layout displayed
in Layout mode.

The relative size of each of the layout parts can be changed by clicking anywhere on the horizontal boundary line between two layout parts and dragging the line up or down the layout.

An empty layout part can be removed by highlighting the part label and pressing the Delete or Backspace key. A warning dialog box will appear if the layout part contains any information. A layout can be deleted using the menu option Layouts>Delete Layout.

Note that a file must contain at least one layout and a layout must consist of at least one part.

In the next section we'll use FileMaker's built-in layout wizard to create a set of layouts for the Business Cards database, with the options for each discussed.

The Standard Form Layout

The standard form layout is ideal for displaying a single record on the screen. The entire screen area could be used to display descriptive fields for a record. As will be shown later in the case studies, a standard form layout can be adapted to include a portal as a means of displaying information on one or more related records from another table.

A slightly more colorful standard form layout can be created for the file by switching to Layout mode and choosing the menu option Layouts>New Layout/Report. The New Layout/Report dialog box will appear, as shown in Figure 6.3. A set of layout types are listed in the dialog box, with an example layout illustration and a short comment on each type of layout and when it might be used.

A series of layout design steps are available with prompts as each Next button is pressed in the New Layout/Report dialog box. These work very much like a wizard to assist with good layout design. All the options selected can be manually altered later using the menu options in Layout mode.

A layout must be based on an underlying table in a file so that FileMaker knows what record set to display with the layout. The layout name can be completely different from the table or file name. A check box allows the lay-out designer to choose whether or not to include the layout in the Layout menu. This can be useful when a layout is not used for data entry or record searching. A script can be used to gain temporary access to a layout that is not displayed in the Layout menu.

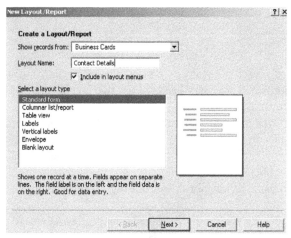

Figure 6.3:
The New
Layout/Report
dialog box.

If the Standard form layout option is highlighted, the Specify Fields screen appears when the Next button is clicked. Fields from the current table, global fields, or fields from any related tables can be included in the layout. The fields and their relative order on the layout can be selected. In Figure 6.4, the

Move All button has been clicked to include all fields from the underlying table in the standard form layout.

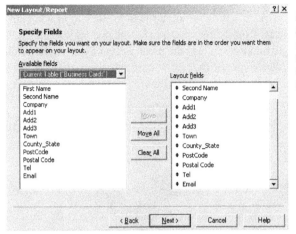

Figure 6.4:
Specifying the
fields and their
order for a
standard form
layout.

If the Next button is clicked again, a theme can be selected from a displayed list for the new layout. The theme list is shown in Figure 6.5.

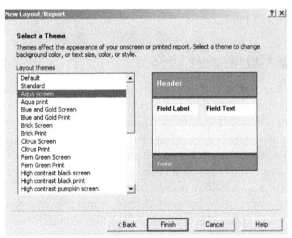

Figure 6.5:
The layout theme
selection screen.

When the Finish button is clicked, the new layout will appear in Layout mode.

If the standard form layout is only going to be used to display a single record on the screen at a time, the header and footer parts are not essential to the layout and can easily be deleted. If the body part has been given a fill color after choosing a theme for the new layout, this will appear as a background color when records are printed using this layout.

There are two easy ways to avoid printing a background color on a record or report. One option is to design a similar layout with no fill color and a script that switches to the plain layout before printing begins, then switches back to the original layout. The second option is to draw a new rectangle layout object, using the Tools palette. Give this new rectangle a fill color and use the menu option Arrange>Send to Back to prevent any fields or other layout objects from being obscured by the rectangle. Finally, with the colored rectangle highlighted, use the menu option Format>Set Sliding/Printing to open the dialog box of the same name and check the "Do not print the selected objects" option, as shown in Figure 6.6.

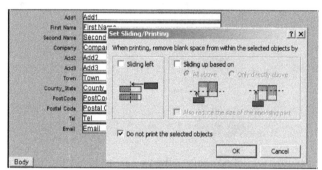

Figure 6.6:
The Set Sliding/
Printing dialog.

The position and size of the fields on the layout can be adjusted, and the field labels can be removed or changed.

The Columnar List/Report Layout

List reports are used when you want to display a set of records in a row on screen or as a printed report. If a list report is to be printed, it is important to restrict the overall dimensions of the fields in a layout to the printer's page dimensions. Simple list layouts at minimum consist of a body layout part and usually include a header and footer. More complex list layouts may include summary parts. A summary layout part can be placed at the start or end of a set of records, either as a leading grand summary above the body part or as a trailing grand summary below the body. A third summary layout part is a sub-summary, which is sorted by a specific field. Sub-summary parts, and any fields contained within them, will only be displayed correctly in Preview mode or when a report is printed if the record set has been sorted by at least the same field as is referenced in the sub-summary part. Usually a sub-summary part is used to display descriptive or summary field information, which is based on the same sort field as the part's definition and relates to the current set of records.

1. Create a new layout, choose the **Columnar list/report** option for the layout type in the New Layout/Report dialog box, and click the **Next** button.

The Choose Report Layout screen, shown in Figure 6.7, gives you the option of selecting a simple columnar list report or a more complex grouped report with summary field data.

The "Constrain to page width" check box enables you to constrain the fields on the layout to the currently selected page width. The orientation and dimensions of the page can be adjusted later using the File>Print Setup menu option.

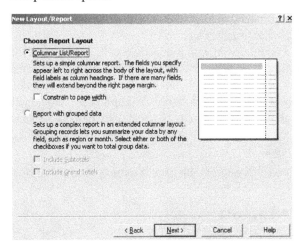

Figure 6.7: The Choose Report Layout screen.

If a simple columnar list/report is selected, subsequent dialog box screens will ask which fields to include in the list layout, whether to sort the records in a particular order, and which theme, if any, to use.

The next screen gives the option to include header and footer part information, such as a report title or page number. The Header and Footer Information screen is shown in Figure 6.8.

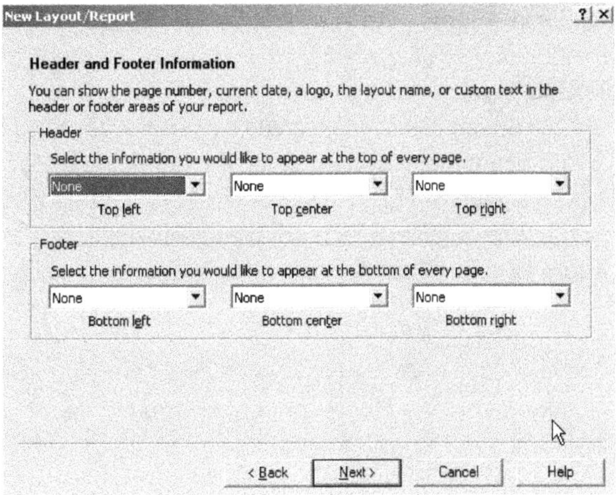

Figure 6.8: The Header and Footer Information screen for columnar/list reports.

It should be noted that if no header or footer information is selected, these parts will not be included in the list layout.

2. Leave the Header and Footer areas of the screen set to **None**, and click **Next**.

The next dialog box screen gives the option to create a script for the new layout. This can be a great advantage as several steps can be automated using a script. For example, the correct layout can be selected, the records sorted by the right field order, and Preview mode selected to display any summary parts correctly.

If a report layout with grouped data is selected, the dialog box gives the option to include sub-totals and grand totals in the completed layout. This can enable quite a complex report to be generated. For example, you could include a sales summary figure for an individual and a company, all in the same report. The veterinary practice management solution case study in Chapter 21 includes some examples of sub-summary report layouts.

3. For now, simply accept the default settings by clicking **Next** and **Finish**.

Table View Layouts

It is possible to view records in a layout as a form, as a list, or as a table. A set of records viewed as a table in FileMaker is similar to how data is displayed in a spreadsheet. While a list or form layout have similar characteristics when viewed in Browse or Layout mode, a layout that has been specified to display records as a table need not resemble the underlying layout when viewed in Browse or Preview mode.

A Table view layout is an excellent method for displaying a set of records. It gives the user greater flexibility than a simple list layout, as field labels are displayed as column headings. The order of the columns can be easily changed and columns can also be resized or used to sort the displayed records, all with a mouse click.

A Table view layout can be selected using the New Layout/Report dialog box. After a table layout has been created, it can be customized using the Layouts>Layout Setup menu option. In the Layout Setup dialog box, click the Views tab, as shown in Figure 6.9. For any layout in the file, the Layout Setup dialog box Views tab can be used to control whether a database user can select Form, List, or Table view from the View menu when in Browse mode.

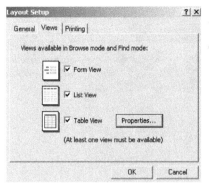

Figure 6.9:
The Layout Setup
dialog box.

Click the Properties button to the right of the Table View check box. The Table View Properties dialog box has additional check boxes to control whether header or footer layout parts will be included when the Table view layout is displayed in Browse, Find, or Preview mode. The parts must already exist in the Table view layout.

The columns can be colored by giving the fields a fill color in Layout mode.

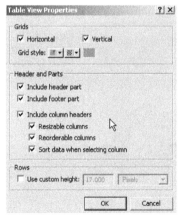

Figure 6.10:
The Table View
Properties dialog
box.

Label Layouts

FileMaker has many standard label sizes preset in a label layout wizard. If the Labels option is selected as the layout type for a new layout, a list of standard labels will be displayed as a drop-down list. Alternatively, a custom label size can be designed, as shown in Figure 6.11.

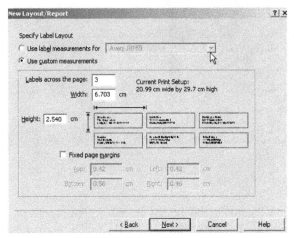

*Figure 6.11:
Selecting a
pre-formatted or
custom size label
with FileMaker.*

When the Next button is clicked, the Specify Label Contents screen appears.
As this layout will not be used for data entry or record searches, the best
method for displaying fields in a label layout is by means of merge fields.
Merge fields ensure that gaps in an address are closed when a label is printed.
The Specify Label Contents screen is shown in Figure 6.12.

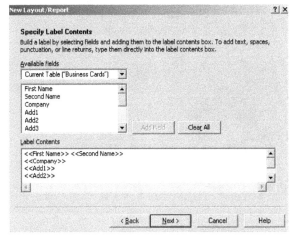

*Figure 6.12:
Adding merge
fields to a new
label layout.*

Additional layout objects, such as a company logo, can be added to the label
layout later, and additional merge fields can be included using the menu
option Insert>Merge Field in Layout mode.

Envelope Layouts

Envelope layouts are created in a very similar way as labels, with merge fields used to add contact details to the envelope layout. The size of the envelope can be modified later by moving the layout part boundaries and checking what paper size has been specified in the Print Setup dialog box.

A completed envelope layout with merge fields is shown in Figure 6.13.

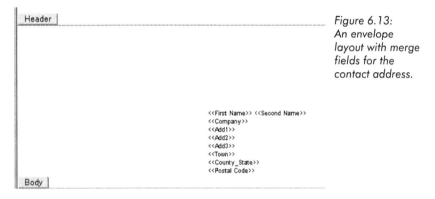

Figure 6.13:
An envelope layout with merge fields for the contact address.

Blank Layouts

A blank layout is a common starting point for most new layouts. The database designer has complete control over the content of a layout from the beginning by selecting the Blank layout option in the New Layout/Report dialog box.

A new named layout will appear with a header, body, and footer part. Parts can be resized or removed from the blank layout and fields or layout objects added as needed.

When you are designing custom layouts, it is a good idea to turn off the "Add newly defined fields to current layout" check box in the Preferences dialog box. You may also wish to turn on "Save layout changes automatically" while you are designing new layouts in a file.

The Color Palette area of the Preferences dialog allows you to choose options for cross-platform design and web publishing of a FileMaker database.

Figure 6.14: The Layout tab in the Preferences dialog box.

Fields, parts, and layout objects can be added to a blank layout using the Status area tools or the Insert menu options to add company logos or customize the look of a layout.

Adding Parts to a Layout

Layout parts are somewhat restricted in the relative order in which they can appear on a layout.

A part can be added to a layout by dragging the Part button into the Status area or by selecting the Insert>Part menu option. A layout part can only exist once on a layout with the exception of sub-summary parts, which can exist for the same sorted field above the body part as a leading sub-summary part and below the body part as a trailing sub-summary part.

The Part Definition dialog box, which appears when an existing part label is double-clicked or the Part button is dragged onto the layout, is a useful guide for adding layout parts and for determining what parts can still be added to a layout, which are shown as solid radio buttons. The Part Definition dialog box is shown in Figure 6.15. Additional features include the ability to break pages or restart page numbers for new record occurrences in the same layout part. For example, a sales report could start on a new page for every sales territory if the records are sorted by this field.

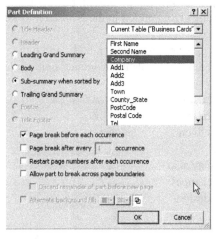

Figure 6.15:
The Part Definition
dialog box.

The order in which parts appear in a layout can be viewed and modified, within the rules of FileMaker's part restrictions, using the menu option Layouts>Part Setup. If a layout part is not locked, as indicated by the padlock symbol shown in Figure 6.16, the part can be moved by using the mouse to click and drag on the vertical double arrows.

Figure 6.16:
The Part Setup
dialog box.

Printing with Layouts

While the database layout designer has complete freedom over what fields to include in a layout, there may be fields and other layout objects that appear on screen that should not appear in print. Examples might include a field with comments on customer payment history or navigation buttons at the top of a layout, which are of great benefit on screen but are unnecessary and use up toner when printed.

There are two options to change the way a data entry layout looks when printed. The first is to design separate layouts for data entry and printing in your FileMaker solution. The design of each layout should fit its purpose, with navigation buttons and background colors on the data entry layout to assist colleagues, and perhaps plain fields on a blank background for the layout that is used to print records. However, this method requires the database developer to spend extra time designing additional layouts for the same underlying record set. A simpler but less flexible option is to use the same database layout for data entry and printed reports, and the menu option Format>Set Sliding/Printing to prevent highlighted layout objects and fields from being printed. The Set Sliding/Printing dialog box is shown in Figure 6.17.

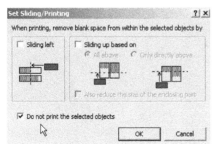

Figure 6.17:
The Set Sliding/
Printing dialog box.

Label layouts are special in that they can print in more than one column on a page.

The Printing tab of the Layout Setup dialog box is shown in Figure 6.18. A custom label layout can be modified to include an extra column or to use fixed page margins.

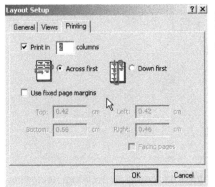

Figure 6.18:
The Layout Setup
dialog box.

Working with Fields in a Layout

Fields are added to a layout at the time it is created, or later by using the Field tool in the Status area. Click and drag the field object to the position on the layout where you want to place the new field. When you let go of the mouse button, the Specify Field dialog box appears with a list of fields from the table that the layout is based on. Fields from other layouts can be selected from the drop-down list near the top of the dialog box, as shown in Figure 6.19.

Figure 6.19:
The Specify Field
dialog box.

Once a field is added to a layout it can be displayed in one of several different styles. The layout designer can also decide whether a user can select a field in Browse or Find mode by highlighting an existing field in a layout and selecting the Format>Field/Control>Setup menu option. With FileMaker Pro 8, a field can be customized to display on a layout as an edit box (or normal field), a drop-down list of selected values, a pop-up menu, a check box set, or a radio button set. In addition, a field can be modified to display a drop-down calendar.

A field can also be displayed on a layout as a merge field by using the menu option Insert>Merge Field. A merge field cannot be selected for editing in Browse mode or searching in Find mode.

The layout designer can also prevent a field from being selected in Browse or Find mode by using the menu option Format>Field/Control>Behavior, which opens the Field Behavior dialog shown in Figure 6.20. Additional check boxes control what keys the user can use to move to the next layout object.

Figure 6.20:
The Field Behavior
dialog box.

It is important to design an effective data entry order, or Tab order, for a layout that will be used to capture new records. In Layout mode, the menu option Layouts>Set Tab Order is used to set up the data entry sequence for a layout. The Tab order can be changed by clicking into each field in the preferred order. The Set Tab Order dialog box is shown in Figure 6.21.

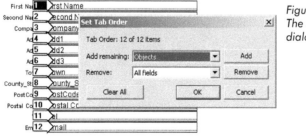

Figure 6.21:
The Set Tab Order
dialog box.

The business database case studies in this book include applied examples of how field entry is controlled and how fields are displayed in layouts.

Chapter 7

Relational Database Design

In this chapter:

Introduction

FileMaker Pro 8 enables you to create a relational database for your business easily and without having to spend a great deal of time researching the theory and background of relational database design.

A relationship adds value to information in one or more record sets. With a relationship you can link data in one or more tables based on common field values, different field values, or a comparison of values in two or more fields.

A relational database consists of two or more tables that have at least one field in common. A few examples of relational data tables for business include organizations to contacts, customers to invoices, and suppliers to orders.

A well-designed relational database is a great asset to a business. Retyping the recipient's address every time you want to send a new letter to an existing customer or adding up a row of invoice line items to work out the total invoice figure is time consuming and prone to error. With a little planning, a FileMaker database can be designed to store customer details and link them to standard sales letters or to automate the conversion of a job sheet into a new invoice with line items and line totals for all billable items.

What's the point of a relational database? A relational database is designed to avoid the problem of redundant or duplicate data, where the same business information is stored in more than one field or in more than one table. Ideally, data should be stored and retrieved from one place only to avoid duplication or false or out-of-date information. For professional database designers, the process of designing a table structure that minimizes or eliminates duplicate data is known as data normalization.

Small firms and workgroups have the fewest resources for retyping and checking existing data at each stage of production or service delivery. The flipside of this is that it is often the small business that can derive the biggest competitive advantage from introducing a FileMaker relational database solution.

This chapter examines how a relational database is designed with FileMaker, when to use related data in a record, and when to use a lookup to derive a value from another table for a field.

A significant change in relational database design occurred with the release of FileMaker Pro 7 and subsequently FileMaker Pro 8. Prior to version 7, a FileMaker file was limited to one table. While relationships could be established between files, the words "table," "file," and "database" were interchangeable, as FileMaker developers were accustomed to the single table per file restriction. With FileMaker Pro 7 and 8, a database file can consist of up to 1,000,000 tables. While this chapter examines relationships between two tables in the same file, the same techniques can be used to create relationships to tables in other FileMaker Pro files.

Designing a Relationship between Two Tables with Key Fields

To start applying relational database techniques, let's consider the simple requirement to link a single organization record with many staff records. The organization has a single name, a main office address, and a company registration and sales tax number. We may be interested in this organization because it could be a new business prospect, an existing client, or a supplier. Our business does not deal directly with the company, but with contacts who represent the company. Details on the name, job title, direct phone number, and email address for a contact cannot be held in the Organization table, as we will have to overwrite these details when we want to capture information on another person at the same company. These contact details need to be held in fields within the Contacts table. We could replicate all the company field details in the Contacts table, but this could be prone to error. If the company announces a takeover and a change of name next year, we will have to ensure that the company name is modified in all relevant contact records for individuals who work for that company. It would be far easier and less time consuming if we made FileMaker do the work of linking organization information with contact details using a relationship between the two tables.

Since in this case there is only one company record and many contact records, the common link between companies and contacts is called a "one-to-many" relationship.

We need to make use of a common, or key, field in both tables to match up a company record with many contact records.

It may seem obvious at first to use the company name as the key field between Organization and Contacts. However, problems will arise later if the company changes its name or merges with another company. As you type a new name into the Organization field, you will risk losing all the existing contact records. They will still be in the Contacts file, but it will be hard to associate them with the revised company name. A similar problem would arise if you were to design a relational database based on staff names and training courses attended. If a colleague's surname changes, the old training course records will no longer be associated with the staff record.

Ideally, we want to create a key field for every record in a database that is unique and never changes for that record. Even if a record for an organization is deleted, its key field value will never be used again. In business there are some data tables that already have a unique identifier that we could use as a key field, such as a social security number for a staff database. This isn't always the case, though, and it is far easier if we make use of FileMaker's field options to make the application do the work and create a unique key field for every record in a database table.

In order to relate two tables together, we need two distinct types of key fields: a primary key and a foreign key. On the "one" table side of a one-to-many relationship, a primary key value will be valid (or never empty) and unique for every record in the table. For a relationship to work for certain records, or be valid, a foreign key field value in another table must be the same as a primary key field value in the original table. In a one-to-many relationship, the same foreign key value can occur more than once in a table. In our example, the records for all staff who work for the same organization will share the same foreign key field value and, for the relationship to be valid and work, this value needs to be the same as the primary key field value in the Organization table.

The table row, or record, that contains the unique primary key is sometimes called the *parent record*, while the table rows, or records, that include a foreign key are sometimes called *child records*. The analogy is taken further, where if a parent record is deleted from a table, the child records are called orphan records. To avoid the problem of orphan records when you design relationships, FileMaker gives you the option of deleting records in an associated table when a record in the current table is deleted.

It is at this point that relational database design has to fit in with how your organization wants to manage business data. For example, do you want to capture contact details when they are in the parent organization record? Also, we want the design to allow us to delete an invoice that has not yet been posted, and also remove any associated line items in another table, but deleting a single line item record should not erase the parent invoice record.

Any table in a FileMaker database solution should have one primary key field. In the present example, the Contacts table should have its own primary key field for designing further relationships, perhaps to correspondence sent, training courses, or meetings attended.

Assigning a Primary Key Field Value with FileMaker

While it is not critical to do so, number fields make excellent primary key fields for relational database design. It is straightforward to create a serial number, usually incrementing by one, and a number field will sort records in an expected numeric order.

To become familiar with defining primary and foreign key fields, we can create a basic FileMaker database that will contain two tables: Clients and Contacts.

1. Launch FileMaker if it is not already open and create a new database called **Clients.fp7**.

    The Define Database dialog box will open with the Fields tab displayed and the default table, Clients, selected, as shown in Figure 7.1.

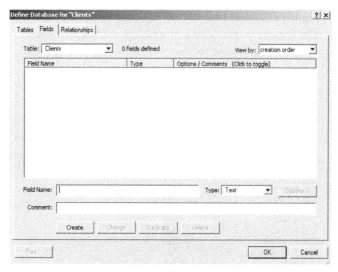

Figure 7.1: The Define Database dialog box.

2. Create a new field called **PKey Client** and select **Number** as the field type. Click the **Create** button.

3. Click the **Options** button to open the Options for Field dialog box. Select the **Auto-Enter** tab, as shown in Figure 7.2.

4. Click the **Serial number** check box, and choose the **On creation** option for Generate. Choose the default next value of **1** and increment by **1**. To prevent the auto-entered PKey field value from being modified, click the **Prohibit modification of value during data entry** check box.

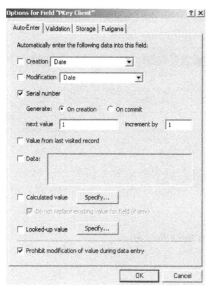

Figure 7.2: Defining the primary key field to be a serial number.

Further field data controls are available by clicking the Validation tab. The options on the Auto-Enter tab are sufficient to create a unique primary key field value for every record in the Clients table.

5. Add the additional descriptive fields to the Clients table as shown in Figure 7.3.

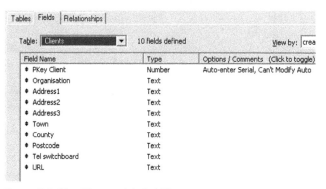

Figure 7.3: The Clients table field list.

Building a One-to-Many Relationship with FileMaker

To capture individual contact details, we are going to add another table called Contacts to the Clients file and build a relationship between the two tables.

1. In the Define Database dialog box, click the **Tables** tab and create a new table called **Contacts**.

2. Click the **Fields** tab and, with the Contacts table highlighted in the drop-down list, add the following fields:

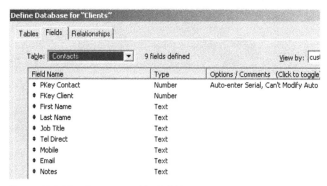

Figure 7.4: The Contacts table field list.

The PKey Contact field uses exactly the same method as the PKey Client field to create a unique serial number value for every record in the Contacts table.

We are now able to create a relationship between the two tables in the file.

3. Click on the **Relationships** tab at the top of the Define Database dialog box.

The relationships graph will appear with our two tables displayed, as shown in Figure 7.5.

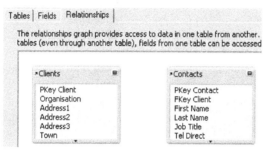

Figure 7.5: The relationships graph showing the two tables in the file.

We can now create a relationship between the two tables by drawing a relationship line between the PKey Client field in the Clients table and the FKey Client field in the Contacts table.

4. Click the mouse on the **PKey Client** field and, holding the mouse button down, drag the relationship line so that it stops on the **FKey Client** field in the Contacts table. FileMaker will change the appearance of the table icons in the graph so that the key fields used in a relationship appear in new boxes at the top of the table, as shown in Figure 7.6.

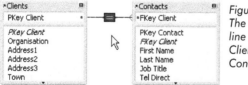

Figure 7.6: The relationship line between the Clients and Contacts tables.

You may notice that FileMaker has added three split lines, or a crow's foot, to the Contacts side of the relationship line. This is because the PKey Client field is set to be a unique number, so FileMaker is assuming, in this case correctly, that the Contacts table is the "many" side of the "one-to-many" relationship, based on the PKey Client and FKey Client fields.

It is worth remembering at this stage that the tables seen in the relationships graph are table occurrences, based on the underlying, or base, tables in a file. The distinction is important as it is possible to have any number of table occurrences in the relationships graph for the same underlying table. As discussed later in this chapter, as more relationships are added in a file, the relationships graph can start to appear quite crowded and some design rules are worth following to make the graph easier to work with.

Populating the Foreign Key Field with FileMaker

We have now built a relational database consisting of a "one-to-many" relationship between the Clients and the Contacts tables. It is perfectly possible to now click the OK button to close the Define Database dialog box and start adding new client and contact records to the file.

Your colleagues may not find this an altogether rewarding experience as they have to remember what client foreign key field value should be added to a new contact record so as to get a match field and make the relationship valid. They may start to feel that using the organization name might have been a more sensible approach; after all, we deal with names in the real world, not unique serial numbers.

To maintain user confidence in the new database and to minimize data error, we need to find a way to place the correct value into the FKey Client field. This is an issue to be resolved for any relational database design.

There are four basic methods for populating the FKey Client field with the correct value for the associated client record. These are:

■ Select an FKey value from a value list in a Contact Details layout.

■ Select a "hidden" FKey value disguised as the client name in a Contact Details layout.

■ Create a new contact record through a portal in a Client Details layout.

■ Use a script to automate the creation of a new related contact record.

Examples of all these methods are used in the case studies described later in this book.

An example of each is presented here for our basic file.

Select an FKey Value from a Value List in a Contact Details Layout

We will need some sample records to demonstrate each of the four basic methods for populating the FKey Client field in the Contacts table.

1. Let's begin by creating two or three sample organization records using the Clients layout. Each time you create a new record, you will notice the value in the PKey Client field increments by one.

2. When you have created two or more sample client records, switch to the
    Contacts layout using the Layout menu in the Status area and select **Lay-
    out mode**.

    The Contacts layout should appear as shown in Figure 7.7.

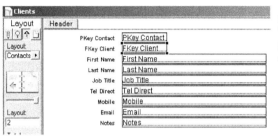

Figure 7.7:
The Contacts
layout in the
Clients file.

3. Highlight the **FKey Client** field, click the right mouse button, and select
    the **Field/Control>Setup** menu option.

4. In the Field/Control Setup dialog box that appears next, choose
    Drop-down List as the display type, and select **Define Value Lists** in
    the Display values from box, as shown in Figure 7.8.

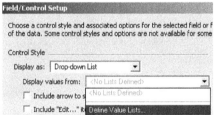

Figure 7.8:
Detail of the
Field/Control
Setup dialog box.

5. The Define Value List dialog box will now appear. Click the **New** button
    to open the Edit Value List dialog. Type **Client List** into the Value List
    Name box, and click the **Use values from field** option.

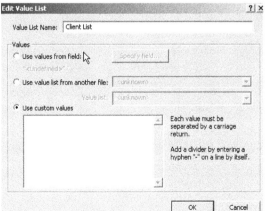

Figure 7.9:
Using field values
for the client list.

6. The Specify Fields for Value List dialog box will then appear, as shown in Figure 7.10. Choose **Clients** from the drop-down list on the left and highlight the **PKey Client** field in the left-hand field list box. Leave the Value List Content option of "Include all values" selected, which is the default setting. Click the **Also display values from second field** check box, and highlight the **Organisation** field in the right-hand field list box. For the moment, leave the Display Options set to **Sort by first field**.

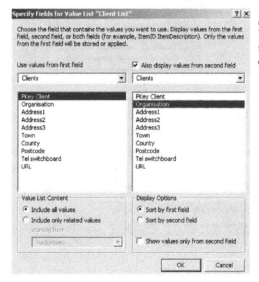

Figure 7.10:
The Specify Fields
for Value List
dialog box.

7. Click **OK** and click the subsequent three **OK** buttons to return to the Contacts layout.

8. Switch to Browse mode and add a new record by using the Ctrl+N keys, the toolbar icon, or the menu option Records>New Record. Now, when the FKey Client field is selected with the mouse or tabbed into, a value list should appear with your organizations listed, similar to Figure 7.11.

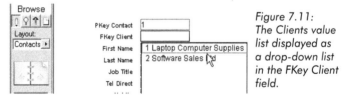

Figure 7.11:
The Clients value
list displayed as
a drop-down list
in the FKey Client
field.

This is a perfectly good method for populating the FKey Client field to relate contact records to a client record.

Select a "Hidden" FKey Value Disguised as the Client Name in a Contact Details Layout

You may have noticed that the Specify Fields for Value List dialog box had additional options to customize how a list is displayed.

1. Select the menu option **File>Define>Value Lists** to open the Define Value Lists dialog box. Highlight **Client List** and click the **Edit** button.

2. The Edit Value List dialog box will appear. Click the **Specify Field** button, then click the **Show values only from second field** check box, as shown in Figure 7.12.

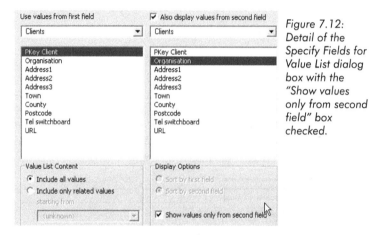

Figure 7.12:
Detail of the
Specify Fields for
Value List dialog
box with the
"Show values
only from second
field" box
checked.

3. Click the **OK** buttons in each of the dialog boxes to return to the Contacts layout in Browse mode.

    You can now test how your changes have altered the value list, as shown in Figure 7.13.

Figure 7.13:
The revised client
list displayed as
a drop-down list.

The client records are sorted by name, and any confusion caused by using the PKey Client field value is avoided.

Create a New Contact Record through a Portal in a Client Details Layout

A portal is a special FileMaker layout object that enables you to view and work with one or more related records. Portals are an ideal method for displaying selected fields as rows for more than one related record.

We can add a portal to our Clients layout and use it to display, and in the present example also create, related contact records.

1. Select the Clients layout and switch to Layout mode. Select the **Portal** tool from the Status area, as shown in Figure 7.14.

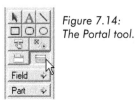
Figure 7.14:
The Portal tool.

2. Move the cursor across the Clients layout and draw a rectangle similar in size to the one shown in Figure 7.15. The Portal Setup dialog will open when you release the mouse button.

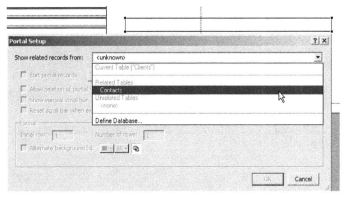

Figure 7.15: The Portal Setup dialog box with the portal area highlighted on the Clients layout.

3. In the Portal Setup dialog box, select **Contacts** from the Show related records from drop-down list. You may at this stage want to check the boxes to sort portal records, allow deletion of portal records, or add a vertical scroll bar. The latter is imperative if more related records will exist than can be shown on the screen.

4. Select how many related records you want to display at one time by typing a number in the Number of rows box.

5. Click **OK** and the Add Fields to Portal dialog box will appear on the screen. Add some fields to the portal from the Contacts table, as shown in Figure 7.16.

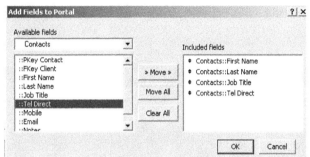

Figure 7.16: Choosing the fields to add to the Contacts portal.

6. Click the **OK** button and the new portal will be displayed in the layout as shown in Figure 7.17. FileMaker does not automatically add field titles to the portal, but these can be added later.

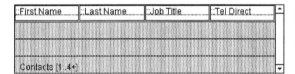

Figure 7.17: The Contacts portal in the Clients layout.

We now have to make a modification to the relationship in the Clients file so that new contact records can be added via the portal.

7. Choose the menu option **File>Define>Database** and click on the **Relationships** tab at the top of the Define Database dialog box.

8. Double-click anywhere on the relationship line between the two table icons in the graph to open the Edit Relationship dialog box, as shown in Figure 7.18. In the Contacts area, click the **Allow creation of records in this table via this relationship** check box.

9. Click both **OK** buttons to return to the Clients layout.

If you switch to Browse mode, you will notice that you can now select the First Name field in the first row of the portal and type in details for a new related contact record.

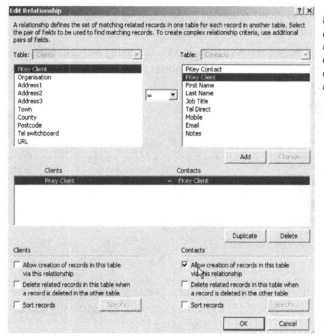

Figure 7.18:
Modifying a
relationship to
enable the
creation of
related records.

Use a Script to Automate the Creation of a New Related Contact Record

A slightly more complicated method for populating the FKey Client field and creating a new related contact record for a client is to write a script that can automate the task.

The benefit of using a script is that it gives the database designer more control over how a new contact record is created and in what order any related data should be captured.

Before we write a script to add a new contact record from within the Clients layout, we need to add a global field to the Clients table.

1. Use the menu option **File>Define>Database** to open the Define Database dialog box and click the **Fields** tab.

2. Select the **Clients** table from the drop-down list and add a new number field called **gPKey Client**.

3. Click the **Options** button and select the **Storage** tab, then click the **Use global storage** check box, as shown in Figure 7.19.

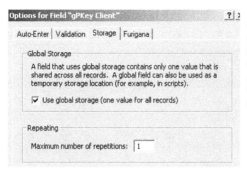

Figure 7.19:
A field can be set
to use global
storage in the
Storage tab of
the Options for
Field dialog box.

The contents of a global field can be referenced across any table in a database. We will use this global field in a script to temporarily store the PKey Client value for a record.

4.   To create a new script, choose the menu option **Scripts>ScriptMaker**. In the Define Scripts dialog box, click the **New** button.

5.   Type **Add a New Contact** in the Script Name box and use the script steps shown in Figure 7.20 to create the script.

To recreate the script shown in Figure 7.20, each of the steps shown should be selected from the script steps list. Highlight each script step in the list, and click the **Move** button to add the selected step to the script. Use the Script Step Options section to replicate the finished script shown in Figure 7.20. A more detailed discussion of how scripts can be used to automate FileMaker is presented in Chapter 9.

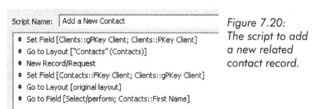

Figure 7.20:
The script to add
a new related
contact record.

The script can be described as follows:

First the gPKey global field is set to have the same value as the PKey field for the current record. The script then switches to the Contacts layout in order to create a new blank contact record. The FKey Client field in the new contact record is set to be the same as the gPKey Client field which, being a global field, can be referenced anywhere in the database. Finally, the script switches back to the original layout, Clients, and selects the First Name field from the Contacts table.

It is important to check that the Contacts portal has been preset to sort related records by first name. If this is the case, then null, or empty, values in FileMaker always appear at the top of a sort order. The script then knows it has selected the new blank contact record, as the blank first name always appears at the top of a portal. If this is too much of an assumption, the script can be simplified to stay in the Contacts layout to enable details for the new record to be captured.

It is not a good idea to leave a script in a PKey or FKey field. There is a risk that the database user will inadvertently erase or modify the key field value.

The script can be triggered by selecting it from the Scripts menu, or from a button or other layout object that is added to the Clients layout and set to run the script when clicked on.

Slightly more complex scripts to create new related records are included in the case studies. They only differ in that some of them make use of custom dialog messages asking the database user to confirm that he or she wants to create a new related record.

Avoiding Accidental Deletion or Modification of Related Record Data

While this chapter is concerned with relational database design, it is worth noting how the Field Behavior dialog box can be used to avoid accidental deleting or editing of information displayed in a layout in fields from a related record.

If we were to add the Organisation field to the Contacts layout to display the organization name, we wouldn't want the contents of this field to be modified by accident.

To avoid accidental modification of data in a related field, highlight the field and select the menu option Format>Field Control>Behavior. In the Field Behavior dialog box, you can decide whether any field can be selected in Browse or Find mode. In the example shown in Figure 7.21, the Organisation field can be searched to find all contacts at a particular organization, but the field cannot be edited in Browse mode.

Figure 7.21: The Field Behavior dialog box.

More Complex Relationships

It is probably true to say that the one-to-many relationship is the relationship most commonly used in database design projects. However, you should also understand the other relationship types and how to manage them in a File-Maker solution. A many-to-many relationship is frequently required in a business database, while a self-join relationship can exist in stock control systems or personnel database files.

Many-to-Many Relationships

The event management case study that is described in Chapter 17 also addresses the issue of a many-to-many relationship. Imagine that you are tasked with designing a staff training database for your company. Your completed database file is going to need a table to hold staff details (Contacts) and a table for course information (Courses). The problem then arises of how these two tables can be related. You need to define relationships to display what courses a staff member has attended and, in the Courses details layout, which colleagues are enrolled in the course.

The easiest way to manage a many-to-many relationship is to include an intermediate, or join, table between the Contacts table and the Courses table. The join table could be called Bookings, as each record in this table should have a related staff name and course title. The Bookings table could be used as the basis for a portal in the Contacts details layout to show all course enrollments for an individual. The Bookings table could also be used as the underlying table for another portal in the Courses details layout to show all students in the course.

The way in which this "many-to-many" relationship is tackled in the relationships graph is shown in Figure 7.22.

You may notice that FileMaker has again symbolized the "many" side of the relationship with the FKey Contacts and FKey Course fields.

Figure 7.22: A basic many-to-many relationship to link Contacts with Courses.

Self-Join Relationships

A self-join relationship occurs when both match fields, the primary and foreign key fields, exist in the same table. An example could be for managers and reporting staff who might all exist as records in an employee database. In such a case, the relationship would need to be based on an Employee ID primary key field, which is unique for all staff records, and a Manager ID foreign key field, which would be the same value for all staff who report to the same manager.

If you wish to define a self-join relationship in FileMaker's relationships graph, you need to add a new table occurrence for the same base table in the graph. FileMaker does not permit you to create a circular relationship on the graph as it would be unable to evaluate the relationship.

Multiple Criteria Relationships

Earlier versions of FileMaker would only let the database designer create relationships if a foreign key field had the same value as the primary key field. These relationships are known as *equijoins*. FileMaker Pro 7 and 8 enable the designer to improve the functionality of relationships by using multiple join types. A relationship can now be defined that is only valid if two or more fields are the same value. In addition, a relationship can be defined based on a value that is less than, greater than, or not equal to values in the related table. These are called *non-equijoin relationships*. An example of this is used in the event management case study in Chapter 17, where an event value list is filtered via a relationship that includes the current date in order to only show future event titles.

It is only really possible to get FileMaker to populate the foreign key field and create new related records for equijoin relationships. FileMaker can be customized to know what a matching foreign key value must be; however, it is much harder to make FileMaker decide what a foreign key field value must not be.

Using Entity Relationship Diagrams to Plan a FileMaker Database

Like most activities in business, some prior planning can be of great benefit when designing a relational database with FileMaker.

Before starting to add tables to a FileMaker file, it is a good idea to consider what information is to be captured, managed, and reported by the database. As a business or workgroup manager, you may already have clear views on this, or you might like to arrange meetings and interviews with colleagues to make sure that all data collection and analysis requirements are addressed when planning a new database.

An entity relationship diagram is an excellent planning tool that should ideally be sketched out before starting work on a FileMaker database.

An entity relationship (ER) diagram is a data modeling technique used to create a graphical representation of all the required entities and how they are related in the business process. Each entity, or table, appears only once in an ER diagram. With FileMaker, a representation of the same table can occur more than once in the relationships graph. This distinction is important. As is discussed later in this chapter, the inclusion of many table occurrences in the relationships graph for the same base table can be a great benefit for clarity and for designing data entry and report layouts.

An ER diagram usually consists of a set of data tables represented by rectangles and labeled with brief descriptions of the entities. Where applicable, these rectangles are connected by a line to indicate where key fields will be used to create a relationship. Each end of the relationship line may include a symbol to indicate whether the relationship is one-to-one, one-to-many, or many-to-many. Often a crow's-foot symbol is used to indicate the "many" side of a relationship. Further notation is sometimes used to indicate whether a relationship must be valid. For example, an invoice line child record must have an invoice parent record. This is sometimes called the *cardinality* of a relationship.

A sample ER diagram is shown in Figure 7.23, indicating the tables needed for a booking database and their relationships and cardinality.

A single line connecting with a rectangle at one end of a relationship indicates that only one related record exists in that table for any record in the table at the other end of the line. A split line, or crow's foot, connecting with a rectangle indicates that there are potentially many related records in that table for any record in the table at the other end of the relationship line. The circle, or "O" symbol, across one end of a relationship line is used to indicate that the relationship does not always have to be valid and that a related record does not always have to exist. A short intersecting line, or "|" symbol, at right angles to one end of the relationship line is used to indicate that the relationship must be valid and that at least one related record must exist at all times in this table.

In Figure 7.23 a contact record does not have to have a related booking record but can have many. A booking record must always have one and only one contact record. The same rules apply for an event, which does not have to have a booking record but can have several. A booking record must always have one and only one event record.

A booking record does not always have a related invoice item record; a booking may be free of charge for students or unpaid contacts, for example. An invoice item should always relate to one booking record. If an invoice is raised, it should always have at least one related invoice item. An invoice item should always have one, and only one, invoice.

Booking Database ER Diagram

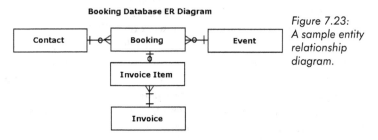

Figure 7.23:
A sample entity relationship diagram.

A well-designed ER diagram can act as a useful focal point for designing a relational database with FileMaker for your business.

The following section introduces the concept of using multiple occurrences of the same underlying table in FileMaker's relationships graph to improve relationship management in the database and to help with layout design table occurrence groups. It may be of particular interest to users of earlier versions of FileMaker who are used to a tabular display of relationships rather than the graphical approach provided by the relationships graph in FileMaker 7 and 8.

Managing the Relationships Graph with FileMaker Pro 8

Part I — Avoiding a Relationships Graph "Spiderweb"

Perhaps the most important difference between FileMaker Pro 7 and 8 and earlier versions of the application is the ability to create multiple tables in a single FileMaker Pro file. This welcome feature has an important effect on the best method for designing relationships between tables in FileMaker. In previous versions of FileMaker, a database designer could define and name a relationship between any two FileMaker files. Since version 7, relationships are no longer defined in the traditional sense. Instead, table occurrences associated with an underlying table are added to the relationships graph in a FileMaker file, and the designer can only name the table occurrence, not the relationship.

The distinction is illustrated in Figures 7.24 and 7.25. In FileMaker Pro 6 and earlier, the designer named the relationships, or the edges. Since FileMaker Pro 7, the database architect names the table occurrences, or the nodes.

To make matters even more complicated, in Figure 7.24 for FileMaker Pro 6 and earlier, relationships are "one way," while in Figure 7.25 for versions 7 and 8, a developer can make use of the relationship to access record data in either direction.

Relationships provide access to data in other files.		2 relationship(s)
	View by: creation order ▼	

Relationship Name	Relationship	Related File
✦ Letters	Record ID = ::Record ID	DLetters.fp5
✦ DPasswords	Company 1 = ::Unique Name	DUniqueOrganisations.fp5

Figure 7.24: The tabular representation of one-way relationships in FileMaker Pro versions 3 to 6, where the designer names the relationship.

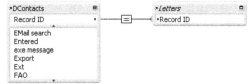

Figure 7.25:
The graphic representation of two-way relationships in FileMaker Pro versions 7 and 8, where the designer names the table occurrence.

Unless some thought and planning is put into the naming of table occurrences in the relationships graph, it can be extremely difficult to decide which table occurrence to use in designing a new layout, a portal within a layout, a sub-summary report, or a conditional value list in a pop-up menu.

Prior to FileMaker Pro 7, fields could be added to any layout from the same file or from any related FileMaker database. For FileMaker 7 and later, any layout, portal, or related records value list must be associated with a unique table occurrence in the relationships graph of a particular file.

Anyone who has converted an older FileMaker solution with several related files to version 7 or 8 may recognize the problem raised by a crowded and complicated relationships graph. Figure 7.26 shows a particularly grue-some example of what many developers call a "spiderweb" relationships graph.

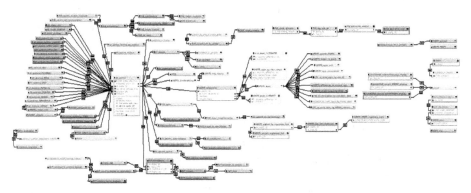

Figure 7.26: The relationships graph for a complex FileMaker solution with multiple relationships.

Anyone having to work with this file is likely to spend considerable time checking which table occurrence to use for a layout, a portal, or the Go to Related Record ScriptMaker step.

A solution to this problem is to group table occurrences into discrete clusters, based on relationships that have a clearly defined route and direction between the table occurrences. The name table occurrence group (TOG) is used for these table occurrence clusters.

Part II — Turn Your Spiders into Squids or Anchor/Buoys

Two similar solutions have been proposed by professional FileMaker devel-opers Kevin Frank (http://www.kevinfrank.com/demo-files-user-group.html) and Jonathan Stark (http://www.jonathanstark.com/pages/article_squids.php). The former has coined the phrase "anchor/buoy" for designing easy-to-read TOGs, while the latter uses the term "squids." Both descriptions are designed to distinguish the left-hand leading table occurrence in any TOG as the "anchor" or "squid head," while any related table occurrences flowing out to the right of the relationships graph are termed the "buoys" or "tentacles."

Key to understanding TOGs is the acceptance that any table occurrence in a relationships graph is not a table itself but only a representation of an underlying, or base, table. It is possible for the graph to have many table occurrences for the same base table. The set of records displayed in Browse mode and the information displayed for those records is dictated by the table occurrence associated with any particular layout. Furthermore, the table occurrence will be influenced by any relationships with linked table occurrences.

To make it easier to recognize a table occurrence in context, any table occurrences that are to the right of an anchor or squid head should be labeled with the name of the first underlying table followed by a separator such as "to" or "_", and the table occurrence's own underlying table. Figure 7.27 shows an example of a timesheet solution.

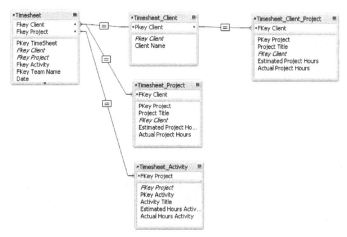

Figure 7.27: The squid head or anchor table occurrence is labeled Timesheet. The squid leg or buoy table occurrences have any preceding table occurrences prefixed in their title and the "_" separator.

Both the squid and anchor/buoy TOG methods have a few simple rules that make the transition from FileMaker Pro 6 to 7 or 8 a lot easier. These rules are as follows:

- The underlying table occurrence for any data layouts should be a squid head or anchor.

- Calculations should be based on a squid head or anchor table occurrence.

- Related value lists should be based on a squid head or anchor table.

- The underlying table occurrence for any portals should be from a squid leg or a buoy.

If each squid or anchor/buoy TOG is placed directly underneath the previous one, with the root table placed on the left-hand side of the relationships graph, it is far easier to print out and use the graph as a project reference document. This is shown for a more complex example in Figure 7.28.

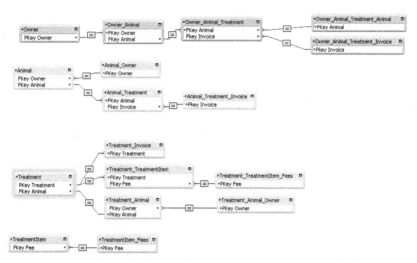

Figure 7.28: A set of well laid out table occurrence groups (TOGs) with the anchor or squid head table occurrence on the left-hand side.

As an applied example, the technique outlined above makes it a lot simpler to choose the correct relationship for a conditional value list. In the example shown in Figure 7.29, a timesheet database designer only wants to show a list of related activity codes that are associated with a project code that has already been selected on any particular timesheet record. In the Specify Fields for Value List dialog box, the table occurrence Timesheet_Activity is selected to display only related activity code values.

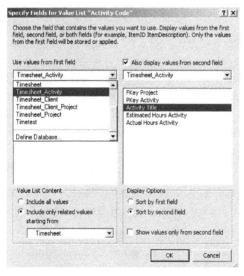

Figure 7.29: Applying the squid or anchor/buoy technique for creating a related value list of timesheet activity codes.

In the timesheet example, the drop-down list of table occurrence "relation-ships" sorted alphabetically in Figure 7.29 is reassuringly similar to how a relationship was selected in older versions of FileMaker.

Chapter 8

Using Calculation Fields

Introduction

The inclusion of calculation fields in a FileMaker database can seem like a big step for new or novice database users. Calculation fields can do a lot of the work in manipulating and reporting business information, and it is well worth becoming familiar with common calculation formulas and their use. If you have ever used the Sum function to add up a row of figures in a spreadsheet application, FileMaker's Calculation dialog box should look reassuringly familiar.

A calculation field does nothing more than derive a value from the contents of other fields in the same table or in other tables in the current file or in other referenced files. For any of the records in a set, the calculation result is determined by the formula that you create for the calculation field. The data in a calculation field result can be in the form of a number, text, date, time, timestamp, or container.

The procedure for creating calculation fields is described in this chapter. Examples include calculating information from related fields, and some of the more common and useful calculation formulas for business solutions are presented.

Defining Calculation Fields

Calculation fields are one of the eight field types in a FileMaker database, and arguably the most useful and powerful, given the wealth of formulas, operators, and functions that can be included in a calculation field's definition.

As with any new technique, the best way to gain familiarity and confidence with FileMaker calculation fields is to have an applied database issue that you wish to resolve.

A new calculation field is added to a table using the Define Database dialog box, with the Fields tab selected. Then type a name for the new calculation field, choose Calculation from the field type drop-down list, and click the Create button.

As with any other type of field, the name used for a calculation field should be chosen carefully. FileMaker will warn you when you create a new field if the field name contains problem characters. If the field itself is later to be used in another calculation, FileMaker will have trouble evaluating the formula if the field name contains any of the characters shown in Figure 8.1.

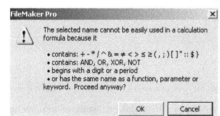

Figure 8.1:
FileMaker Pro
prefers that these
characters are
not included in
calculation or
other field
names.

If you are planning to use FileMaker to create business invoices, it is likely that you will want it to do the work of adding up all invoice lines to produce a total invoice figure. Back in a customer details layout, it is probable that you would like to see the summary total figure for all invoices sent to a customer, the total amount of any payments received, and the difference, if any. You might then like to send a statement or a letter to the client contact to request any outstanding payment.

All of these data manipulation requirements can be managed using calculation fields.

We can use the client and invoice example to add some useful calculation fields to a FileMaker file.

A simple FileMaker database can be used to demonstrate calculation fields that reference related fields.

1. Launch FileMaker and create a new database called **ClientBilling**.

2.   Add the tables shown in Figure 8.2 to the file.

Figure 8.2:
Add these tables
to the ClientBilling
file.

3.   With the Fields tab selected, add the fields shown in Figure 8.3 to the
      Client table.

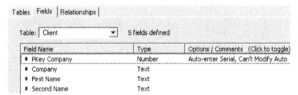

Figure 8.3:
Initial fields added
to the Client table.

We can add a calculation field to the Client table that is used to join
together, or concatenate, a first and second name field using the amper-
sand (&) operator.

4.   Type **Full Name** into the Field Name box, choose **Calculation** from the
      Field type drop-down list, and click the **Create** button. The Specify Cal-
      culation dialog box will appear, as shown in Figure 8.4.

5.   Double-click on the **First Name** field in the upper-left window of the
      Specify Calculation dialog box. The First Name field should be added to
      the formula area.

6.   Single-click on the **&** operator button to add it to the formula, then click
      on the **" "** (double quotes) operator button. A set of quotes should appear
      in the formula.

7.   Place the cursor between the quotes in the formula like so, "|" , and press
      the Spacebar to add a space between the two quotes like so, " ".

8.   Move or click the cursor to the right and outside the quote marks, then
      single-click on the **&** operator button again.

9.   Finally, double-click on the **Second Name** field, and your formula box
      should look like the one in Figure 8.4.

The & symbol is used to concatenate fields together. The double quote
symbol is used to wrap literal text in a formula. If the First Name and
Second Name fields were not separated by the symbols & " " &, then the

calculation field would display names like JeffTracy rather than Jeff Tracy.

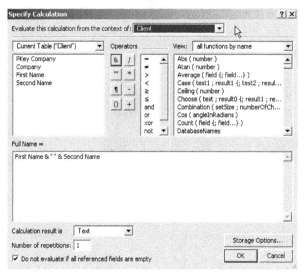

Figure 8.4:
The Full Name calculation field formula.

The calculation result is set to text, and the calculation is set to evaluate from the context of the Client table.

10. Click the **OK** button, and the new Full Name calculation field will be displayed in the table field list, as shown in Figure 8.5.

✦ PKey Company	Number	Auto-enter Serial, Can't Modify Auto
✦ Company	Text	
✦ First Name	Text	
✦ Second Name	Text	
✦ Full Name	Calculation	= First Name & " " & Second Name

Figure 8.5:
The new Full Name field in the Client table list.

The Specify Calculation Dialog Box

Now that we have added our first calculation field to the ClientBilling file, before adding more calculation fields it may be of benefit to examine the Specify Calculation dialog box in more detail.

The parts of the Specify Calculation dialog box are described in Figure 8.6 and in the text that follows.

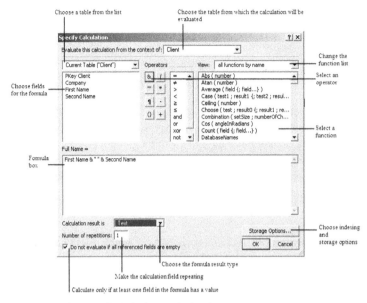

Figure 8.6: The Specify Calculation dialog box.

The drop-down list at the top of the dialog box labeled "Evaluate this calcula-tion from the context of" is populated by all table occurrences in the relationships graph based on the current table. The context is the table in the relationships graph from which a relationship is evaluated. When you define a calculation in a source table and the table has more than one occurrence in the relationships graph, you must specify the context from which you want the calculation to evaluate.

Each context choice represents a different table in the relationships graph and a different perspective on your data; when you choose the context for a calculation, you tell FileMaker Pro to evaluate the calculation starting from that table occurrence. Because each context choice represents a different association of related tables and fields, choosing the evaluation context for your calculation is critical to getting the results you expect.

To avoid the risk of unexpected calculation results and to make calcula-tion formulas easy to read at a later stage, it is a good idea to always evaluate a formula using the anchor table occurrence from the relationships graph.

The Specify Calculation dialog box contains three large boxes. The top-left box displays a list of fields for the selected table. You can change the table using the drop-down list at the top of the field box. The top-right box displays a list of FileMaker functions that can be used in a calculation field's formula. A drop-down list above the function box enables you to change the order of the function list and filter displayed functions by family type. Between the field box and the function box are a series of buttons for text and mathematical operators and a vertical list of comparison and logical operators. The large box in the lower part of the dialog box is the formula box. This is where the calculation field formula is written.

Below the formula box, the calculation field designer can choose the formula result data type from a drop-down list. Additionally, the calculation field can be made into a repeating field, which is of great benefit when referencing repeating fields in the formula. FileMaker can be told not to evaluate a result if all of the fields referenced in the formula are empty.

The Storage Options button opens the dialog box shown in Figure 8.7. It is possible to make the calculation result a global value, which can be useful if the calculation field is to be used later as part of a relationship formula. Indexing is required by FileMaker if a field is to be used in a relationship formula, unless the field is to use global storage. It is not possible to index a calculation field that references fields from other tables in the calculation formula.

With certain calculations, such as Age, which might be based on the subtraction of the date of birth field contents from the current date, it is a good idea not to store the calculation result, as it will be recalculated correctly every time the Age field is displayed on a layout for a given record.

For everyday use, it's best to select None or Minimal in the indexing options, and to check the "Automatically create indexes as needed" option.

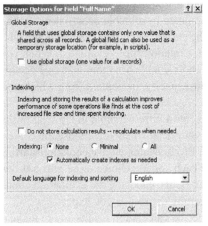

Figure 8.7:
The Storage
Options for Field
dialog box.

A Conditional Calculation — Contact Age

A common use for a calculation field is to record a subject's age in a FileMaker solution. Personnel and education databases usually need to record the ages of employees and students. If you add a date field to capture the date of birth of an individual, it is an easy matter to make FileMaker calculate the subject's age by subtracting the date of birth year from the current year.

As an example, in the ClientBilling file, add a date field called Date of Birth to the Client table and create a new calculation field called Age, with the formula shown in Figure 8.8.

The Year function is chosen from the Date function list. The Get (Current Date) function is used to capture today's date according to the computer system's calendar. The positions of the left and right parentheses are quite important to ensure that both the Year and Get (Current Date) functions evaluate correctly. Check that the calculation result is set to be a number.

Figure 8.8:
The basic Age
formula.

While the Age calculation formula does work in evaluating the difference in years between someone's birth year and the current year, it will add an extra year to the age if the birthday has not yet occurred in the current year. To avoid upsetting any 29-, 39-, or 49-year-olds, the formula can be improved by using the If function to calculate the age accurately.

The If function is an example of a logical function and is used to create conditional formulas and conditional options in FileMaker scripts.

The If function looks like this:

If (test ; result1 ; result2)

The formula returns one of two possible results depending on the value of the test. If the test is true (any non-zero numeric result), the calculation formula returns result1. If test is false (0), result2 is returned. The test must be an expression that returns either a numeric or a Boolean (true or false) result.

We can improve the Age formula with the If function as shown in Figure 8.9. FileMaker Pro 8 uses the the semicolon character as a separator for all functions.

The greater than comparison operator has been used in the test to see if the birthday falls on a date later than today in the current year. If it does, then 1 is subtracted from the difference in years between the two dates.

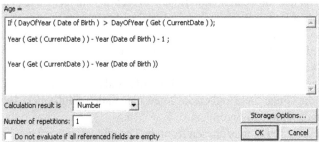

Figure 8.9:
The improved Age calculation formula using the If function to test whether a birthday has occurred in the current year.

If you make a mistake when writing a formula, FileMaker is quite helpful and will provide a dialog prompt with guidance on correcting the error. An example of this is shown in Figure 8.10, where a parenthesis is missing in the formula.

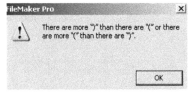

Figure 8.10:
The FileMaker calculation field formula error prompt.

You may like to try rewriting the Age formula with the Case function. The Case function is written as follows:

Case (test1 ; result1 ; test2 ; result2 ; default result)

The Case function returns one of several possible results based on a set of tests.

With a Case function, each test expression is evaluated in order and, when a true expression is found, returns the value specified in the result for that expression. You can include a default result at the end of the parameter list. If none of the expressions evaluate to true, the Case function returns the value specified for the default result. If no default result is supplied, the Case function returns an "empty" result. A big advantage of the Case function over an If function is that it avoids the problem of creating a nested set of If functions for several tests in a formula. Each test in a Case function can follow from the previous one.

The revised Age calculation field formula written with a Case function is shown in Figure 8.11.

Figure 8.11: The Age formula written using the Case function.

Calculation Fields in a Business Database Solution

The point of calculation fields is to make FileMaker do the work of adding value to captured information accurately and quickly.

A basic FileMaker file holding client, invoice, and payment information can provide several examples of the most common calculation field formulas for a business database solution. Similar calculation field formulas will be used in all the case study database solutions introduced in this book.

We will use our ClientBilling file to create a series of calculation fields, first using fields in the same table and then using related fields from other tables.

Using Fields from the Same Table in Calculation Fields

Let's start with some examples of calculation fields that reference fields from the same table in their formula.

1. Open the ClientBilling file if it is not already open, use the menu option **File>Define>Database** to open the Define Database dialog box, and, with the **Fields** tab selected, choose the **InvoiceLine** table from the drop-down table list.

2. Add the number fields shown in Figure 8.12 to the InvoiceLine table.

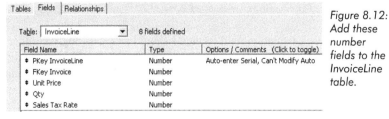

Figure 8.12: Add these number fields to the InvoiceLine table.

PKey InvoiceLine is a primary key field and has its auto-enter options set to insert a uniqe serial number value for each new record, as described in Chapter 7.

3. Add three calculation fields to the InvoiceLine table for Net Line Price, Sales Tax Line Price, and Inclusive Line Price. These three new calculation field formulas are displayed in Figures 8.13, 8.14, and 8.15. The parentheses are used in the Sales Tax Line Price formula to manage the order in which the formula is calculated.

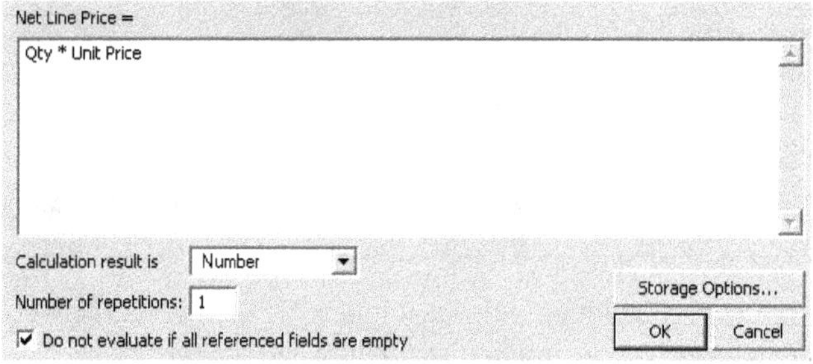

Net Line Price =

Qty * Unit Price

Calculation result is   Number

Number of repetitions: 1   Storage Options...

☑ Do not evaluate if all referenced fields are empty   OK   Cancel

Figure 8.13: The Net Line Price calculation field formula.

Sales Tax Line Price =

Net Line Price * (Sales Tax Rate/100)

Calculation result is   Number

Number of repetitions: 1   Storage Options...

☐ Do not evaluate if all referenced fields are empty   OK   Cancel

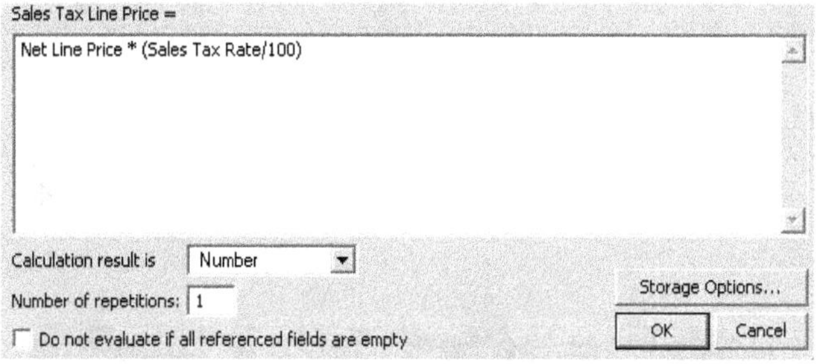

Figure 8.14: The Sales Tax Line Price calculation field formula.

Inclusive Line Price =

Net Line Price + Sales Tax Line Price

Calculation result is   Number

Number of repetitions: 1   Storage Options...

☐ Do not evaluate if all referenced fields are empty   OK   Cancel

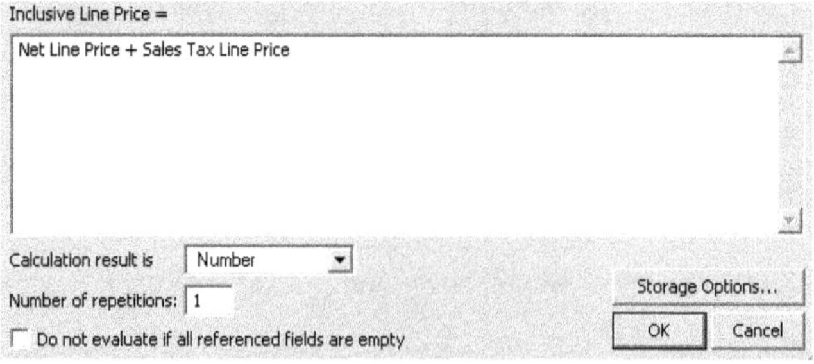

Figure 8.15: The Inclusive Line Price calculation field formula.

These calculation field formulas should be reassuringly familiar if you are used to inserting formulas into spreadsheet cells. The principal difference is that fields are referenced in the formula rather than cell coordinates.

Using Related Fields in Calculation Fields

The calculation fields created for the InvoiceLine table can be referenced in the Invoice table using additional calculation fields to derive a total net, sales tax, and inclusive figure for an invoice.

Before this can be done, a relationship must be created in the relationships graph between a table occurrence for the Invoice table and one based on the InvoiceLine table. We can apply the technique described in Chapter 7 for creating a table occurrence group based on "anchor" and "buoy" tables.

1. A table occurrence named Invoice already exists in the ClientBilling file's relationships graph. Add a new table occurrence to the graph using the Add Table button tool, which shows a table icon with a green cross and is located in the bottom left of the relationships graph (⬚). In the Specify Table dialog box, select the **InvoiceLine** table and name the new table occurrence **Invoice_InvoiceLine**, as shown in Figure 8.16.

Figure 8.16: Adding a new table occurrence to the relationships graph using the Specify Table dialog box.

2. Place the new table to the right of the existing Invoice table occurrence and, holding the mouse button down, draw a new relationship line between the PKey Invoice field in the Invoice table occurrence and the FKey Invoice field in the Invoice_InvoiceLine table occurrence. The relationship line should look similar to the one in Figure 8.17.

You may notice that FileMaker has automatically included a crow's-foot symbol at the InvoiceLine end of the relationship. This is an assumption based on the fact that the FKey Invoice field does not have any auto-enter or validation options set, while the PKey Invoice field is set to auto-enter a unique serial number.

Figure 8.17:
The Invoice to
InvoiceLine
relationship.

3. Before we define calculation fields for the Invoice table, double-click on the relationship line to open the Edit Relationship dialog box. We will want to add new invoice lines for an invoice from within an invoice details layout. This can be done using a portal based on the Invoice_InvoiceLine table occurrence.

    To create new invoice line records, we check the box labeled **Allow creation of records in this table via this relationship** on the InvoiceLine side of the relationship, as shown in Figure 8.18.

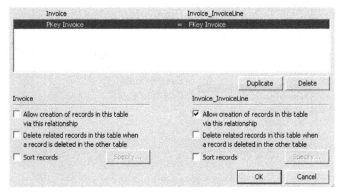

Figure 8.18: Detail of the Edit Relationship dialog box, with the "Allow creation of records in this table via the relationship" option checked.

We can now gain access to fields in the InvoiceLine table to use them within calculation formulas for fields in the Invoice table.

4. Select the **Fields** tab in the Define Database dialog box. Select **Invoice** from the Table drop-down list and create a new calculation field called **Invoice Net Total**.

    The two most widely used functions for calculation fields that reference related table fields are the Sum and Count functions. The Sum function will add up the individual values in a referenced field for each related record, and the Count function can be used to display how many related records exist based on a matching foreign key field in the record set.

5. Enter the Sum function shown in Figure 8.19 for the Invoice Net Total calculation field formula. The formula is designed to derive the total or sum value of the Net Line Price for all related InvoiceLine records. This value can be displayed on an invoice details layout.

When a related field is included in a formula, FileMaker prefixes the field name with a double colon symbol (::) and the name of the table occurrence in the relationships graph. Related fields can be selected for inclusion in the formula box by selecting the related table from the drop-down list of tables above the list of fields in the Specify Calculation dialog box. The calculation result data type for the Invoice Net Total field should be set to Number.

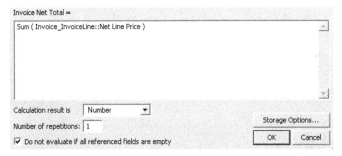

Figure 8.19: The Invoice Net Total calculation field formula in the Invoice table.

6. Click **OK** and type the name of another calculation field called **Invoice Sales Tax Total**. The formula for this field will prefix the Sum function with the Round function. The Round function is used by FileMaker to return a number rounded to a set number of decimal places specified as the precision number in the calculation.

7. Enter the Invoice Sales Tax Total formula as shown in Figure 8.20.

The sales tax line total is evaluated based on the line price multiplied by the sales tax percentage. To maintain accuracy and avoid an odd number of decimal places, the Round function is used to force FileMaker to calculate the value to only two decimal places for pence or cents. The Round function can be selected from the full list of functions or from the Number type function list.

As the formula is created using selected functions and fields, FileMaker should place the separator parentheses in the correct positions. The parentheses should pair up, so that the total number of left parentheses in a formula is the same as the total number of right parentheses.

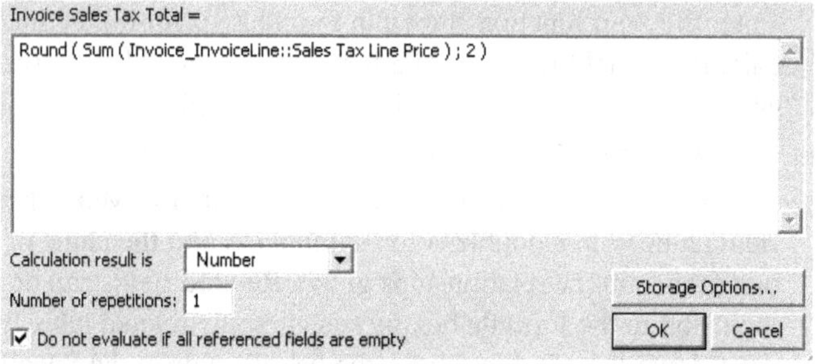

Invoice Sales Tax Total =

Round (Sum (Invoice_InvoiceLine::Sales Tax Line Price) ; 2)

Calculation result is   Number

Number of repetitions: 1   Storage Options...

☑ Do not evaluate if all referenced fields are empty   OK   Cancel

Figure 8.20: The Invoice Sales Tax Total calculation field formula.

We have created two calculation fields to derive the total net and sales tax figures for an invoice. Now, as so often is the case with FileMaker, we have a choice of how to calculate a total invoice figure.

The first option is to create a new calculation field called Invoice Inclusive Total in the Invoice table. The formula for the Invoice Inclusive Total is shown in Figure 8.21. The formula again uses the Sum function to derive a total Inclusive Line Price for all the related InvoiceLine records.

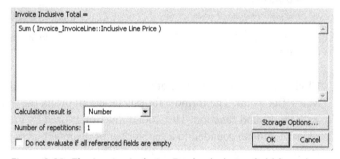

Invoice Inclusive Total =

Sum (Invoice_InvoiceLine::Inclusive Line Price)

Calculation result is   Number

Number of repetitions: 1   Storage Options...

☐ Do not evaluate if all referenced fields are empty   OK   Cancel

Figure 8.21: The Invoice Inclusive Total calculation field formula.

Another way of deriving the same value for the total invoice value is to create a calculation field whose formula simply adds up the two subtotal fields in the Invoice table. This formula is shown in Figure 8.22, and simply uses the + operator to add the Invoice Net Total and the Invoice Sales Tax Total together.

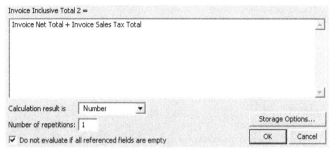

Figure 8.22: Adding the two sum calculation fields together to derive the invoice total.

8. Create the new Invoice Inclusive Total field using one of the methods shown above.

    After all this work creating an Invoice table that automatically calculates an invoice total, we would ideally like to view a total for all invoices for a particular client back in the Client table.

9. To be able to reference invoice fields and to display invoice data in a client details layout, we need to switch back to the relationships graph and create a new relationship between Client and a new table occurrence based on the Invoice table called **Client_Invoice**. Add the new table occurrence to the graph on the right side of the Client table occurrence and draw a relationship line from PKey Company in the Client table occurrence to FKey Client in the Client_Invoice table occurrence. The new relationship should look similar to Figure 8.23.

Figure 8.23: The Client to Client_Invoice table relationship.

    We can now reference invoice fields as part of calculation field formulas in the Client table.

10. Let's start by using the Count function to display how many invoice records exist for any particular client record. Create a new calculation field called **Count Invoices** in the Client table, with the formula shown in Figure 8.24.

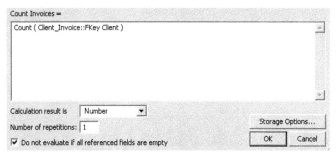

Figure 8.24: The Count Invoices calculation field formula.

11. Add two additional calculation fields to the Client table to display the total net and inclusive invoice totals for each client. These are shown in Figures 8.25 and 8.26.

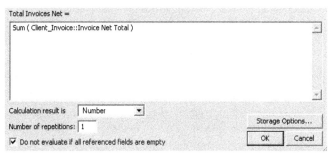

Figure 8.25: The Total Invoices Net calculation field formula in the Client table.

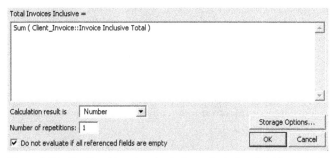

Figure 8.26: The Total Invoices Inclusive calculation field formula in the Client table.

You might now like to start experimenting with other operators and functions as part of a calculation formula. In Figure 8.27, the division of the Total Invoices Inclusive field by the Count Invoices field is used to derive a mean invoice value.

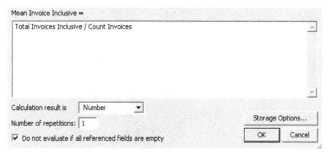

Figure 8.27: The Mean Invoice Inclusive calculation field formula in the Client table.

A summary field can, of course, be created for a calculation field; for example, to display a total of all invoices in the footer of a client list layout.

If client payments are being recorded in another table called Payments, a calculation field can be used to display whether or not the client has outstanding payments due.

12. In the Define Database dialog box, select the **Payments** table from the drop-down list in the Fields tab and add the fields shown in Figure 8.28 to the Payments table.

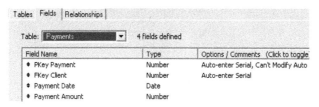

Figure 8.28: The Payments table field list.

13. Now click the **Relationships** tab and add a new table occurrence to the graph called **Client_Payments**, based on the Payments table.

14. Create a new relationship between Client and Client_Payments using the PKey Company and FKey Client fields, as shown in Figure 8.29. The three table occurrences now form a Client table occurrence group (TOG).

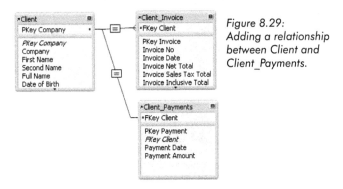

Figure 8.29:
Adding a relationship
between Client and
Client_Payments.

15. Back in the Client table, add a new calculation field called **Total Payments** with the formula shown in Figure 8.30.

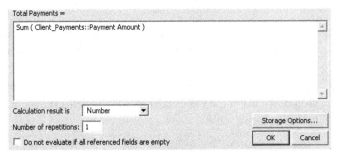

Figure 8.30: The Total Payments calculation field formula in the Client table.

16. Add a calculation field called **Total Outstanding** in the Client table with the simple subtraction formula shown in Figure 8.31.

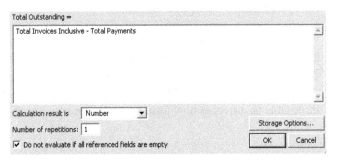

Figure 8.31: The Total Outstanding calculation field formula.

When layouts are designed for the ClientBilling database, you might want to capture new payments in a portal within the client details layout. If this is the case, then the relationship to the Client_Payments table occurrence will need to be edited to allow the creation of new payment records.

Text and number fields can be combined in calculation fields. An example calculation field called chase paragraph is shown in Figure 8.32. The chase paragraph calculation field formula uses the Case function to test whether a client owes any money, by the test Total Outstanding > 0. If the client does owe money, the text and combined fields shown in the formula will be displayed in the field. If the client has no outstanding invoices or has a balance of 0 or less, no text will appear. Like so many business systems, this one won't tell a client that an overpayment has been made. You might like to have a go at modifying this Case statement to do this — go on, build a better mousetrap!

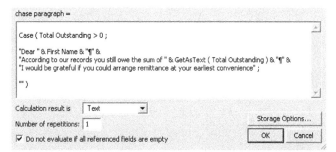

Figure 8.32: The chase paragraph calculation field formula combining text and fields in a calculation result.

Conclusion

Hopefully, this chapter has given you some ideas for including calculation fields in your own business database and shown you the benefits of getting FileMaker to do the work of deriving values based on other field contents.

The sample case study database files that are available to download from the publisher's website at www.wordware.com/files/fmapps and the author's website at www.aweconsultancy.com contain many examples of calculation fields that can be used to improve the functionality of a FileMaker database.

Familiarization with a range of calculation functions is useful when you are deciding how to tackle a business data management project. This is also a transferable skill, as many of the calculation functions are also available in ScriptMaker, FileMaker's built-in scripting language.

Chapter 9

Using ScriptMaker

In this chapter:

- Introduction
- Using Buttons and Scripts to Automate Tasks
- Creating a New Script in FileMaker
- Displaying Scripts in the Scripts Menu
- Conditional Scripts
- Conclusion

Introduction

Scripts are used in FileMaker to manage one or several automated tasks.

Although designing scripts with ScriptMaker may seem daunting for new users of FileMaker, it is actually quite simple. Scripts are built in the Edit Script dialog box by selecting from a list of script steps. To run the script, a layout object such as a button or a field, or some text that is defined as a button, is clicked, or the script is chosen from the Scripts menu.

Many business database solutions can be constructed in FileMaker without needing to create a single script. The Timesheet database case study that is described in Chapter 12 was written without a single script.

Using Buttons and Scripts to Automate Tasks

A basic scripting facility has existed in FileMaker since the earliest versions of the database application. More recent versions have seen the number of available commands or script steps greatly increase, to the stage where extremely powerful automated tasks can be included in a FileMaker business solution and designed by a database author with no prior programming experience. It could even be said that having a programming background may be a hindrance when you first launch ScriptMaker and open the Edit Script dialog box. An experienced programmer might find the script step list rather quirky.

A large number of the script steps are based on familiar FileMaker menu options, which should quickly become familiar to even a novice FileMaker user.

FileMaker scripts can save you time by automating tasks and help colleagues to use a database by providing a familiar and expected outcome every time the script is run.

Almost any layout object can be assigned to be a button, and a button can be defined to perform a single automated task. A button can also be used to launch a script that performs a series of tasks.

In Layout mode, if a new button is added to a layout using the Button tool from the Status area, the Button Setup dialog box will appear, as shown in Figure 9.1.

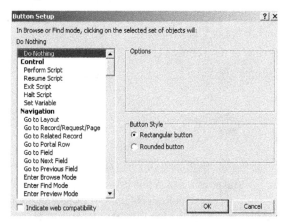

Figure 9.1: The Button Setup dialog box.

The button can be set to run any of the commands in the list. Buttons are ideal to help colleagues with file navigation. For example, a button can be set to switch to a main menu layout, change from Browse to Find mode to search the database, or open the Print dialog box to print a record.

A button's drawback is that it can only perform a single automated task. If you wanted to automate the process of finding all business contacts, change the layout to a list report, sort the list by last name and organization name, and then finally print the set of records in landscape mode, a single button can't help you. A set of buttons could do each of these required tasks in turn; however, you might soon fill up your layout with rows of single task buttons. A far easier solution would be to write a script that could perform a series of automated tasks in the correct order. The humble button does redeem itself by being able to launch a specified script when clicked on. This is the first command in the Control section of the list shown in Figure 9.1 — Perform Script.

Creating a New Script in FileMaker

Let's start by writing a script that carries out all the tasks mentioned previously for finding all records in a table, sorting them by a preset order, and printing them using a particular layout. We can add our new script to a database created with the Contact Management template that comes with FileMaker Pro 8.

1. Launch FileMaker Pro or, if it is already open, select the menu option **File>New Database**. The New Database dialog box should appear, as shown in Figure 9.2.

   If it does not, select the menu option **Edit>Preferences** to open the Preferences dialog box. Select the **General** tab and check the **Show templates in New Database dialog box** option. When you next select the New Database command, the template list should appear.

2. Select **Create a new file using a template** and, in the templates list, select the **Contact Management** template from the Business - People & Assets list. Click the **OK** button and choose a location to save the new file, then click the **Save** button.

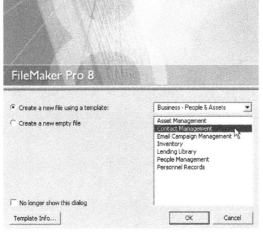

Figure 9.2:
Select the
Contact
Management
template in the
Business - People
& Assets list.

3. Add two or three sample contacts with company names to the file, as shown in Figure 9.3.

Figure 9.3: Add sample records to the Contact Management file.

We are now ready to add our new script for printing a contact list from the file.

4. Select the **Scripts** menu and choose the **ScriptMaker** menu option. The Define Scripts dialog box will appear, as shown in Figure 9.4.

    A series of existing scripts that have already been included in the template file can be seen. At a later stage, you may like to examine some of these scripts by highlighting the script and clicking on the Edit button.

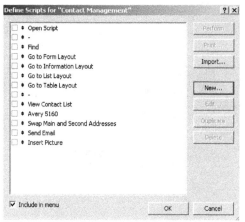

Figure 9.4: The Define Scripts dialog box.

5. To add our new script, click the **New** button and the Edit Script dialog box will appear, as shown in Figure 9.5.

    There are three important sections within the Edit Script dialog box. The first is the long vertical box to the left, which contains a list of script steps. A script step can be double-clicked on to add it to the current script, or you can use the >>Move>> button. The second is the large box on the right, which displays the script itself as a series of steps. The third section is the smallest, located directly below the script and labeled

Script Step Options. This section will display different check boxes and pop-up menus, depending on what script step is highlighted in the main script box.

6. The new script should be given a unique name that explains what it is designed to do. This will help you pick the right script from the list using the Button Setup dialog box later. Name the new script **Print Landscape Contact List**.

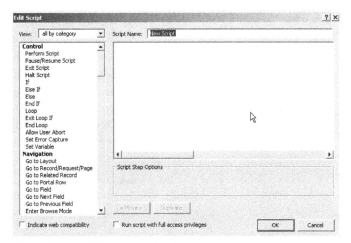

Figure 9.5: The Edit Script dialog box.

It is worth investing some time in trying out each of the script steps, ideally with a copy of your business database solution. You may find it beneficial to write out what you want the script to do in plain English before building the script with the appropriate script steps.

An example of this could be:

- Find all the records.
- Sort them by company name, surname, and first name.
- Switch to an appropriate list layout.
- Print the records with the required fields displayed — switch to landscape paper orientation to maximize the available space on the paper.

7. Making use of the existing fields and layouts in the Contact Management template file, the script steps to do the above are shown in Figure 9.6. Click on each script step in turn and use the >>Move>> button or double-click the step to add it to the

Figure 9.6: The newly created script.

script. If the script step order gets mixed up in the script box, click on the double arrow icon to the left of the script step name to move a script step up or down.

The script steps are required to do each of the following:

- To ensure that the contact layout is currently being viewed in Browse mode, we enter Browse mode to start the script.
- We then select all records.
- The records are then sorted by the selected field order.
- When the Sort Records script step is added to a script, the step is highlighted. The Script Step Options section then displays items specific to the Sort Records script step, such as the "Perform without dialog" option, which can be checked if you do not want the database user to choose fields, and a Specify button, which will open the Sort Records dialog box, shown in Figure 9.7. Here, fields can be added to the Sort Order in the required order.

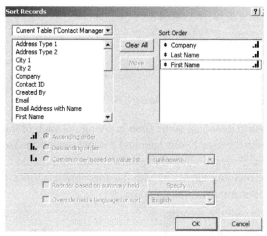

Figure 9.7:
The Sort Records dialog allows you to specify the sort order for the Sort Records script step.

- An existing List view layout is then selected, which will be used to print the records.
- The Print Setup script is used to open the Print Setup dialog box. The options for printer type and paper orientation are preserved in this script and used every time the script is run.
- The Print script step stores the option to only print the current record or to print all the records currently being browsed.
- If the script is to be run by clicking on a button, it is a good idea to include the Go to Layout script step and select the Original Layout option in the layout drop-down list. The database user is then returned to the original layout after the script has been run.

■   It is possible that other records will be printed using portrait orientation, so the Print Setup script step is used again at the end of the script to switch back to portrait orientation.

8.   Click **OK** and the Define Scripts dialog box will reappear, with the new script included in the list.

Displaying Scripts in the Scripts Menu

A script can be run by three methods. A script may be referenced in another script using the Perform Script step. This is a useful feature and can be used to "daisy chain" scripts together in a set order or to reuse the automated tasks of one script in many others. A script can also be run by clicking on a button in a layout.

The third option is to include the script in the Scripts menu.

A script can be displayed in the Scripts menu by checking the box to the left of the script name in the Define Scripts dialog box. If all the scripts are checked to display in the Contact Management file, the Scripts menu will appear as shown in Figure 9.8.

You may have noticed that the first 10 scripts in the menu also have a keyboard shortcut displayed in the form Ctrl+x. Up to 10 scripts can therefore also be run using the Ctrl+1...0 keyboard shortcuts. You can assign whatever script you wish to each of the shortcuts. This is done by changing the order of scripts in the Define Scripts dialog box using the double arrow icon. Check that the order of the checked script in the Define Scripts dialog box matches the keyboard number you want to assign.

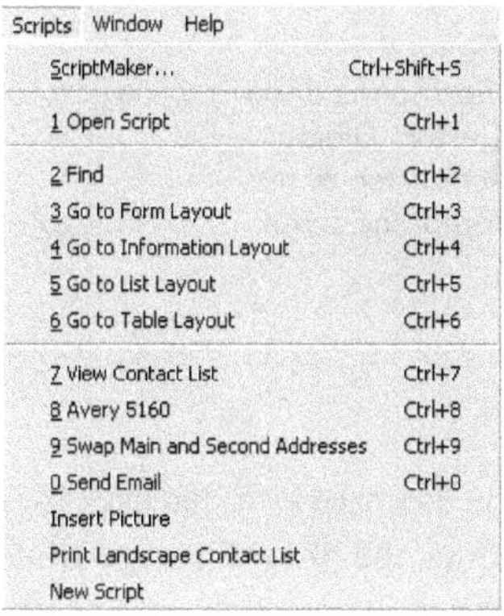

Scripts Window Help	
ScriptMaker...	Ctrl+Shift+S
1 Open Script	Ctrl+1
2 Find	Ctrl+2
3 Go to Form Layout	Ctrl+3
4 Go to Information Layout	Ctrl+4
5 Go to List Layout	Ctrl+5
6 Go to Table Layout	Ctrl+6
7 View Contact List	Ctrl+7
8 Avery 5160	Ctrl+8
9 Swap Main and Second Addresses	Ctrl+9
0 Send Email	Ctrl+0
Insert Picture	
Print Landscape Contact List	
New Script	

Figure 9.8: The Scripts menu displays any scripts checked in the Define Scripts dialog box.

Conditional Scripts

A script can be designed to have more than one outcome, depending on information contained in fields or choices made by the database user when the script is run. This ability to design scripts that have difference branches, depending on what conditions are in place, can be used to design powerful business software.

We can modify the script created earlier to include a conditional script step based on how the database user responds to a Show Custom Dialog script step.

1. With the Contact Management file open, select **ScriptMaker** from the Scripts menu and highlight our new script called **Print Landscape Contact List**. Click the **Edit** button to open the Edit Script dialog box.

    The script in its current form will always select all records, sort them, and print them using the specified layout and page orientation. What if we were to give the database user a chance to confirm the decision to print this report? The best place to raise this question is at the beginning of the script, before FileMaker starts to sort records or switch to a different layout. We can use the Show Custom Dialog script step to enable the user to confirm printing the report.

2. Scroll down the list of available script steps in the Edit Script dialog box until you see the Miscellaneous script step category displayed in bold. This category contains a script step called **Show Custom Dialog**. Add this script step to the script and use the vertical arrows if necessary to place it at the beginning of the script, as shown in Figure 9.9.

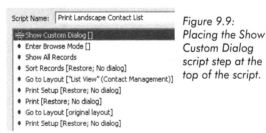

Figure 9.9:
Placing the Show
Custom Dialog
script step at the
top of the script.

3. We need to design a message for the database user that asks for confirmation to print the report. Double-click the **Show Custom Dialog** script step at the start of the script, or highlight it and click the **Specify** button in the Script Step Options section.

4. The Show Custom Dialog Options dialog will appear, as shown in Figure 9.10. In the General tab we can create a title for the dialog box and

display a message for the database user. Up to three buttons can be included in the custom dialog box.

Type the title and message shown in Figure 9.10. Leave the Default Button on the left-hand side as **OK** and Button 2 as **Cancel**.

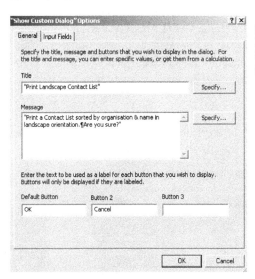

Figure 9.10:
The Show Custom
Dialog Options
dialog box.

5. Click **OK**; the changes to the Show Custom Dialog step will be displayed in the Edit Script dialog box.

6. We now need to add an If statement to the script so that the script can take one of two branches, depending on which of the custom dialog buttons is selected by the user.

   Double-click on the **If** script step, near the top of the list under the Control category, to add it to the list of steps. When an If step is added to a script, an End If step is also automatically added to assist you in closing a conditional branch that is performed when the If statement is true.

   The script should look like Figure 9.11. The If step is placed immediately below the Show Custom Dialog step and the End If step dragged down to the bottom of the script.

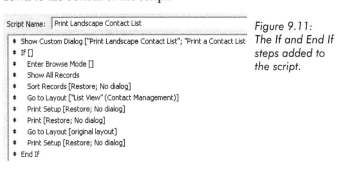

Figure 9.11:
The If and End If
steps added to
the script.

7. Double-click on the **If** step, or highlight it and click the **Specify** button in the Script Step Options section. A Specify Calculation dialog box will appear, looking exactly the same as for a calculation field.

8. We need to use the Get (LastMessageChoice) function to test which button the database user chose when the custom dialog box appeared: button 1 or button 2. Insert the **Get (LastMessageChoice)** function into the formula box, as shown in Figure 9.12. Type = **1** after the closing parenthesis so that the If statement tests to see if button 1, which is labeled OK and is the default button in the custom dialog box, was indeed selected by the user.

   If the If statement is true and button 1 was pressed, the script will continue to run all the steps below the If statement until another If statement, an End If, or an Else If script step is reached.

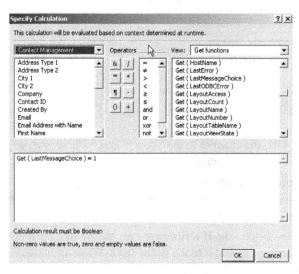

Figure 9.12: Using the Get (LastMessage-Choice) function in an If statement.

9. Click **OK** to add the function to the If step and close the Specify Calculation dialog.

   The modified script is shown in Figure 9.13.

Figure 9.13: The script now includes an If script step that if true, meaning button 1 is selected, all the following steps in the script will be run.

10. Click **OK** in the Edit Script dialog to save the script changes and return to the Define Scripts dialog.

Now, when the Print Landscape Contact List script is run, the custom dialog box appears, as shown in Figure 9.14.

Figure 9.14:
The custom dialog box generated by the script.

You may also want to run the script from a new button in the Form view layout.

Script research and experimentation (on an expendable copy of your business database) can be a helpful exercise. The decision of what to do with the default button in a custom dialog box is worth some thought. Whenever the script is going to do something that cannot be undone or canceled, such as deleting a record, it is good practice to make the default button choice be the Cancel button. That way, the database user must read the message and respond to it by selecting a button with the mouse. This can help to avoid "Friday afternoon" record deletions!

Conclusion

Scripts can pay huge dividends in automating a FileMaker database and making a file easier for workgroup colleagues to use.

The best way to become familiar with scripts is to have a repetitive database issue that you or a colleague would like to simplify. Try out some script steps to see if the issue can be simplified and automated. The scripts that are included in the FileMaker templates are a good source for ideas of how a script can be applied to meet your own requirements.

The If script step and the Show Custom Dialog Options dialog box both crop up frequently in the case studies presented in this book.

Chapter 10

Planning a FileMaker Business Solution

In this chapter:
- Introduction
- Database Usability
- Documentation and Support
- Introduce a Backup Procedure
- An Introduction to the FileMaker Case Study Chapters

Introduction

I'm guessing a little here, but I am assuming you are doing a great job managing your workgroup team or running your small business. You also make great business decisions. After all, you are already using, or planning to use, FileMaker Pro to manage information in your business, and you've also bought a copy of this book (if this is a library copy, I'll let you off).

On a more serious note, it's likely that nobody understands your business data management requirements better than you do. At the same time you are managing your day-to-day business and your team, you are proactively planning how you want to develop your business while reacting to project revisions, supplier issues, and client requests.

If you want to deploy a FileMaker (or any other) database application in your work environment, some planning is essential to maximize the benefit of the software and optimize the added value that can be derived from your business data. Because of your position in the business, you are the best person to initiate and coordinate the database solution planning exercise.

Imagine if you were to employ the services of one of the big global management accounting and consulting firms (virtually all of whom use FileMaker in at least one department, by the way) as part of a management reorganization and software implementation exercise. It is likely that you have already thought of the questions that they will want to ask you and your staff. What is it that your firm does? How do you do it currently? How do you manage the business workflow? In what way could improved data management help you to run the business?

These are broad-brush questions. More specifically, you may have considered how and where data comes into and flows out of your business. Do you purchase prospect data electronically or on paper? How and where in the business do you manage client details and client communication? Who manages orders or projects? How are changes to these orders logged? Is anybody re-entering information in one department that already exists electronically in another part of the firm? Is purchase and sales data rekeyed into an accounting software package when it already exists in FileMaker or another application?

If you want to put an existing information management system in your organization to the test, see how quickly the current software (or you, if you don't have a current system) can answer the following:

- What is your biggest market sector?
- Who are your top five clients?
- What was your average invoice amount last year?
- Who is your most reliable supplier for matching purchase invoices to purchase orders and on-time arrival of goods?
- Which item of stock do you most frequently hold in surplus or run out of?

Provided the relevant information is being captured in the correct fields in the appropriate tables, a well-designed FileMaker database should be able to answer these types of questions in seconds.

Database Usability

Before we can start to build a FileMaker database to resolve our business data management requirements, we need to spend a little time thinking about how the database will fit into our work and business environment.

There are three database usability stages to consider: a solid database architecture, a means of getting information into the database, and accurate reporting of information from the database.

An entity relationship (ER) diagram, which was introduced in Chapter 7, might be considered the blueprint for the database structure; however, it is rare to get the design of an ER diagram right the first time. A certain amount of iteration might be needed to ensure that all representative entities for your business process are included in the diagram, with the correct relationships mapped out.

You may want to add some of the important descriptive fields to each of the tables identified in the ER diagram as a way of testing whether the database will be able to accurately describe your business information before you commit to adding a large number of fields to tables in a FileMaker file.

Key colleagues may wish to be involved in the design of data input layouts. Information on business suppliers, prospects, and clients may have to be captured in a certain order. Your team may also have ideas on when value lists, in the form of drop-down lists or pop-up menus on a layout, may be a great benefit in speeding up data capture.

As the business owner or workgroup manager, you might have some design ideas in mind for listing records and the best layout format for a sales or project status report. You may also need to physically extract records from the database in the form of an export file in order to insert the data into a spreadsheet to create a graph, or to import invoice values into an accounting package.

Bear in mind that while the introduction of a new software application into a work environment is never easy, FileMaker is an extremely forgiving application to use. If you realize that an important descriptive field has been omitted from a table, or even a table from a file, you can easily take an extra backup copy of the file and add new fields, tables, relationships, and scripts as required. You don't have to worry about breaking elements of code or recompiling the file, as you would need to if the database was written using a programming language.

Documentation and Support

FileMaker Pro can give you a new hat at work. As well as managing your team and your business, you are now the business database developer as well. While you deserve to bask in the kudos and glory that come with writing your own software for your business, you may also find yourself being called up frequently by colleagues wanting to know whether an individual record should be captured before a company or which button to press for the weekly "work in progress" report.

The database is supposed to work for you. To avoid it being the other way around, with constant support issues for colleagues, it is worth writing some form of documentation describing how to open the database, how to work through the data capture layouts, what the buttons do, and how to close the file safely with a Quit button or with the File>Quit menu option. A user guide can be something as simple as a word processor document describing these processes and illustrated with screen shots.

If you are planning on expanding your business and delegating this task (hopefully the introduction of your new database is going to make this more rather than less likely!), you might consider writing two user guides: one for database users and one for a database manager who will need to know how to modify scripts, layouts, value lists, fields, or relationships.

In addition to a printed or PDF file support document, you might also consider adding your contact details to a custom dialog box that appears as part of a script when a button is clicked in a menu layout. If all your hard work pays off and you sell your business solution for a zillion dollars or the corporate office adopts your database solution for other workgroups, it would be good if your name appeared in an "About this solution" dialog message. Each of the case study solutions includes an About script that does this.

Introduce a Backup Procedure

While a FileMaker file is reasonably robust, there are certain steps that cannot be undone using the Ctrl+Z keyboard command. The most obvious one is when a record is accidentally deleted it cannot be brought back. Unless you have a backup of the database file, your only recourse is to retype the record, which may not be a simple matter because a new record in that table will have a different primary key field. This means that the relationship will no longer be valid to any previously related records, or worse, records in other tables may also have been deleted if a relationship was edited to delete records in the related file.

You should make a backup copy of the file as often as you think necessary. Give yourself an estimate of how dynamic your data is. Know how many new records you are creating in an hour and how many other records you are modifying over the same period. If you only back up once per day, know how long it would take you to recapture that amount of data.

Unless you are using FileMaker Server to share your database files over your business network, which is described in Chapter 23, you need to close the FileMaker file before you begin a backup. There are commercial software applications that will automate backups of selected files on your computer. At the very least, you should drag a copy of the database to a hard disk on another computer or to an external drive. The latter can be argued to be a better option, as leaving copies of your database across the office network runs the risk that an old version may be opened by mistake in the morning, with records being added and modified in two files at the same time.

Frequently test to be sure the backed-up copy of the database file works or your automated backup software can restore the file from a backup archive. If you are really organized, you may want to have separate folders for named daily and weekly backups.

Remember that the better the database you design, the more your company will be reliant on it, and the more you need a backup.

An Introduction to the FileMaker Case Study Chapters

This book includes 11 example FileMaker business projects. Each project addresses the data management requirements of a different business sector. While the reader may wish to start with the case study chapter that most closely matches his or her own business, it is recommended that the Customer Relationship Management and the Timesheets case studies be read first, as both of these chapters emphasize some of the new relational database techniques available in FileMaker Pro 8.

With the exception of the first two case studies, the other nine database projects follow a set database design procedure that can be described by the following steps:

1. Determining the data management requirement for the business sector.
2. Building the entity relationship diagram.
3. Adding tables to the database file.
4. Adding preliminary fields to the tables.
5. Adding relationships and table occurrence groups to the file.
6. Adding additional calculation fields that make use of the relationships.
7. Designing data entry and list report layouts for the file.
8. Automating the file where appropriate with scripts.

As this method for database design is adhered to for the majority of the case studies, there are some paragraphs that are repeated in each chapter. Sections that describe the method for adding key fields to the tables and the procedure for creating table occurrence groups in the relationships graph are the same for each case study. While this may be a bit of an annoyance to the reader who follows each chapter, it also means that the example database projects can be studied in any preferred order.

For the sake of reference and to examine any field, script, or relational design techniques introduced in the case study projects, complete copies of all the FileMaker Pro database files are available to download from the publisher's website at www.wordware.com/files/fmapps and the author's website at www.aweconsultancy.com. The administrator password for each of the files is described in the introduction section of each of the case study chapters.

FileMaker Project Case Studies

Chapter 11

Customer Relationship Management

Introduction

While FileMaker is used to manage a myriad of tasks in business, client or customer relationship management (CRM) is one of its more common uses. If you want to do more business with existing customers and convert more prospects into new business, knowing which members of your team said what to who and when is fairly essential.

In a modern sense, customer relationship management can be defined as an integrated approach to identifying, acquiring, and retaining customers. I think Kipling did a good job defining the key requirements of CRM 100 years ago with his "six honest serving-men":

> I Keep six honest serving-men
> (They taught me all I knew);
> Their names are What and Why and When
> And How and Where and Who.

Rudyard Kipling — "The Elephant's Child," 1902

FileMaker is ideal for recording contact details for prospects and customers. By using well-designed layouts that include portals, it is easy to see if your team has approached other individuals at the same organization, which can help leverage a purchase decision, or at least avoid treading on a sales colleague's toes! With the simple use of date fields to record when a contact was added to a database and on what date a product or service was first purchased, you can also make FileMaker report on performance indicators such as average prospect conversion times.

As with any FileMaker relational database project, we need to start with a clear definition of what prospect/customer information we wish to capture and how this data should be linked together, or related.

FileMaker's ability to index fields and storage capacity of up to 2 gigabytes of data in a single text field gives you the option of going for a minimalist approach in your database design. I recently came across a firm whose CRM solution consisted of one single text field on screen, with each contact assigned to a separate record. In its simplicity this contact database did work well. In FileMaker, the sales team could search for a contact's last name, and all notes and telephone numbers would appear on screen with the found record. This simple system worked, as the sales team mainly used the database to react to incoming customer calls to retrieve contact notes. However, if the database designer was asked to provide a more proactive approach to the file by providing mailing labels, email addresses, or salutation fields for a mail merge document, the single field approach would become unstuck.

The CRM Entity Relationship Diagram

As with any FileMaker project that requires the design of relationships between tables, it is good practice to start with an entity relationship (ER) diagram, showing what tables are required for the project and how records in the tables are related to each other.

As detailed in Chapter 7, an ER diagram is not the same as the relationships graph, which is constructed in FileMaker using table occurrences. An ER diagram describes how the underlying tables are related to each other as part of the overall solution design.

The first stage of designing the CRM ER diagram is to map out all the entities, or tables, that will be required to create an effective method to manage customer or prospect communications and activities. Remember that an entity is the item itself, such as a company or a contact. The item is described by attributes, such as staff surname or client company name. Attributes are the equivalent of fields in a FileMaker table.

Let's start by defining what entities or types of records we are going to want to manage in a reasonably simple CRM solution.

Our **Sales Staff** need to manage **Communication To**, **Communication From**, and planned **Actions** for targeted prospect and customer **Contacts** who are based at various address **Locations** within **Organisations**. Each of these entities, highlighted in bold, can be drawn as a rectangle representing each table. Lines can then be drawn between the tables to indicate how they are related to each other. The crow's-foot symbol at one end of a relationship line linked to a single line at the other indicates a one-to-many relationship.

A big decision for any CRM project is whether to split out organization details into a separate table from individual contacts and organization addresses. Relational database professionals would consider this approach to be correct as it avoids the problem of repeating organization and address details in every contact record, or redundant data, as discussed in Chapter 7. There may still be valid reasons to consider using a single table to capture company names, addresses, telephone numbers, and individual names. You may be considering purchasing prospect target data from a commercial list rental company, or business information from professional agencies such as Dun and Bradstreet or Standard and Poor. If provided electronically, it is likely that mailing lists will be in a delimited table format, with a tab, comma, or other character used to separate field values. The easiest way of importing such data into FileMaker is into a single table consisting of matching fields. The use of import and export features to get data in and out of FileMaker is discussed in Chapter 25.

For the CRM example in this chapter, we will work with separate tables to manage organizations, contacts, addresses, communication out, and communication in. We will also create a staff table for our own colleagues and an action table to flag sales team activities. An ER diagram for these entities is shown in Figure 11.1.

CRM ER Diagram

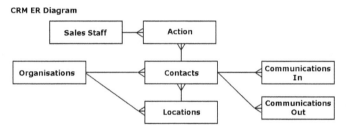

Figure 11.1: A customer relationship management ER diagram.

An organization record has several contacts and possibly more than one site address. A contact is only likely to have one site address, and more than one contact will be at this location.

In our ER diagram, the related record actions, communication to and communication from, are associated with an individual in the Contacts table, not the Organisations table. To avoid the problem of sales colleagues "treading on toes," as mentioned earlier, it would be good if we can see actions and communications with any related contacts from within the organization record on screen.

We can now start to create our CRM file, beginning with the required tables. As with all the case studies in this book, a copy of the completed FileMaker Pro 8 database file, **CRM**, is available to download from the publisher's website at www.wordware.com/files/fmapps and the author's website at www.aweconsultancy.com. You may find it easier to examine some of the FileMaker features and techniques discussed in this chapter in a copy of the completed file.

The default database password for the Admin account is **CUSTOMER** (all capitals). The database file options have been preset to open with the active Guest account (with read-only access to the file). To open the file with full access privileges, hold down the Shift key (Windows) or Option key (Mac OS) while the file is opening. Type the word **Admin** in the Account Name box and type the password in the box below. You can change the default password at a later stage. More information on database security issues, passwords, accounts, and privileges is given in Chapter 24.

Building the CRM File

Step 1: Adding Tables to the CRM File

We are now ready to start building the underlying tables that we will need for our CRM solution. As was discussed in Chapter 7, the best way to build relationships between tables in FileMaker is to base the relationships on primary and foreign keys that are automatically managed by FileMaker and cannot be edited or replaced over time. We will want to create a single primary key field and the required number of foreign key fields in all the necessary tables. One of the best methods for creating a primary key field is to add a number field to the table and use FileMaker's field options settings to automate the insertion of a serial number. The Options for Field dialog box can be used to prohibit later modification of auto-entered values by database users. If relationships and values in key fields are not carefully designed and secured against accidental modification, contacts and their organization links can be lost, or individuals may be associated with the wrong company.

We need to start by creating a new FileMaker file and adding a table for each of the boxes, or entities, in Figure 11.1. In addition, FileMaker will always create a default table for any new database file, with the same name as the file. Although it is possible to delete or rename this table, it can be used as the underlying table for any welcome menu or reports screen that might be added to the finished solution.

Let's start by creating a new file in FileMaker called CRM.fp7.

1. If FileMaker is already open, choose the menu option **File>New Database**. If your preferences are set so that when a new database is selected, the templates window appears, you can choose the **Create a new empty file** option. The templates window can be switched on or off by choosing the menu option **Edit>Preferences>General>Show templates in New Database dialog box**.

2. Type **CRM.fp7** into the File name box, choose the folder in which you wish to create the file, such as the Desktop at this stage, and click the **Save** button.

    FileMaker will then open the new file and the Define Database dialog box, as shown in Figure 11.2. The Fields tab will be selected for the single default table in the file. When we begin working on the file, the single default table has the same name as the file.

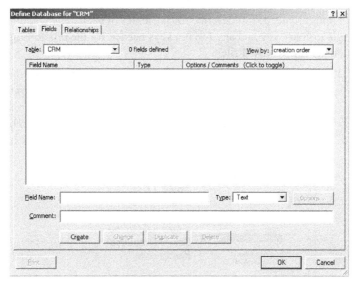

Figure 11.2: The Define Database dialog box for a new file with the Fields tab selected for the default table.

3. The Define Database dialog has three tabs: Tables, Fields, and Relationships. Click the **Tables** tab and add the tables shown in Figure 11.3 to the file.

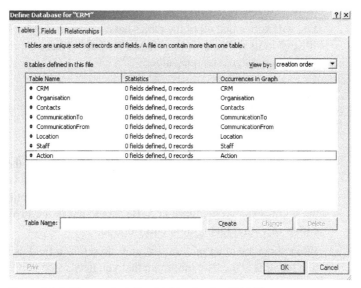

Figure 11.3: The newly defined tables for the CRM file.

Step 2: Adding Fields to the CRM File Tables

We are now ready to add fields to our newly created tables in the CRM file. Fields are needed to describe the attributes of each table and to provide a single primary key and any foreign keys needed for the relationships that we create for the CRM file.

1. To add fields to each of the tables within the file, choose the **File>Define>Database** menu option and the **Fields** tab of the Define Database dialog box. It is important to ensure that the correct table is selected prior to adding new fields. Each of the tables can be selected from the drop-down list near the top of the dialog box, as shown in Figure 11.4.

Figure 11.4: Selecting the relevant table for a new field in the Define Database dialog box.

2. Add the initial fields to each table as shown in Figures 11.6 to 11.12. Later, when we have established relationships between these tables, using table occurrences in the relationships graph, we will add additional fields to the tables to improve the functionality of the file.

    You will notice that all of the tables have a primary key with the prefix "PKey" in its field name. We can use the field options settings to make FileMaker assign a unique value.

Note: The "fields defined" field at the top of the windows reflects the number of fields defined after all the fields have been defined, not just the ones added initially.

3. When you have created a new primary key field, such as the **PKey Organisation** field shown in Figure 11.5, click the **Options** button and choose the **Auto-Enter** tab. Check the **Serial number** option and choose the settings shown in Figure 11.5. Be sure to check the **Prohibit modification of value during data entry** option.

    While there are other options that you can set for a field using the Validation tab, this is the bare minimum that you need to do to prevent users from accidentally modifying a FileMaker assigned primary key value.

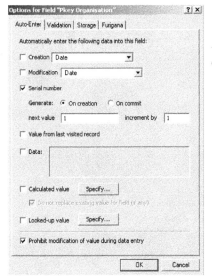

*Figure 11.5:
The field options
settings for a
primary key field
in all the tables.*

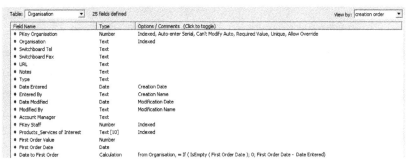

Figure 11.6: The fields for the Organisation table.

Figure 11.7:
The fields for the
Contacts table.

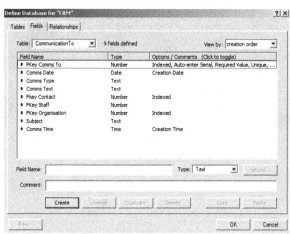

Figure 11.8:
The fields for the
CommunicationTo
table.

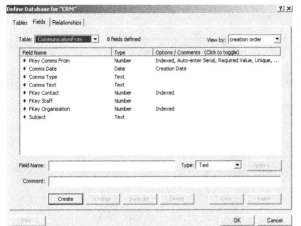

Figure 11.9:
The fields for the
Communication-
From table.

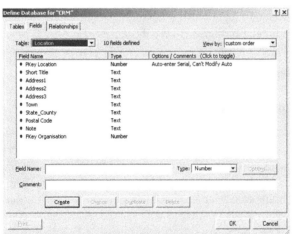

Figure 11.10:
The fields for the
Location table.

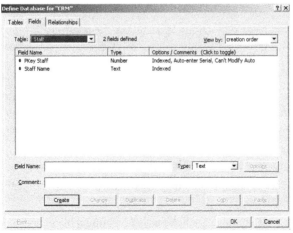

Figure 11.11:
The fields for the
Staff table.

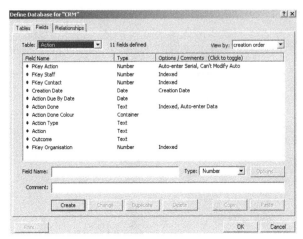

Figure 11.12:
The fields for the
Action table.

We can now select the Relationships tab of the Define Database dialog box and start creating relationships between the tables.

Step 3: Adding Relationships within the CRM File

3.1: Building an Initial Table Occurrence Group

By linking the tables within the CRM file we can make FileMaker do much of the work in terms of making it easy to capture contact records, communication details, and sales or marketing activities. As discussed in Chapter 7, with FileMaker we do not link the underlying base tables directly in the relationships graph. Instead, relationships are built up between table occurrences, which are representations of the base tables in the relationships graph. For design purposes and often to aid clarity, it is possible to have any number of table occurrences on the relationships graph for the same underlying base table.

Chapter 7 introduced the idea of designing the relationships graph as a series of discrete table occurrence groups, or TOGs. Each TOG should have a main or "anchor" table occurrence on its left-hand side, with any number of linked "buoy" tables related to the anchor table spread out on the right-hand side. To ease relationship design at the outset and to assist you or any colleagues who may work on the file at a later stage, a number of fundamental rules should be followed when using relationships in any FileMaker solution:

- As a general rule, any relationships graph will have one anchor table occurrence for every base table in the file.

- All data entry layouts should only be based on an underlying anchor table occurrence.

- Any portals on layouts should be based on buoy table occurrences.

■ To assist with documenting a complex FileMaker project, it is a good idea to limit the dimensions of any TOGs in the relationships graph to a single page in width but any number of pages in length.

1. If we click on the **Relationships** tab within the Define Database dialog box, we will see that a table occurrence for each of the tables in the CRM file has been added to the relationships graph, as shown in Figure 11.13. Note that in the example shown, to reduce the space used we have clicked on the button on the table header to toggle the display of the table and collapse it to its title only.

Figure 11.13: The relationships graph will, by default, contain one table occurrence for each table in a file.

To get the required functionality from our CRM solution, we now need to add some new TOGs to the relationships graph.

2. For the sake of reference, it is a good idea to leave at least one table occurrence for each source table in a file displayed at the top of the graph. Note that an underscore (_) has been added to each of the source table occurrences so that the original table name can be used as an anchor table occurrence. Each table occurrence must have a unique name in the graph. A table occurrence can be renamed by double-clicking on it to open the Specify Table dialog box, or by highlighting the table occurrence and clicking the **Edit** button at the bottom of the graph (the button with a yellow pencil icon).

A series of TOGs must now be added to the relationships graph. The most complex of all the TOGs we are about to build in the CRM file will be the one built from the underlying Organisation table. This is because the completed CRM solution will enable users of the file to add new records for contacts, locations, communication to, communication from, and action items, all created from within layout portals from the Organisation table.

Using the anchor/buoy or squid head and tentacles idea developed in Chapter 7, we need to start with a table occurrence based on the Organisation table and add table occurrences for associated tables flowing out to the right in the relationships graph.

If we are consistent in naming our linked table occurrences with the name of any preceding, or "upstream," table occurrences in each title, we should be able to follow the TOG format, both now and with any future improvements to the CRM file.

3.   Let's get started by adding the new **Organisation** table occurrence to the relationships graph and placing a set of table occurrences to the right of it for **Contacts, Location, CommunicationTo, CommunicationFrom, Staff**, and **Action**. Each of these table occurrences to the immediate right of Organisation should follow the naming convention Organisation_Contacts, Organisation_Location, etc.

The Organisation TOG at this stage should look similar to Figure 11.14.

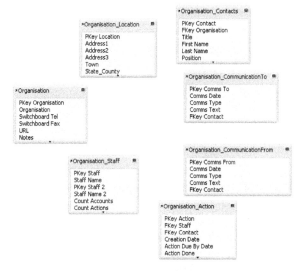

Figure 11.14: The initial Organisation TOG in the relationships graph.

4.   Begin adding relationships by clicking on the **PKey Organisation** field in the Organisation table occurrence and, keeping the mouse button down, dragging the relationship line that appears across to the **FKey Organisation** field in each of the other table occurrences, with the sole exception of **Organisation_Staff**. You may need to increase the vertical length of the other table occurrences by dragging the lower edge or scroll the table to find the FKey Organisation field.

5. We need to use the **FKey Staff** field in the **Organisation** table to link to the **PKey Staff** field in the **Organisation_Staff** table occurrence. The Staff table is used to select an account manager of each organization from our own staff. Unlike the other tables, we do not intend to add new staff records from an organization layout. We do need to create a relationship to the Staff table to display the staff account manager name in an organization layout.

When all the initial relationship lines have been drawn with the mouse, the relationships graph should look similar to Figure 11.15.

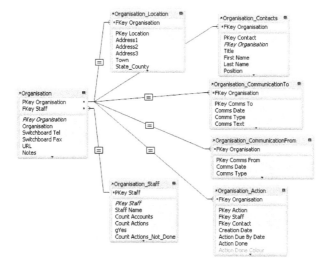

Figure 11.15: The initial Organisation TOG with relationships added.

6. As mentioned, we want to design a CRM system that makes it easy for colleagues to add new associated records for contacts, locations, communications, and actions.

To facilitate adding new records in the linked tables, with the sole exception of Staff, we need to double-click on each of the **PKey Organisation** relationship lines and select **Allow creation of records in this table via this relationship** from the Edit Relationship dialog box, as shown in Figure 11.16.

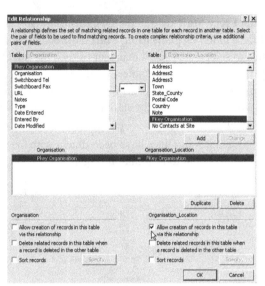

Figure 11.16:
Checking the
option to create
related records
via the
relationship.

3.2: Adding Additional Table Occurrences to Assist with Displaying Related Record Data

In order to assist colleagues in using our CRM solution, we now need to add some additional table occurrences to the Organisation TOG. These additional tables are not required for adding new related records; their purpose is solely to help users of the database in seeing additional related record information. For example, we have added a table occurrence called Organisation_CommunicationTo. This will be used to display all letters, emails, phone calls, and meetings to any contacts for the currently viewed organization as a portal within an organization layout. The portal can be sorted by date order, with the most recent communication at the top, and can show us the approaches that have been made to specific contacts within an organization and on what dates. However, without further table occurrences in the Organisation TOG in our relationships graph, we cannot easily display the full names of the contacts concerned or the name of the staff member who made the approach. This is because the CommunicationTo table only has foreign key fields for Contacts and Staff, not the full names of either. While this method of relational database design is "correct" because it avoids duplication of data within tables, we do still wish to display in our FileMaker layouts more detail on a related record than just foreign key values. To make this possible, we need to add additional table occurrences to the right, or downstream, of the table occurrence that holds a foreign key.

1. In the present example of making a planned CommunicationTo portal display full names, we need to join two more table occurrences to the **Organisation_CommunicationTo** table. Add two more tables to the

graph based on the Contacts and Staff tables, following the usual path naming convention of **Organisation_CommunicationTo_Contacts** and **Organisation_CommunicationTo_Staff**.

2. New relationships can be drawn to these new tables using the **FKeys** to **PKey** for **Contacts** and **Staff** respectively, as shown in Figure 11.17.

   Here, to make the relationship as clear as possible, we have toggled the display of the table to display only match fields used in relationships by clicking the button in the header of each table occurrence.

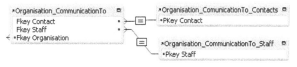

Figure 11.17: Additional table occurrences are used to display more details on related records.

We need to add additional table occurrences to the Organisation TOG whenever it would benefit the user to see additional information on related records. The alternative to this, and the only method available in previous versions of FileMaker, is to "pipe through" related data across files using several calculation fields. It is arguable that what is gained in minimal and less cluttered table field definitions is conceded slightly in complex relationships graphs. However, if a consistent naming convention is used for table occurrences, even the biggest "spider web" relationships graph can be followed.

3.3: Using Multiple Fields in a Relationship Definition

Thus far we have used primary and foreign key fields to link records in separate tables. These relationships make use of a single field. In relational database jargon they are known as *equijoins*, where any foreign key with the same or equal value as a primary key must be a related, or joined, record. We can use FileMaker to build more sophisticated relationships that may help us in displaying or reporting CRM data.

As an example, when we start to display our CRM data, we may want to show two summary values, one for all actions linked to an organization and one for all actions that have not yet been completed. We can gather this sort of information using a multi-criteria relationship. In this CRM project, we are going to make use of multi-criteria relationships to summarize the number of incomplete actions for organizations and contacts.

1. We need to add a new field to the Organisation table that has a text value of "No" for all organization records. Let's add the field by clicking the **Fields** tab in the Define Database dialog box and selecting the **Organisation** table from the drop-down table list. Add a new calculation field called **gNo** whose formula is **"No"**, with a calculation result of **Text**, and

whose storage option is set to **Use global storage**, as shown in Figure 11.18.

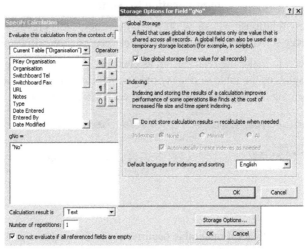

Figure 11.18: Adding a gNo global calculation field to the Organisation table.

2. We can now use this new global field in a multi-criteria relationship between the Organisation and Action tables. Click the **Relationships** tab in the Define Database dialog box to open the relationships graph. Add a new table occurrence based on the underlying **Action** table and name it **Organisation_Action__to do**. The final text of the table's title, preceded by a double underscore, is designed to indicate that a particular field is being used in the relationship.

3. Click and drag a new relationship from the **Organisation** table to **Organisation_Action__to do** table, linking the PKey Organisation field to the FKey Organisation field. Now double-click on this relationship in order to edit it.

4. In the Edit Relationship dialog box, as shown in Figure 11.19, highlight the **gNo** field in the Organisation table and the **Action Done** field in the Organisation_Action__to do table, then click the **Add** button. You should see the relationship definition has a new line added, so that the complete relationship definition is PKey Organisation = FKey Organisation AND gNo = Action Done.

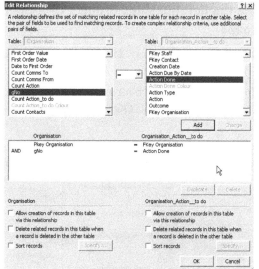

*Figure 11.19:
The multi-criteria
relationship between
Organisation and
Organisation_Action__
to do.*

5.   After you have clicked the **OK** button to return to the relationships graph, you may notice that the relationship line between the two table occurrences is now split at both ends to indicate that more than one field is used in the relationship definition, as shown in Figure 11.20.

The box in the middle of the line, known as the *relational operator*, still shows an equal sign, as both pairs of fields have to be of equal value for the relationship to be valid.

*Figure 11.20: The multi-criteria relationship displayed
between the Organisation and the Organisation_
Action__to do table occurrences.*

We can now add the remaining table occurrences to the Organisation TOG and design TOGs for Contacts and any other tables for which a layout will be designed.

3.4: Completing the Relationships Graph's Collection of Table Occurrence Groups

1. Add the TOGs shown in Figures 11.21 to 11.28 to the relationships graph.

2. Use the **Color Wheel** tool at the bottom of the Relationships Graph dialog box to vary the color of each TOG and make the graph easier to follow.

3. Toggle the display for the table occurrences to only display match fields that are used in relationships to make the TOGs easier to follow.

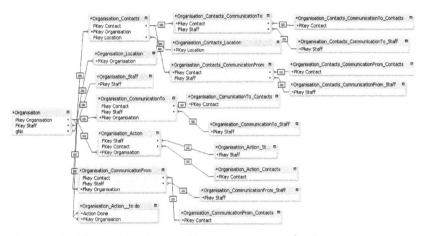

Figure 11.21: The completed CRM table occurrence group for Organisation.

Before building the Contacts TOG, you may want to try designing a relationship that uses multiple match criteria that must not be equal to make the relationship valid. This is indicated in the Relationship operator box by an X. We previously made use of a global calculation field in the Organisation table with a value of "No".

4. As an introduction to using a non-equality condition in a relationship, we can add a global calculation field to the Contacts table whose value is set to **"Yes"**. We can then include in our Contacts TOG a multi-criteria relationship between **Contacts** and **Actions** with the formula shown in Figure 11.22. Notice that the "not equal to" symbol is used between gYes and Action Done in the relationship formula.

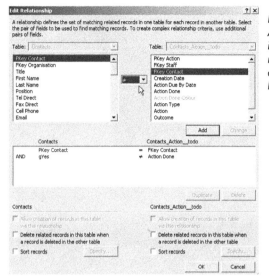

*Figure 11.22:
A non-equality condition
in a multi-criteria
relationship to identify
contacts and actions that
have not been done.*

5. We can deploy this new relationship as part of our Contacts TOG, which can be seen in Figure 11.23.

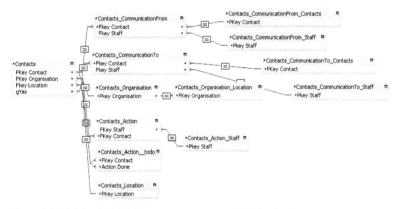

Figure 11.23: The CRM table occurrence group for Contacts.

Figure 11.24: The CRM table occurrence group for CommunicationTo.

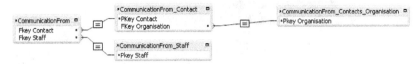

Figure 11.25: The CRM table occurrence group for CommunicationFrom.

Figure 11.26: The CRM table occurrence group for Location.

Figure 11.27: The CRM table occurrence group for Staff.

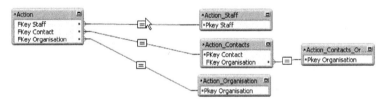

Figure 11.28: The CRM table occurrence group for Action.

The database designer must make the decision of which relationships should make use of the "Allow creation of related records" feature in the Edit Relationship dialog box. When this feature is used to populate records in related tables, any portals that make use of this relationship to display related records will have a blank line ready to accept data for a new related record. In this CRM example, we are going to make use of this feature to populate related tables directly from an organization layout.

We are now ready to design the layouts for our data entry screens.

Step 4: Designing an Organisation Details Layout with Tab Panels for the CRM File

The way in which we have designed our relationships graph with the structure of the TOGs does have an influence on the design of our CRM layouts. The number of relationships flowing from the Organisation file indicates that most new related records will be created from an Organisation layout. For this example CRM project, we are going to make extensive use of portals and the Tab Control tool, which is new to FileMaker Pro 8, in our layout design.

We will start with a new blank layout called Organisation Details, based on the Organisation table.

1. Switch to Layout mode and select the menu option **Layouts>New Layout/Report**. In the New Layout/Report dialog box, show records from **Organisation**, select the **Blank layout** type, and name the layout **Organisation Details**, as shown in Figure 11.29.

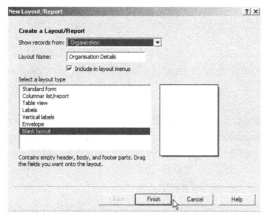

Figure 11.29:
Creating a new blank Organisation Details layout.

2. We are going to create a simple Form view layout that does not require a header or footer layout part. We can highlight and delete these parts by pressing the **Backspace** key, and we are left with a blank body part.

3. We can begin by giving the body a background color by highlighting the **Body** label and selecting a color from the Fill Color palette in the Status area.

4. Now let's add a merge field for the organization name to make it easy to identify which record we are browsing. Choose the menu option **Insert>Merge Field** or press **Ctrl+M**. Select the **Organisation** field from the Specify Field dialog box and click **OK**.

5. We can make FileMaker do much of the layout design work by using the Tab Control tool. Click the **Tab Control** tool and you will find that the mouse pointer has switched to a crosshair on the layout. With the mouse button held down, draw a large rectangle across the layout and then release the mouse button. The Tab Control Setup dialog box should now appear on screen. Add tab names for **Details, Contacts, Location, Communication To, Communication From,** and **Action**.

6. Now you can start to add fields from the Organisation table into the layout, as shown in Figure 11.30.

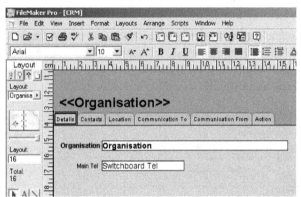

Figure 11.30: The Organisation layout with tab names and fields added to the Details tab panel.

We'll soon want to make use of all that hard work in the relationships graph. We want to add an initial location address for the organization record. We can do this by adding fields from the related Organisation_Location table into the Organisation layout. We can add further addresses later by use of a portal we will add to the Location tab panel.

7. Add address fields from the **Organisation_Location** related table onto the layout as shown in Figure 11.31. Notice that the address fields all have a double colon (::) before the field name to signify that the fields exist in a related table and not in the table this layout is based on. A check box has been created for the field labeled "Address Type." This has been done to make sure that the first related location address is given a "Head Office" short title description.

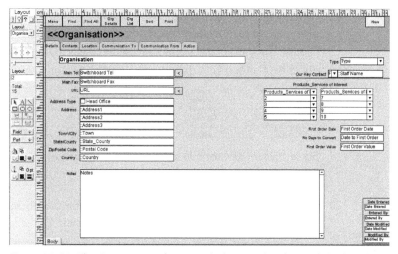

Figure 11.31: The Organisation layout with the Details tab panel displayed in Layout mode.

8. The **Staff Name** field from the **Organisation_Staff** table occurrence has been added to the layout to the right of the FKey Staff field. This field displays a pop-up list of staff names, with only the words "staff name" showing at the time of selection. This is a useful feature in populating the foreign key in a related table. Most of us prefer to work with real names rather than serial numbers. Use the settings in the Specify Fields for Value List dialog as shown in Figure 11.32.

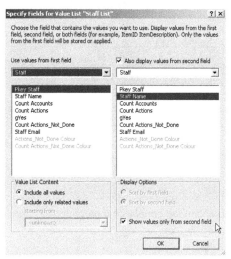

Figure 11.32: The Staff List value list is set to only show Staff Name values.

9. Other fields have been added to the Organisation table to indicate how many related records there are in other tables for each organization record. These make use of the calculation field Count function, as shown in Figure 11.33.

Field	Type	Definition
◆ gNo	Calculation	Global, from Organisation, = "No"
◆ Count Comms To	Calculation	Unstored, from Organisation, = Count (Organisation_CommunicationTo::FKey Organisation)
◆ Count Comms From	Calculation	Unstored, from Organisation, = Count (Organisation_CommunicationFrom::FKey Organisation)
◆ Count Action	Calculation	Unstored, from Organisation, = Count (Organisation_Action::FKey Organisation)
◆ Count Action_to do	Calculation	Unstored, from Organisation, = Count (Organisation_Action__to do::FKey Organisation)
◆ Count Contacts	Calculation	Unstored, from Organisation, = Count (Organisation_Contacts::FKey Organisation)

Figure 11.33: Calculation fields added to the Organisation table to count how many related records exist for each organization.

10. Continue adding fields to the other tab panels for the Organisation Details layout as shown in Figures 11.34 to 11.38.

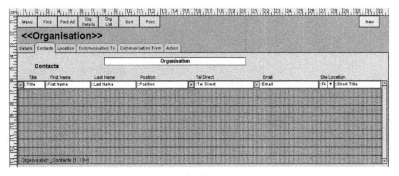

Figure 11.34: The Contacts tab panel with a portal to the Organisation_Contacts table occurrence.

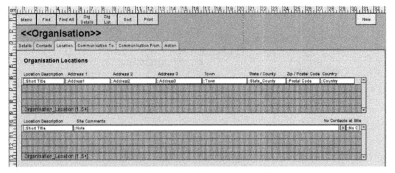

Figure 11.35: The Location tab panel with a portal to the Organisation_Location table occurrence.

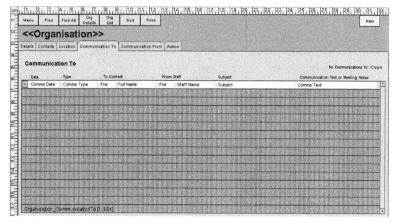

Figure 11.36: The Communication To tab panel with a portal to the Organisation_CommunicationTo table occurrence.

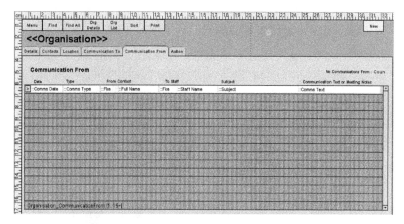

Figure 11.37: The Communication From tab panel with a portal to the Organisation_CommunicationFrom table occurrence.

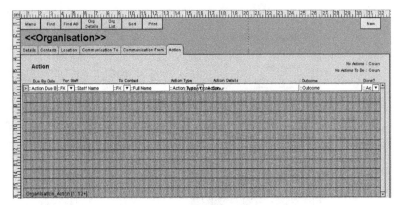

Figure 11.38: The Action tab panel with a portal to the Organisation_Action table occurrence.

Step 5: Adding a Welcome Menu Layout with a Customization Wizard

As with any FileMaker file, it is reassuring if the same screen appears each time a user first opens the file. We can tell FileMaker to perform a range of steps each time a file is opened. As a start, let's design a new Welcome Menu layout and tell our CRM file to always open this layout first.

1. Switch to **Layout** mode and create a new blank layout titled **CRM Welcome Menu**, showing records from the unused **_CRM** table occurrence. Delete the header and footer layout parts, and give the body part a friendly background color.

2. Add a set of menu buttons with text labels to indicate the destination layout when the button is selected. A large title button can be added to the layout and set to **Do Nothing** in the Button Setup dialog box. A welcome message or CRM title can be added to this display box.

    The basic Welcome Menu layout is shown in Figure 11.39.

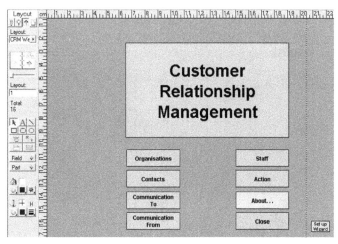

Figure 11.39: A basic CRM Welcome Menu layout.

The CRM file can be customized to display your company's contact details and logo in selected output layouts. Rather than type in your company details in all these screens, we can make use of FileMaker's global field indexing feature to capture our company details and perhaps a company logo for letterhead and fax layout design.

3. Add the text and container fields shown in Figure 11.40 to the CRM table.

Table: CRM ▼	16 fields defined	
Field Name	Type	Options / C
✦ gCompany Name	Text	Global
✦ gCompany Logo	Container	Global
✦ gAddress 1	Text	Global
✦ gAddress 2	Text	Global
✦ gAddress 3	Text	Global
✦ gTown	Text	Global
✦ gCounty_State	Text	Global
✦ gPostcode	Text	Global
✦ gTel	Text	Global
✦ gFax	Text	Global
✦ gURL	Text	Global
✦ gEmail	Text	Global
✦ gLetter Footer	Text	Global
✦ gLayout Name	Text	Global
✦ gColours	Container [10]	Global
✦ gCountry	Text	Global

Figure 11.40: Text and container fields with global storage are used to provide your own company details in any of the CRM layouts.

Notice that the container field called **gColours** is set to be a repeating field with a maximum of 10 repetitions. This field is going to be used to store two status colors —green and red — depending on whether an action record has its "done" field set to "Yes" or "No".

4. We need to create a layout containing the global fields, which can be populated with our company information. Figure 11.41 shows the **Setup Wizard** layout containing both the text and container global fields.

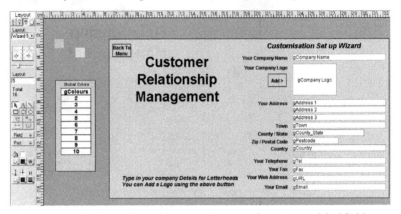

Figure 11.41: The Setup Wizard layout with text and container global fields.

5. The **gColours** container has been added to the layout with all 10 repetitions displayed. For any repeating field, you can choose how many of the defined repetitions you want to display in a layout using the **Format>Field/Control>Setup** menu option and choosing the settings shown in Figure 11.42.

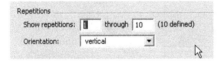

Figure 11.42: Displaying all repetitions for a repeating field in the Field/ Control Setup dialog box.

6. With the **gColours** field selected, click the right mouse button and choose the **Graphic Format** menu option. Select the **Reduce or Enlarge** image to fit frame option and leave the "Maintain original proportions" box unchecked, as shown in Figure 11.43. This is how a small graphic object can be used to fill a large container field in Browse mode.

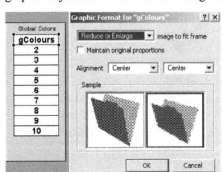

Figure 11.43: Using the Graphic Format dialog to make a graphic object fill a container field.

7. We need to add a basic green and red color to the first two rows of our gColours container field. In Layout mode, draw a small square with sides of about **25** pixels. Use the **Fill Color** tool to give the square a green color. Duplicate the layout object when it is still selected by pressing **Ctrl+D**, and give the new square a red color. Copy each square in turn and switch to **Browse** mode. Paste the green and red squares into the first and second repetitions of the gColours field. The contents of this field will be used to change the background color of an action field.

8. We need to add a button called **Setup Wizard** to take the user from the Welcome Menu layout to the Wizard layout, and another button labeled **Back to Menu** to return to the main menu.

9. We can now incorporate our new global fields into the Welcome Menu layout and into letter and fax layouts based on the CommunicationTo table. Global fields can be incorporated into any layout in the same file, regardless of whether the global field table and the table underlying the layout are related. FileMaker will still display a global field correctly on the layout, without the usual <Unrelated Table> message appearing in Browse or Preview modes.

10. The button labeled **Add>** next to the gCompanyLogo container field has been set to run a script that selects the right field and opens the Insert Picture dialog box. We are forced to write a script to do this rather than use a simple button command, which can only perform one command. In this case we want to make sure the gCompanyLogo field has been selected by the user before the Insert Picture command is run; otherwise, FileMaker will not know where to insert an image and will therefore not open the Insert Picture dialog box. If we are going to the trouble of writing a script anyway, we might as well make it a conditional one, offering the user the choice of canceling the request or going ahead and inserting a logo into the gCompanyLogo field. Our new script is shown in Figure 11.44.

Script Name: | Import Logo

* Show Custom Dialog ["Add Logo"; "Add a logo for your company letterheads etc?\""]
* If [Get (LastMessageChoice) = 1]
*   Halt Script
* End If
* Go to Field [_CRM::gCompany Logo]
* Insert Picture [Reference]

Figure 11.44: The Import Logo script for the Wizard layout.

11. In Browse mode, we can now add our company data to the global fields, which are shown for an example company in Figure 11.45. FileMaker will have created a blank record for the CRM table when the file was first created. If you accidentally deleted this record, you will need to create a new one before populating the global fields.

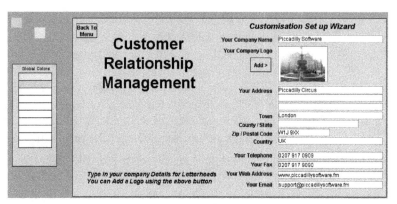

Figure 11.45: The completed Wizard record.

12. To make the CRM file always open with the Welcome Menu layout, we need to select the menu option **File>File Options**, check the **Switch to layout** option, and select the **CRM Welcome Menu** from the drop-down list of layouts.

13. There is no reason why we need to show the Status area when the Welcome Menu appears on screen. We can write an opening script that will hide the Status area in addition to switching to the Welcome Menu. The Opening script is shown in Figure 11.46.

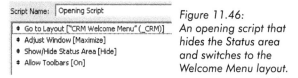

Figure 11.46: An opening script that hides the Status area and switches to the Welcome Menu layout.

14. Choose both the **Switch to layout** and **Perform script** options as shown checked in Figure 11.47.

Figure 11.47: The File Options dialog box settings to perform the Opening Script when the CRM file is launched.

We can now add the remaining data entry screens to the CRM file.

Step 6: Completing the CRM Data Entry Layouts

As a bare minimum, a FileMaker database should include layouts to browse records in Form view with details on a single record displayed, and in List view with reduced details on a set of records visible on screen. If a portal is adequate to display information on related records, it is not always necessary to display List views for all tables. Similarly, if all relevant information on a record can be viewed in a List report, such as for Staff details in our CRM example, it is not always necessary to have a Form view or details layout for every table in a file.

1. A series of List view and Form view layouts has been added to the CRM file to assist the user in data entry and in viewing related records.

2. A set of navigation and function buttons has been added to the top of each layout and, where appropriate, adjacent to a field in the layouts.

3. We can enhance a basic Organisation List layout by including a count of the number of related contacts, communication, and action records that are linked to each organization. This is shown in Figure 11.48.

4. The navigation buttons at the top of the layout are labeled to assist the user. The smaller buttons in the body have been formatted to switch to the Organisation Details layout; open the website for an organization; or display any related contacts, communication, action, and action "to do" records.

Figure 11.48: The Organisation List layout.

5. A calculation field called **Count Action_to do Colour** has been added to the Organisation table, with the formula shown in Figure 11.49. The result of the calculation is set to be a container field. This field can be placed immediately behind the Count Action_to do field. If the latter is not given a fill color, its background color will appear to change based on whether there is one or more related action records whose Action Done field does not have "Yes" as its contents.

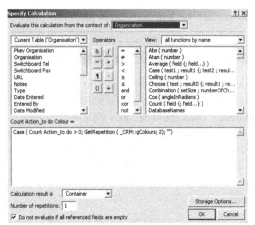

Figure 11.49:
The formula for the
Count Action_to do
Colour field.

6. The buttons marked with a right arrow (>), which take the user to any related records, all have a very similar formula that makes use of the Go to Related Record button function. The Go to Related Record option must have a related record target table occurrence and needs to be instructed which layout to use to display any related records. We need to choose the relevant target table occurrence that holds related records and display these with a layout that uses the same underlying base table. In the example shown in Figure 11.50, we are in an Organisation layout and wish to view any related contact records via the related table occurrence Organisation_Contacts. To display the related contacts, we have selected to use the **Contact List** layout. In the Result Options section of the dialog box, the **Show only related records** option is checked. This means that only contacts related to the currently viewed organization record will be displayed.

This method of getting related records from a linked table occurrence and displaying the record set using a layout from the same base table is used many times in the CRM solution and other case studies in this book.

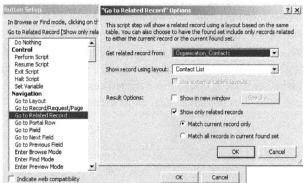

Figure 11.50:
The Go to
Related Record
button function
used to get
related
contacts from
within an
Organisation
layout.

7. The **Staff List** layout is used to display staff records. Three Go to Related Record buttons enable the user to navigate to any related organization records for which the staff record is the nominated key contact, any action records, or any actions that remain to do. The **Count Actions_Not_Done** field makes use of a multi-criteria relationship between staff and action records that are not equal to "Yes" in the Action Done field. A calculation field is used to display a green or red color depending on whether or not the Count Actions_Not_Done field is greater than 0.

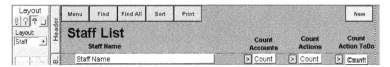

Figure 11.51: The Staff List layout.

8. The **Fax, Letter, Outgoing Email**, and **Meeting Phone Call Report** layouts shown in Figures 11.52 to 11.55 are all based on the CommunicationTo table occurrence. These layouts are designed for creating faxes, letters, emails, or meeting notes linked to an individual contact. The Fax and Letter layouts make extensive use of merge fields to manage how contact information is laid out on the printed page. Buttons and other layout objects are set to not print by highlighting them, choosing the menu option **Format>Set Sliding/Printing**, and checking the **Do not print the selected objects** option in the dialog box.

9. Extensive use has been made of merge fields in the communication layouts. These are displayed in Layout mode with the field name enclosed by double open (<<) and close (>>) angle brackets. You can add a merge field to a layout by pressing **Ctrl+M** on the keyboard or by selecting the menu option **Insert>Merge Field**. Merge fields enable you to combine field data with static text. A merge field automatically shrinks or expands to fit the amount of text in a field for each record. This means that a personal line in a letter layout, such as Dear <First Name>, always looks like it has been typed as a single text block with no excess spaces in Browse and Preview modes. When a merge field is on a line by itself and the field contains no text, FileMaker Pro removes the blank line from the text block, which improves the appearance of the text when browsed on screen or printed.

A script can be used to enhance navigation to any of these outgoing communication layouts. Ideally we would like to be able to click on a single button to view any CommunicationTo correspondence and have FileMaker work out the best layout to use to display the record. This script is described in the next section of this chapter.

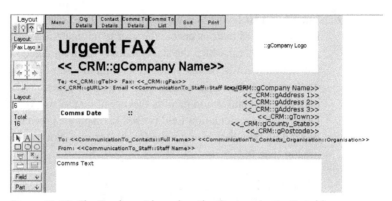

Figure 11.52: The Fax layout based on the CommunicationTo table occurrence.

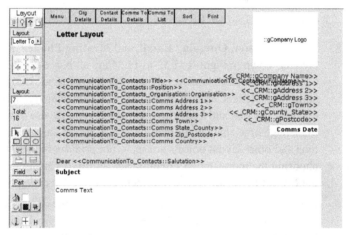

Figure 11.53: The Letter layout based on the CommunicationTo table occurrence.

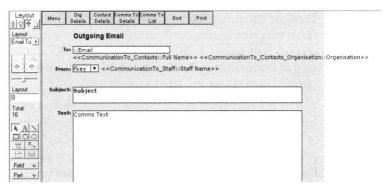

Figure 11.54: The Outgoing Email layout based on the CommunicationTo table occurrence.

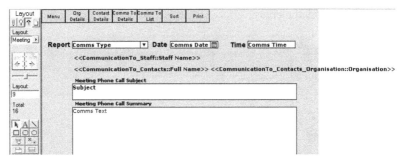

Figure 11.55: The Meeting Phone Call Report layout based on the CommunicationTo table occurrence.

10. The **Contact Details** layout is similar to the Organisation layout in that it makes use of a Tab control to display related records for any contact record within portals. If we want to create new related records for CommunicationTo, CommunicationFrom, or Action, we need to modify these relationships to allow creation of related records. In this solution, new related communication and action records can be created from the Organisation layout or the Contact Details layout.

11. A set of fields for a contact's personal address has been added to the **Contacts** table. The **Preferred Address** field uses a value list to ask the user whether this contact prefers to use an organization address or personal address for correspondence. A further set of calculation fields called **Comms Address 1** to **Comms Country** have then been added to the Contacts table. Each of these makes use of a simple calculation formula as follows:

Case (Preferred Address = "Organisation"; Contacts_Location:: Address1; Pers Address 1)

The Case function is similar to the If function and, if true, runs any number of tests with an associated result. If none of the tests are true, the default result applies. In this case, the personal address for a contact is used as the contents of the Comms Address field unless the user selects "Organisation" in the Preferred Address field.

12. Exactly the same technique is used to discern whether we should be writing to this individual as "Dear Dr. Lewis" or "Dear Susan." A field called **Formal_Informal** has been added to the Contacts table and displayed in the Contacts layout with the radio button value list as seen in Figure 11.56. A calculation field called **Salutation** has the formula:

Case (Formal_Informal = "Informal"; First Name ; Title & " " & Last Name)

This makes it easier to use a single field called Salutation for letters and mail merges.

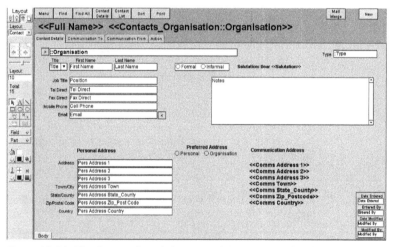

Figure 11.56: The Contact Details layout and Contact Details tab panel.

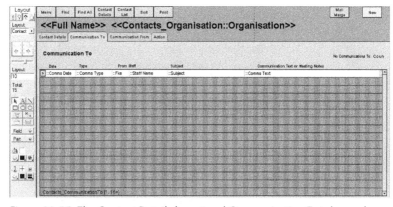

Figure 11.57: The Contact Details layout and Communication To tab panel.

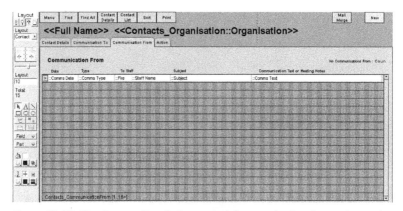

Figure 11.58: The Contact Details layout and Communication From tab panel.

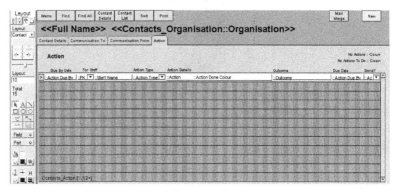

Figure 11.59: The Contact Details layout and Action tab panel.

13. A **Communication From** layout is used to display any item of communication received from a contact. There are third-party plug-ins available
for FileMaker that will automatically import emails from Outlook,
Entourage, and other email packages. The plug-ins are available on
FileMaker's website at www.filemaker.com/downloads/. For the basic
CRM solution we are building, it is assumed that you will have to cut
and paste relevant emails into new Communication From records, or
type in letter or fax summaries, or meeting or phone call notes. The
Communication From layout is shown in Figure 11.60.

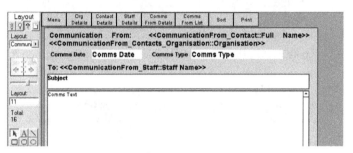

Figure 11.60: The Communication From layout.

14. A series of additional list layouts can be added to the CRM file to display
a set of records on screen. The list layouts for **Action**, **Contacts**, **Communication From**, and **Communication To** are shown in Figures 11.61
to 11.64.

Figure 11.61: The Action List layout.

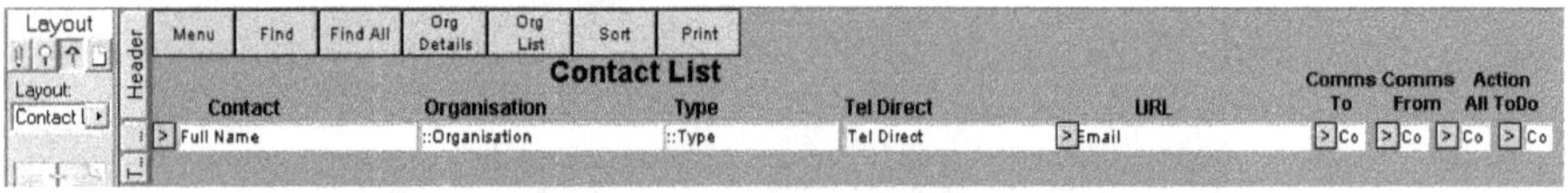

Figure 11.62: The Contact List layout.

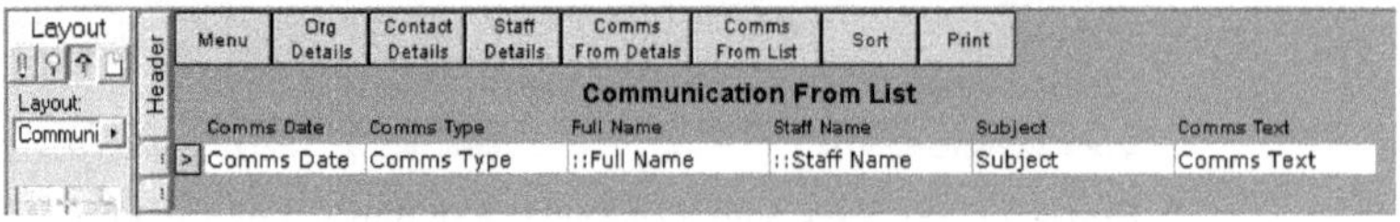

Figure 11.63: The Communication From List layout.

Figure 11.64: The Communication To List layout.

Step 7: Enhancing the CRM Solution with Scripts and Script Parameters

Buttons added to a FileMaker layout can be defined to perform a single task or run a predefined script. As discussed in Chapter 9, a script is used to run a series of tasks. There are several examples of where scripts can be used to enhance our basic CRM solution to assist colleagues in working with the file.

The Organisation, Contacts, and Staff layouts all have a green button labeled "New" that is designed to create a new record for each of these three tables. We could simply define this button to perform the New Record/Request command; however, we decide that this is too easy a way to add new records to the file and a warning message might be a good enhancement. With previous versions of FileMaker, we would need to add three new scripts to the file, with a custom dialog in each asking whether the user wished to create a new organization, contact, or staff record. With FileMaker Pro 8, we can take advantage of the new ScriptParameter feature, which enables us to use a single new record script for all three layouts.

1. We can start by writing the **New Record** script shown in Figure 11.65.

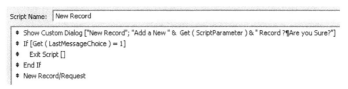

Figure 11.65: The New Record script makes use of the FileMaker Pro 8 ScriptParameter function.

2. In the **Show Custom Dialog** script step, the message includes the contents of the ScriptParameter between the words New and Record. We can use a ScriptParameter to customize the new record description that is inserted here: Organisation, Contact, or Staff.

The Show Custom Dialog Options dialog box is shown in Figure 11.66.

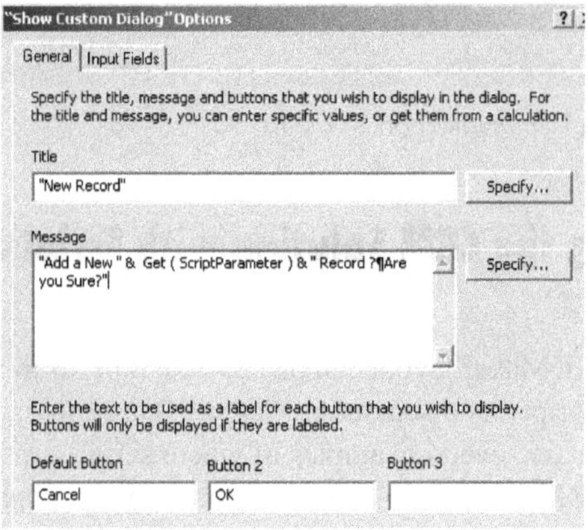

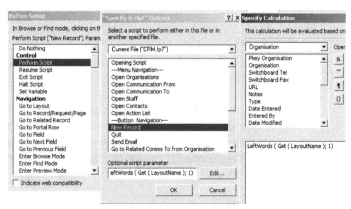

Figure 11.66:
The Show Custom
Dialog Options
dialog uses the
ScriptParameter
contents in the
dialog message.

The easiest way to do this is to add part of the relevant layout name to the ScriptParameter each time the script is run.

3. We can add a ScriptParameter to our New Record button setup. In Layout mode, add the **New Record** button by using the **Button** tool or by duplicating an existing button and renaming it.

4. Select the menu option **Format>Button Setup** or double-click on the button to open the Button Setup dialog box, then highlight the **Perform Script** button command and select the **New Record** script.

5. In the Specify Script Options dialog box, click the **Edit** button next to the "Optional script parameter" setting and add the function **LeftWords (Get (Layout Name); 1)**, as shown in Figure 11.67.

Figure 11.67: Adding an optional script parameter to a Perform Script button command.

While FileMaker is perfectly capable of producing letters to contacts, it is also able to export record data into other applications, such as a word processor for producing a mail merge document.

6. A script called **Mail Merge Found Set** can be written to export the selected set of contact records into a new merge document, which can be used to perform a mail merge using Microsoft Word. This script can be performed by a button in the Contact Details screen.

   The script makes use of FileMaker's ability to export field contents as a merge file (.mer). The Mail Merge Wizard, accessed from the Microsoft Word Tools menu, will recognize a .mer file exported from FileMaker as a valid data source. However, you may have to select Files of Type "All Files" in Word's Select Data Source dialog box to display the target merge file.

7. You can even make FileMaker open Microsoft Word (or most other applications) by using the **Send Event** script step shown in Figure 11.68.

Figure 11.68: Using the Send Event script step to launch other application .exe files from FileMaker.

The completed Mail Merge Found Set script is shown in Figure 11.69.

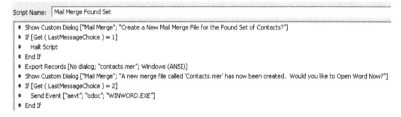

Figure 11.69: The Mail Merge Found Set script.

Taking the Solution Further

As with all FileMaker database projects, new fields, layouts, and functionality can be added to the basic CRM file as and when required. For example, you may want to use the New Layout/Report dialog box to add a mailing label layout to the Contacts table.

The CRM file can be used as part of a wider management system written in FileMaker that might include additional tables or tables in other files that hold details on projects, quotations, orders, and invoices. Having a "live link" to orders and invoices through portals when you are speaking to a contact is a great way to have related information available during your conversation. Your control department colleagues may be grateful that you can tactfully remind a client if an outstanding payment is due at the same time that you are taking details on a new order, for example.

The vast majority of FileMaker solutions have some form of contact management as their hub. Hopefully, you can apply the relationship and layout designs discussed in this chapter for your own CRM projects.

Chapter 12

Timesheets

Introduction

A timesheet solution written in FileMaker is a great example of how conditional, or filtered, value lists can be used to assist colleagues in entering accurate information into a record. Completing a timesheet log can be an onerous chore; however, FileMaker can ensure that only the active project and activity information appears on screen. The task may then be less burdensome and it is more likely that accurate information will be entered, which could later be used for invoicing or client activity reports.

A timesheet solution can also be used to demonstrate how an effective database solution can be built by using reasonably simple relationships between tables, standard layouts, and FileMaker's built-in button commands. In its basic form, the file does not require any scripts.

This solution is designed to assist a workgroup in logging the time spent and activities undertaken by staff on projects that have been commissioned by clients. As with most FileMaker relational database design projects, it is a good idea to start with a clear breakdown of a) what data is to be recorded, b) who will be responsible for the data capture, and c) who will wish to query and report on the information that can be extracted from this data.

For a timesheet solution, the information to be recorded is the time spent by individuals on activities on a particular day. Ideally, each person will be responsible for entering his or her own timesheet records. The solution should be able to report on timesheet entries in such a way that the organization's management can find out how much time has been spent by whom, on what activity, for which project, on behalf of which client.

As with the other case studies in this book, a copy of the completed FileMaker Pro 8 database file, **TimeSheets**, is available to download from the publisher's website at www.wordware.com/files/fmapps and the author's website at www.aweconsultancy.com. You may find it easier to examine some of the FileMaker features and techniques discussed in this chapter in a copy of the completed file.

The default database password for the Admin account is **HOURLY** (all capitals). The database file options have been preset to open with the active Guest account (with read-only access to the file). To open the file with full access privileges, hold down the Shift key (Windows) or Option key (Mac OS) while the file is opening. Type the word **Admin** in the Account Name box and type the password in the box below. You can change the default password at a later stage. More information on database security issues, passwords, accounts, and privileges is given in Chapter 24.

The Timesheet Entity Relationship Diagram

As with any FileMaker project that requires the design of relationships between tables, it is good practice to start with an entity relationship (ER) diagram showing what tables are required for the project and how records in the tables are related to each other.

As detailed in Chapter 7, an ER diagram is not the same as the relationships graph, which is constructed in FileMaker using table occurrences. An ER diagram describes how the underlying tables are related to each other as part of the overall solution design.

The first stage of designing the ER diagram is to map out all the entities, or tables, that will be required to create an effective method of both capturing and reporting on timesheet records. Remember that an entity is the item itself, such as a colleague or a client. The item is described by attributes, such as staff surname or client company name. Attributes are the equivalent of fields in a FileMaker table.

A colleague or **Team** member needs to record in a **Timesheet Entry** the time expended on a **Role**, which is part of an **Activity**, which is part of a **Project** that has been commissioned by a **Client**. Each of these entities, highlighted in bold, can be drawn as rectangles representing each table. Lines can then be drawn between the tables to indicate how they are related to each other. The crow's-foot symbol at one end of a relationship line linked to a vertical line (|) at the other indicates a "one-to-many" relationship.

The Timesheet ER diagram is shown in Figure 12.1. An individual client can commission many projects. Each project has many activities. Each activity has several roles. A role is the involvement of a team member on a particular project activity. The time spent on roles by a team member is recorded in a timesheet entry.

Timesheet ER Diagram

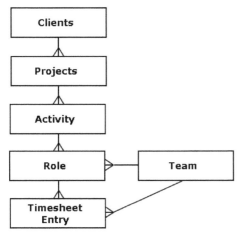

Figure 12.1: The Timesheet ER diagram.

Building the TimeSheets File

Step 1: Adding Tables to the TimeSheets File

We are now ready to start building the underlying tables that we will need for our timesheet solution in FileMaker.

As discussed in Chapter 7, the best way to build relationships between tables in FileMaker is to base the relationships on primary and foreign keys that are automatically managed by FileMaker and cannot be edited or replaced over time. We will want to create a single primary key field for each table and the foreign key fields that are needed in the tables. The best method for creating a primary key field is to create a number field and use FileMaker's field options settings to automate the insertion of a serial number that cannot later be edited or deleted. If relationships and values in key fields are not carefully designed and secured against accidental modification, billable time for a project can be lost or incorrectly allocated at a later stage when reports are printed or client invoices are generated.

We need to create a table for each of the entities shown in Figure 12.1. In addition, a table for the solution will be created, which can be used as the underlying table for any welcome menu or report screens that might be added to the finished solution.

Let's start by creating a new file in FileMaker called TimeSheets.fp7.

1. Open FileMaker and choose the menu option **File>New Database**. If your preferences are set so that when a new database is selected, the

templates window appears, you can click the radio button labeled **Create a new empty file**. The templates window can be switched on or off by choosing the menu option Edit>Preferences>General and clearing or checking the "Show templates in New Database dialog box" option.

2. Type **TimeSheets.fp7** into the File name box, choose the folder in which you wish to create the file, such as the **Desktop** at this stage, and click the **Save** button.

FileMaker will then open the new file and the Define Database dialog box, as shown in Figure 12.2. The Fields tab will be selected for the single default table in the file. When we begin working on the file, the single default table has the same name as the file.

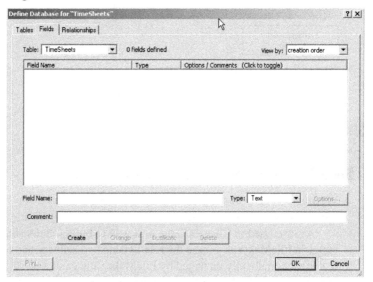

Figure 12.2: The Define Database dialog box for a new file with the Fields tab selected for the default table.

3. The three tabs at the top of the dialog box — Tables, Fields, and Relationships — manage which one of these screens is displayed within the Define Database dialog box. Click the **Tables** tab and add the tables shown in Figure 12.3 to the file.

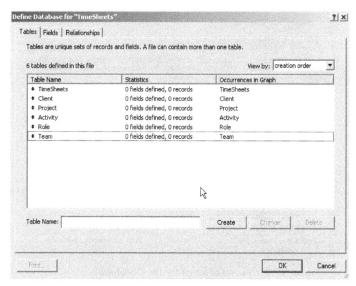

Figure 12.3: Create these tables for the TimeSheets file.

Step 2: Adding Fields to the TimeSheets File Tables

We are now ready to add fields to the TimeSheets file tables. Fields are needed to describe the attributes of each table and to provide a primary key and any foreign keys needed for the relationships that we create for the TimeSheets file.

1. To add fields to each of the tables within the file, choose the **File> Define>Database** menu option and the **Fields** tab of the Define Database dialog box. It is important to ensure that the correct table is selected prior to adding new fields. Each of the tables can be selected from the drop-down list near the top of the dialog box, as shown in Figure 12.4.

Figure 12.4: Selecting the relevant table for a new field in the Define Database dialog box.

2. Add the initial fields to each table as shown in Figures 12.5 to 12.10. Later, when we have established relationships between these tables using table occurrences in the relationships graph, we will add additional fields to the tables to improve the functionality of the file.

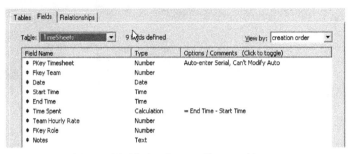

Figure 12.5: The initial fields for the TimeSheets table.

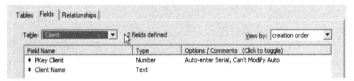

Figure 12.6: The initial fields for the Client table.

Tables | Fields | Relationships

Table: Project   6 fields defined   View by: creation order

Field Name	Type	Options / Comments (Click to toggle)
PKey Project	Number	Auto-enter Serial, Can't Modify Auto
Project Title	Text	
Fkey Client	Number	
Estimated Project Hours	Time	
Actual Project Hours	Time	
Project Notes	Text	

Figure 12.7: The initial fields for the Project table.

Tables | Fields | Relationships

Table: Activity   6 fields defined   View by: creation order

Field Name	Type	Options / Comments (Click to toggle)
Pkey Activity	Number	Auto-enter Serial, Can't Modify Auto
Fkey Project	Number	
Activity Title	Text	
Estimated Activity Hours	Time	
Actual Activity Hours	Time	
Activity Notes	Text	

Figure 12.8: The initial fields for the Activity table.

Tables | Fields | Relationships

Table: Role   7 fields defined   View by: creation order

Field Name	Type	Options / Comments (Click to toggle)
PKey Role	Number	Auto-enter Serial, Can't Modify Auto
Role	Text	
FKey Activity	Number	
FKey Team	Number	
Role Comments	Text	
Estimated Role Hours	Time	
Actual Role Hours	Time	

Figure 12.9: The initial fields for the Role table.

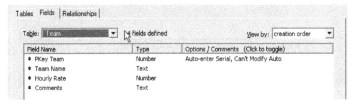

Figure 12.10: The initial fields for the Team table.

Step 3: Adding Relationships within the TimeSheets File

By linking the tables within the TimeSheets file we can make FileMaker do much of the work in terms of making it easy to capture timesheet entries and report on the total time expended by colleagues on specific projects and activities. With FileMaker we do not link the underlying base tables directly in the relationships graph. Instead, relationships are built up between table occurrences, which are representations of the base tables in the relationships graph. For design purposes and often to aid clarity, it is possible to have any number of table occurrences on the relationships graph for the same underlying base table.

Chapter 7 introduced the idea of designing the relationships graph as a series of discrete table occurrence groups, or TOGs. Each TOG should have a main or "anchor" table occurrence on its left-hand side, with any number of linked "buoy" tables related to the anchor table spread out on the right-hand side. To ease relationship design at the outset and to assist you or any colleagues who may work on the file at a later stage, a number of fundamental rules should be followed when using relationships in any FileMaker solution:

- As a general rule, any relationships graph will have one anchor table occurrence for every base table in the file.
- All data entry layouts should only be based on an underlying anchor table occurrence.
- Any portals on layouts should be based on buoy table occurrences.
- To assist with documenting a complex FileMaker project, it is a good idea to limit the dimensions of any TOGs in the relationships graph to a single page in width but any number of pages in length.

1. Click on the **Relationships** tab within the Define Database dialog box to see that a table occurrence for each of the tables in the TimeSheets file has been added to the relationships graph, as shown in Figure 12.11.

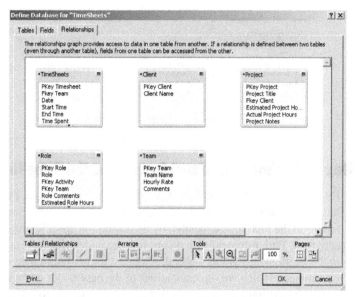

Figure 12.11: The relationships graph will, by default, contain one table occurrence for each table in a file.

To get the required functionality from our TimeSheets solution, we now need to add some new TOGs to the relationships graph.

2. For the sake of reference, it is a good idea to leave at least one table occurrence for each source table in a file displayed at the top of the graph. To reduce the space used, the button on the table header can be clicked to toggle the display of the table and collapse it to its title only, as shown in Figure 12.12.

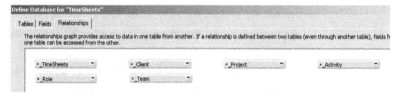

Figure 12.12: Collapsing the source tables to show their titles only at the top of the relationships graph.

3. Add an underscore (_) to each of the source table occurrences so that the original table name can be used as an anchor table occurrence. Each table occurrence must have a unique name in the graph. A table occurrence can be renamed by double-clicking on it to open the Specify Table dialog box, or by highlighting the table occurrence and clicking the **Edit** button at the bottom of the graph (the button with a yellow pencil icon).

4. Add the TOGs shown in Figure 12.13 to the relationships graph. Use the **Color Wheel** tool to vary the color of each TOG and make the graph easier to follow.

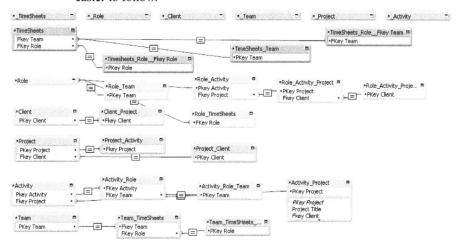

Figure 12.13: The TimeSheets relationships graph.

5. To make it easier to add related records in the data entry screens, set the relationships to the left of **Client_Project**, **Project_Activity**, and **Activity_Role** to **Allow creation of records in this table via this relationship**. This can be done by double-clicking anywhere on the relevant relationship line and selecting the check box shown in Figure 12.14.

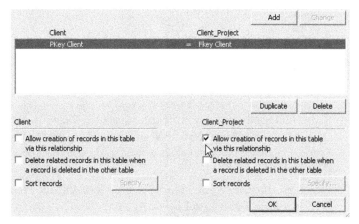

Figure 12.14: Modifying a relationship to allow creation of records in a related table in the Edit Relationship dialog box.

We are now ready to design the data entry screens.

Step 4: Designing Data Entry Layouts for the TimeSheets File

Before we can begin to capture timesheet records and start to deploy conditional value lists for data entry, we need to add some records to the tables in our TimeSheets solution. Prior to recording timesheet entries, we first need to design suitable data entry layouts to input records for clients, projects, activities, roles, and workgroup colleagues in the Team table.

As previously mentioned, it is good design to base data entry layouts on anchor table occurrences, or the leftmost table occurrence in any table occurrence group.

1. Open the **Define Database** dialog box if necessary and save the changes to the relationships graph by clicking the **OK** button. You will notice that FileMaker has automatically created a standard form layout for each table in the file. These appear in the Layout pop-up menu in the Status area, as shown in Figure 12.15.

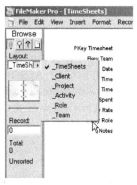

Figure 12.15: FileMaker automatically adds a standard form layout for each table in the file.

In order to have complete control over the look of our data entry layouts, we will create new layouts for record capture. We will need to add new layouts to record information on clients and associated project information, together with team names as well as the central timesheet entry screen.

2. Start creating a new layout by selecting **View>Layout Mode** and then choosing **Layouts>New Layout/Report**. The New Layout/Report dialog box will appear, as shown in Figure 12.16.

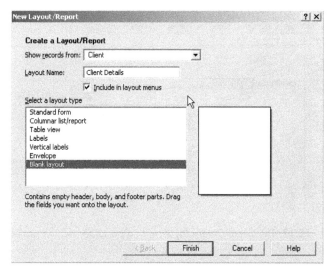

Figure 12.16: The New Layout/Report dialog box with the underlying Client table occurrence selected, a suitable name given, and a blank layout selected.

3.   Choose to show records from an anchor base table, such as **Client**, and choose a suitable layout name, such as **Client Details**. As we are going to have complete control over the record entry layouts, select **Blank layout** from the list of layout types, then click **Finish**.

4.1: The Client Details Layout

For our TimeSheets solution, we want to make it easy to add client records and associate projects with clients. To do this we are going to add a portal showing related project records for each client. There is no reason to show primary key fields in any of the record entry screens since a unique value for each primary key field is automatically given to a new record by FileMaker.

   The most important field in the Client Details layout is the **Client Name** field, together with details on any projects in a portal. Figure 12.17 shows the basic Client Details layout with a portal added to show project details from the Client_Project related table occurrence. As we have already indicated that we want to allow creation of related records through this relationship, we can add new project records to the last row in the project portal. This basic layout is only being used for record capture, so the header and footer layout parts that FileMaker automatically adds to a new blank layout have been deleted by highlighting each part and pressing the **Delete** key.

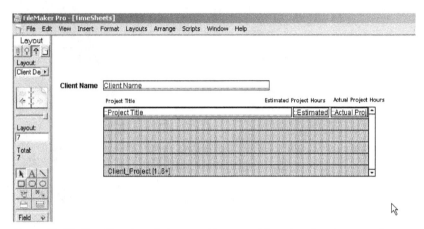

Figure 12.17: The Client Details layout with a portal for related project records.

4.2: The Project Details Layout

As a minimum, the Project Details layout should include fields for the project title, the associated client, the estimated and actual project hours, and project notes, and a portal showing related activities for a specific project. The portal, which is constructed using the Project_Activity table occurrence, contains fields for the activity title, the estimated hours, and the actual hours, and is shown in Figure 12.18.

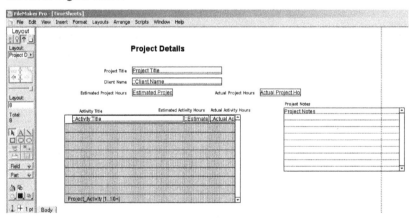

Figure 12.18: The Project Details layout.

The related **Client Name** field in the Project Details layout is selected from the Project_Client table occurrence. As is often the case, the database designer will not want users to accidentally change the value of a field from within a related record. In this case, an inexperienced user may inadvertently click into the Client Name field and permanently change the original name in the field (or delete the value). This problem can be avoided in a number of ways, such as limiting access privileges for certain users. The easiest method is simply to choose the menu option **Format>Field/Control>Behavior** in Layout mode and uncheck the option that allows a particular field to be entered in Browse mode, as shown in Figure 12.19.

Field Behavior for "Client Name"   ? ✕

Allow field to be entered: ☐ In Browse mode   ☑ In Find mode

☐ Select entire contents of field on entry

☐ Set input method to: Synchronize with field's font

Go to next object using
☑ Tab key   ☐ Return key   ☐ Enter key

OK   Cancel

Figure 12.19: The Field Behavior dialog box can be used to restrict access to selected fields.

4.3: The Activity Details Layout

Workgroup colleagues in the Team table can be assigned to work on a particular project through the Activity Details layout by including a portal to the Activity_Role table occurrence.

1. Design the **Activity_Role** portal to allow a team member to be allocated to a role within an activity. Use the **FKey Team** field to relate role records to an individual in the **Team** table. It is possible to include the team name in the portal row alongside the FKey Team field by adding the **Team Name** field from the Activity_Role_Team table occurrence.

    The Activity Details layout is shown in Figure 12.20.

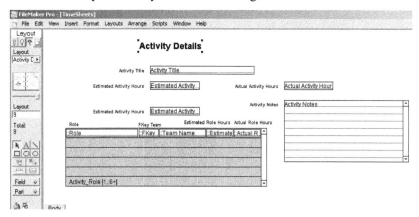

Figure 12.20: The Activity Details layout.

Ideally we would like a team list to appear in the Role portal when we click on the FKey Team field. This will assist data entry when assigning individuals to roles within an activity, and means that the user does not have to remember unique primary key values for each team.

2. To assign a Team value list to the FKey Team field, switch to Layout mode and highlight the **FKey Team** field. Select the **Format> Field/Control>Setup** menu option to open the Field/Control Setup dialog box, as shown in Figure 12.21.

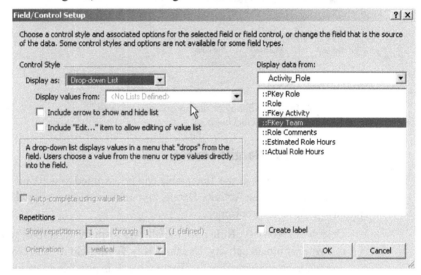

Figure 12.21: The Field/Control Setup dialog box with the Drop-down List display option selected.

3. Under Control Style, click in the Display as box. Select **Drop-down List** and create a new value list called **Team Name**.

4. In the Display values from box, select **Define Value List** and create a new value list named **Team Name**.

5. Select the **Use Values from Field** radio button to open the Specify Fields for Value List dialog box. Use the **PKey Team** and **Team Name** fields from the **Team** table, as shown in Figure 12.22. Select the **Show values only from second field** option so that the value list will only show easily recognized colleague names and not leading serial numbers. This can help with accurate data entry.

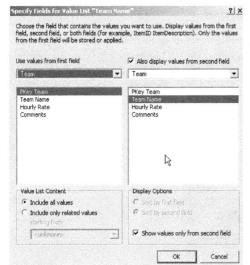

Figure 12.22:
The Team Name
value list.

4.4: The Role Details Layout

Team members are assigned to roles in the Activity Details layout, as described previously. If we now create a new layout based on the underlying Role table, we can add a portal to this layout and view individual timesheet entries that are related to each role. The Role Details layout includes the field FKey Team and, from the related Role_Team table occurrence, the Team Name field.

The Role Details layout, with a portal showing related records from the Role_TimeSheets table occurrence, can be seen in Figure 12.23.

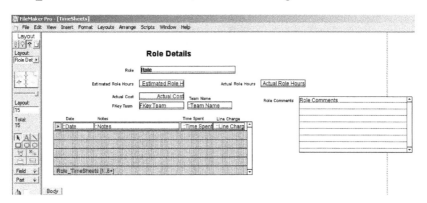

Figure 12.23: The Role Details layout.

4.5: The Team List Layout

We need to create a layout to capture team information. Since we are only interested in the name, hourly rate, and perhaps a brief comment on each team member, a list layout can be created instead of a columnar list/report layout.

The basic Team List layout is shown in Figure 12.24.

Figure 12.24: The Team List layout.

Step 5: Adding Sample Records to the Tables in the TimeSheets File

We can now add sample records to the tables in the database prior to designing the TimeSheets entry screen itself. To test if the portals are working correctly in allowing the creation of related records, start by adding a client, and then add a couple of projects into the Project portal. Switch to the Project Details layout and add some activities to each project. Add records for individual colleagues in the Team List layout, and then switch to the Activity Details layout and assign roles for team members in the Role portal.

If any of the portals are not allowing you to add related records, it is most likely that the relationship needs to be edited to allow creation of records via the relationship. This can be checked by double-clicking anywhere along the relevant relationship line in the relationships graph and ensuring that the "Allow creation of records..." option is checked.

At this stage you might want to type in values for the estimated hours needed for projects, activities, and tasks. We will soon be able to compare these values against actual timesheet entries.

Step 6: Designing the TimeSheets Entry List Layout

We should now design the most important layout in our solution, the TimeSheet Entry List layout.

1. In Layout mode, add a new columnar list/report layout called **TimeSheet Entry List** to show records from the TimeSheets table occurrence.

2. Add fields to the list layout as shown in Figure 12.25. Notice that the Team Name and Role fields, both shown grayed out, have been taken from the related table occurrences TimeSheets_Team and TimeSheets_Role_FKey Role.

Figure 12.25: The TimeSheet Entry List layout.

We can now start to assist colleagues in entering accurate timesheet entries by making use of conditional value lists and using scripts to automate data entry. We can start by making the FKey Team field a pop-up list based on the Team Name value list that we previously created for the Role portal in the Activity Details layout.

3. Switch to Layout mode, highlight the **PKey Team** field and right-click, then select the **Field/Control>Setup** menu option. Choose **Drop-down list** for the control style and select the **Team Name** value list.

We want to assist colleagues in displaying activity roles that they are actively involved in for each timesheet record entry. This will require us to create a conditional value list that is based on a relationship between TimeSheets and Role records that both have the same FKey Team value. In the example shown in Figure 12.26, when Mary Peters' FKey Team value is selected for a timesheet record, only Mary's roles should appear in the FKey Role value list.

Figure 12.26: Items in the FKey Role value list are related to the FKey Team value selected for each timesheet record.

4. Create the related value list and attach it to the FKey Role field by switching to Layout mode and selecting the **FKey Role** field. Right-click the field and choose the **Field/Control>Setup** menu option. Create a new value list called **Team Roles List** using values from the **PKey Role** and **Role** fields in the **TimeSheets_Role__FKey Team** related table occurrence, as shown in Figure 12.27. It is important to specify that only related values starting from the **TimeSheets** table occurrence are used.

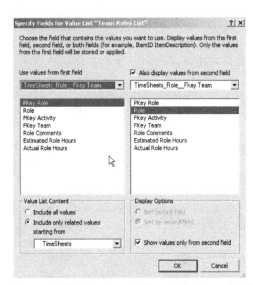

Figure 12.27: Creating the Team Roles List value list using related records only.

6.1: Using Lookups in Preference to Related Fields

The TimeSheets Entry List layout has a field called Team Hourly Rate, which records the amount we charge for a team member at the time that the timesheet record is created. This is an important distinction from simply using the related field for hourly rate in the Team table. What would happen if you increased your team's rates by 50% next month?

Despite all the benefits of using a relationship between two tables, it is often important to preserve information that was current only at the time a record was created. Last month's timesheets should preserve the hourly rate that was applicable then. Similarly, last year's invoices should preserve the line item prices that were used at that time, which may not be the same as today's prices. In this situation the contents of the Team Hourly Rate field in the TimeSheets table should be inserted using a lookup rather than by making direct use of the Hourly Rate field in the Team table.

With the exception of calculation and summary fields, all field types can be set as a lookup, where the contents of a field in one table is "looked up" from the contents of a field in another table, based on the relationship's key field values matching. It is important to note that a looked-up value in a field will not subsequently change, unless the data in the same table's foreign key field is modified or refreshed by clicking into the key field and selecting the menu option Records>Relookup Field Contents. For example, if another staff number was selected in the FKey Team field, the corresponding hourly rate for the team member will be "relooked up" into the Team Hourly Rate field.

The Options for Field settings to make Team Hourly Rate a looked-up value based on the TimeSheets_Team relationship are shown in Figure 12.28.

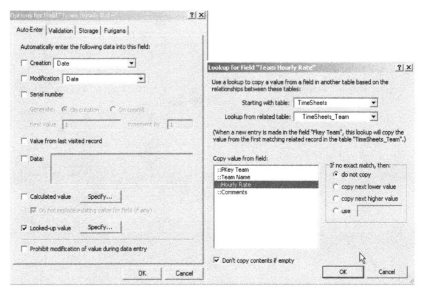

Figure 12.28: The Team Hourly Rate field in the TimeSheets table is a lookup value based on the TimeSheet_Team table occurrence relationship.

6.2: Improving the Pop-up Lists in the TimeSheets Entry List Layout

The FKey Role value list only gives limited information. While the value list is conditional on the selected team name for each timesheet entry and only shows the relevant roles for the chosen name, it doesn't help the user by showing the project title or client name.

As a default value, lists will only show a maximum of two linked fields. To increase the amount of relevant information for each item in a value list, we can create a calculation field that concatenates the contents of two or more other fields.

We need to make the Activity Title, Project Title, and Client Name field contents available in the Team Roles value list. To do this we need to make use of the relationships between the Role table occurrence in the relationships graph and the table occurrences we created for Role_Activity, Role_Activity_Project, and Role_Activity_Project_Client, as shown in Figure 12.29.

Figure 12.29: New table occurrences based on the Activity, Project, and Client base tables are related to each other using the FKey and PKey fields from Role_Activity, Role_Activity_Project, and Role_Activity_Project_Client.

If users would like to check that they are choosing the correct role for a timesheet entry by also seeing details on the project title and the associated client, we need to create a new calculation field called **Role_Activity_Project_Client** in the Role table, as shown in Figure 12.30.

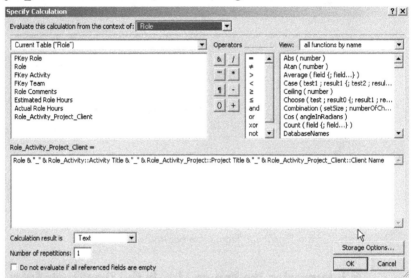

Figure 12.30: The Role_Activity_Project_Client calculation field in the Role table with its contents derived from three table occurrences related to the Role table occurrence.

The definition for the Team Role value list can now be updated to use the new field as the only field that is displayed, as shown in Figure 12.31.

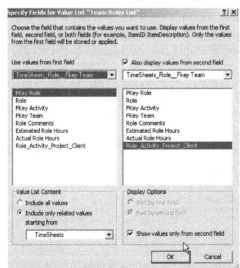

Figure 12.31: The revised Team Roles List definition, which now uses Role_Activity_Project_Client as its contents in the second field.

When the OK button is clicked, you may see a message box like the one in
Figure 12.32, indicating that this value list will not work as the second field
chosen cannot be indexed. This is because it uses fields from related tables in
its definition.

This will not create a problem for displaying the value list as only the
contents of the first field, PKey Role, is stored and used in the FKey Role
field in the TimeSheets table.

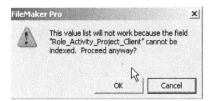

Figure 12.32: The value list index warning box.

If you go back to the TimeSheets Entry List layout in Browse mode and now
select the FKey Role field for the selected team name, the value list contents
will give a lot more information on the activity, project, client, and role for
that time period. The revised value list is displayed in Figure 12.33.

Fkey Team	Team Name	Date	Start Time	End Time	Time Spent	FKey Role	Role	Team Hourly Rate	Notes
1	Mary Peters	07/11/2005	9:00	20:10:18	11:10:18	2	Assistant	60	
					Printer Liaison/Confirm Page Design Software with current Printers/Classic Car Magazine Relaunch/Eastern					
					Project Leader/Agree Design Brief with Client/Classic Car Magazine Relaunch/Eastern Magazine Group					

Figure 12.33: The revised value list that appears when the FKey Role field is selected.

Step 7: Enhancing the Basic Timesheet Solution

We have now created a basic method by which timesheet entries can be used
by colleagues to allocate time against allocated project activity roles. A little
enhancement will make the files more user friendly, help to capture accurate
data, and report on actual project time and cost resources.

A good place to start would be by making the data entry layouts easier to
navigate with an improved interface by adding navigation buttons.

Each of the data entry screens can be given a similar look with a standard
set of navigation buttons at the top of each layout. We can also add a Welcome Menu layout and ensure that it is the first screen that appears when the
TimeSheets file is opened.

Figure 12.34 shows a Welcome Menu layout, with a series of buttons
that will open the corresponding data entry layouts, provide a help dialog box
for colleagues, and close the file. Each of these buttons has been created
using the Button tool in Layout mode. The data entry buttons all make use of
the Go to Layout button command, while the About button uses the Show
Custom Dialog command to open a new dialog box. A dialog box is often

used by developers to provide contact details such as the phone number and email address of the database author. The Quit button provides an easy method for users to close the TimeSheets file and makes use of the Close File button command.

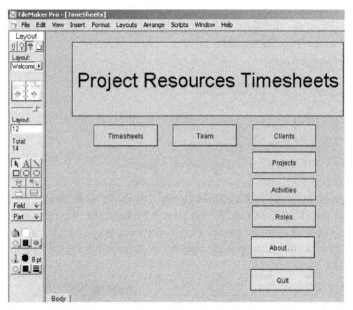

Figure 12:34: Adding a Welcome Menu layout to the TimeSheets database.

The Welcome Menu screen can be set to always appear when the TimeSheets file is opened by selecting the **File>File Options** menu choice, checking the **Switch to layout** check box, and selecting the **Welcome Menu** layout, as shown in Figure 12.35.

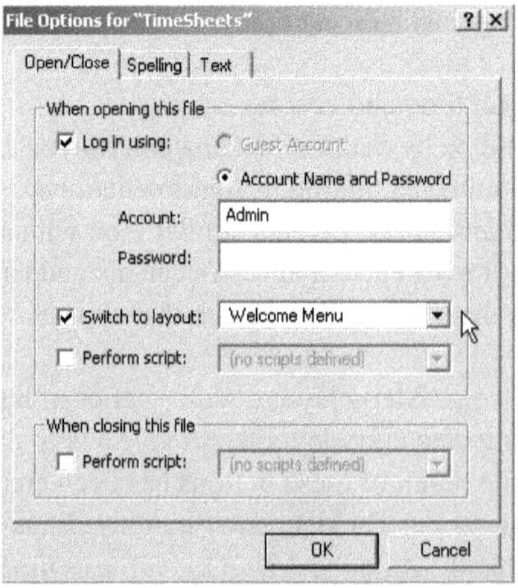

Figure 12.35: The File Options dialog settings to switch to the Welcome Menu layout when the file is opened.

For each of the data entry screens, a set of buttons can be added to assist colleagues in adding new records and navigating to related records in the file. The revised Team List layout is shown in Figure 12.36.

Figure 12:36: Data entry layouts such as Team List can be enhanced with standard navigation buttons and consistent background colors.

Step 8: Using Calculation Fields to Report on Timesheet Resources

Within the TimeSheets solution, the Team table includes a field for the hourly rate charged for team members, while each record in the TimeSheets table records the start and stop time for a team member undertaking a selected role. By defining some simple calculation fields, this information can be used to report on the total time to date spent on a role, activity, and project. By converting each time period into the equivalent charge out time, the total amount to be charged for each project, activity, and role can also be calculated and displayed.

Let's start by calculating the time spent for each timesheet entry. We need to create a simple calculation formula that subtracts the start time from the end time.

1. Choose the menu option **File>Define>Database** and, with the **Fields** tab selected, choose the **TimeSheets** table in the drop-down list of tables.

2. Create a new calculation field called **Time Spent** with the formula shown in Figure 12.37. We need to tell FileMaker to evaluate this calculation from the context of the **TimeSheets** table occurrence and select the fields **End Time** and **Start Time** from the same table (this is the current table in the table drop-down list).

3. After inserting the End Time and Start Time fields into the formula window by double-clicking on the fields, insert the subtract symbol between the two fields in the formula by using the keyboard or by selecting the "–" operator key in the middle of the dialog box.

4. It is important that we tell FileMaker the result of this calculation should be a unit of time by selecting **Time** in the "Calculation result is" drop-down list.

5. Click the **OK** button to add the new Time Spent calculation field to the TimeSheets table.

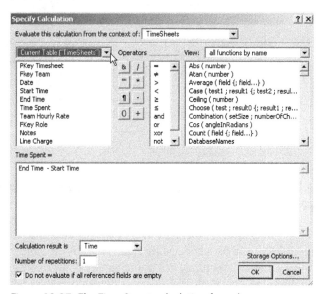

Figure 12.37: The Time Spent calculation formula.

We can now calculate the line charge for every timesheet entry. This is the basic building block for all subsequent charge summaries that we may wish to report on by role, activity, project, and client.

6. Create another calculation field called **Line Charge** with the formula shown in Figure 12.38. Choose **Number** from the "Calculation result is" drop-down list.

The formula uses FileMaker's Hour, Minute, and Seconds functions to convert the time spent for each record into an equivalent line charge using the looked-up team hourly rate. (You may feel that calculating the time to the second to be a bit too precise, or penny pinching! It is used here to demonstrate the function.) Notice that this time we want the calculation result to be a number to correctly calculate the amount charged for each timesheet entry.

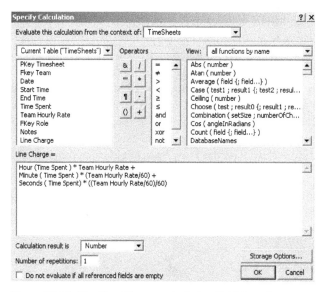

Figure 12.38: The Line Charge calculation field formula.

We can now create Summary Time and Charge fields in all the related tables to report on resources spent, the rate scale of a role for an activity and a project, and the total for each client.

When we first created our tables, we included fields for actual hours spent and actual cost in the Project, Activity, and Role tables. We can now redefine these fields to be calculation fields based on the data in related timesheet records.

7. In the Role table, highlight the **Actual Role Hours** field, choose **Calculation** in the Type drop-down list, and click the **Change** button. A message box as shown in Figure 12.39 will appear, warning that contents of the field will be replaced with the result of the formula.

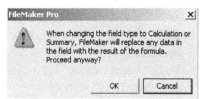

Figure 12:39: Before an existing field can be changed into a calculation or a summary field, FileMaker displays a warning that any existing data will be replaced by the result of the formula.

8. Click the **OK** button and the Specify Calculation dialog box appears. Choose to evaluate the calculation from the context of the **Role** table. Use FileMaker's **Sum** function to calculate the total time spent for all related timesheet records using the formula shown in Figure 12.40. We want to calculate the total time for all timesheet records that are related to a role record. Therefore, we need to choose the Time Spent field in the related table Role_TimeSheets. This field can be inserted into the formula by choosing the **Role_TimeSheet** table in the drop-down list and double-clicking on the **Time Spent** field when the correct table's field list appears in the window.

9. As this summary data will be a unit of time, the calculation result must have **Time** selected as the field type.

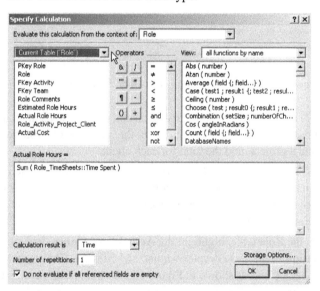

Figure 12:40: The Actual Role Hours calculation formula.

10. The Actual Cost formula in the Role table should also be changed to a calculation field with the formula shown in Figure 12.41. As before, the formula makes use of FileMaker's Sum function and uses the **Line Charge** field from the related **Role_TimeSheets** table.

Summary fields for actual time and actual cost can also be added to the Activity, Project, and Client tables.

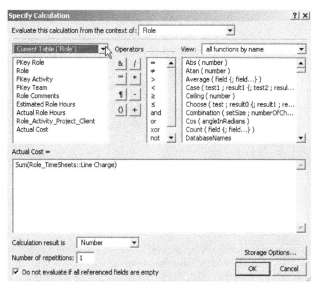

Figure 12:41: The Actual Cost formula.

11. Add calculation fields to the relevant data entry layouts to report on time and costs logged at each scale of interest in the TimeSheets file. The Role Details layout is shown in Figure 12.42 with the new fields added. The Activity, Project, and Client Details layouts have been similarly enhanced.

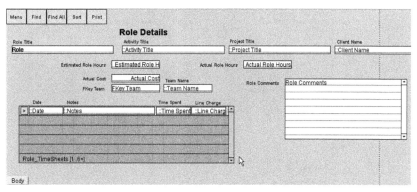

Figure 12:42: The enhanced Role Details layout with Actual Cost and Actual Role Hours fields added and a portal that displays related TimeSheets records.

12. Add a new Team layout that includes a field called **Most Recent Timesheet**, which shows the most recent timesheet date that has been entered for each staff name, as shown in Figure 12.43. This can be used as a gentle reminder that colleagues may not have updated their timesheets for a day or two.

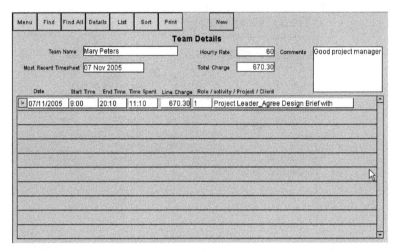

Figure 12:43: The Team Details layout shows the most recent timesheet date and a portal with related timesheet entries.

The Most Recent Timesheet calculation formula uses FileMaker's Max function and is shown in Figure 12.44.

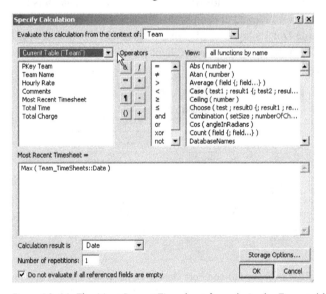

Figure12:44: The Most Recent Timesheet formula in the Team table.

Taking the Solution Further

No scripts have been used in the TimeSheets solution. It is, of course, possible to continue to improve the file and apply your newly acquired FileMaker techniques to add user accounts and privileges so that work colleagues are unable to accidentally delete timesheet records or modify existing client and project information. We could then create a New Record script that would automatically insert the correct staff name for a new timesheet entry.

The solution could be incorporated into a job bag system for managing projects in more detail, and could also be used as the basis for invoicing clients based on the chargeable time recorded. The other case study projects should hopefully give you some ideas on how to enhance the TimeSheets solution.

Chapter 13

Job Bag I — Creative Design Management

Introduction

FileMaker is used by over 100,000 creative professionals worldwide. Every creative agency and design studio will have its own methods for tracking projects and assignments. The client will be expecting an original response to the creative assignment from a design team. The design team will expect a database application to keep up with their methods for getting the work done. FileMaker is easy to use, can be adapted to new methods of design management, and is accessible over all desktop systems, handheld PDAs, and the web. You will be hard pressed to find an advertising or design firm that does not contain a workgroup using FileMaker.

It is rare to find creative teams that adhere to common or formal business methods for managing commissioned assignments. Good creative designers are often the least interested in departmental budget management or financial ledgers. FileMaker excels in this environment with its options to create a database that can help manage the creative team while still providing reports for the firm's financial department. As no two workgroups will ever approach a creative assignment in exactly the same way, the precise requirements of a job bag will vary across firms. Three case study chapters in this book are dedicated to the subject of job bags. The first case study addresses the needs of creative design management, the second focuses on print and production management, and the third develops a solution for job estimating and cost tracking.

In this chapter, a FileMaker database called OnTrack is developed to help manage the design and production process of a firm that specializes in broadcast and print advertisement production. The database is used to link clients to work orders, work orders to job sheets, job sheets to tasks, and tasks to actions. Team members who are involved at each stage of ad production can track their resource commitments.

Custom or standard templates for job sheets to manage the stages and timeline for broadcast and print advertisement production can be used and adapted as necessary.

As with the other case studies in this book, a copy of the completed FileMaker Pro 8 database file, **OnTrack**, is available to download from the publisher's website at www.wordware.com/files/fmapps and the author's website at www.aweconsultancy.com. You may find it easier to examine some of the FileMaker features and techniques discussed in this chapter in a copy of the completed file.

The default database password for the Admin account is **JOBBAG1** (all capitals). The database file options have been preset to open with the active Guest account (with read-only access to the file). To open the file with full access privileges, hold down the Shift key (Windows) or Option key (Mac OS) while the file is opening. Type the word **Admin** in the Account Name box and type the password in the box below. You can change the default password at a later stage. More information on database security issues, passwords, accounts, and privileges is given in Chapter 24.

We should start by defining what entities or tables are needed for the file to manage the firm's creative procedures.

The Broadcast and Ad Production Entity Relationship Diagram

We can recognize each entity that will require its own table in the database by describing the production process.

Clients give work to a team of creative and production professionals within an agency to create advertisements for printed media and for broadcasting. This work is commissioned in the form of **Work Orders** for the various **Brands** that a client owns. Each work order is subdivided into a series of **Job Sheets**. A Job Sheet in turn consists of a series of **Tasks**, ending with the completed ad or the date that an advertisement is broadcast. Some of these Tasks within a Job Sheet are **Milestones**. Each Task consists of a number of **Actions**. Each Action is linked to a single member of the **Design Staff**. The firm does have tried and tested methods for successful design management. These methods are held in the form of a **Job Sheet Template**, which is linked to several **Template Tasks**.

The way in which these tables are related can be drawn as an entity relationship diagram, as shown in Figure 13.1.

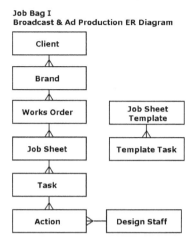

Job Bag I
Broadcast & Ad Production ER Diagram

Figure 13.1: The Broadcast and Ad Production ER diagram.

Building the Broadcast and Ad Production File

Step 1: Adding Tables to the OnTrack File

1. Launch FileMaker and create a new file called **OnTrack**.

   FileMaker will automatically open the Define Database dialog box with the Fields tab selected for the default OnTrack table, as shown in Figure 13.2.

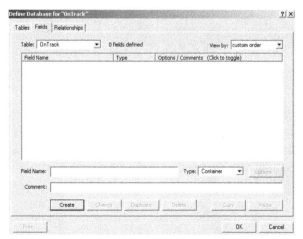

Figure 13.2: The Define Database dialog box for a new file with the Fields tab selected for the default table.

2. Click on the **Tables** tab at the top of the Define Database dialog box and
    add the additional 10 tables listed in Figure 13.3.

OnTrack
Client
WorksOrder
JobSheet
Task
Action
Staff
TimePlan
TimePlanTask
Contacts
Brand

Figure 13.3: The tables
needed for the OnTrack file.

Step 2: Adding Fields to the OnTrack File Tables

As with the other case studies in this book, we need to add a primary key
field to each of the tables that will contain records by using FileMaker's ability to automatically assign a unique serial number to each record in each
table. In addition, we will need to add foreign key fields to any of the tables
to which we need to establish a relationship.

1. To add fields to each of the tables within the file, choose the
    File>Define>Database menu option and the **Fields** tab of the Define
    Database dialog box. It is important to ensure that the correct table is
    selected prior to adding new fields. Each of the tables can be selected
    from the drop-down list near the top of the dialog box, as shown in Fig-
    ure 13.4.

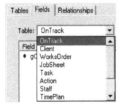

Figure 13.4:
Selecting the
relevant table for
a new field in the
Define Database
dialog box.

We will add the initial fields to each table as shown in Figures 13.5 to
13.24. Later, when we have established relationships between these
tables using table occurrences in the relationships graph, we will add
additional fields to the tables to improve the functionality of the file.

2. Global fields in a FileMaker file can be used in any layout, irrespective
    of whether the global field's table is related to a layout's underlying
    table. Add a global container field with 10 repetitions to store a set of
    background colors. These colors can later be used to highlight completed

tasks or milestones. The global container field called **gColours** can be added to the **OnTrack** table, as shown in Figure 13.5.

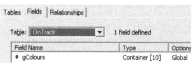

Figure 13.5:
The global gColours
field in the OnTrack
table.

3. While the **gColours** field is highlighted, click the **Options** button to open the Options for Field dialog box. Click the **Storage** tab and click the **Use global storage** check box. Type **10** for the "Maximum number of repetitions setting," as shown in Figure 13.6.

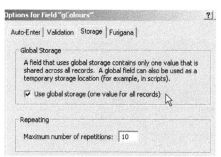

Figure 13.6:
Setting the gColours
field to be a global
field with 10
repetitions.

We can paste a set of background fill colors into the gColours field once we have created an OnTrack Menu layout.

4. Select the **Client** table from the Table drop-down list and add the fields shown in Figure 13.7. To maximize the functionality of the OnTrack database, we will need to add some additional fields to the Client table, and others in the file, once we have established relationships between the various tables. The **gClientPKey** field is a global number field and will be used later in a script to create new work order records for a client.

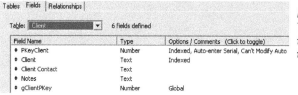

Figure 13.7:
The initial fields
for the Client
table.

5. All the tables that are designed to hold records in the OnTrack solution contain a primary key field, such as the Client table's primary key field called **PKeyClient**. We can use FileMaker's built-in field options to auto-enter a serial number for each primary key field, as shown in Figure 13.8. The serial number is set to increment by **1**. There is no reason to

display primary key fields in a layout, which prevents the accidental modification of an auto-entered value. Despite this, it is a good idea to check the **Prohibit modification of value during data entry** option.

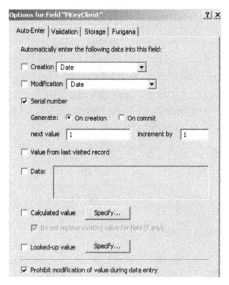

Figure 13.8:
Field options of
the PKeyClient
primary key
field.

6. Switch to the **WorksOrder** table and add the fields shown in Figure 13.9. The **Works Order No** field can be set to start at any number, and the table contains a calculation field called **Status Display**.

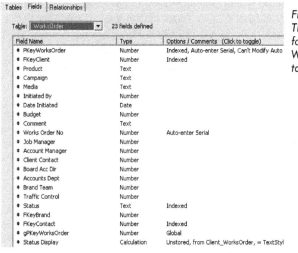

Figure 13.9:
The initial fields
for the
WorksOrder
table.

Field Name	Type	Options / Comments (Click to toggle)
PKeyWorksOrder	Number	Indexed, Auto-enter Serial, Can't Modify Auto
FKeyClient	Number	Indexed
Product	Text	
Campaign	Text	
Media	Text	
Initiated By	Number	
Date Initiated	Date	
Budget	Number	
Comment	Text	
Works Order No	Number	Auto-enter Serial
Job Manager	Number	
Account Manager	Number	
Client Contact	Number	
Board Acc Dir	Number	
Accounts Dept	Number	
Brand Team	Number	
Traffic Control	Number	
Status	Text	Indexed
FKeyBrand	Number	
FKeyContact	Number	Indexed
gPKeyWorksOrder	Number	Global
Status Display	Calculation	Unstored, from Client_WorksOrder, = TextStyl

The formula for the Status Display calculation field makes use of FileMaker Pro 8's text formatting functions to change the display color of the calculation field's text result depending on the contents of the Status field. If the Status field contains the text "In Progress," the contents of the Status field will be displayed in green. Otherwise, the contents of the Status field will be displayed in red. The calculation result is set to **Text**. The Status Display formula is shown in Figure 13.10.

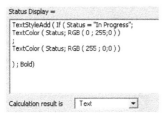

Status Display =

```
TextStyleAdd ( If ( Status = "In Progress";
TextColor ( Status; RGB ( 0 ; 255;0 ) )
;
TextColor ( Status; RGB ( 255 ; 0;0 ) )
) ; Bold)
```

Calculation result is   Text

Figure 13.10:
The Status Display
calculation field
formula for the
WorksOrder table.

7.   Add the fields shown in Figure 13.11 to the **JobSheet** table.

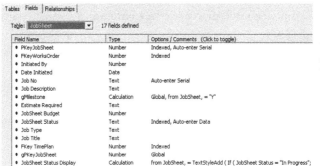

Tables Fields Relationships

Table: JobSheet   17 fields defined

Field Name	Type	Options / Comments (Click to toggle)
PKeyJobSheet	Number	Indexed, Auto-enter Serial
FKeyWorksOrder	Number	Indexed
Initiated By	Number	
Date Initiated	Date	
Job No	Text	Auto-enter Serial
Job Description	Text	
gMilestone	Calculation	Global, from JobSheet, = "Y"
Estimate Required	Text	
JobSheet Budget	Number	
JobSheet Status	Text	Indexed, Auto-enter Data
Job Type	Text	
Job Title	Text	
FKey TimePlan	Number	Indexed
gPKeyJobSheet	Number	Global
JobSheet Status Display	Calculation	from JobSheet, = TextStyleAdd (If (JobSheet Status = "In Progress";

Figure 13.11:
The initial
fields for the
JobSheet
table.

A calculation field called **JobSheet Status Display** is included in the JobSheet table with a very similar formula to the Status Display field in the WorksOrder table. The contents of the JobSheet Status Display field are displayed in green or red, depending on whether or not the field contents are "in progress." The Job Sheet Status Display formula is shown in Figure 13.12.

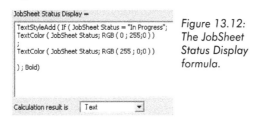

JobSheet Status Display =

```
TextStyleAdd ( If ( JobSheet Status = "In Progress";
TextColor ( JobSheet Status; RGB ( 0 ; 255;0 ) )
;
TextColor ( JobSheet Status; RGB ( 255 ; 0;0 ) )
) ; Bold)
```

Calculation result is   Text

Figure 13.12:
The JobSheet
Status Display
formula.

8. Select the **Task** table and add the fields shown in Figure 13.13.

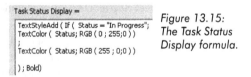

Tables	Fields	Relationships

Table: Task ▾   19 fields defined

Field Name	Type	Options / Comments (Click to toggle)
PKey Task	Number	Indexed, Auto-enter Serial, Can't Modify Auto
FKeyJobSheet	Number	Indexed
Milestone	Text	Indexed
Manager Title	Text	
Task Manager	Text	
Title	Text	Indexed
Planned Duration Days	Number	
Status	Text	Indexed, Auto-enter Data
Planned Start Date	Date	
Planned Completion Date	Date	
Actual Start Date	Date	
Actual Completion Date	Date	
Comment	Text	
gPKey Task	Number	Global
Milestone Colour	Calculation	Unstored, from Task, = Case (Milestone = "Y";
gDate	Date	Global
Task Status Display	Calculation	from Task, = TextStyleAdd (If (Status = "In Pr

Figure 13.13: The initial fields for the Task table.

The global color field called gColours, which was added to the OnTrack table, is referenced in the **Milestone Colour** calculation field. The formula for the Milestone Colour field is displayed in Figure 13.14. The calculation result must be set to **Container**.

Milestone Colour =

```
Case ( Milestone = "Y"; GetRepetition ( OnTrack::gColours; 4) ; GetRepetition ( OnTrack::gColours;
1) )
```

Figure 13.14: The Milestone Colour calculation field formula.

In contrast, the **Task Status Display** calculation field uses text formatting functions to display the Status field contents in either red or green, depending on whether or not a task is "in progress." The Task Status Display field formula is shown in Figure 13.15. The calculation result should be set to **Text**.

Task Status Display =

```
TextStyleAdd ( If ( Status = "In Progress";
TextColor ( Status; RGB ( 0 ; 255;0 ) )
;
TextColor ( Status; RGB ( 255 ; 0;0 ) )
) ; Bold)
```

Figure 13.15: The Task Status Display formula.

9. Add the fields listed in Figure 13.16 to the **Action** table.

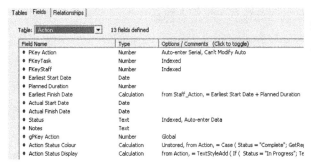

Figure 13.16:
The fields for the
Action table.

The formula for the **Action Status Colour** calculation field is shown in Figure 13.17.

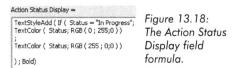

Figure 13.17: The Action Status Colour field formula.

The **Action Status Display** calculation field is similar to the Status Display field created for the other tables, and is shown in Figure 13.18.

Action Status Display =

```
TextStyleAdd ( If ( Status = "In Progress";
TextColor ( Status; RGB ( 0 ; 255;0 ) )
;
TextColor ( Status; RGB ( 255 ; 0;0 ) )
) ; Bold)
```

Figure 13.18:
The Action Status
Display field
formula.

10. Select the **Staff** table and add the fields listed in Figure 13.19.

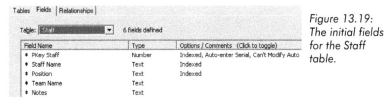

Figure 13.19:
The initial fields
for the Staff
table.

11. Two fields can be added to the **TimePlan** table at this stage. These are shown in Figure 13.20.

Tables Fields Relationships

Table: TimePlan ▼	3 fields defined	
Field Name	Type	Options / Comments (Click to toggle)
PKeyTimePlan	Number	Indexed, Auto-enter Serial, Can't Modify Auto
TimePlan Title	Text	Indexed

Figure 13.20:
The initial fields
for the TimePlan
table.

12. Add the fields for the **TimePlanTask** table as shown in Figure 13.21.

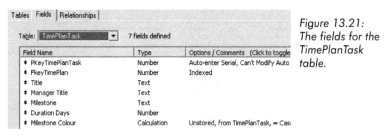

Figure 13.21: The fields for the TimePlanTask table.

The formula for the **Milestone Colour** calculation field in the TimePlanTask table is displayed in Figure 13.22. The field will be used to create a background color for the Milestone field.

```
Milestone Colour =
Case ( Milestone = "Y"; GetRepetition ( OnTrack::gColours; 4)); GetRepetition ( OnTrack::gColours;
1 ) )
```

Figure 13.22: The Milestone Colour calculation field formula.

13. Add the fields for the **Contacts** table as shown in Figure 13.23.

Tables Fields Relationships

Table: Contacts ▼   8 fields defined

Field Name	Type	Options / Comments (Click to toggle)
◆ PKeyClientContact	Number	Indexed, Auto-enter Serial, Can't Modify Auto
◆ Contact Title	Text	
◆ Contact First Name	Text	Indexed
◆ Contact Second Name	Text	
◆ Full Name	Calculation	from Contacts, = Contact First Name & " " & Contact Second Name
◆ Full Name Surname	Calculation	Indexed, from Contacts, = Contact Second Name & " " & Contact First Name
◆ Job Title	Text	
◆ FkeyClient	Number	Indexed

Figure 13.23: The fields for the Contacts table.

The **Full Name** and **Full Name Surname** calculation fields will be used later in value lists.

14. The **Brand** table is used to hold details on brands owned by clients. Add the three fields needed for the Brand table as shown in Figure 13.24.

Tables Fields Relationships

Table: Brand ▼   3 fields defined

Field Name	Type	Options / Comments (Click to toggle)
◆ PKeyBrand	Number	Indexed, Auto-enter Serial, Can't Modify Auto
◆ Brand Name	Text	
◆ Fkey Client	Number	Indexed

Figure 13.24: The fields for the Brand table.

We can now use the primary and foreign key fields from the tables to create a series of relationships using FileMaker's relationships graph. We will then be able to add some additional calculation fields to the tables that use related tables in their formulas and redefine some text and number fields to use lookup values.

Step 3: Adding Relationships within the OnTrack File

At each stage of the broadcast and print ad production process, the creative team will want to view information on screen, with related records displayed by using portals or available to "jump to" using the Go to Related Record command. This functionality can be achieved by designing a series of table occurrence groups, or TOGs, in the relationships graph, and data entry layouts that match the method by which the team manages work orders and job sheets.

1. If the Define Database dialog box is not open, select the menu option
    File>Define>Database and click the **Relationships** tab at the top of the
    dialog box. The 11 base tables that we have created for the OnTrack file
    will be visible as table occurrences, as shown in Figure 13.25.

Figure 13.25: The initial relationships graph for the OnTrack file showing the 11 base tables.

As with the other case study FileMaker solutions, we do not link the underlying base tables directly in the relationships graph. Instead, relationships are built up between table occurrences, which are representations of the base tables in the relationships graph. It is possible to have any number of table occurrences on the relationships graph for the same underlying base table.

As introduced in Chapter 7, our aim is to refine the relationships graph into a series of discrete TOGs. Each TOG should have a main or "anchor" table occurrence on its left-hand side, with any number of linked "buoy" tables related to the anchor table spread out on the right-hand side. To ease relationship design at the outset and to assist you or any colleagues who may work on the file at a later stage, a number of fundamental rules should be followed when using relationships in any FileMaker solution:

- As a general rule, any relationships graph will have one anchor table occurrence for every base table in the file.

- All data entry layouts should only be based on an underlying anchor table occurrence.

- Any portals on layouts should be based on buoy table occurrences.

- To assist with documenting a complex FileMaker project, it is a good idea to limit the dimensions of any TOGs in the relationships graph to a single page in width but any number of pages in length.

To get the required functionality from our design management solution, we now need to add some TOGs to the relationships graph.

2. For the sake of reference, it is a good idea to preserve at least one table occurrence for each base table within the file displayed at the top of the relationships graph. To reduce the space used, the button on the table header can be clicked on to toggle the display of the table and collapse it to its title only, as shown in Figure 13.26.

3. Note that an underscore (_) has been added to the base table occurrences so that the original table name can be used as an anchor table occurrence. Each table occurrence must have a unique name in the graph. A table occurrence can be renamed by double-clicking on it to open the Specify Table dialog box, or by highlighting the table occurrence and clicking the **Edit** button at the bottom of the graph (the button with a yellow pencil icon).

Figure 13.26: The reference base tables collapsed to display only the table title.

3.1: The Client TOG

1. The creative team wants to add new contacts, brands, and work order records from within a Client Details layout. To make this possible, a Client TOG must include relationships from the Client table occurrence to **Brands**, **WorksOrder**, and **Contacts**.

2. To display additional descriptive information in each portal row, further table occurrences must be added to the Client TOG, as displayed in Figure 13.27.

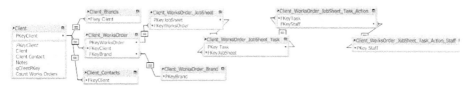

Figure 13.27: The Client table occurrence group.

3. To enable new brand and contact records to be created through a portal, the relationships to these table occurrences must be modified to enable the creation of related records. Double-click anywhere on the relationship line between Client and Client_Brands and check the **Allow creation of records in this table via this relationship** option. This part of the Edit Relationship dialog box is highlighted in Figure 13.28.

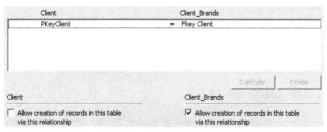

Figure 13.28: Modifying the relationship between Client and Client_Brands to allow the creation of new records in the Client_Brands table.

The design team decides that a warning message should be issued in a script prior to creating a new work order record. As new work order records will be created via a script, the relationship between Client and Client_WorksOrder can be left unmodified.

3.2: The TimePlan TOG

A relationship from a TimePlan table occurrence and one based on the TimePlanTask table is needed to manage and display records for TimePlan templates. The TimePlan TOG is shown in Figure 13.29.

Figure 13.29: The TimePlan table occurrence group.

The design team wants to add new related TimePlanTasks through a portal. To make this possible in a layout based on the TimePlan table occurrence, the relationship in Figure 13.29 must be modified to allow the creation of related records.

3.3: The WorksOrder TOG

Within a WorksOrder data entry layout, the design team will want to see the related client, brand, and client contact for any work order record. A warning message will be issued using a script before a new related job sheet record is created for a work order. Therefore, none of the relationships in the WorksOrder TOG need to be modified to create related records. The WorksOrder TOG is shown in Figure 13.30.

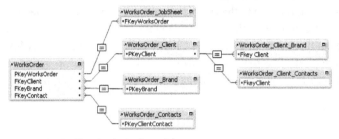

Figure 13.30: The WorksOrder table occurrence group.

3.4: The JobSheet TOG

Each job sheet record is related to a single work order. The job sheet may use a TimePlan template with standard tasks for broadcast or print advertising workflow. Each job sheet will include one or more tasks, and it would be good to identify which, if any, of these tasks are milestones.

The design team doesn't want to create new related task records using a portal from the job sheet. Instead another script with a warning message is preferred. The JobSheet TOG, with the relationships needed to get the required functionality for job sheet records, is shown in Figure 13.31. None of the relationships are used to automatically create new records.

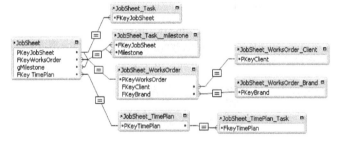

Figure 13.31: The JobSheet table occurrence group.

The design manager has requested that milestone tasks be displayed in a special portal once a JobSheet data entry layout is designed. A specific relationship to flag milestone tasks needs to be established between the JobSheet and JobSheet_Task table occurrences. This relationship makes use of the **gMilestone** global calculation field in the JobSheet table, which is set to have a global value of **"Y"**. The relationship is only valid when a related task record contains the value "Y" in the Milestone field. The relationship is shown in Figure 13.32.

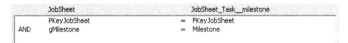

Figure 13.32: The JobSheet to JobSheet_Task__milestone relationship.

3.5: The Task TOG

A task record is directly related to a parent job sheet record. Each task record can also consist of one or more action records, which in turn is allocated to an individual creative staff member. The Task TOG is shown in Figure 13.33.

Figure 13.33: The Task table occurrence group.

3.6: The Staff TOG

In order to display descriptive information for related action, task, job sheet, and work order records within the Staff Details layout, several table occurrences must be related to the Staff table occurrence. The Staff TOG is shown in Figure 13.34.

Figure 13.34: The Staff table occurrence group.

3.7: The Action TOG

Each action record is related to a single task and staff record. To display job sheet details for the related task, a further relationship must be established to a table occurrence for the JobSheet table.

The Action TOG is displayed in Figure 13.35.

Figure 13.35: The Action table occurrence group.

Additional calculation fields that make reference to fields in these table occurrences in their formula can now be added to the OnTrack tables.

Step 4: Adding Calculation Fields to the OnTrack Tables

The addition of a few calculation fields that make use of the Count function will help to report on how many related records exist for each stage of the broadcast and print ad production process.

If the Define Database dialog box is not open, select the **File>Define> Database** menu option. Click the **Fields** tab to return to the fields list for each of the tables in the OnTrack database.

4.1: An Additional Field for the Client Table

In the Client table, we can add a calculation field called **Count Works Orders**, which displays how many related orders exist for a client record. The formula for the Count Works Orders field is shown in Figure 13.36.

Figure 13.36: The Count Works Orders field calculation formula for the Client table.

4.2: Additional Fields for the JobSheet Table

Select the JobSheet table and add two calculation fields called **Count Tasks** and **Count Milestones**. The formulas for these fields are shown in Figures 13.37 and 13.38.

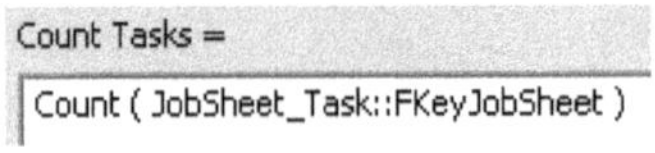

Count Tasks =	Count Milestones =
Count (JobSheet_Task::FKeyJobSheet)	Count (JobSheet_Task__milestone::FKeyJobSheet)

Figure 13.37: The Count Tasks calculation field formula in the JobSheet table.

Figure 13.38: The Count Milestones calculation field formula in the JobSheet table.

4.3: Additional Fields for the Task Table

Two calculation fields can be added to the Task table to display the number of related Action and Action Days for a task record. The formulas for the **Count Actions** and **Account Action Days** calculation fields are displayed in Figures 13.39 and 13.40.

Count Actions =

Count (Task_Action::FKeyTask)

Count Action Days =

Sum (Task_Action::Planned Duration)

Figure 13.39: The Count Actions calculation field formula in the Task table.

Figure 13.40: The Count Action Days calculation field formula in the Task table.

4.4: An Additional Field for the Staff Table

A calculation field called **Count Tasks** can be added to the Staff table. The formula, which makes use of the Staff_Action relationship in the Staff TOG, is shown in Figure 13.41.

Count Tasks =

Count (Staff_Action::FKeyStaff)

Figure 13.41: The Count Tasks calculation field formula in the Staff table.

4.5: An Additional Field for the TimePlan Table

The total number of related task records for any TimePlan template can be displayed by creating a new calculation field called **Count Tasks** in the TimePlan table. The formula for the Count Tasks field is shown in Figure 13.42.

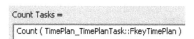

Count Tasks =

Count (TimePlan_TimePlanTask::FkeyTimePlan)

Figure 13.42: The Count Tasks calculation field formula in the TimePlan table.

We can now design a series of data entry and report layouts for the OnTrack solution.

Step 5: Designing Data Entry, List, and Report Layouts for the OnTrack File

It is important that data entry and report layouts in a FileMaker file are sufficiently well designed so that the information in a displayed record can be easily viewed and understood by the database user. The process of "good design" for layouts can be particularly challenging when working on a database that will be used by creative professionals. With a little bit of time and effort, FileMaker layouts can be made to look appealing and clearly convey information contained in the records for the viewer.

As discussed in Chapter 7, with FileMaker it is a good idea to base any data entry and report layouts on anchor table occurrences. The anchor table occurrence is the one to the far left of every table occurrence group in our relationships graph.

Let's start by creating a Main Menu layout for the database.

5.1: The OnTrack Welcome Menu Layout

The design team will want to work with the database at various levels. It is a good idea to include a Main or "Welcome" Menu layout that is accessible from all the data entry, list, and report layouts. The Welcome Menu layout can also be the first layout that appears when a file is first opened to assist new database users with navigation and getting to know the file.

1. The Welcome Menu layout is shown in Figure 13.43. The layout contains a number of buttons that are labeled in accordance with the layouts they will be set to open using scripts.

Figure 13.43:
The Welcome
Menu layout.

While the scripts will be described in detail later in this chapter, two scripts that are directly linked to the Welcome Menu layout are described in this section.

2. The green About button is designed to provide more information on the solution and details about the author. The **About...** script, which is triggered by this button, is a good example of a conditional script. The Show Custom Dialog script step can display up to three buttons and, when combined with the LastMessageChoice function, the user's choice can be monitored by the script with a different outcome depending on which button is selected. In this case, the user can choose to open one of two websites. The About... script is shown in Figure 13.44.

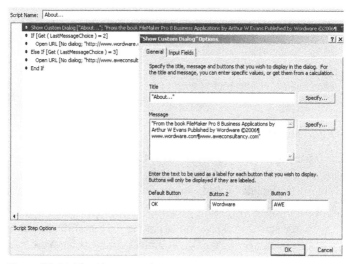

Figure 13.44: The About... script.

3. The red button labeled Quit is used to run a script with the same name. The **Quit** script also uses the Show Custom Dialog script step to create a conditional script. Depending on which button is selected, the user can choose to close the OnTrack file or quit FileMaker. The Quit script is shown along with the Show Custom Dialog Options dialog box in Figure 13.45.

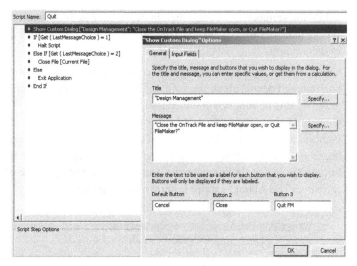

Figure 13.45: The Quit script is triggered by the button of the same name in the Welcome Menu layout.

5.2: The Client Details Layout

The starting point for data capture is Client Details. A client record must exist before a work order and a subsequent job sheet can be assigned to the same client. The default Client layout that was created by FileMaker can be adapted as shown in Figure 13.46.

1. Add a series of navigation buttons at the top of the layout to assist the user in navigating the file. A green button labeled **New** is defined to create a new record, and a red button labeled **Delete** is set to run a script with a warning message before deleting the record.

2. Include in the Client Details layout three portals that can be used to enter new records for contacts, brand names, and new work orders — all associated with the current client record. Both contacts and brand records can be created by typing into a new portal row. New related work orders will be created via a script that will be triggered using the small green **New** button just to the left of the Client_WorksOrder portal.

3. Add a small gray button labeled with a right arrow (**>**) to the left side of the works order portal that uses the Go to Related Record button command to open the related work order records. Add a small red button labeled with an **X** to the right side of the works order portal and set it to run a script that deletes the selected work order record.

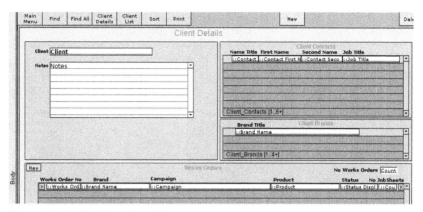

Figure 13.46: The Client Details layout.

5.3: The Client List Layout

A new columnar list/report layout can be created in the OnTrack database to display a list of client records. The Client List layout shown in Figure 13.47 uses the same navigation buttons in the layout header as the Client Details layout. The button to the left of the layout body switches to the Client Details layout.

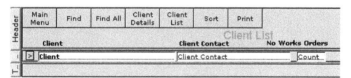

Figure 13.47: The Client List layout.

5.4: The Works Order Details Layout

The default Works Order layout that FileMaker has already created in the OnTrack database can be modified to display work order records and related job sheets in a portal.

The Works Order Details layout is shown in Figure 13.48.

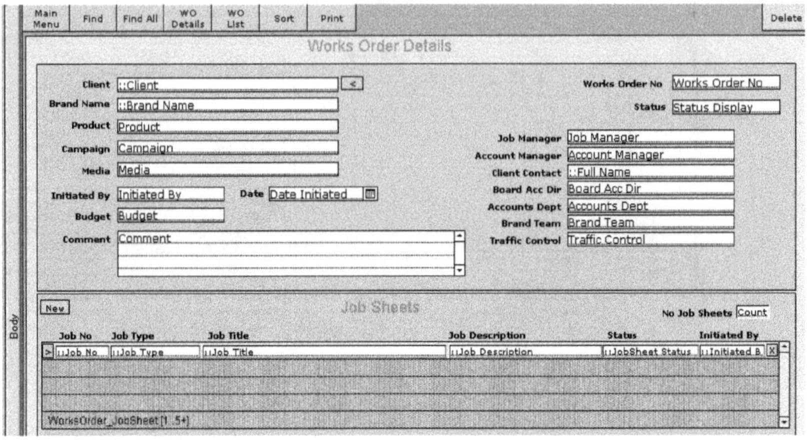

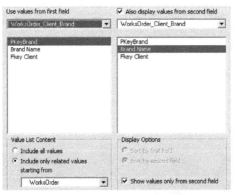

Figure 13.48: The Works Order Details layout.

When a new work order record is created with a script that is launched in the Client Details layout, the database user will want to choose the brand name the work order is for. A list of related brand names for the selected client can be chosen in the Works Order Details layout, using a value list that is displayed when the "almost-hidden" FKeyBrand field from the WorksOrder table is selected.

Note: The FKeyBrand field is created normally, then its size is set to one pixel and it is placed just to the left of the Brand Name field to "hide" it. This is described in detail below.

1. A new value list called **Brand Codes for Client in WorksOrder** needs to be created. The value list should only display related brands for the chosen client record. The field settings for the value list are shown in Figure 13.49. Only the brand name will appear when the value list is displayed.

Figure 13.49: The settings for the Brand Codes for Client in WorksOrder value list.

2. The **FKeyBrand** field must now be highlighted and set so that the field will display the new value list as a drop-down list when the field is selected using the menu option **Format>Field/Control>Setup**.

3. There is no reason to make the FKeyBrand field too obvious on the layout as the brand name can be displayed using the field from the WorksOrder_Brand table occurrence. To disguise and "hide" the FKeyBrand field, its width can be set to be one pixel while the field is highlighted by using the menu option **View>Object Size**. Make sure the unit of measurement is **pixels** by clicking the unit of measurement displayed in the Object Size dialog box until **px** is displayed. Then type **1** in the width box, and press the **Return** or **Enter** key. While the field is still selected, move the FKeyBrand field so that it is just to the left side of the Brand Name field, as shown in Figure 13.50.

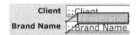

Figure 13.50: The "almost-hidden" FKeyBrand field is called out in dark gray here to show its position to the left of the Brand Name field.

4. The user cannot be expected to find or select the "hidden" FKeyBrand field, so define the **Brand Name** field as a button that will run a script that selects the FKeyBrand field. The script will only need to consist of the Go to Field script step.

The value list that originates from the "hidden" FKeyBrand field is shown in Figure 13.51.

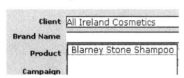

Figure 13.51: The value list displayed when the Brand Name field is clicked on.

To avoid data entry errors, the same technique for an "almost-hidden" value list is also used in the Works Order layout to enable the client name to be changed if the wrong client was originally selected for a work order. The related client contact list is displayed with the same technique using an FKeyContact field that is only one pixel wide just to the left of the Full Name field.

5.5: The Works Order List Layout

A new layout can be created to display a list of work orders as shown in Figure 13.52.

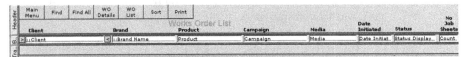

Figure 13.52: The Works Order List layout.

5.6: The JobSheet Details Layout

1. A layout called JobSheet already exists in the OnTrack file. This can be modified to display details on a JobSheet record. The top part of the layout is used to display information on the client and the work order to which this job sheet record is related. A series of small gray buttons, labeled with a left arrow (<), make use of the Go to Related Record command to switch to the related work order or client record.

2. Include two portals in the JobSheet Details layout, as displayed in Figure 13.53, to display related tasks and milestone task records. The buttons on the layout to create new task records, use a template, or adjust the date projection for a job sheet schedule will all be set to run scripts shortly.

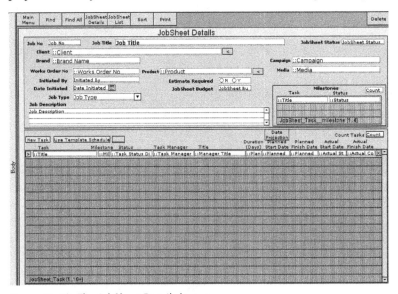

Figure 13.53: The JobSheet Details layout.

5.7: The JobSheet List Layout

A list layout to display job sheet records can be added to the file. The same navigation buttons as for the JobSheet Details layout can be copied and pasted into the header part of the JobSheet List layout, which is shown in Figure 13.54.

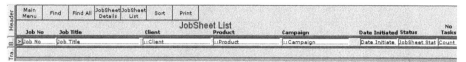

Figure 13.54: The JobSheet List layout.

5.8: The TimePlan Templates Layout

A standard task procedure is available for broadcast and print advertisement production job sheets. The TimePlan Templates layout is designed to display details on a standard timeplan template, and any related timeplan tasks using a portal. A field in the portal enables a task to be described as a milestone by using a drop-down list.

The TimePlan Templates layout is shown in Figure 13.55.

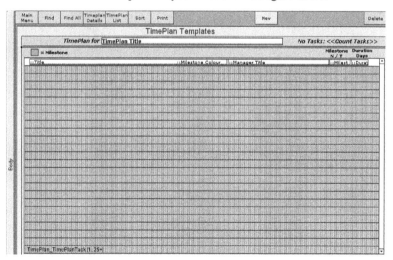

Figure 13.55: The TimePlan Templates layout.

5.9: The TimePlan Templates List Layout

A TimePlan Templates List layout is used to display the timeplan template records. The TimePlan Templates List layout is displayed in Figure 13.56.

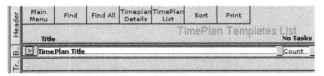

Figure 13.56: The TimePlan Templates List layout.

5.10: The Staff Details Layout

Details on the creative team are displayed using the Staff Details layout, shown in Figure 13.57. Related action records for individual members of the team can be displayed using a portal.

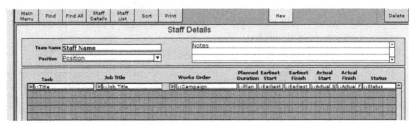

Figure 13.57: The Staff Details layout.

5.11: The Staff List Layout

Staff records can also be displayed using the Staff List layout, which includes the Count Task field. The Staff List layout is shown in Figure 13.58.

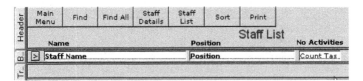

Figure 13.58: The Staff List layout.

5.12: The Task Details Layout

A job sheet record will contain one or more tasks. Tasks are displayed in the Task Details layout, which can be seen in Figure 13.59.

A task can have one or more actions related to it, which are displayed in the Task Details layout using a portal to display records from the Task_Action table occurrence.

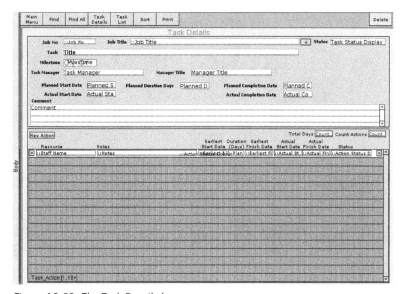

Figure 13.59: The Task Details layout.

The **Milestone** field has been set to display a radio button set for "Y" or "N" and a background calculation field called **Milestone Colour** has been placed immediately behind the Milestone field. The user can be prevented from accidentally clicking into the Milestone Colour field by highlighting the field and preventing its selection in Browse or Find mode using the **Format> Field/Control>Behavior** menu option.

5.13: The Task List Layout

The Task List layout provides a quick List view of several task records, with milestone description, task status, and schedule dates displayed.

The Task List layout is shown in Figure 13.60.

Figure 13.60: The Task List layout.

5.14: The Action Details Layout

Details on individual action records are the final point of interest for the creative design team. An action record forms part of a task and is linked to a selected member of the team.

The Action Details layout is displayed in Figure 13.61.

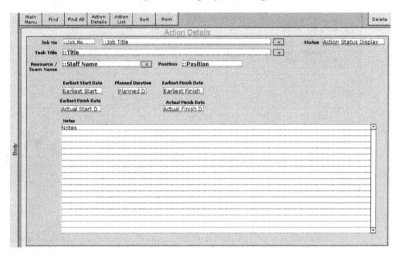

Figure 13.61: The Action Details layout.

5.15: The Action List Layout

The Action List layout shows most important fields for an action record, including the staff name, the task title, and related job title.

The Action List layout is shown in Figure 13.62.

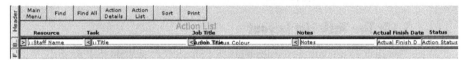

Figure 13.62: The Action List layout.

5.16: The Reports Menu Layout

A big advantage to having the OnTrack file for the creative team is the ability to run status reports on work orders, job sheets, tasks, and related resources.

A new layout based on the default OnTrack table occurrence is used to create a Reports Menu layout, which is shown in Figure 13.63.

A series of report scripts will be written that make use of the list layouts to present selected record information.

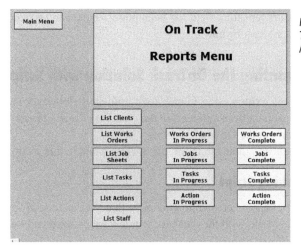

1. Add the global field **gColours** to the far right of the Reports Menu layout in order to populate the container field's 10 repeating values with a contrasting set of fill colors. The gColours field is shown in Figure 13.64.

2. Set the field to display all 10 repetitions using the **Field/Control>Setup** dialog box.

3. The gColours container field now needs to be populated with varying colors that will be used in background color calculation fields. While still in **Layout** mode, draw a small rectangle on the layout and color it using the **Fill Color** palette. The rectangle can be duplicated by pressing **Ctrl+D** or by using the **Edit>Duplicate** menu option. Give each copy of the rectangle a new color.

4. Copy each of these colored rectangles to the clipboard, switch to **Browse** mode, and paste the rectangle into the next repetition of the gColours field.

Figure 13.64:
Drawing a series
of rectangles to
populate the
gColours global
container field in
the Reports Menu
layout.

Once the gColours repeating field has been populated, it can be removed from the Reports Menu layout.

Step 6: Automating the OnTrack Solution with Scripts

A series of scripts written using FileMaker's built-in ScriptMaker facility would be of great benefit in automating the creation of related records and displaying reports in the OnTrack database.

These scripts and their use in the file are described in this section.

6.1: The Opening Script

An opening script can be created to guarantee that the database always opens on the Welcome Menu with the database window maximized and the Status area hidden.

The Opening script is shown in Figure 13.65.

Figure 13.65:
The Opening
Script/Open
Menu script.

6.2: Navigation Scripts to Open Data Entry and List Layouts

We will want to see the Status area when each of the data entry and list layouts is opened from the Welcome Menu layout.

A series of scripts can be created to open the various data entry layouts and show the Status area. As an example, the script to open the Client Details layout is shown in Figure 13.66.

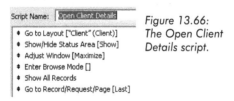

Figure 13.66:
The Open Client
Details script.

6.3: Creating a New Work Order Record from within the Client Details Layout

A script can be used to display a dialog box that asks the user to confirm the addition of a new work order record for a client and then proceeds to create the new work order record. The script is shown in Figure 13.67 and makes use of the global field gClientPKey to store the primary key value for the client record and make the FKeyClient field in the WorksOrder table the same value. The script finishes by selecting the FKeyBrand field, so the user can select which client brand the work order is for.

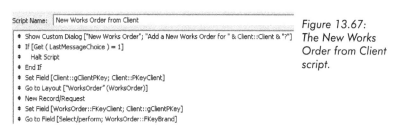

Figure 13.67:
The New Works
Order from Client
script.

6.4: Scripts that Create a New Related Record Using a Global Field and a Custom Dialog Box

Several of the data entry layouts include buttons that will create a related record after first presenting the user with a dialog box to confirm that the new record is required. The New Action from Task script is a good example of how this type of script is put together.

The script starts by opening a custom dialog box that asks the database user to confirm the creation of a new action for the named task. The script then sets the global gPKey Task field to have the same value as the PKey field for the current task record. The script then switches to the Action Details layout, creates a new record, and sets the FKeyTask foreign key field to be the same value as the gPKey field. The script then returns to the Task layout and goes to the last portal row, where the new blank action record is displayed. Finally, the "almost-hidden" FKeyStaff field is selected, which displays a drop-down list of staff to allocate a name for the new action record.

The New Action from Task script is shown in Figure 13.68.

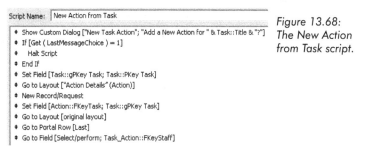

Figure 13.68:
The New Action
from Task script.

6.5: Scripts to Display a Foreign Key Field Value List

The Go to Field script step will select any target field that exists on a FileMaker layout. The script step will override the behavior settings for a field. Even if a field has been set so that it cannot be selected in Browse or Find mode by using the menu option Format>Field/Control>Behavior, the target field will be selected. A series of scripts that only use the Go to Field script step can be written to assist with targeting a "hidden" foreign key field. The script can be triggered by clicking on the descriptive field from the related table occurrence. As an example, the Client field in the Works Order layout has been formatted as a button that will run the Display Client Code Value List in WorksOrder script, as shown in Figure 13.69.

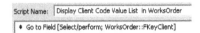

Script Name: | Display Client Code Value List in WorksOrder

♦ Go to Field [Select/perform; WorksOrder::FKeyClient]

Figure 13.69: The Display Client Code Value List in WorksOrder script.

6.6: The Add Tasks from Template Script

It is possible to have custom dialog box "overload" in a script. The Add Tasks from Template script is triggered by a button in the JobSheet layout. The script is designed to use a selected JobSheet template title to populate a related set of task records with a set of template tasks. In the basic OnTrack solution, templates exist for standard broadcast and print ad production job sheets.

The design manager is worried that a member of the team may inadvertently delete existing tasks if a template for a job sheet is chosen at a later stage. To avoid any confusion, a couple of dialog box reminders are requested in a script that automates the importing of a template task set of records.

As the script is quite convoluted, it has been broken into sections using several comment script steps. These appear in bold and are numbered for ease of reference.

Although the dialog box messages are not too serious and will probably be removed in time, it is a good way of giving colleagues a heads up that the templates do affect any related data for an existing job sheet record.

The Add Tasks from Template script is shown in Figure 13.70.

Script Name: | Add Tasks from Template

```
♦ Set Error Capture [On]
♦ Go to Layout ["JobSheet" (JobSheet)]
♦ #1 Check no existing records exist before adding template
♦ If [Count ( JobSheet_Task::FKeyJobSheet ) > 0]
♦    Show Custom Dialog ["Tasks Already Exist"; "WARNING! Using A Tasking Template will Delete any Existing Tasks for th
♦    If [Get ( LastMessageChoice ) = 1]
♦       Halt Script
♦    Else
♦       Show Custom Dialog ["Career Decision"; "The Brand Manager may not thank you for this.¶This is a Career Decision.¶
♦       If [Get ( LastMessageChoice ) = 1]
♦          Halt Script
♦       End If
♦    End If
♦    Go to Related Record [Show only related records; From table: "JobSheet_Task"; Using layout: "Task Details" (Task)]
♦    Delete All Records [No dialog]
♦ End If
♦ #2 Ask which template is required
♦ Go to Layout ["JobSheet" (JobSheet)]
♦ Show Custom Dialog ["Select a Template"; "Please select a Task Template from the pop up list and press Continue..."]
♦ Go to Field [Select/perform; JobSheet::FKey TimePlan]
♦ Pause/Resume Script [Indefinitely]
♦ #3 Check a Timeplan has been selected
♦ If [IsEmpty ( JobSheet::FKey TimePlan )]
♦    Perform Script ["Add Tasks from Template"]
♦ End If
```

Figure 13.70: The Add Tasks from Template script (Part 1).

```
♦ #4 Set global PKey Job Sheet
♦ Set Field [JobSheet::gPKeyJobSheet; JobSheet::PKeyJobSheet]
♦ #5 Get the Timeplan Tasks Isolated for importing into Tasks
♦ Go to Related Record [Show only related records; From table: "JobSheet_TimePlan"; Using layout: "TimePlan" (TimePlan)]
♦ Go to Layout ["TimePlan" (TimePlan)]
♦ Go to Related Record [Show only related records; From table: "JobSheet_TimePlan_Task"; Using layout: "TimePlanTask" (TimePlanTask)]
♦ #6 Import the Templates Tasks  into Tasks
♦ Go to Layout ["Task List" (Task)]
♦ Import Records [No dialog; "OnTrack.fp7"; Add; Windows ANSI]
♦ #7 Replace the FKey JobSHeet with the stored Global Value
♦ Replace Field Contents [No dialog; Task::FKeyJobSheet; JobSheet::gPKeyJobSheet]
♦ Go to Layout [original layout]
```

Figure 13.70: The Add Tasks from Template script (Part 2)

6.7: Using Loops — The Forward Project Task Dates Script

The Loop and End Loop script steps, which are always set as a pair in a script with a course of action in between, can be a great way to manipulate data across a record set, often in combination with a global field. A global field can be used as a temporary storage facility for a field value, which can be tested in subsequent records in a found set. Use this method of temporary storage to get rid of duplicate records, for example, or to use in a calculation with the value in the next record. The latter technique is used to create a forward projected date schedule for a job sheet's related tasks.

Advertisement production for broadcast or printed media has critical deadlines. If the duration of each task for a job sheet is recorded, it is possible to write a script that will calculate the end date for a project based on the accumulated number of task days.

A script can be written to automate this, which is shown in Figure 13.71. If no start date is given in the first task record, the current date is used.

With any loop script step, it is important to check that the loop has an end point. In this case, the Go to Record/Request/Page script step has the "Exit after last" option checked.

```
Script Name:   Forward Project Task Dates

♦ Set Error Capture [On]
♦ Show Custom Dialog ["Forward Project Dates"; "Forward Project Dates for this Job Sheet, based on the Earliest Start Date and task durations?"]
♦ If [Get ( LastMessageChoice ) = 1]
♦    Halt Script
♦ End If
♦ Go to Related Record [Show only related records; From table: "JobSheet_Task"; Using layout: "Task Details" (Task)]
♦ If [IsEmpty ( Task::Planned Start Date )]
♦    Set Field [Task::Planned Start Date; Get ( CurrentDate )]
♦ End If
♦ Loop
♦    Set Field [Task::Planned Completion Date; Task::Planned Start Date + Task::Planned Duration Days]
♦    Set Field [Task::gDate; Task::Planned Completion Date]
♦    Go to Record/Request/Page [Next; Exit after last]
♦    Set Field [Task::Planned Start Date; Task::gDate]
♦ End Loop
♦ Go to Layout [original layout]
```

Figure 13.71: The Forward Project Task Dates script.

6.8: Reports Scripts

Several of the list layouts are used as the basis for reports in the OnTrack solution. A series of reports scripts will select a predefined set of records by using the Perform Find script step and display these, often in a particular sort order, using the list layouts.

The List Works Orders In Progress script shown in Figure 13.72 is an example of a report script.

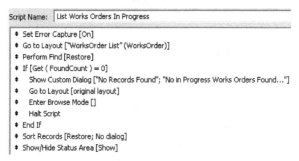

Script Name: List Works Orders In Progress

```
♦ Set Error Capture [On]
♦ Go to Layout ["WorksOrder List" (WorksOrder)]
♦ Perform Find [Restore]
♦ If [Get ( FoundCount ) = 0]
♦    Show Custom Dialog ["No Records Found"; "No in Progress Works Orders Found..."]
♦    Go to Layout [original layout]
♦    Enter Browse Mode []
♦    Halt Script
♦ End If
♦ Sort Records [Restore; No dialog]
♦ Show/Hide Status Area [Show]
```

Figure 13.72: The List Works Orders In Progress script.

The script switches to the WorksOrder List layout and carries out a specified find request, which has been customized in the script. The find request is designed to only show work orders whose status field contains the text "In Progress." The Specify Find Requests dialog box can be seen in Figure 13.73.

Specify Find Requests

Use this panel to edit the Find Requests. Find Requests are executed in the order that they appear.

Action	Criteria
Find Records	WorksOrder::Status: ["In Progress"]

Figure 13.73: The Specify Find Requests dialog for the Perform Find script.

The sort order of the found record set can be customized in the script using the Sort Records step. If the **Specify** button is clicked when the Sort Order step is highlighted, a Sort Records dialog box will appear, which enables the sort order to be embedded into the script. You may find it easier to be on a layout that is based on the same underlying table occurrence as the required record set, so that the correct set of fields appears in the Sort Records dialog box. The fields for the sort order are displayed in Figure 13.74.

Sort Order

```
♦ Client                        .ıl
♦ WorksOrder::Works Order No    .ıl
```

Figure 13.74: The sort order fields selected for the Sort Records script step.

Taking the Solution Further

The OnTrack database solution should be capable of evolving if the creative team discovers improved methods for tracking advertisement production projects.

The database does not currently have fields to capture budget information and report on resource expenditures as a project progresses. Fields to capture anticipated and actual work orders and job sheet costs could easily be added to the file.

The Staff, Action, and Task tables in the OnTrack file are not currently linked to a timesheet system. Additional tables, such as those in the timesheet solution introduced in the previous chapter, could be incorporated into the database.

Chapter 14

Job Bag II — Print and Production Management

Introduction

The print, print brokerage, and print management industries have seen significant changes over the last decade. The traditional role and services offered by commercial print and design firms have changed, while boundaries between design managers and printers have become blurred. More clients expect a managed service or "one-stop shop" for integrated print services and corporate design. The project could vary from a business card to an exhibition stand, an annual report to a website.

FileMaker can provide a perfect solution for managing the job tracking needs of a print and production company. Supplier quotes, purchase orders, and client invoices can all be managed from the same database, while the specific production requirements of each job can be logged and tracked.

As with the other case studies in this book, a copy of the completed FileMaker Pro 8 database file, **PrintProdMgt**, is available to download from the publisher's website at www.wordware.com/files/fmapps and the author's website at www.aweconsultancy.com. You may find it easier to examine some of the FileMaker features and techniques discussed in this chapter in a copy of the completed file.

The default database password for the Admin account is **JOBBAG2** (all capitals). The database file options have been preset to open with the active Guest account (with read-only access to the file). To open the file with full access privileges, hold down the Shift key (Windows) or Option key (Mac OS) while the file is opening. Type the word **Admin** in the Account Name box and type the password in the box below. You can change the default password at a later stage. More information on database security issues, passwords, accounts, and privileges is given in Chapter 24.

We will start by considering the tables needed for the print and production management file, based on a method by which orders are managed from initial proposals and quotes to a final invoice.

The Print and Production Management Entity Relationship Diagram

A database is required to assist the team within a busy print and corporate design production firm. The firm will want to store details for a **Client** and any related **Contact** names for the organization. The team wants to be able to create a new **Quote** for a client, and will want to be able to **Communicate** with client contacts at each stage of the production process. If a quote is accepted by the client, it is turned into a new **Job Bag**. Part or all of a job will be subcontracted out to one or more **Suppliers**. They will be asked for a **Supplier Quote** for part or all of a job. If a Supplier Quote is accepted, it is converted into a new **Supplier Purchase Order**. The supplier service is captured as a new **Outwork** record for a job. An **Invoice** record will be created for a job. Each chargeable item for a job will be included as a new **Invoice Item**.

The basic way in which these tables are related can be viewed in the entity relationship diagram shown in Figure 14.1.

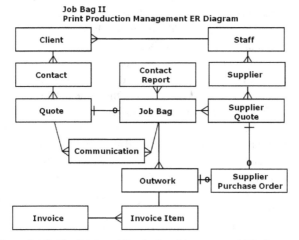

Figure 14.1: The Print and Production Management ER diagram.

Each of these entities can be added as tables to a new FileMaker database.

Building the Print and Production Management File

Step 1: Adding Tables to the Print and Production Management File

1. Launch FileMaker and create a new file called **PrintProdMgt**.

    FileMaker will automatically open the Define Database dialog box with the Fields tab selected for the default PrintProdMgt table, as shown in Figure 14.2.

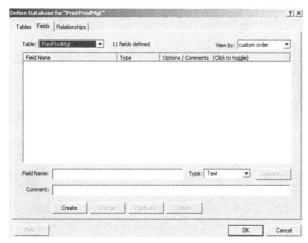

Figure 14.2: The Define Database dialog box for a new file with the Fields tab selected for the default table.

2. Click on the **Tables** tab at the top of the Define Database dialog box and add the additional 13 tables listed in Figure 14.3.

    PrintProdMgt
    Client
    Contact
    Supplier
    JobBag
    Staff
    Contact Report
    SupplierQuote
    SupplierPO
    Comms
    Outwork
    Invoice
    InvoiceItem
    Quote

    Figure 14.3: The tables needed for the PrintProdMgt file.

Step 2: Adding Fields to the PrintProdMgt File Tables

As with the other case studies in this book, we need to add a primary key field to each of our tables using FileMaker's ability to automatically assign a unique serial number to each record in each table. In addition, we will need to add foreign key fields to any of the tables to which we need to establish a relationship.

1. To add fields to each of the tables within the file, choose the **File> Define>Database** menu option and the **Fields** tab of the Define Database dialog box. It is important to ensure that the correct table is selected prior to adding new fields. Each of the tables can be selected from the drop-down list near the top of the dialog box, as shown in Figure 14.4.

Figure 14.4: Selecting the relevant table for a new field in the Define Database dialog box.

2. Add initial fields to each table as shown in Figures 14.5 to 14.20. Later, when we have established relationships between these tables using table occurrences in the relationships graph, we will add additional fields to the tables to improve the functionality of the file.

3. We will want to customize the solution business details for a print production firm. We can do this by creating a series of global text fields in the PrintProdMgt table.

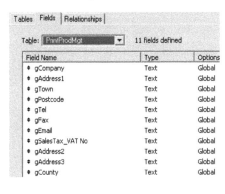

Figure 14.5: The global fields used to customize a file for a print production firm.

Add the global text fields shown in Figure 14.5 to the PrintProdMgt table. For each text field, click the **Options** button to open the Options for Field dialog box. Click the **Storage** tab at the top of the dialog box and select the **Use global storage** option, as shown in Figure 14.6.

Figure 14.6:
Selecting the
global storage
option for a field.

Setting the global storage option means that the text fields for the firm's name and address can be displayed in any layout, without the need to create a relationship from that layout's underlying base table to the table that holds the global fields.

In this solution, we will also make use of global number fields to temporarily store the contents of a record's primary key field when we create new related records in another table. For example, a global number field will be used to store a treatment event's primary key field value, which can then be placed as the treatment event's foreign key field value in a new related invoice record.

4. FileMaker can allocate a unique serial number for each record's primary key, or PKey, field, which is required for each of the data tables in the solution. For example, after creating a new number field called **PKey Client** for the Client table, click the **Options** button in the Define Fields dialog box. Select the **Auto-Enter** tab, check the **Serial number** box, and set an initial value of **1** and an increment of **1**.

5. By careful use of value lists in conjunction with foreign key fields, there is no reason to display the PKey field in any of the layouts in our solution. This means that there is little chance of the unique serial number field value being modified, duplicated, or erased by a user accidentally clicking into the field in a layout. Despite this, it is good practice to also check the **Prohibit modification of value during data entry** option, as shown in Figure 14.7.

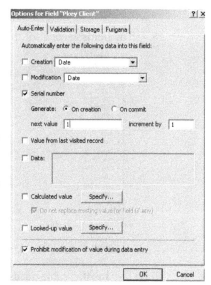

Figure 14.7: The auto-enter options for all primary key fields in the file.

6. The initial fields required for the **Client** table are shown in Figure 14.8.

Figure 14.8: The initial fields for the Client table.

7. Select the **Contact** table and add the fields shown in Figure 14.9.

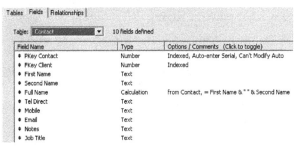

Figure 14.9: The fields for the Contact table.

8. The fields needed for the **Supplier** table are displayed in Figure 14.10.

Figure 14.10: The initial fields for the Supplier table.

9. The **JobBag** table needs a large number of descriptive fields. The initial fields needed for the JobBag table are listed in Figure 14.11.

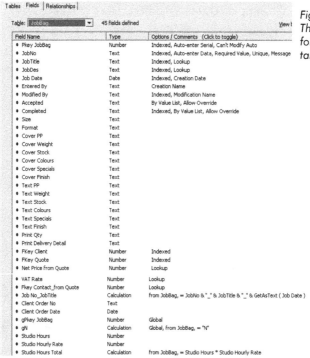

Figure 14.11: The initial fields for the JobBag table.

10. The **Staff** table is used to capture records on the print production team. The fields for the Staff table are shown in Figure 14.12.

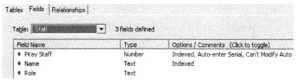

Figure 14.12: The fields for the Staff table.

11. Add the fields listed in Figure 14.13 to the **Contact Report** table.

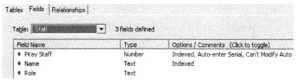

Figure 14.13: The fields for the Contact Report table.

12. Add the **SupplierQuote** table fields listed in Figure 14.14.

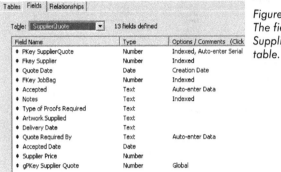

Figure 14.14:
The fields for the
SupplierQuote
table.

13. The **SupplierPO** table is used to record details on supplier quotes that are accepted and converted into supplier purchase orders. The initial fields for the SupplierPO table are shown in Figure 14.15.

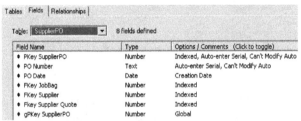

Figure 14.15:
The initial fields
for the
SupplierPO
table.

14. The **Comms** table will be used to capture client and contact communication records. The fields needed for the Comms table are listed in Figure 14.16.

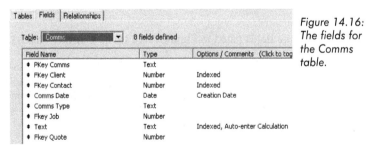

Figure 14.16:
The fields for
the Comms
table.

15. The print manager wants to include some calculation fields in the **Outwork** table to indicate the profit for a job. The fields required for the Outwork table are shown in Figure 14.17.

Figure 14.17:
The initial fields
for the Outwork
table.

16. The **Invoice** table requires the initial fields displayed in Figure 14.18.

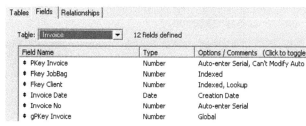

Figure 14.18:
The initial fields
for the Invoice
table.

17. The fields needed for the **InvoiceItem** table are listed in Figure 14.19.

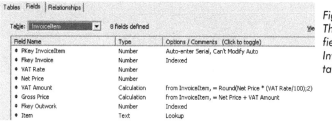

Figure 14.19:
The initial
fields for the
InvoiceItem
table.

18. Finally, we need to add the initial fields displayed in Figure 14.20 to the
Quote table.

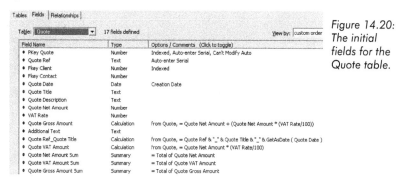

Figure 14.20:
The initial
fields for the
Quote table.

We can now use the primary and foreign key fields from the tables to create a series of relationships using FileMaker's relationships graph. We will then be able to add to the tables some additional calculation fields that use related tables in their formulas, and redefine some text and number fields to use lookup values.

Step 3: Adding Relationships to the PrintProdMgt File

To manage the various stages of communicating with a client contact, quoting for work, creating a new job bag, requesting supplier quotes, generating purchase orders, and invoicing for the work, some well-designed table occurrence groups, or TOGs, need to be created in the PrintProdMgt file using FileMaker's relationships graph.

1.   If the Define Database dialog box is not open, select the menu option **File>Define>Database** and click the **Relationships** tab at the top of the dialog box. The 14 base tables that we have created for the PrintProdMgt file will be visible in the relationships graph as table occurrences.

Figure 14.21: The initial relationships graph for the PrintProdMgt file showing the 14 base tables.

As with the other case study FileMaker solutions, we do not link the underlying base tables directly in the relationships graph. Instead, relationships are built up between table occurrences, which are representations of the base tables in the relationships graph. It is possible to have any number of table occurrences on the relationships graph for the same underlying base table.

As introduced in Chapter 7, our aim is to refine the relationships graph into a series of discrete TOGs. Each TOG should have a main or "anchor" table occurrence on its left-hand side, with any number of linked "buoy" tables related to the anchor table spread out on the right-hand side. To ease relationship design at the outset and to assist you or any colleagues who may work on the file at a later stage, a number of fundamental rules should be followed when using relationships in any FileMaker solution:

■   As a general rule, any relationships graph will have one anchor table occurrence for every base table in the file.

■ All data entry layouts should only be based on an underlying anchor table occurrence.

■ Any portals on layouts should be based on buoy table occurrences.

■ To assist with documenting a complex FileMaker project, it is a good idea to limit the dimensions of any TOGs in the relationships graph to a single page in width but any number of pages in length.

To get the required functionality from our Print and Production Management solution, we now need to add some TOGs to the relationships graph.

2. For the sake of reference, it is a good idea to preserve at least one table occurrence for each base table within the file displayed at the top of the relationships graph. To reduce the space used, click the button on the table header to toggle the display of the table and collapse it to its title only, as shown in Figure 14.22.

3. Note that an underscore (_) has been added to some of the base table occurrences so that the original table name can be used as an anchor table occurrence. Each table occurrence must have a unique name in the graph. A table occurrence can be renamed by double-clicking on it to open the Specify Table dialog box, or by highlighting the table occurrence and clicking the **Edit** button at the bottom of the graph (the button with a yellow pencil icon).

Figure 14.22: The reference base tables collapsed to display only the table title.

3.1: The Client TOG

The print production team decides that a data entry layout based on the Client table occurrence will form the central information "hub" of the database. The Client TOG will need to include relationships to table occurrences for most of the other record sets in the file.

1. The Client TOG is shown with the Client table occurrence as the anchor table on the left-hand side in Figure 14.23.

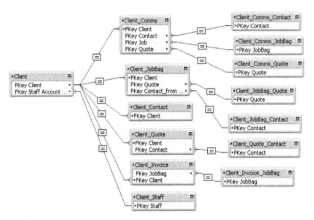

Figure 14.23: The Client table occurrence group.

2. With the exception of the Invoice and Staff table occurrence relation-
    ships in the Client TOG file, all the other relationships will be used to
    create related records. Open the Edit Relationship dialog box for each of
    these relationships by double-clicking anywhere on the relationship line.
    As shown in Figure 14.24, click the check box labeled **Allow creation of
    records in this table via this relationship**.

3. For some of the Client TOG relationships, such as **Communications**,
    you'll want to sort the related records by checking the **Sort records**
    option and specifying the appropriate field. In Figure 14.24, we sort by
    the **Comms Date** field.

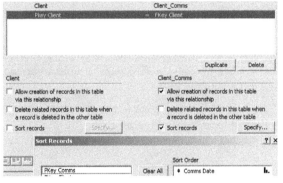

Figure 14.24:
Changing the
settings in the
Edit Relationship
dialog box.

3.2: The JobBag TOG

A job bag record will be related to most of the other data tables in the file. To facilitate this, the design of the JobBag TOG is shown in Figure 14.25.

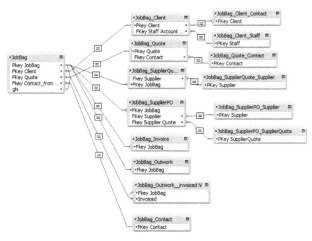

Figure 14.25: The JobBag table occurrence group.

The only relationship in the database that is not a straightforward equijoin, where the value in the field on one side of the relationship is the same as that on the other, is that between the JobBag and the JobBag_Outwork__Invoice N table occurrence. This relationship, which is displayed in Figure 14.26, is only valid if the FKey JobBag foreign field is the same as the PKey JobBag primary field and the Invoiced field value in the outwork record is "N". This relationship will be used to identify outwork records that have not yet been invoiced.

JobBag		JobBag_Outwork__invoiced N
	Pkey JobBag	= Fkey JobBag
AND	gN	= Invoiced

Figure 14.26: The relationship between the JobBag and JobBag_ Outwork__invoiced N table occurrences in the JobBag TOG.

The relationships from JobBag to the Outwork and Supplier Quote table occurrences need to be modified to allow the creation of related records.

3.3: The SupplierQuote TOG

The Supplier Quote TOG is required to display related record information for supplier purchase orders, supplier details, and job details in a SupplierQuote Details layout.

The SupplierQuote TOG is displayed in Figure 14.27.

Figure 14.27: The SupplierQuote table occurrence group.

None of the relationships in the SupplierQuote TOG need to be modified to allow the creation of related records.

3.4: The SupplierPO TOG

A supplier purchase order record will also need to display related record information. The relationships necessary to facilitate this in the SupplierPO TOG are shown in Figure 14.28. As with the SupplierQuote TOG, as the relationships are used purely for data display purposes only, none of the SupplierPO TOG relationships need to be modified to allow the creation of related records.

Figure 14.28: The SupplierPO table occurrence group.

3.5: The Supplier TOG

When viewing a supplier record on screen, it would be of benefit to see any related quote requests or purchase orders by using portals. A member of the design team can also be allocated to be a point of contact for the supplier.

The Supplier TOG is shown in Figure 14.29.

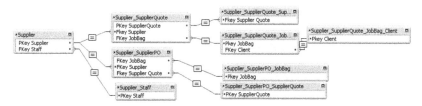

Figure 14:29: The Supplier table occurrence group.

New supplier quote and purchase order records will be created using the JobBag TOG, so none of the relationships in the Supplier TOG will be used to create related records.

3.6: The Outwork TOG

Outwork records will need to display related field contents from related JobBag and SupplierPO records. In addition, it is important to track whether or not an outwork record has been invoiced by testing whether a related record exists in an InvoiceItem table occurrence.

The Outwork TOG is shown in Figure 14.30.

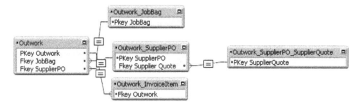

Figure 14.30: The Outwork table occurrence group.

3.7: The InvoiceItem TOG

The InvoiceItem TOG consists of a single relationship between table occurrences for the InvoiceItem and Outwork tables. It will be used to create a lookup field in the InvoiceItem table for a chargeable outwork item.

The InvoiceItem TOG is shown in Figure 14.31.

Figure 14.31: The InvoiceItem table occurrence group.

3.8: The Quote TOG

A quote record will need to display information from related fields in the JobBag, Client, and Contact tables.

The Quote TOG is displayed in Figure 14.32.

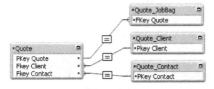

Figure 14.32: The Quote table occurrence group.

3.9: The Comms TOG

The Comms TOG is required so that a communication record shows the correct related information for a client, contact, job bag record, or quote record, depending on which one is relevant.

The Comms TOG is shown in Figure 14.33.

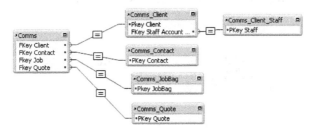

Figure 14.33: The Comms table occurrence group.

3.10: The Contact TOG

A Contact TOG is needed to display details about an individual within a company.

The Contact TOG is shown in Figure 14.34.

Figure 14.34: The Contact table occurrence group.

Additional calculation and lookup fields that make use of these table occurrences in their definition can now be added to the PrintProdMgt file tables.

Step 4: Adding Calculation and Lookup Fields to the PrintProdMgt File Tables

We can improve the functionality of the PrintProdMgt database and its ability to manage print production by using calculation fields. For example, we'll add fields to total an invoice or look up the outwork fee for an invoice item.

If the Define Database dialog box is not open, select the **File>Define> Database** menu option. Click the **Fields** tab to return to the fields list for each of the tables in the PrintProdMgt database.

4.1: Additional Fields for the Client Table

In the Client table, we can add a set of calculation and summary fields that count the number of related records for a client in the other tables.

The additional fields for the Client table are listed in Figure 14.35.

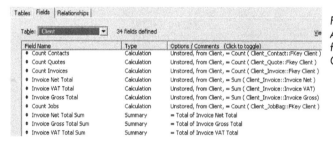

Figure 14.35: Additional fields for the Client table.

4.2: Additional Fields for the Supplier Table

Two calculation fields can be added to the Supplier table, as listed in Figure 14.36, to count how many related supplier quote and purchase order records exist for each supplier record.

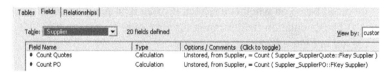

Figure 14.36: Additional fields for the Supplier table.

4.3: Additional Fields for the JobBag Table

Four calculation fields and three summary fields can be added to the JobBag table to display totals for related invoice records.

The additional fields for the JobBag table are shown in Figure 14.37.

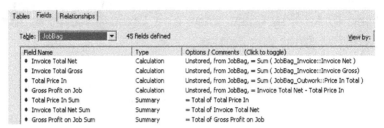

Figure 14.37: Additional fields for the JobBag table.

4.4: An Additional Field for the SupplierPO Table

A single new calculation field called **Count Outwork** can be added to the SupplierPO table. The formula for the Count Outwork field is shown in Figure 14.38.

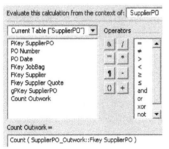

Figure 14.38:
The Count Outwork
calculation field
formula in the
SupplierPO table.

4.5: An Additional Field for the Outwork Table

A new calculation field called **Count InvoiceItem** is needed in the Outwork table. It will be used to test whether or not an outwork record has been invoiced based on whether a related invoice item record exists.

The calculation field formula for the Count InvoiceItem field is displayed in Figure 14.39.

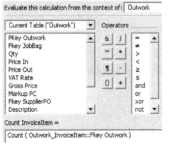

Figure 14.39:
The Count
InvoiceItem
calculation field
formula in the
Outwork table.

4.6: Additional Fields for the Invoice Table

The **Invoice Net**, **Invoice VAT**, and **Invoice Gross** fields can now be added with calculation fields that summarize the values in any related invoice item records. Summary totals fields can also be created for these items.

The new fields for the Invoice table are shown in Figure 14.40.

Figure 14.40: Additional fields for the Invoice table.

4.7: An Additional Field for the InvoiceItem Table

The **Item** text field in the InvoiceItem table can be set to look up the description value in a related outwork record using the InvoiceItem TOG.

The Lookup settings for the Item field are displayed in Figure 14.41.

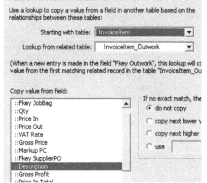

Figure 14.41: The Lookup settings for the Item field in the InvoiceItem table.

4.8: An Additional Field for the Quote Table

It is decided to create a field that displays whether or not a quote has been accepted by a client, based on whether a related job bag record exists.

The calculation field formula for the **Accepted** field in the Quote table is shown in Figure 14.42.

Figure 14.42: The Accepted calculation field in the Quote table.

Step 5: Designing Data Entry and Report Layouts for the PrintProdMgt File

A series of data entry and list reporting screens now need to be designed. As discussed in Chapter 7, with FileMaker it is a good idea to base any data entry and report layouts on anchor table occurrences. The anchor table occurrence is the one to the far left of every table occurrence group in our relationships graph.

5.1: Creating a Wizard Layout to Capture Information about the Print Firm

We need to create a layout the production manager can use to capture contact details for the firm. As this information is captured in global fields within the PrintProdMgt table, the information can be used in any layout, regardless of any underlying relationships.

1. Open the **PrintProdMgt** file, if it is not already open, select the menu option **View>Layout Mode** to switch to Layout mode, and create a new layout.

2. Choose the menu option **Layouts>New Layout/Report** to open the New Layout/Report dialog box. Choose to show records from the **PrintProdMgt** table, type **Wizard** in the Layout Name box, and select **Blank layout**, as shown in Figure 14.43.

Figure 14.43: The New Layout/Report dialog box settings for the Wizard layout.

3. Delete the layout header and footer parts in the Wizard layout by highlighting the part label for each and pressing the **Backspace** or **Delete** key.

4. As shown in Figure 14.44, give the layout body a fill color and use the **Button** tool to display the global fields on a background tile.

5. A button to link the Wizard layout back to a main menu has been added to the upper-left corner of the layout.

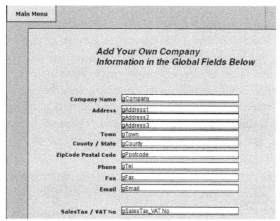

Figure 14.44:
The PrintProdMgt
Wizard layout.

5.2: The PrintProdMgt Main Menu Layout

As with all the case study solutions, the team members tasked with using the database are more likely to gain confidence using the software if the same main menu or welcome screen appears every time the file is launched.

1. Create a Main Menu layout that includes a set of navigation buttons to open the various data entry and list layouts. In addition, add buttons to provide technical support, open the Wizard layout, and safely close the database or quit FileMaker.

The Main Menu layout is shown in Figure 14.45.

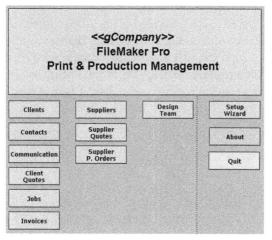

Figure 14.45:
The PrintProdMgt
Main Menu
layout.

While scripts will be described in detail later in this chapter, two scripts that are directly linked to the Main Menu layout are described in this section.

2. The green About button is designed to provide more information on the solution and details about the author. The **About...** script, which is triggered by this button, is a good example of a conditional script. The Show Custom Dialog script step can display up to three buttons and, when combined with the LastMessageChoice function, the user's choice can be monitored by the script with a different outcome depending on which button is selected. In this case, the user can choose to open one of two websites. The About... script is shown in Figure 14.46.

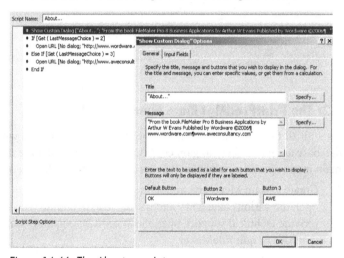

Figure 14.46: The About... script.

3. The red button labeled Quit is used to run a script with the same name. The **Quit** script also uses the Show Custom Dialog script step to create a conditional script. Depending on which button is selected, the user can choose to close the PrintProdMgt file or quit FileMaker. The Quit script is shown along with the Show Custom Dialog Options dialog box in Figure 14.47.

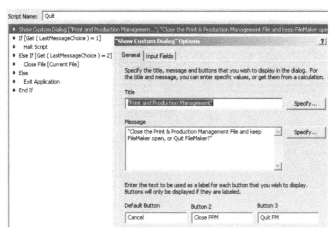

Figure 14.47: The Quit script is triggered by the button of the same name in the Main Menu layout.

5.3: The Client Details Layout

The Client Details layout is designed to act as an information "hub" for the print and production management team, allowing members to view contact details for a client, together with related contacts, communications, quotes, job bags, and invoice records, all in one screen view. The Client Details layout makes use of portals to show any records for the firm currently being viewed.

To manage the space needed to display so many related record sets, the new tab panel feature of FileMaker Pro 8 has been used to segment related records in one Client Details layout.

A series of standard navigation buttons at the top of the Client Details layout will be copied and used in a similar form in most of the file's layouts to help users work with the file. The small gray buttons, labeled with ">" and located to the left of a portal row, make use of the Go to Related Record button command to switch to any related records and display them using the correct data entry layouts.

Each tab panel in the Client Details layout is shown in Figures 14.48 to 14.53.

Several value lists are used to capture field data in the Client Details layout.

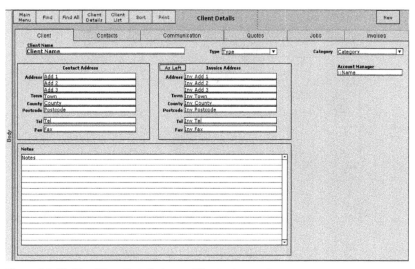

Figure 14.48: The Client Details layout Client tab panel.

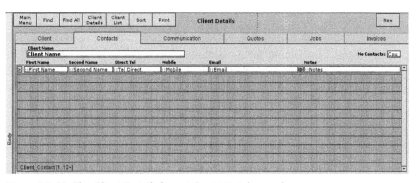

Figure 14.49: The Client Details layout Contacts tab panel.

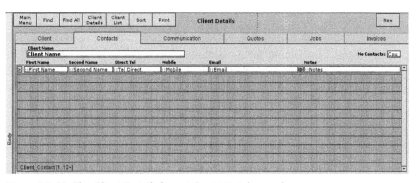

Figure 14.50: The Client Details layout Communication tab panel.

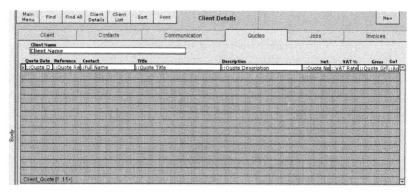

Figure 14.51: The Client Details layout Quotes tab panel.

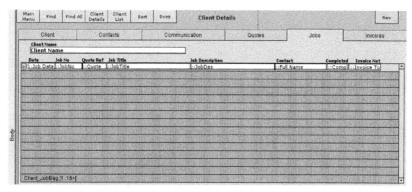

Figure 14.52: The Client Details layout Jobs tab panel.

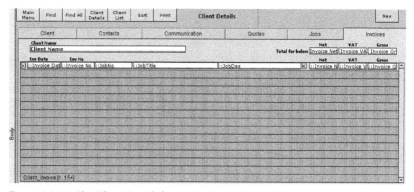

Figure 14.53: The Client Details layout Invoices tab panel.

5.4: The Client List Layout

The Client Details layout navigation buttons can be copied and pasted into a new list layout to display several client records on the screen. A series of small buttons, labeled with "<", next to each related record count make use of the Go to Related Record command to switch to any related records and display them in the correct data entry layout.

Invoice Net and **Gross** summary fields are included in a trailing grand summary layout part.

The Client List layout is shown in Figure 14.54.

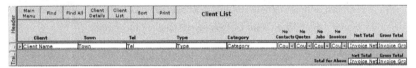

Figure 14.54: The Client List layout.

5.5: The Contact List Layout

A Contact List layout is used to display a set of individual contacts on screen, with a **Client Details** navigation button in the layout to switch to the related Client Details layout.

The Contact List layout is shown in Figure 14.55.

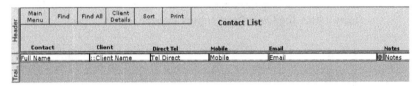

Figure 14.55: The Contact List layout.

5.6: The Supplier Details Layout

It would be of great benefit to view any related quote requests or purchase orders next to a supplier's details on screen. This can be achieved by including two portals in the Supplier Details layout, which is shown in Figure 14.56.

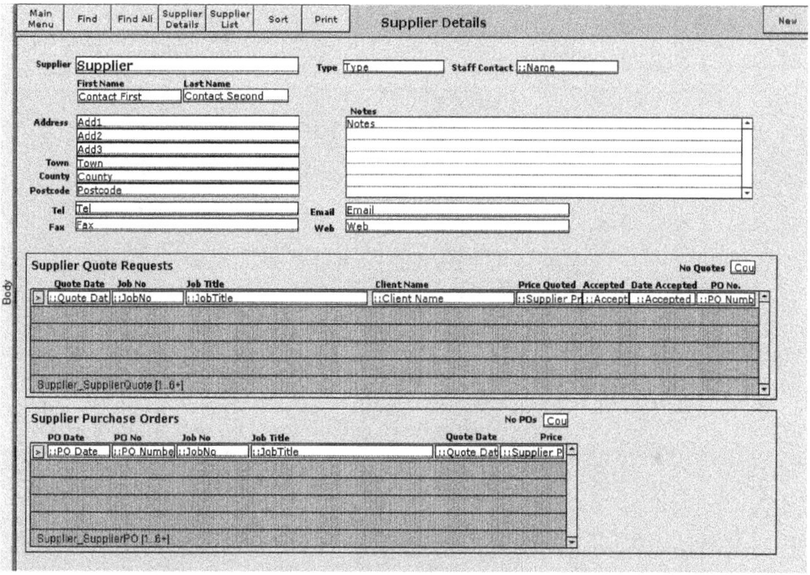

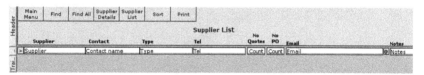

Figure 14.56: The Supplier Details layout.

5.7: The Supplier List Layout

As with clients, the Supplier List layout, shown in Figure 14.57, shares the same navigation buttons as the Supplier Details layout.

Figure 14.57: The Supplier List layout.

5.8: The Job Details Layout

The Job Details layout needs to display details on a job and any related supplier quotes, purchase orders, chargeable items, and invoice records. The Job Details layout, shown in Figure 14.58, includes four portals to display related records. The portals for supplier quotes and chargeable items can be used to create new related records.

The two green buttons, labeled **Charge** and **Create Invoice**, will be set to run scripts that automate the creation of related outwork and invoice records.

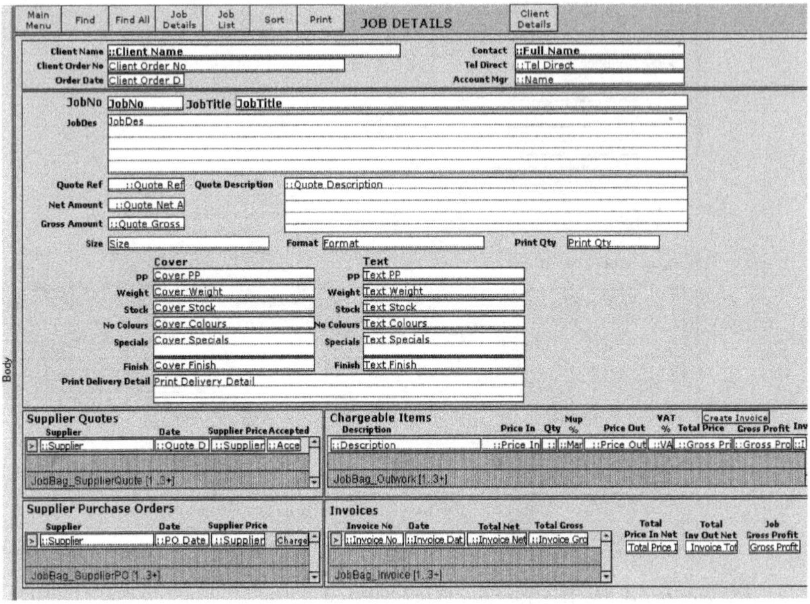

Figure 14.58: The Job Details layout.

5.9: The Job List Layout

A set of job records can be viewed on screen using a Job List layout, which is displayed in Figure 14.59. Summary fields that calculate fees, costs, and profit are included in a trailing grand summary layout part.

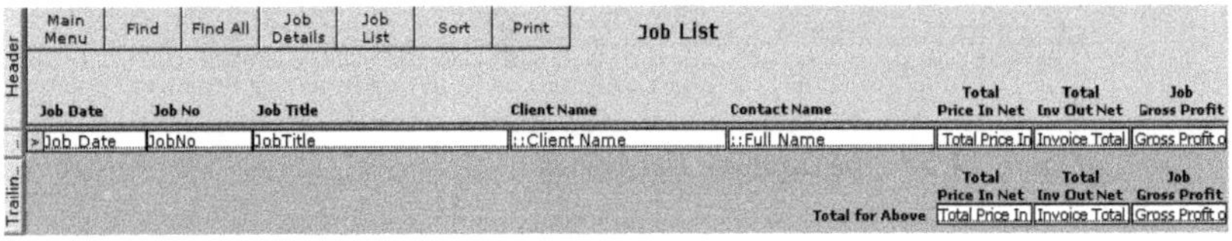

Figure 14.59: The Job List layout.

5.10: The Quote Request Layout

The Quote Request layout displays records from the SupplierQuote table occurrence. New quote request records are created from the portal in the Job Details layout. The green **Create POrder** button will be set to run a script that converts the supplier's quoted price and includes it in a new related supplier purchase order record.

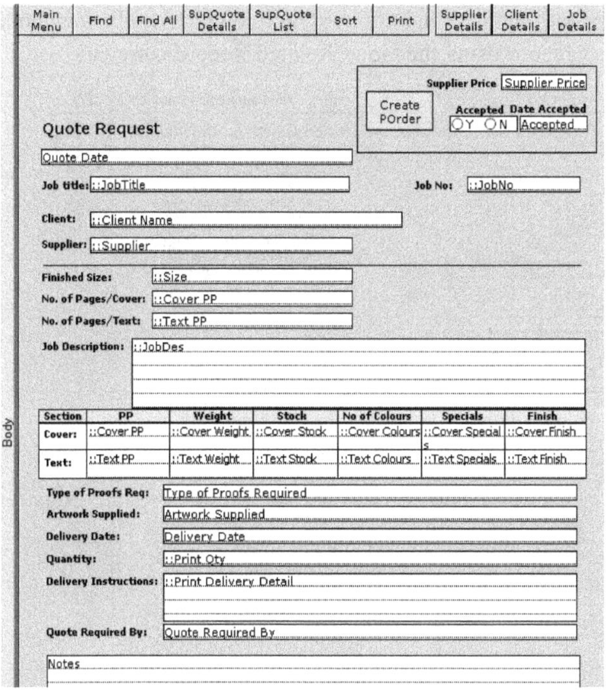

Figure 14.60: The Quote Request layout.

5.11: The Supplier Quote Requests List Layout

A list layout based on the SupplierQuote table is used to display several supplier quote records. The Supplier Quote Requests List layout is shown in Figure 14.61.

Figure 14.61: The Supplier Quote Requests List layout.

5.12: The Communication Details Layout

Communication records for emails and letters sent to a client contact are held in the Comms table. A Communication Details layout, shown in Figure 14.62, can be used to display the contents of a letter or email record.

Merge fields are used to display the firm's address, the client contact address fields, and reference information on the related job or quote record.

A set of four navigation buttons switch to the related client, contact, quote, or job record using the Go to Related Record command.

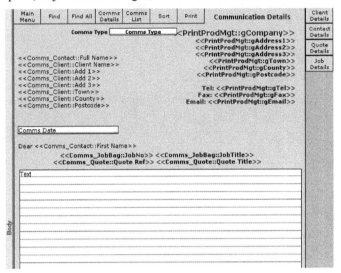

Figure 14.62: The Communication Details layout.

5.13: The Communication List Layout

A set of communication records can be displayed as a single line record using a Communication List layout, which can be seen in Figure 14.63.

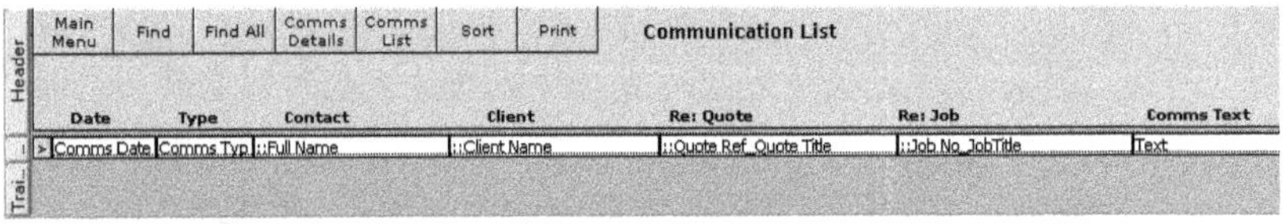

Figure 14.63: The Communication List layout.

5.14: The Invoice Details Layout

The Invoice Details layout needs to display contact fields for the print company and the client and any related InvoiceItem records in a portal. The **Invoice Net**, **Invoice VAT**, and **Invoice Gross** fields also need to be displayed.

The Invoice layout is displayed in Figure 14.64.

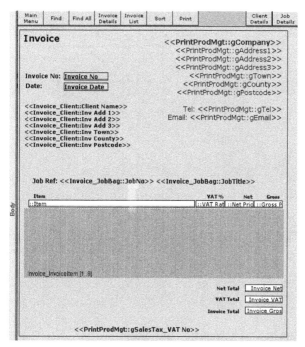

Figure 14.64: The Invoice Details layout.

5.15: The Invoice List Layout

The Invoice List layout shares the same navigation buttons as the Invoice Details layout. Additionally, smaller buttons can switch to the related client or job record.

The Invoice List layout is shown in Figure 14.65.

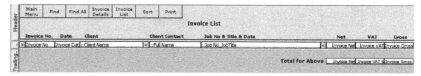

Figure 14.65: The Invoice List layout.

5.16: The Quote Details Layout

New quote records are created in the Client Details layout. The Quote Details layout displays a quote record on screen with fields to describe and itemize the quote for the client.

The Quote Details layout is shown in Figure 14.66.

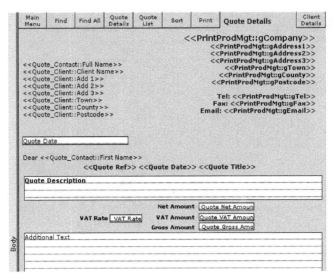

Figure 14.66: The Quote Details layout.

5.17: The Quote List Layout

The Quote List layout is shown in Figure 14.67 and includes summary fields in a trailing grand summary layout part.

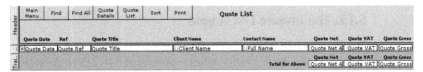

Figure 14.67: The Quote List layout.

5.18: The Design Team List Layout

A list of staff names is needed to create a value list that can be used to assign staff to clients or suppliers as account managers. The Design Team List layout is shown in Figure 14.68.

Figure 14.68: The Design Team List layout.

5.19: The Purchase Order Details Layout

In terms of data flow, supplier purchase order records exist "downstream" from supplier quote requests and are created when a supplier quote is accepted.

The Purchase Order Details layout includes buttons to switch to the related supplier quote, supplier, client, or job bag records.

The Purchase Order Details layout is shown in Figure 14.69.

Many of the descriptive fields in the Purchase Order Details layout are taken from the related supplier quote and job bag records.

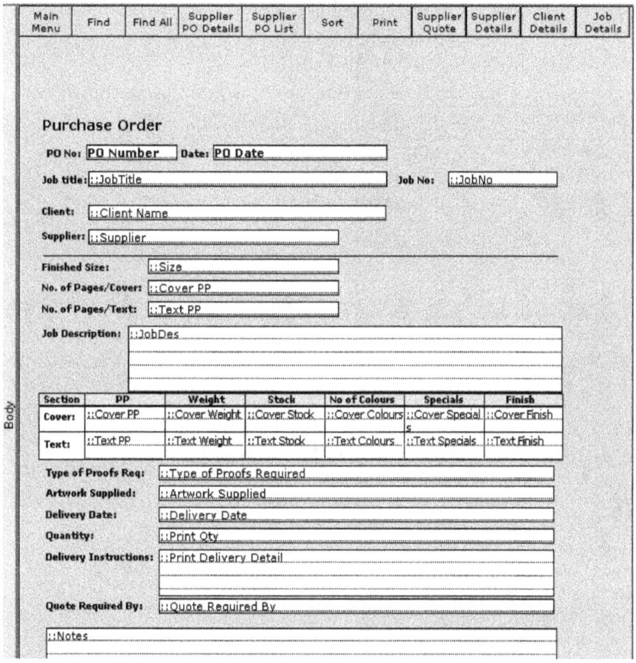

Figure 14.69: The Purchase Order Details layout.

5.20: The Supplier Purchase Order List Layout

A list layout can be created based on the SupplierPO table occurrence to display a set of supplier purchase order records. The Supplier Purchase Order List layout is shown in Figure 14.70.

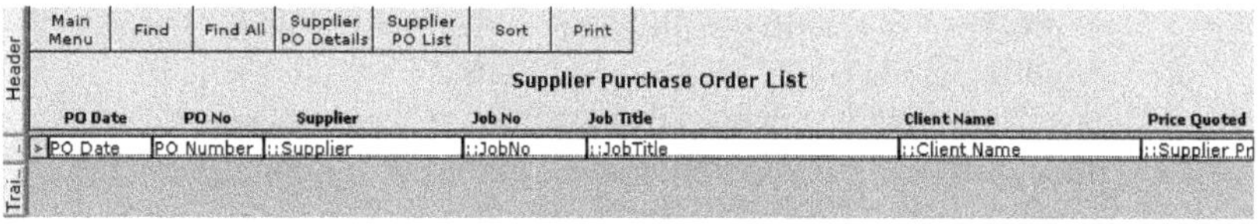

Figure 14.70: The Supplier Purchase Order List layout.

Step 6: Automating the Print and Production Management Solution with Scripts

Before the print production team starts using the solution, a series of scripts would be of great benefit to aid with navigation around the file and to assist with the creation of new related records.

6.1: The Opening Script

An opening script can be created to guarantee that the database always opens on the Welcome Menu with the database window maximized and the Status area hidden.

The Opening script is shown in Figure 14.71.

Figure 14.71:
The Opening
Script/Open
Menu script.

6.2: Navigation Scripts to Open Data Entry and List Layouts

The production team will want to view the Status area in each of the data entry and list layouts.

A series of scripts can be created to open the various data entry layouts. As an example, the Open Client Details script is shown in Figure 14.72.

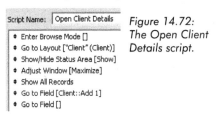

Figure 14.72:
The Open Client
Details script.

6.3: Creating New Purchase Orders from a Supplier Quote Record

New supplier quotes are created using a portal in the JobBag Details layout. A script is needed to automate the process of turning an accepted supplier quote into a new supplier purchase order. The Create Purchase Order from Supplier Quote script is shown in Figure 14.73.

The script first checks that the current supplier quote record contains a price, before a purchase order can be created. If a purchase order for this quote already exists, indicated by the quote having a related supplier purchase order record, the script will halt. The script will then display a dialog box asking the database user to confirm the creation of a new purchase order for the current quote record. If the user goes ahead, a global field is used to store the primary key value for the supplier quote and set this value for the foreign key field in a new supplier purchase order record. The relationship back to the supplier quote record is used to set a value for the supplier foreign key field in the new purchase order record. Another global field in the JobBag table is used to set the job bag foreign key field value for the new purchase order record.

Figure 14.73: The Create Purchase Order from Supplier Quote script.

6.4: Turning the Supplier Purchase Order into a New Outwork Record for a Job Bag

A green button in the purchase order portal within the JobBag Details layout is labeled Charge. When clicked on, this button is designed to create a new related outwork record for a job based on the contents of the selected supplier purchase order. A script is needed to automate this and prevent subsequent outwork records from being added for the same purchase order by accident. The Add Supplier PO to Outwork script is shown in Figure 14.74.

The script first checks to see that an outwork record has not already been created from the current supplier purchase order, using the Count Outwork field from the JobBag_SupplierPO table occurrence. A custom dialog box then asks the database user to confirm the creation of a new outwork record for the current purchase order. If the user selects the button to go ahead, two global fields are used to store the primary key field values for the job bag and the supplier purchase order. These fields are used to set the FKey JobBag and FKey SupplierPO fields in a new outwork record. The Description field in the new outwork record is set to be the same as the related JobDes field in the JobBag table.

```
Script Name:  Add Supplier PO to Outwork

  •  Set Error Capture [On]
  •  If [JobBag_SupplierPO::Count Outwork > 0]
  •     Show Custom Dialog ["Supplier Purchase Order Charge..."; "ERROR:  This Purchase Order has already been allocated to Outwork in the JobBag..."]
  •     Halt Script
  •  End If
  •  Show Custom Dialog ["Add Purchase Order to Outwork"; "Add this Purchase Order to a NEW OUTWORK item for this JobBag?"]
  •  If [Get ( LastMessageChoice ) = 1]
  •     Halt Script
  •  End If
  •  Set Field [JobBag::gPkey JobBag; JobBag::Pkey JobBag]
  •  Set Field [JobBag_SupplierPO::gPKey SupplierPO; JobBag_SupplierPO::PKey SupplierPO]
  •  Go to Layout ["Outwork" (Outwork)]
  •  New Record/Request
  •  Set Field [Outwork::Fkey JobBag; JobBag::gPkey JobBag]
  •  Set Field [Outwork::Description; Outwork_JobBag::JobDes]
  •  Set Field [Outwork::Fkey SupplierPO; SupplierPO::gPKey SupplierPO]
  •  Go to Layout ["JobBag" (JobBag)]
```

Figure 14.74: The Add Supplier PO to Outwork script.

6.5: Creating New Invoices for Outwork Items

Once outwork records have been created for a job, it would be good if a script could collect any outwork records that have not yet been invoiced and include them as invoice line items for a new invoice record. The script called Invoice Outstanding Outwork Items is designed to do this. The script is shown in Figure 14.75.

The script will be run using a button in the JobBag Details layout. The script first checks that there are outwork records for a job that have not yet been invoiced. A custom dialog box then appears, asking for confirmation before creating a new related invoice record. The global field gPKey JobBag is then used to store the PKey JobBag field value. The outwork items that have not been invoiced are then isolated using the Go to Related Record script step. A new invoice record is then created and related to the job bag record by making the FKey JobBag field value the same as the gPKey JobBag global field value. The script then switches to an InvoiceItem blank layout, based on the InvoiceItem table occurrence, and imports the found set of outwork records that have not been invoiced. The FKey Invoice field contents in the newly imported InvoiceItem records are then set to be the same as the new invoice record using the global field gFKey Invoice. The Invoiced field for the found set of outstanding outwork records is then automatically set to be "Y" using the Replace Field Contents script step. Finally the script opens the new Invoice layout.

```
Script Name:  Invoice Outstanding Outwork Items

  ● Set Error Capture [On]
  ● If [Count ( JobBag_Outwork__invoiced N::Fkey JobBag ) = 0]
  ●    Show Custom Dialog ["All Outwork Invoiced"; "ERROR: All Outwork Items have been invoiced..."]
  ●    Halt Script
  ● End If
  ● Show Custom Dialog ["Create Invoice"; "Create a NEW INVOICE for all non charged Outwork Items in this JobBag"]
  ● If [Get ( LastMessageChoice ) = 1]
  ●    Halt Script
  ● End If
  ● Set Field [JobBag::gPkey JobBag; JobBag::Pkey JobBag]
  ● Go to Related Record [Show only related records; From table: "JobBag_Outwork__invoiced N"; Using layout: "Outwork" (Outwork)]
  ● Go to Layout ["Invoice" (Invoice)]
  ● New Record/Request
  ● Set Field [Invoice::gPKey Invoice; Invoice::PKey Invoice]
  ● Set Field [Invoice::Fkey JobBag; JobBag::gPkey JobBag]
  ● Go to Layout ["InvoiceItem" (InvoiceItem)]
  ● Import Records [No dialog; "PrintProdMgt.fp7"; Add; Windows ANSI]
  ● Replace Field Contents [No dialog; InvoiceItem::Fkey Invoice; Invoice::gPKey Invoice]
  ● Go to Layout ["Outwork" (Outwork)]
  ● Replace Field Contents [No dialog; Outwork::Invoiced; "Y"]
  ● Go to Layout ["Invoice" (Invoice)]
```

Figure 14.75: The Invoice Outstanding Outwork Items script.

6.6: Printing or Emailing a Client Communication Record

A script in the database can be used to determine whether a new communication record to a client should be printed or emailed, depending on the contents of the Comms Type field for a record.

The Print or Send Comms script is shown in Figure 14.76. The script uses an If script step to check whether or not the Comms Type field contains the word "Letter." If it does, a custom dialog box will appear in order to advise the user to check the print settings. To avoid accidentally printing all records being browsed, the script shows all records, omits the current record, then shows only the omitted record. If the If statement is false and the Comms Type field does not contain the word "Letter," an alternative custom dialog box will appear, informing the user that the email can still be edited in the email application.

```
Script Name:  Print or Send Comms

  ● Set Error Capture [On]
  ● Enter Browse Mode []
  ● If [Comms::Comms Type = "Letter"]
  ●    Show Custom Dialog ["Print Letter"; "Please check your Print Set Up for this letter"]
  ●    Show All Records
  ●    Omit Record
  ●    Show Omitted Only
  ●    Print []
  ● Else
  ●    Show Custom Dialog ["Send Email"; "This email can be edited before sending"]
  ●    Send Mail [To: Comms_Contact::Email; Subject: Case ( Count ( Comms_JobBag::Pke
  ● End If
```

Figure 14.76: The Print or Send Comms script.

The Send Mail script step settings are shown in Figure 14.77. The email recipient is based on the related Email field in the related Comms_Contact table occurrence. The Subject field is based on a calculation formula that is displayed in Figure 14.78.

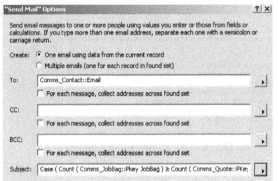

Figure 14.77:
The Send Mail
dialog box in the
Print or Send
Comms script.

The Subject formula is designed to test whether the communication record has a related job bag or quote record. The Subject field contents will be based on either the job reference and job title, or the quote reference and quote title.

```
Case ( Count ( Comms_JobBag::Pkey JobBag ) ≥ Count ( Comms_Quote::PKey Quote );
PrintProdMgt::gCompany & " Job Ref " & Comms_JobBag::JobNo & " " & Comms_JobBag::JobTitle ;
PrintProdMgt::gCompany & " Quote Ref " & Comms_Quote::Quote Ref & " " &
Comms_Quote::Quote Title)
```

Figure 14.78: The Subject calculation field formula for the
Send Mail script step.

Taking the Solution Further

Currently, the chargeable items portal in the job bag record includes design work and charged out items. It could be extended to include staff time sheets or even press run costs. Unlike some of the other case studies in this book, client payment details are not currently captured in the database.

In this example, the descriptive fields in the JobBag layout are specifically designed to record paper size and weight values for printed brochure type media. The fields for cover and text paper parameters could, of course, be extended or changed for other media.

Hopefully, the methods presented in this solution for converting new client quote records into a job bag with related supplier quotes and purchase orders, other chargeable items, and an invoice at the end of the data flow will provide you with a source of ideas for your own job bag requirements.

Chapter 15

Job Bag III — Job Sheet Management

Introduction

Job management is not solely the preserve of the creative, design, and print business sector. Small businesses that are involved in custom manufacturing, plumbers, builders, and craftsmen/women may all need to record quote letters that have been sent to clients and, if the quote is accepted, the agreed job specification for the finished article. A price list for parts and services rendered may be referred to and used in a worksheet to calculate prices for a quote.

If a repeat order for additional work is requested from the same client in the future, a database is ideal for recording the work that was done in the past and what parts or materials were used for the original job. The database itself can be used to generate repeat business for those trades that offer periodic or annual inspections.

This case study will address the database management requirements for a small business that sells and installs windows and stained glass. The firm would like to automate the process of writing quote letters to residential and commercial clients, calculating the cost of a job using a worksheet, and generating an invoice for the work. Currently the firm enters the customer's address in a word processor every time a new letter to an existing customer is written, and uses a spreadsheet to calculate the cost of glass and associated materials for a job. Invoices are also currently typed into a word processor.

The firm is looking to FileMaker to assist with customer communication, improve the accuracy of job quotes, calculate how much material is needed, and automatically generate invoices.

The job sheet management database should hopefully be found to be applicable for other small businesses that provide clients with quote letters and need to calculate job costs and transfer job information into an invoice. Plumbers, kitchen or bathroom contractors, and metal workers may find the database solution developed in this case study has a great deal in common with their own data management requirements.

As with the other case studies in this book, a copy of the completed FileMaker Pro 8 database file, **FMGlass**, is available to download from the publisher's website at www.wordware.com/files/fmapps and the author's website at www.aweconsultancy.com. You may find it easier to examine some of the FileMaker features and techniques discussed in this chapter in a copy of the completed file.

The default database password for the Admin account is **JOBBAG3** (all capitals).

The database file options have been preset to open with the active Guest account (with read-only access to the file). To open the file with full access privileges, hold down the Shift key (Windows) or Option key (Mac OS) while the file is opening. Type the word **Admin** in the Account Name box and type the password in the box below. You can change the default password at a later stage. More information on database security issues, passwords, accounts, and privileges is given in Chapter 24.

We will start by considering the tables needed for the job sheet management file, based on how the glass company wishes to communicate with clients, quote for new work, and generate invoices.

The Job Sheet Management Entity Relationship Diagram

A database is required for a small, specialized glass company to capture **Client** details and information on a site. The firm needs to calculate the cost of a **Job** based on the type of glass and associated materials needed. A job cost is calculated based on the sum of individual **Line Items**. Material costs are held in a **Price List**. The job costs are presented to the client in a written quote. If the quote is accepted, the work is carried out and an **Invoice** is presented to the client. The invoice consists of one or more **Invoice Line Items**.

The Job Sheet Management entity relationship (ER) diagram is shown in Figure 15.1.

The crow's-foot symbol in the ER diagram is used to denote a "one-to-many" relationship. As an example, a client may have received several job quotes. The line with a circle at one end and a perpendicular line (|) at the other, such as the one between the Job and Invoice tables, is used to demonstrate that not all job records will turn into an invoice, while any invoice and invoice items records will have one associated job record and job line item record, respectively.

Job Bag III
Job Sheet ER Diagram

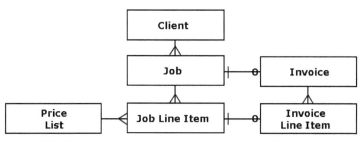

Figure 15.1: The Job Sheet Management entity relationship diagram.

These entities can now be incorporated into a FileMaker Pro 8 file as separate tables.

Building the Job Sheet Management File

Step 1: Adding Tables to the FMGlass File

1. Launch FileMaker and create a new file called **FMGlass**.

   FileMaker will automatically open the Define Database dialog box with the Fields tab selected for the default FMGlass table, as shown in Figure 15.2.

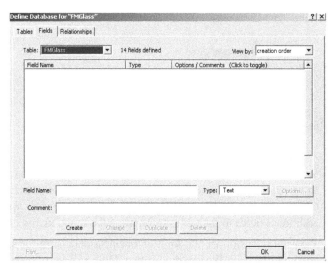

Figure 15.2: The Define Database dialog box for a new file with the Fields tab selected for the default table.

2.   Click on the **Tables** tab at the top of the Define Database dialog box and
     add the additional four tables listed in Figure 15.3.

FMGlass
PriceList
Client
JobSheet
Invoice

Figure 15.3: The tables needed for the FMGlass file.

Step 2: Adding Fields to the FMGlass File Tables

As with the other case studies in this book, we need to add a primary key
field to each of our tables using FileMaker's ability to automatically assign a
unique serial number to each record in each table. In addition, we will need to
add foreign key fields to any of the tables to which we need to establish a
relationship.

1.   To add fields to each of the tables within the file, choose the **File>
     Define>Database** menu option and then the **Fields** tab of the Define
     Database dialog box. It is important to ensure that the correct table is
     selected prior to adding new fields. Each of the tables can be selected
     from the drop-down list near the top of the dialog box, as shown in Fig-
     ure 15.4.

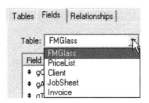

*Figure 15.4: Selecting the relevant table for a
new field in the Define Database dialog box.*

We will be adding the initial fields to each table as shown in Figures 15.5
to 15.16. Later, when we have established relationships between these
tables, using table occurrences in the relationships graph, we will add
additional fields to the tables to improve the functionality of the file.

2.   We want to customize the solution business details for the stained glass
     and window firm. We can do this by adding a series of global text fields
     to the **FMGlass** table. Add the global fields shown in Figure 15.5.

Figure 15.5: The global fields used to customize the file for a glass and window firm.

3. For each text field, click the **Options** button to open the Options for Field dialog box. Click the **Storage** tab at the top of the Options for Field dialog box and select the **Use global storage** option, as shown in Figure 15.6.

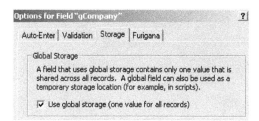

Figure 15.6: Selecting the global storage option for a field.

Setting the global storage option means that the text fields for the firm's name and address can be displayed in any layout, without the need to create a relationship from that layout's underlying base table to the table that holds the global fields.

In this solution, we will also make use of global number fields to temporarily store the contents of a record's primary key field when we create new related records in another table. As an example, a global number field will be used to store a client's primary key field value, which can then be placed as the client foreign key field value in a new related job record.

4. FileMaker can allocate a unique serial number for each record's primary key, or PKey, field, which is required for all the data tables in the solution. For example, after creating a new number field called **PKey Client** in the Client table, click the **Options** button in the Define Fields dialog box. Select the **Auto-Enter** tab, check the **Serial Number** option, and set an initial value of **1** and an increment of **1**.

5. By careful use of value lists in conjunction with foreign key fields, there is no reason to display the primary key field in any of the layouts in our solution. This means that there is little chance of the unique serial number field value being modified, duplicated, or erased by a user accidentally clicking into the field in a layout. Despite this, it is good practice to also check the **Prohibit modification of value during data entry** option, as shown in Figure 15.7.

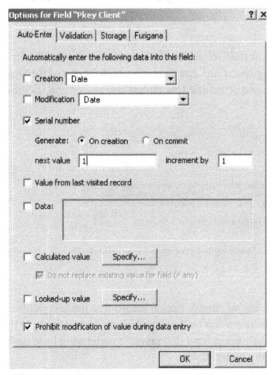

Figure 15.7: The auto-enter options for all primary key fields in the file.

6. Add the initial fields required for the **Client** table as shown in Figure 15.8.

Tables Fields | Relationships |

Table: [Client ▼]   36 fields defined

Field Name	Type	Options / Comments (Click to toggle)
♦ PKey Client	Number	Indexed, Auto-enter Serial, Can't Modify Auto
♦ Add1	Text	
♦ Add2	Text	
♦ Add3	Text	
♦ Town	Text	
♦ County	Text	
♦ Postcode	Text	
♦ Tel Day	Text	
♦ Fax	Text	
♦ Client Type	Text	
♦ Salutation	Text	
♦ Site Detail	Text	
♦ Directions	Text	
♦ Map	Container	
♦ Notes	Text	
♦ Car Parking	Text	
♦ Mobile	Text	
♦ Email	Text	
♦ Ladder	Text	
♦ Name Title	Text	
♦ First Name	Text	
♦ Second Name	Text	
♦ Organisation	Text	
♦ Tel Eve	Text	
♦ Full Name	Calculation	from Client, = Name Title & " " & First Name & " " & Second Name
♦ Dear_	Calculation	from Client, = Case (Salutation = "Informal"; "Dear " & First Name
♦ gPKey Client	Number	Global
♦ View in Multimap	Calculation	Unstored, from Client, = "http://www.multimap.com/map/browse.

Figure 15.8: The initial fields for the Client table.

The **Dear_** calculation field uses a formula to determine how a client contact should be addressed in a letter, depending on the contents of the Salutation field. The calculation formula is shown in Figure 15.9.

Dear_ =

    Case (Salutation = "Informal"; "Dear " & First Name;"Dear " & Name Title & " " & Second Name)

Figure 15.9: The calculation formula for the Dear_ field in the Client table.

The **View in Multimap** calculation field contains the URL code from the www.multimap.com website. The URL code can be used to search for and display a location map for a UK postcode. This formula could be adapted to work with other country zip or postal codes. At the time of this book's publication, Multimap grants the website user permission to make up to 10 copies of their maps for personal use only. The calculation formula for the View in Multimap field is shown in Figure 15.10.

View in Multimap =

    "http://www.multimap.com/map/browse.cgi?client=public&search_result=&db=pc&cidr_client=none&l
    ang=&keepicon=true&pc=" & Postcode & "&advanced=&client=public&addr2=&quicksearch="
    &Postcode & "&addr3=&addr1="

Figure 15.10: The View in Multimap field.

The **Map** container field could be used to store a direction map for a client's location. This information, if pulled from a mapping website, may be copyrighted and should only be used in accordance with the online mapping company's terms and conditions of use.

7.   The **PriceList** table should now be selected using the Table drop-down list in the Fields tab. Add the fields shown in Figure 15.11 to the PriceList table.

Field Name	Type	Options / Comments (Click to toggle)
✦ PKey Item	Number	Indexed, Auto-enter Serial, Can't Modify Auto
✦ Family	Text	Indexed
✦ Glass Type	Text	Indexed
✦ Supply Only	Number	Indexed
✦ Supply_Fit	Number	
✦ Family_Glass Type	Calculation	Indexed, from PriceList, = Family & "/" & Glass Type

Tables   Fields   Relationships

Table: PriceList ▼   6 fields defined

Figure 15.11: The fields for the PriceList table.

The JobSheet table will be used to store a significant amount of information for a job record. The glass company is reasonably confident that it will never produce a quote for a client with more than a dozen individual line items to describe materials needed for a job. To avoid creating another table for job sheet line items, repeating fields will be used in the JobSheet table to store and calculate the material cost for up to 12 lines of data.

A FileMaker field can be turned into a repeating field by clicking the **Options** button when a field is highlighted, clicking on the **Storage** tab in the Options for Field dialog, and typing a number greater than 1 into the "Maximum number of repetitions" box. This is shown in Figure 15.12.

Options for Field "FKey Item"

Auto-Enter   Validation   Storage   Furigana

Global Storage

A field that uses global storage contains only one value th shared across all records. A global field can also be used temporary storage location (for example, in scripts).

☐ Use global storage (one value for all records)

Repeating

Maximum number of repetitions: 12

Figure 15.12: Setting the FKey Item field in the JobSheet table to be a repeating field with up to 12 repetitions.

8. Add the initial fields needed for the **JobSheet** table listed in Figure 15.13. The repeating fields are marked with square brackets that contain the maximum number of repetitions in the Type column.

Field Name	Type	Options / Comments (Click to toggle)
PKey JobSheet	Number	Indexed, Auto-enter Serial, Can't Modify Auto
FKey Client	Number	Indexed
FKey Item	Number [12]	
Family	Text [12]	Lookup
Glass Type	Text [12]	Lookup
Width	Number [12]	
Height	Number [12]	
Sq Metres	Calculation [12]	Unstored, from JobSheet, = Width * Height
Qty	Number [12]	Auto-enter Data
Supply Only Price	Number [12]	Lookup
Supply_Fit Price	Number [12]	Lookup
Line Total	Calculation [12]	Unstored, from JobSheet, = Case (Supply_Fit = "Fit"; Supply_Fit Price * S
Supply_Fit	Text [12]	
Job Extra Item	Text [4]	
Job Extra Item Price	Number [4]	
Extra Item Sub Total	Calculation	from JobSheet, = Sum (Job Extra Item Price)
Line Total Sub Total	Calculation	Unstored, from JobSheet, = Sum (Line Total)
Job Sub Total	Calculation	Unstored, from JobSheet, = Line Total Sub Total +Extra Item Sub Total
VAT Rate	Number	Auto-enter Data
Job Total	Calculation	Unstored, from JobSheet, = Job Sub Total + VAT Amount
Job Description to Print	Text	
One Third Deposit	Calculation	Unstored, from JobSheet, = Round(Job Total / 3;2)
Deposit Amount Paid	Number	
Deposit Date Paid	Date	
Balance to Pay	Calculation	Unstored, from JobSheet, = Job Total - Deposit Amount Paid
Amount Paid	Number [3]	
Job Accepted	Text	
If No Why	Text	
Job No	Text	Indexed, Auto-enter Serial, Can't Modify Auto
VAT Amount	Calculation	Unstored, from JobSheet, = (Job Sub Total * (VAT Rate/100))
Job Date	Date	Creation Date
Start Date	Date	
Size Quoted	Text	
Date Finished	Date	
Notes	Text	
Quote Letter Date	Date	Creation Date
Quote Letter Paragraph One	Text	Auto-enter Data
Total Costs Paragraph	Text	Auto-enter Data
Quote Letter Paragraph 2	Calculation	Unstored, from JobSheet, = Case(One Third Deposit Required = "N";
One Third Deposit Required	Text	Auto-enter Data
gPKey JobSheet	Number	Global
Fkey Invoice	Number	Indexed
Job Total Sum	Summary	= Total of Job Total

Figure 15.13: The initial fields for the JobSheet table.

The **Line Total** calculation formula is shown in Figure 15.14. The calculation result is a number.

Line Total =

Case (Supply_Fit = "Fit"; Supply_Fit Price * Sq Metres * Qty ; Supply Only Price * Sq Metres * Qty)

Figure 15.14: The Line Total calculation field in the JobSheet table.

The **Quote Letter Paragraph 2** calculation field is designed to automate the process of requesting a 1/3 deposit for any commissioned work, as part of the quote letter. The calculation field formula is shown in Figure 15.15.

```
Quote Letter Paragraph 2 =

Case(One Third Deposit Required = "N";

"Assuring of my best attention at all times.¶¶" &
"Yours faithfully¶¶¶" & FMGlass::gSignature Name & "¶" & FMGlass::gJob Title;


"We would require a 1/3 deposit equivalent to £" & GetAsText(GetAsNumber(One Third Deposit)) & " and then the
balance on completion/delivery of the order.¶¶" &
"Assuring of my best attention at all times,¶¶" &
"Yours faithfully¶¶¶" & FMGlass::gSignature Name & "¶" & FMGlass::gJob Title )
```

Figure 15.15: The Quote Letter Paragraph 2 formula.

9.   Add the fields listed in Figure 15.16 to the **Invoice** table. Once relationships have been established between the tables in the FMGlass file, the lookup fields can be correctly defined.

Field Name	Type	Options / Comments (Click to toggle)
♦ Pkey Invoice	Number	Auto-enter Serial, Can't Modify Auto
♦ Invoice No	Text	Auto-enter Serial, Can't Modify Auto
♦ Invoice Date	Date	Creation Date
♦ Family	Text [12]	Lookup
♦ Glass Type	Text [12]	Lookup
♦ Width	Number [12]	Lookup
♦ Height	Number [12]	Lookup
♦ Sq Metres	Calculation [12]	Unstored, from Invoice, = Width * Height
♦ Qty	Number [12]	Auto-enter Data, Lookup
♦ Line Total	Number [12]	Lookup
♦ Job Extra Item	Text [4]	Lookup
♦ Job Extra Item Price	Number [4]	Lookup
♦ Extra Item Sub Total	Calculation	from Invoice, = Sum (Job Extra Item Price)
♦ Line Total Sub Total	Calculation	Unstored, from Invoice, = Sum (Line Total)
♦ Job Sub Total	Calculation	Unstored, from Invoice, = Line Total Sub Total + Extra Item Sub Total
♦ VAT Rate	Number	Lookup
♦ Job Total	Calculation	Unstored, from Invoice, = Job Sub Total + VAT Amount
♦ Deposit Amount Paid	Number	Lookup
♦ Balance to Pay	Calculation	Unstored, from Invoice, = Job Total - Total Amount Paid
♦ VAT Amount	Calculation	Unstored, from Invoice, = (Job Sub Total * (VAT Rate/100))
♦ FKey Job Sheet	Number	Indexed
♦ FKey Client	Number	Indexed, Lookup
♦ Description	Text	Lookup
♦ Full Name	Text	Lookup
♦ Organisation	Text	Lookup
♦ Add1	Text	Lookup
♦ Add2	Text	Lookup
♦ Add3	Text	Lookup
♦ Town	Text	Lookup
♦ County	Text	Lookup
♦ Postcode	Text	Lookup
♦ Deposit Amount Paid Date	Date	Lookup
♦ Amount Paid	Number [3]	
♦ Amount Paid Date	Date [3]	
♦ Total Amount Paid	Calculation	from Invoice, = Sum (Amount Paid) + Deposit Amount Paid
♦ Size Quoted	Text	Lookup
♦ Job No	Text	Lookup
♦ Job Sub Total Sum	Summary	= Total of Job Sub Total
♦ Balance to Pay Sum	Summary	= Total of Balance to Pay
♦ VAT Amount Sum	Summary	= Total of Total Amount Paid
♦ Job Total Sum	Summary	= Total of Job Total

Tables | Fields | Relationships

Table: Invoice   42 fields defined   View

Figure 15.16: The initial fields for the Invoice table.

We now need to create relationships between these tables in order to design the input and reporting screens in our FMGlass job sheet solution, and to finalize some of the field definitions and formulas in the tables at a later stage.

Step 3: Adding Relationships within the FMGlass File

The glass company is hoping that FileMaker will improve the efficiency and accuracy with which quotes are produced and take care of the calculations to derive the total cost in the job sheet. The staff is also looking forward to not having to retype another customer address again in an invoice or quote letter! To make this possible we need to design a series of table occurrence groups, or TOGs, in the relationships graph, and combine these TOGs with easy-to-follow layouts at a later stage.

1. If the Define Database dialog box is not open, select the menu option **File>Define>Database** and then click the **Relationships** tab at the top of the dialog box. The five base tables that we have created in the FMGlass file will be visible as table occurrences, as shown in Figure 15.17.

Figure 15.17: The initial relationships graph for the FMGlass file showing the five base tables.

As with the other case study FileMaker solutions, we do not link the underlying base tables directly in the relationships graph. Instead, relationships are built up between table occurrences, which are representations of the base tables in the relationships graph. It is possible to have any number of table occurrences on the relationships graph for the same underlying base table.

As introduced in Chapter 7, our aim is to refine the relationships graph into a series of discrete TOGs. Each TOG should have a main or "anchor" table occurrence on its left-hand side, with any number of linked "buoy" tables related to the anchor table spread out on the right-hand side. To ease relationship design at the outset and to assist you or any colleagues who may work on the file at a later stage, a number of fundamental rules should be addressed using relationships in any FileMaker solution:

- As a general rule, any relationships graph will have one anchor table occurrence for every base table in the file.
- All data entry layouts should only be based on an underlying anchor table occurrence.
- Any portals on layouts should be based on buoy table occurrences.

■ To assist with documenting a complex FileMaker project, it is a good idea to limit the dimensions of any TOGs in the relationships graph to a single page in width but any number of pages in length.

To get the required functionality from our FMGlass solution, we now need to add some TOGs to the relationships graph.

2. For the sake of reference, it is a good idea to preserve at least one table occurrence for each base table within the file, displayed at the top of the relationships graph. To reduce the space used, click on the button on the table header to toggle the display of the table and collapse it to its title only, as shown in Figure 15.18.

3. Note that an underscore (_) has been added to the base table occurrences so that the original table name can be used as an anchor table occurrence. Each table occurrence must have a unique name in the graph. A table occurrence can be renamed by double-clicking on it to open the Specify Table dialog box, or by highlighting the table occurrence and clicking the **Edit** button at the bottom of the graph (the button with a yellow pencil icon).

Figure 15.18: The reference base tables collapsed to display only the table titles.

3.1: The Client TOG

As with any FileMaker solution, the fundamental business rules within a workgroup or company should dictate how records are captured in the database. A client's details are captured first before a new job sheet and quote letter are created. If the quote is accepted, the job goes ahead and an invoice is generated for the work. The Client TOG is used to manage the relationships between clients, job sheets and, if a quote is successful, invoices.

Create the Client TOG with the Client table occurrence as the anchor table on the left-hand side as shown in Figure 15.19. A table occurrence based on the Invoice table appears twice in the TOG, as the invoice number for a particular job sheet is to be displayed in a job sheet portal.

None of the relationships in the Client TOG need to be modified to allow the creation of related records, as new job sheets will be created via a script.

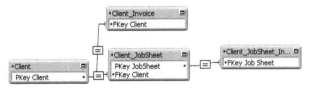

Figure 15.19: The Client TOG.

3.2: The JobSheet TOG

The JobSheet table occurrence needs a relationship to a table occurrence based on the PriceList, Client, and Invoice tables. The JobSheet TOG is shown in Figure 15.20.

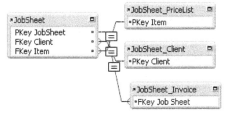

Figure 15.20: The JobSheet TOG.

3.3: The Invoice TOG

An invoice record is only created when a job sheet record is accepted. Each invoice record will have a related job sheet and client record. The Invoice TOG is shown in Figure 15.21.

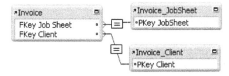

Figure 15.21: The Invoice TOG.

Now that we have finished building the relationships graph, there are some additional calculation fields, based on the relationships we have built, that we need to add to our existing tables.

Step 4: Adding Calculation and Lookup Fields to the FMGlass File Tables

4.1: Additional Fields for the Client Table

There are several calculation and lookup fields that we can now add to the database tables to maximize the solution's effectiveness. For example, we can now get FileMaker to add up all the invoices sent to a particular client.

1. If the Define Database dialog box is not open, select the **File>Define> Database** menu option. Click the **Fields** tab to return to the fields list for each of the tables in the FMGlass database.

2. In the **Client** table, we can now add a set of calculation and summary fields to count how many related job sheet and invoice records exist for a client and total how much the owner has been invoiced, how much has

been paid, and what is still owed. These new fields are displayed in Figure 15.22.

Field Name	Type	Options / Comments (Click to toggle)
◆ Count JobSheets	Calculation	Unstored, from Client, = Count (Client_JobSheet::FKey Client)
◆ Count Invoices	Calculation	Unstored, from Client, = Count (Client_Invoice::FKey Client)
◆ Total Invoiced	Calculation	Unstored, from Client, = Sum (Client_Invoice::Job Total)
◆ Total Paid	Calculation	Unstored, from Client, = Sum (Client_Invoice::Total Amount Paid)
◆ Total To Pay	Calculation	Unstored, from Client, = Sum (Client_Invoice::Balance to Pay)
◆ Total Invoiced Sum	Summary	= Total of Total Invoiced
◆ Total Paid Sum	Summary	= Total of Total Paid
◆ Total To Pay Sum	Summary	= Total of Total To Pay

Figure 15.22: Additional calculation and summary fields added to the Client table.

4.2: Additional Fields for the JobSheet Table

The global container field gColours from the FMGlass table can be used to display a different background color depending on whether or not a job has been accepted.

A calculation field called Job Accepted colour uses a Case function to test whether the Job Accepted field contents are "Y" or "N". A green or red background color can then be displayed depending on the field value. The default color is set to be the third repetition in the gColours repeating field, which is plain or white.

1. Create the **Job Accepted colour** field with the formula shown in Figure 15.23. The calculation result type needs to be set to **Container**.

Job Accepted colour =

```
Case (
Job Accepted = "Y";GetRepetition ( FMGlass::gColours; 1);
 Job Accepted = "N";GetRepetition ( FMGlass::gColours; 2);
GetRepetition ( FMGlass::gColours; 3)


)
```

Figure 15.23: The Job Accepted colour calculation field formula.

A second new calculation field for the JobSheet table is called Final Payment Received Date. This uses the Max function to derive the latest date from the Amount Paid Date repeating field in the Invoice table.

2. Create the **Final Payment Received Date** field with the formula displayed in Figure 15.24. The calculation result type is set to be **Date**.

Final Payment Received Date =

```
Max ( JobSheet_Invoice::Amount Paid Date )
```

Figure 15.24: The Final Payment Received Date calculation field formula.

4.3: An Additional Field for the Invoice Table

A single calculation field can be added to the Invoice table that is designed to display a different background color for a field if an invoice still has an outstanding balance to be paid. The formula for the Invoice Paid Colour field also makes reference to the gColours repeating container field in the FMGlass table.

1. Create the **Invoice Paid Colour** field with the formula shown in Figure 15.25. To address any possible rounding errors, the Case function test is based on a **Balance to Pay** field value of less than a penny. A green color, based on the first repetition contents of the gColours field, is displayed if there is no balance outstanding. A red color, based on the second repetition contents of gColours, is displayed if there is still an amount to pay. The calculation result type is set to be **Container**.

```
Invoice Paid Colour =

 Case ( Balance to Pay < .01; GetRepetition ( FMGlass::gColours; 1) ; GetRepetition ( FMGlass::gColours; 2) )
```

Figure 15.25: The Invoice Paid Colour field calculation formula.

The invoice line repeating fields in the Invoice table can now be set to be lookups based on the Invoice_JobSheet relationship.

Step 5: Designing Data Entry and Report Layouts for the FMGlass File

As discussed in Chapter 7, it is a good idea to base any data entry and report layouts on anchor table occurrences, which are the table occurrences to the far left of the table occurrence groups in our relationships graph.

We are now at the stage with our FMGlass job sheet database project where we need to design layouts to assist us with capturing, managing, and reporting on our business data.

5.1: Creating a Wizard Layout to Capture Glass Company Information

Let's start by creating a new layout to capture business information about the glass firm that is going to use the solution by using the global text and container fields in the FMGlass table.

1. Open the **FMGlass** file if it is not already open and select the menu option **View>Layout Mode** to switch to Layout mode.

2. Choose the menu option **Layouts>New Layout/Report** to open the New Layout/Report dialog box. Choose to show records from **FMGlass**, type **Wizard** in the Layout Name box, and select **Blank layout**, as shown in Figure 15.26.

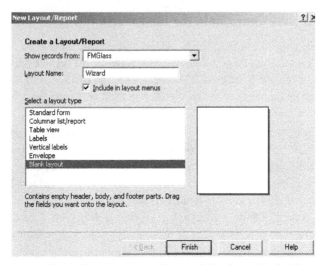

Figure 15.26: The New Layout/Report dialog box with the Show records from, Layout Name, and Select a layout type boxes.

3. Click the **Finish** button. The new blank layout can now be customized to our requirements. As the Wizard layout is not a report and will only be used to capture global field values for the glass company, the header and footer parts can be deleted. Click on the header and footer labels and press the **Backspace** or **Delete** key.

4. Give the body background a color by clicking on the body label and selecting a fill color from the Status area. Additionally, create a background tile effect by using the **Button** tool to draw a large rectangle, then drag the global fields onto this colored area using the **Field** tool. The finished Wizard layout is shown in Figure 15.27.

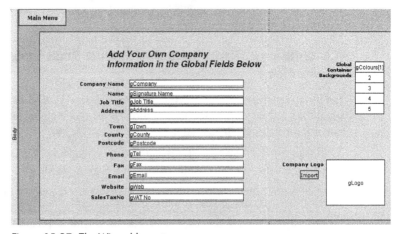

Figure 15.27: The Wizard layout.

5. Add a global container field for the company logo called **gLogo** to the Wizard layout.

6. It is important to highlight the container field in Layout mode and ensure that any graphic held in the container field is displayed correctly. In Layout mode, right-click on the **gLogo** container field and select the **Graphic Format** menu option. In the Graphic Format dialog box, choose **Reduce or Enlarge** image to fit frame and check the **Maintain original proportions** option, as shown in Figure 15.28.

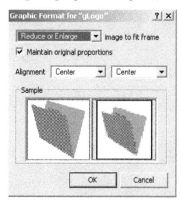

Figure 15.28: The Graphic Format dialog box for a container field.

7. To assist the user of the finished solution, add a small button labeled **Import** next to the gLogo container field. This button can be set to perform a script that will select the gLogo global container field and open the Insert Picture dialog box.

8. Create the **Insert Logo** script as shown in Figure 15.29.

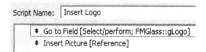

Figure 15.29: The Insert Logo script.

A script that includes the Go to Field command has been used in preference to simply programming the button to perform the menu command Insert Picture. This is because an inexperienced user may have forgotten to initially select the gLogo field as the destination field for the image.

9. Add a button labeled **Main Menu** to return the user to the FMGlass main menu, or welcome layout, to the upper-left corner of the Wizard layout. We can later define this button to switch the user back to the main solution layout. You can see this button in Figure 15.27.

The Wizard layout with example information and a logo for an imaginary glass company is shown in Figure 15.30.

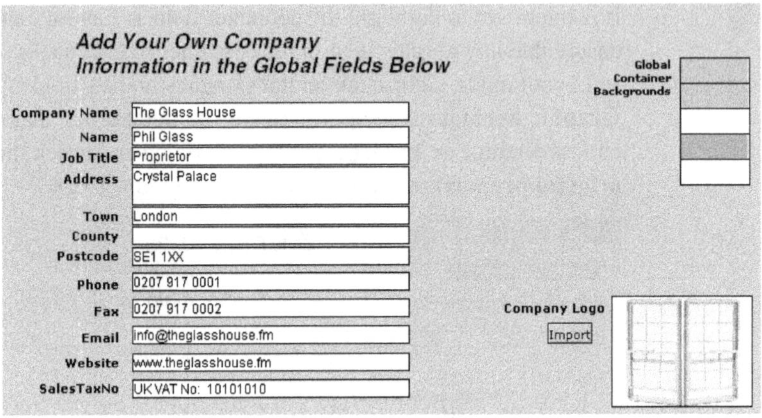

Figure 15.30: The Wizard layout with information added to the global fields.

5.2: The FMGlass Main Menu Layout

As with any FileMaker solution, a welcome screen or main menu layout is a useful starting point for the users of the software. The user can decide which information to work with from this screen. By including a button to return to the main menu from any of the other layouts, the user can always return to this screen.

1. Create a new blank layout based on the FMGlass table and, as with the Wizard layout, delete the header and footer. Highlight the body label and select a fill color from the Status area's **Fill Color** tool.

2. As shown in Figure 15.31, use the **Button** tool to create a background area, and insert the company name as a merge field by using the **Insert>Merge Field** menu option.

3. Add the **gLogo** container field to the layout, as well as a series of standard size buttons created using the **Edit>Duplicate** menu option. These buttons will shortly be defined to run scripts to open the various data entry screens.

   While most of the scripts needed for the file are discussed in Step 6 of this case study, two standard scripts that have been added to the file and form part of the functionality of the Main Menu layout are discussed here. The red Quit button is defined to run the Quit script, and the green About button runs a script that provides contact details for the publisher and author of the database. Both scripts make use of the Show Custom Dialog script step to create a conditional script, where the user decides which choice to select.

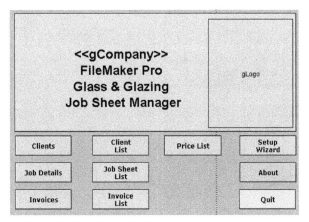

Figure 15.31: The FMGlass Main Menu screen.

4. Create the **Quit** script shown below in Figure 15.32, with the Show Custom Dialog script step highlighted.

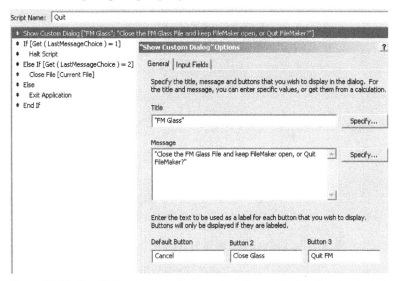

Figure 15.32: The Quit script is performed when the red Quit button is selected from the Main Menu screen.

5. Create the **About...** script, which is triggered by the green About button, as shown in Figure 15.33. The About... script is an example of how web addresses can be opened through a script step.

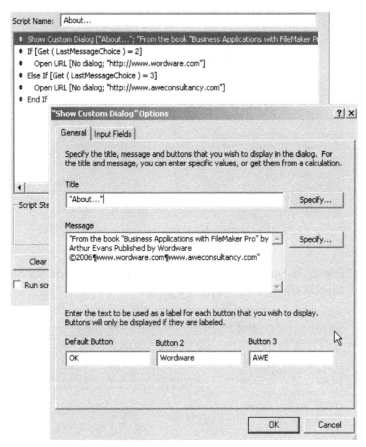

Figure 15.33: The About... script.

The remaining buttons in the Main Menu layout can be set up to open the various data entry screens once the layouts are ready.

5.3: The Client Details Layout

A Client Details layout is needed to display contact details on a client and additional information on directions and resources available on the job site. These include fields called Car Parking and Ladder, which are labeled "Car Parking?" and "Ladder on site?", respectively. "For Canterbury cathedral, the one on the van isn't big enough!" the stained glass craftsman who originally commissioned this solution once told the author. The Client Details layout is based on the Client table.

As with most of the solutions in this book, a series of standard navigation buttons is added to the Client Details layout. As these buttons are consistent through most of the solution layouts, users of the job sheet management software should rapidly become familiar with working through the data entry and report screens.

Two portals are used in the Client Details layout to display related record information on job sheets and invoices. The finished Client Details layout is shown in Figure 15.34.

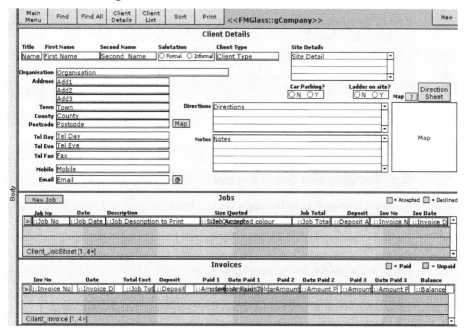

Figure 15.34: The Client Details layout.

The green button labeled New is defined to create a new client record.

Value lists are used to assist the user in selecting a title, the type of client, and closed response ("Y" or "N") questions on certain fields. FileMaker Pro 8's auto-complete field control is a useful feature to help complete the Town and County fields when clients are generally local to the firm.

Job sheet and invoice records cannot be created in the Client Details layout as the business flow is based on creating new job records and subsequent invoices via scripts.

The small buttons labeled with ">" on the left side of the Job No and Inv No portals will switch the user to the correct related record using the Go to Related Record button command once layouts are completed for these records.

5.4: The Client List Layout

The Client List layout is designed to make it easy for the user to view all clients and get a snapshot view of the number of related job records and the value of invoices generated. The Client List layout is based on the Client table. Navigation buttons to the left side of each record in the list and adjacent to the related record count fields will be used to assist navigation around the file. The Client List layout is shown in Figure 15.35.

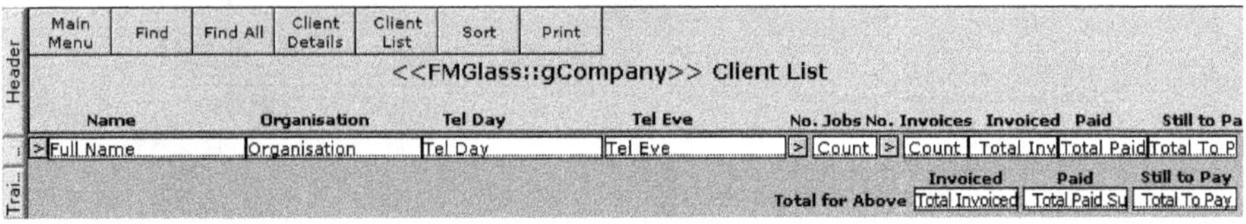

Figure 15.35: The Client List layout.

5.5: The Direction Sheet Layout

To assist the workers in finding a client's house or getting directions to a rural church, a Direction Sheet layout has been designed that can be printed and includes the Map container field. Merge fields are included in the layout for the client name and address. The layout is based on the Client table occurrence and is shown in Figure 15.36.

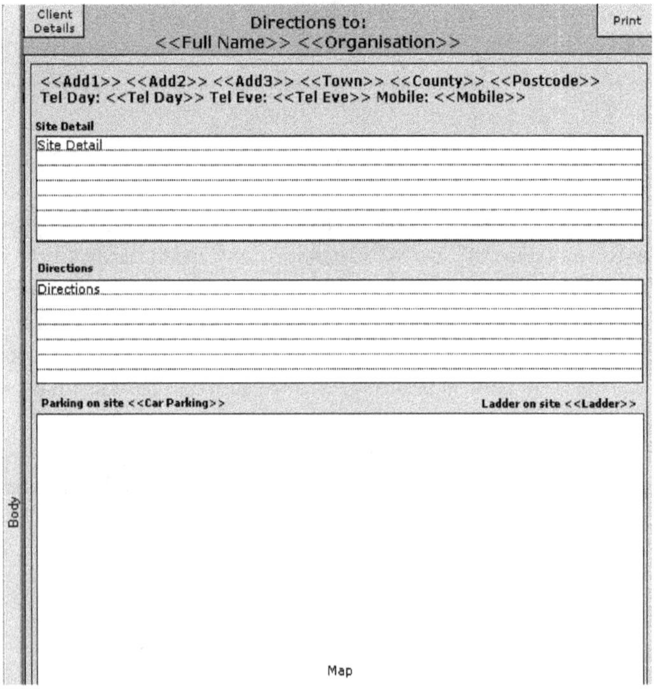

Figure 15.36: The Direction Sheet layout.

5.6: The Price List Layout

A glass job could range from replacing a stained glass panel in a church window to installing a fireproof glass window in a stove. Each product is categorized by a glass family type and has a price for material only and, not surprisingly, a higher price for material and installation.

Pricing information can be stored in a Price List layout, based on the PriceList table occurrence. The Price List layout is shown in Figure 15.37.

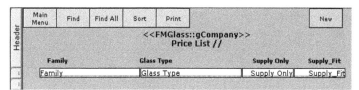

Figure 15.37: The Price List layout.

5.7: The Job Sheet Layout

Each record in the JobSheet table can be displayed in several ways, using different layouts that are all based on the JobSheet table occurrence. Details on the same job record can be displayed as a quote letter, a work sheet, a job sheet, or a deposit receipt.

The glass company doesn't want to change its existing paper filing procedure for archiving job details. A Job Sheet layout, labeled "Contract/Job Form," has therefore been designed that is closely based on the firm's existing paper form. The Job Sheet layout is shown in Figure 15.38.

5.8: The Job Work Sheet Layout

The glass company has a set method for determining the cost of a job. It has already been decided that no single job sheet will ever be greater than 12 charge lines. FileMaker's ability to create repeating fields will be used to create a 12-line table of charges in the Job Work Sheet layout. Radio buttons are used with value lists for the Job Accepted and Supply OR Fit fields.

The green button labeled Create Invoice is set to run a script designed to automate the task of turning a job into an invoice.

The Job Work Sheet layout is shown in Figure 15.39.

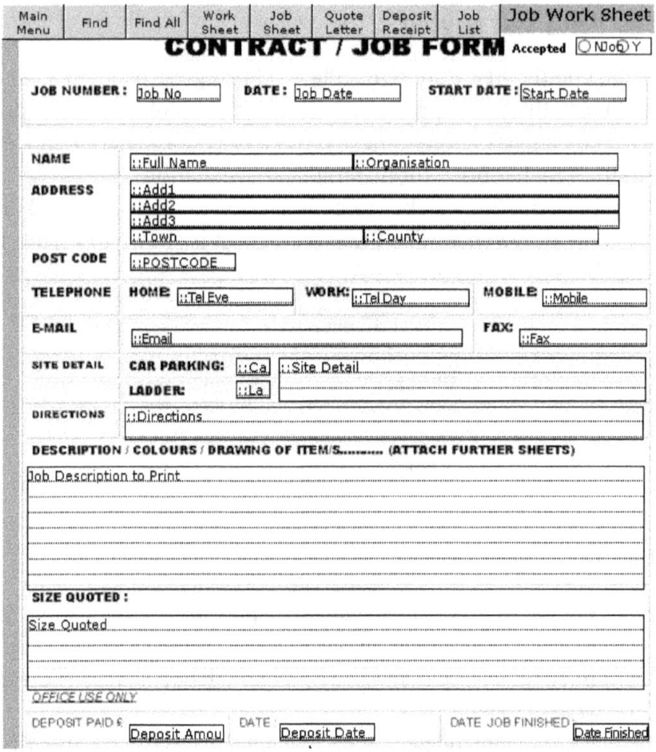

Figure 15.38: The Job Sheet layout.

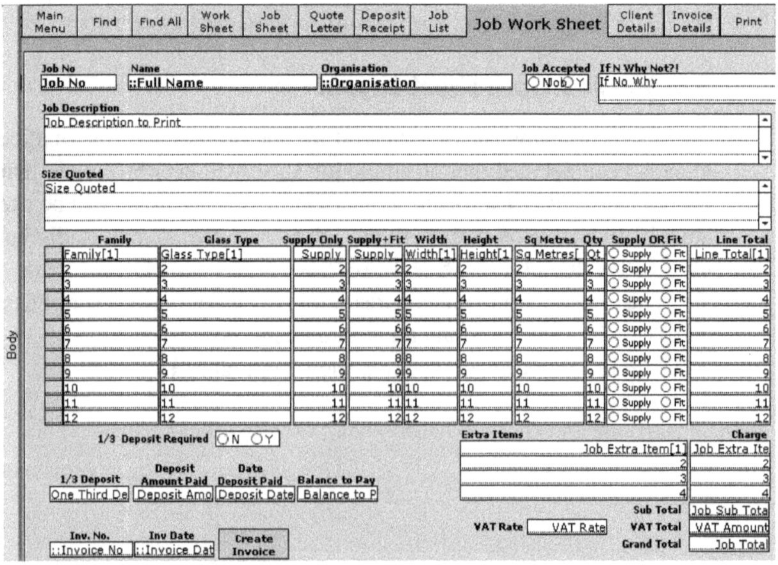

Figure 15.39: The Job Work Sheet layout.

The first repeating field in the table of charges is the FKey Item field. This field can be formatted to display a drop-down list value list for all records in the PriceList field. The field settings for the FKey Glass value list are shown in Figure 15.40. When a new FKey Item value is selected from the value list, any fields set to be lookup values from the Price List table, in the same repeating field row, will be populated with data.

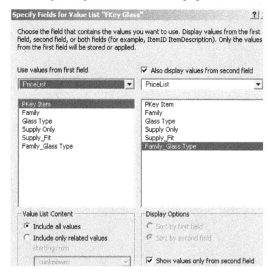

Figure 15.40: The field settings for the FKey Glass value list.

5.9: The Quote Letter Layout

The Quote Letter layout is based on the JobSheet table occurrence and is used to send the client details on the proposed job with prices and text fields to describe the job.

Merge fields are used to display the glass firm's details and the client's address. The 1/3 Deposit Required field is included in the layout as a non-printing object. If "Y" is selected for the deposit field, the calculation field called Quote Letter Paragraph 2 will display the required deposit amount. The Quote Letter layout is shown in Figure 15.41.

5.10: The Receipt Layout

If a job is accepted and a deposit has been requested, a receipt will need to be issued when the deposit is paid. The Receipt layout is based on the JobSheet table occurrence and is shown in Figure 15.42. Merge fields are used extensively in the layout to place the address fields in a precise position for a window envelope and to avoid accidental selection and changes to a job field value.

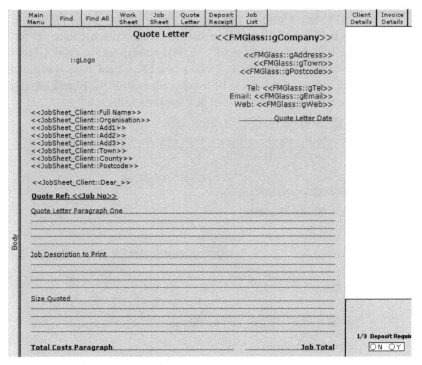

Figure 15.41: The Quote Letter layout.

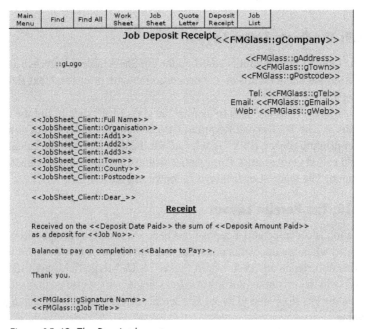

Figure 15.42: The Receipt layout.

5.11: The Job List Layout

The Job List layout is used to display a set of job records on screen. The Job Accepted colour field is used to create a background color across all the other fields in the layout body. The Field Behavior dialog box has been used to prevent the background field from being selected. The Job Total Sum field is included in a trailing grand summary layout part.

The Job List layout is shown in Figure 15.43.

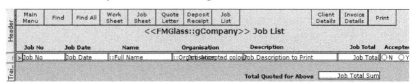

Figure 15.43: The Job List layout.

5.12: The Invoice Layout

The Invoice layout displays details about the glass firm, the client, and the job that is being invoiced. Unsurprisingly, it is based on the Invoice table.

The Invoice layout includes fields to record remittance details when a client pays for all or part of the job. Repeating fields are used for the Amount Paid and the Date Paid.

The invoice lines in the layout are repeating fields that are set to look up their contents based on a relationship between the Invoice and the JobSheet tables, using the FKey JobSheet field.

The Invoice layout is shown in Figure 15.44.

5.13: The Invoice List Layout

The Invoice List layout is used to display a set of invoice records. Summary fields for the Net, VAT, Gross, Paid, and Still to Pay fields are included in the trailing grand summary part of the layout.

The navigation buttons are the same as for the Invoice layout. The Invoice List layout is shown in Figure 15.45.

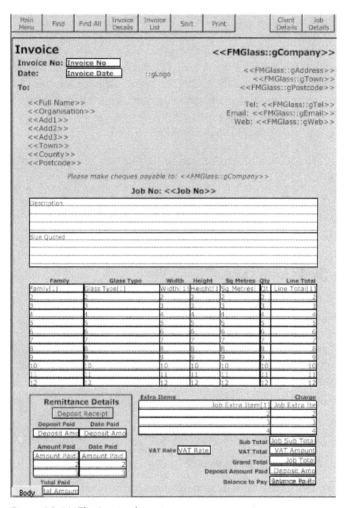

Figure 15.44: The Invoice layout.

	Invoice No.	Date	Client	Organisation	Job No	Net	VAT	Gross	Paid	Still to Pay
>	Invoice No	Invoice Dat	Full Name	Organisation	Job No	Job Sub Total	VAT Amount	Job Total	Total Amount	Balance to Pa
						Net	VAT	Gross	Paid	Still to Pay
					Total for Above	Job Sub Total	VAT Amount	Job Total Su	Total Amount	Balance to Pa

Figure 15.45: The Invoice List layout.

Step 6: Automating the FMGlass Solution with Scripts

A series of scripts would help to make the FMGlass database easy to use and automate the process for creating a new quote for a client and converting an accepted job sheet into a new invoice.

6.1: The Opening Script

As with any FileMaker solution, new user confidence is boosted if the same familiar screen appears every time the file is opened. We want the file to switch to the Main Menu layout and hide FileMaker's Status area when the database is launched.

We can write an Opening script to do this, as shown in Figure 15.46. As this script is relatively simple and does not, for instance, open a series of related files each time it is run, we can also use it as a way of returning to the main menu. The same script is therefore used each time the Main Menu button is clicked in any of the solution layouts.

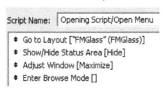

Script Name: Opening Script/Open Menu

* Go to Layout ["FMGlass" (FMGlass)]
* Show/Hide Status Area [Hide]
* Adjust Window [Maximize]
* Enter Browse Mode []

Figure 15.46: The Opening Script/Open Menu script.

To make the Opening script run every time the FMGlass database is opened, choose the menu option **File>File Options**. In the File Options dialog box, check the **Perform script** option and choose **Opening Script/Open Menu**, as shown in Figure 15.47.

File Options for "FMGlass"

Open/Close | Spelling | Text

When opening this file

☑ Log in using: ○ Guest Account

● Account Name and Password

Account: Admin

Password:

☑ Switch to layout: FMGlass

☑ Perform script: Opening Script/Open Menu

Figure 15.47: Customizing the file options for the database to run the opening script when the file is opened.

6.2: Navigation Scripts to Open Data Entry and List Layouts

Since the Status area is now hidden when the Main Menu layout is displayed, a series of scripts will be needed to show the Status area and switch to the correct data entry or list layouts. An example script, which is used to switch to the Client Details layout, is shown in Figure 15.48.

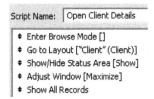

Script Name: Open Client Details

- ☀ Enter Browse Mode []
- ☀ Go to Layout ["Client" (Client)]
- ☀ Show/Hide Status Area [Show]
- ☀ Adjust Window [Maximize]
- ☀ Show All Records

Figure 15.48: The Open Client Details script.

6.3: The New Job From Client Script

While we could have changed the relationship between Client and Client_JobSheet to enable new job sheet records to be created via the portal in the Client Details layout, the glass company would like more control over when a new job record is created.

A script can be written to manage the creation of new related job sheet records for the selected client record.

The New Job From Client script is shown in Figure 15.49.

The database user is first presented with a custom dialog box with a message asking if they wish to go ahead and create a new job sheet for the named client. If the user goes ahead with the script, the global field gPKey Client is used to store the current client's PKey field value. The script switches to the WorkSheet layout, which is based on the JobSheet table occurrence, creates a new record, and sets the FKey Client field in the JobSheet table to be the

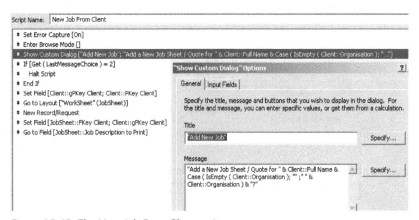

Figure 15.49: The New Job From Client script.

same as the gPKey Client field, thereby creating a new related job sheet record for the client. The script finally switches away from the FKey Client field to avoid the possibility of the contents being deleted or modified.

6.4: The Create Invoice from JobSheet Script

If a job estimate is approved by a client, the work will go ahead. Then the contents of the job costing table, displayed in the WorkSheet layout, will need to be transferred to a new invoice record.

The automated task of creating a new invoice for a job can be managed with a script. The Create Invoice from JobSheet script is displayed in Figure 15.50.

The script begins by checking that an invoice has not already been generated for the current JobSheet, using the Count function for any related records in the Invoice table. If no invoice exists, the database user is presented with a dialog box and asked to confirm the creation of a new invoice for the current job record. If the user goes ahead, the global field gPKey JobSheet is used to store the PKey JobSheet record contents for the current record. The Job Accepted field is set to "Y". A new invoice record is created and the FKey JobSheet field in the Invoice table is set to be the same as the global gPKey JobSheet field in the JobSheet table.

```
Script Name:  Create Invoice from JobSheet

  ✷  Set Error Capture [On]
  ✷  Enter Browse Mode []
  ✷  If [Count ( JobSheet_Invoice::FKey Job Sheet ) > 0]
  ✷     Show Custom Dialog ["Job Invoiced"; "ERROR: This Job has already been invoiced..."]
  ✷     Halt Script
  ✷  End If
  ✷  Show Custom Dialog ["Invoice Job"; "Create a NEW INVOICE for this Job?"]
  ✷  If [Get ( LastMessageChoice ) = 1]
  ✷     Halt Script
  ✷  End If
  ✷  Set Field [JobSheet::gPKey JobSheet; JobSheet::PKey JobSheet]
  ✷  Set Field [JobSheet::Job Accepted; "Y"]
  ✷  Go to Layout ["Invoice" (Invoice)]
  ✷  New Record/Request
  ✷  Set Field [Invoice::FKey Job Sheet; JobSheet::gPKey JobSheet]
```

Figure 15.50: The Create Invoice from JobSheet script.

Taking the Solution Further

Any effective FileMaker database solution should be able to evolve and keep up with the business data management requirements of the firm.

The database could easily be extended to include tables for material suppliers, supplier purchase orders, delivery notes, and stock control. The stock control solution introduced in Chapter 16 could be incorporated into the JobSheet file.

You might like to have a go at writing a script that can revise the price list figures by an annual percentage increase.

The glass company might also want to incorporate photos of site work or historic stained glass plans and sketches within container fields in the JobSheet file.

Chapter 16

Stock Control

Introduction

Accurate recording of stock levels is a critical commercial concern and a legal accounting requirement for most manufacturing businesses. Stock on hand is an important part of a company's balance sheet. Although many production and accounting software packages include modules to manage stock control, often such applications cannot be tailored or customized to the specific sales order and manufacturing procedure of an organization. This can be frustrating to a business owner who may be forced to change the method by which work orders are recorded and fulfilled solely to match the method by which the software manages stock.

FileMaker is ideal for creating a dynamic stock management system, provided that the way in which orders are tracked (the business information flow) is accurately replicated in the design of the database software (the data flow).

To increase the level of stock on hand, a business can either buy more of a stock item with a purchase order issued to a supplier, or it can manufacture the stock item, using component parts to make the assembled product. Stock levels are reduced when an item is included in a sales order. Accurate knowledge of the level of a stock item is critical to knowing when to place a new order with a supplier and whether a new sales order can be filled with the amount of stock on hand.

As an introduction to stock management with FileMaker, this case study does not include subassembly items or part components to calculate stock levels. A stock item is a single unit, with its level increased by purchase orders and deliveries. The stock level is decreased by sales orders and shipments.

As with the other case studies in this book, a copy of the completed FileMaker Pro 8 database file, **StockMgt**, is available to download from the publisher's website at www.wordware.com/files/fmapps and the author's website at www.aweconsultancy.com. You may find it easier to examine some of the FileMaker features and techniques discussed in this chapter in a copy of the completed file.

The default database password for the Admin account is **STOCKCONTROL** (all capitals). The database file options have been pre-set to open with the active Guest account (with read-only access to the file). To open the file with full access privileges, hold down the Shift key (Windows) or Option key (Mac OS) while the file is opening. Type the word **Admin** in the Account Name box and type the password in the box below. You can change the default password at a later stage. More information on database security issues, passwords, accounts, and privileges is given in Chapter 24.

We can translate this method of managing dynamic stock levels with a series of tables for our FileMaker solution.

The Stock Management Entity Relationship Diagram

A business owner wishes to report on the levels of stock items. Items are held in a **Stock** table. Stock items originate from suppliers and new stock items are requested in a **Purchase Order**. A purchase order can consist of more than one **Purchase Order Item**. Each purchase order item record is allocated to a specific stock item. In an ideal world the quantity requested in every purchase order will be delivered to the business. There are often discrepancies between what is requested and what is delivered. A **Delivery In** table will be used to record deliveries received. Each line in a delivery will be recorded in a **Delivery In Item** table.

The business makes money by getting a **Sales Order**. A sales order can consist of more than one **Sales Order Item**. Each sales order item record is allocated to a particular stock item. As with purchase orders, in the real world not all sales orders are filled in the same shipment. A **Despatch Out** table is used to record shipments to a client. Each shipment note will consist of at least one **Despatch Out Item**.

The Stock Management ER diagram is shown in Figure 16.1.

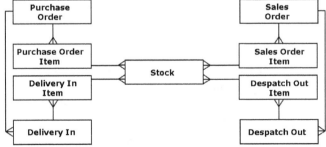

Figure 16.1: The Stock Management entity relationship diagram.

Building the Stock Management File

Step 1: Adding Tables to the Stock Management File

1. Launch FileMaker and create a new file called **StockMgt**.

    FileMaker will automatically open the Define Database dialog box with
    the Fields tab selected for the default StockMgt table, as shown in Figure
    16.2.

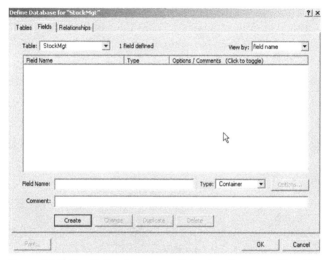

Figure 16.2: The Define Database dialog box for a new file with
the Fields tab selected for the default table.

2. Click the **Tables** tab at the top of the Define Database dialog box, and
    add the additional nine tables to the StockMgt file shown in Figure 16.3.

StockMgt
StockItem
POrder
POrderItem
SOrder
SOrderItem
DeliveryIn
DeliveryInItem
DespatchOut
DespatchOutItem

Figure 16.3: The tables
needed for the StockMgt file.

Step 2: Adding Initial Fields to the StockMgt File Tables

As with the other case studies in this book, we need to add a primary key field to most of our tables using FileMaker's ability to automatically assign a unique serial number to each record in each table. In addition, we will need to add foreign key fields to any of the tables to which we need to establish a relationship.

1. To add fields to each of the tables within the file, choose the **File>Define>Database** menu option and the **Fields** tab of the Define Database dialog box. It is important to ensure that the correct table is selected prior to adding new fields. Each of the tables can be selected from the drop-down list near the top of the dialog box, as shown in Figure 16.4.

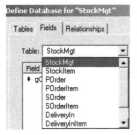

Figure 16.4: Selecting the relevant table for a new field in the Define Database dialog box.

2. Add the initial fields to each table as shown in Figures 16.5 to 16.16.

    Later, when we have established relationships between these tables using table occurrences in the relationships graph, we will add additional fields to the tables to improve the functionality of the file.

    Global fields in a FileMaker file can be used in any layout, regardless of whether the global field's table is related to a layout's underlying table. A global container field with 10 repetitions will be used to store a set of background colors. These colors will later be used to highlight critical stock levels in a Stock List layout.

3. The global container field called **gColours** can be added to the StockMgt table, as shown in Figure 16.5.

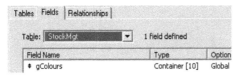

Figure 16.5: The global gColours field in the StockMgt table.

4. While the gColours field is highlighted, click the **Options** button to open the Options for Field dialog box. Click the **Storage** tab, click the **Use global storage** check box, then type **10** for the number of repetitions, as shown in Figure 16.6.

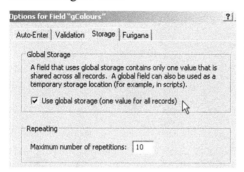

Figure 16.6: Setting the gColours field to be a global field with 10 repetitions.

We will be adding a set of background fill colors to the gColours field once we have created a Stock Menu layout.

5. In the **Fields** tab, select the **StockItem** table and add the fields to the table shown in Figure 16.7.

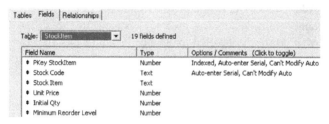

Figure 16.7: The initial fields for the StockItem table.

6. As with all the data tables in the StockMgt file and the other solutions in this book, the StockItem table contains a primary key field. This number field can be set to auto-enter a unique serial number that should not be changed or altered at a later stage. This can be easily defined using FileMaker's field options.

Highlight the **PKey StockItem** field and click the **Options** button. In the Options for Field dialog box, choose the **Auto-Enter** tab and click the **Serial number** check box. The Generate option should be set to **On creation**, and the "next value" and "increment by" settings should be set to **1**. Click the **Prohibit modification of value during data entry** check box, as shown in Figure 16.8.

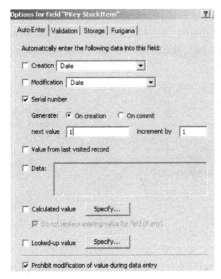

*Figure 16.8:
Setting up a
unique serial
number for the
PKey StockItem
field in the
StockItem table.*

7. The same settings should be applied to the primary key fields in all the data tables in the database.

8. Add the fields shown in Figure 16.9 to the **POrder** table, which will hold details on purchase orders. The calculation field **POrder No_Supplier_Date** will be used for a value list in the Delivery Details layout to ensure that the correct purchase order is referenced for any new supplier delivery.

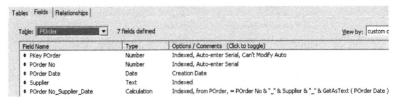

Figure 16.9: The initial fields for the POrder table.

9. The **POrderItem** table is used to record line items in purchase orders. Add the fields shown in Figure 16.10 to the POrderItem table. Once a relationship is established with the StockItem table, the **Unit Price** field can be set to look up a stock item's price.

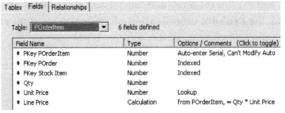

*Figure 16.10:
The fields for the
POrderItem table.*

10. The **SOrder** table is designed to hold details on sales orders. The initial fields for the SOrder table can be seen in Figure 16.11.

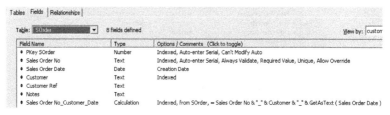

Figure 16.11: The initial fields for the SOrder table.

11. The fields for the **SOrderItem** table are shown in Figure 16.12. The SOrderItem table will hold records on order items. The **Unit Price** field can be set to look up a stock item's price once we have established a relationship between SOrderItem and StockItem.

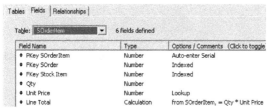

Figure 16.12: The fields for the SOrderItem table.

12. The **DeliveryIn** table is used to record shipments received by the company. The fields for the DeliveryIn table are shown in Figure 16.13.

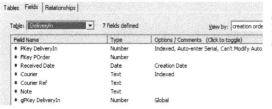

Figure 16.13: The fields for the DeliveryIn table.

13. The **DeliveryInItem** table will be related to the DeliveryIn table and represents individual delivery line items. The fields for the DeliveryInItem table are displayed in Figure 16.14.

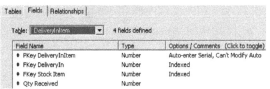

Figure 16.14:
The fields for the
DeliveryInItem
table.

14. The **DespatchOut** table will be used to store records on shipments to clients from the business. The DespatchOut field list can be seen in Figure 16.15.

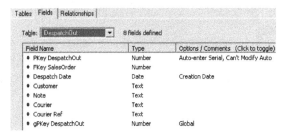

Figure 16.15:
The fields for the
DespatchOut table.

15. Each line item for a dispatch will be held in the **DespatchOutItem** table, the fields for which are shown in Figure 16.16.

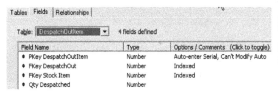

Figure 16.16:
The fields for the
DespatchOutItem
table.

The primary and foreign keys in each of these tables can now be used to create a series of table occurrence groups for the StockMgt file using the relationships graph.

Step 3: Adding Relationships within the StockMgt File

The business manager will want to get a snapshot view of quantities on hand, on order, and allocated for sales for each stock item. The file needs to record details on new purchase orders, deliveries received, new sales orders, and shipment information.

These features can be achieved by first designing a series of table occurrence groups, or TOGs, using the relationships graph. After setting up relationships between the table occurrences, we can design a set of layouts to manage stock movements.

1. If the Define Database dialog box is not open, select the menu option
    File>Define>Database and click the **Relationships** tab at the top of the
    dialog box. The 10 base tables that we have created for the stock man-
    agement file will be visible as table occurrences, as shown in Figure
    16.17.

*Figure 16.17: The initial relationships graph for the StockMgt file showing the 10
base tables.*

As with the other case study FileMaker solutions, we do not link the underlying base tables directly in the relationships graph. Instead, relationships are
built up between table occurrences, which are representations of the base
tables in the relationships graph. It is possible to have any number of table
occurrences on the relationships graph for the same underlying base table.

As introduced in Chapter 7, our aim is to refine the relationships graph
into a series of discrete TOGs. Each TOG should have a main or "anchor"
table occurrence on its left-hand side, with any number of linked "buoy"
tables related to the anchor table spread out on the right-hand side. To ease
relationship design at the outset and to assist you or any colleagues who may
work on the file at a later stage, a number of fundamental rules should be followed when using relationships in any FileMaker solution:

- As a general rule, any relationships graph will have one anchor table
  occurrence for every base table in the file.

- All data entry layouts should only be based on an underlying anchor
  table occurrence.

- Any portals on layouts should be based on buoy table occurrences.

- To assist with documenting a complex FileMaker project, it is a good
  idea to limit the dimensions of any TOGs in the relationships graph to a
  single page in width but any number of pages in length.

To get the required functionality from our stock management solution, we
now need to add some TOGs to the relationships graph.

2. For the sake of reference, it is a good idea to preserve at least one table occurrence for each base table within the file displayed at the top of the relationships graph. To reduce the space used, the button on the table header can be clicked on to toggle the display of the table and collapse it to its title only, as shown in Figure 16.18.

3. Note that an underscore (_) has been added to some of the base table occurrences so that the original table name can be used as an anchor table occurrence. Each table occurrence must have a unique name in the graph. A table occurrence can be renamed by double-clicking on it to open the Specify Table dialog box, or by highlighting the table occurrence and clicking the **Edit** button at the bottom of the graph (the button with a yellow pencil icon).

Figure 16.18: The reference base tables collapsed to display only the table titles.

3.1: The StockItem TOG

The business owner wants to see the current stock quantity for an item and the total number of items ordered, delivered, awaiting delivery, sold, dispatched, and awaiting dispatch. In order to calculate and present these figures, the StockItem TOG needs to relate the StockItem table occurrence to SOrderItem, POrderItem, DeliveryInItem, and DespatchOutItem. If the user wants to query any of these subquantities and view them in detail, a further set of relationships must be included to link to the SOrder, POrder, DeliveryIn, and DespatchOut table occurrences.

The StockItem TOG is shown in Figure 16.19.

Figure 16.19: The StockItem TOG.

3.2: The POrder TOG

Purchase order records, which are held in the POrder table, will consist of one or more line items from the POrderItem table. To display details on a stock item correctly in a printed purchase order, a further relationship will be needed from the POrderItem to the StockItem table occurrence.

The business owner wishes to add new purchase order line items using a portal in the Purchase Order layout. We therefore need to modify the relationship between the POrder and POrder_POrderItem table occurrences to allow creation of records with the relationship.

The POrder TOG is shown in Figure 16.20.

Figure 16.20: The POrder TOG.

3.3: The DeliveryIn TOG

DeliveryIn records will be related to one or more DeliveryInItem records. The paperwork for any DeliveryIn should reference a purchase order given to a supplier. Additional table occurrences are needed to provide more details on a stock item and to assist with automatic record creation if the user wants to auto-fill a new delivery with every item on the original purchase order. The DeliveryIn TOG is displayed in Figure 16.21.

The operator recording new deliveries will need the ability to add new line items to a delivery record, so the relationship between DeliveryIn and DeliveryIn_DeliveryInItem will need modifying to allow creation of records in the latter table.

Figure 16.21: The DeliveryIn TOG.

3.4: The SOrder TOG

In order for new sales orders to appear correctly in a layout based on the SOrder table, a relationship needs to be established from SOrder to the SOrderItem table and to the StockItem table to display the correct stock item details. The SOrder TOG is shown in Figure 16.22.

As with purchase orders, the business owner wishes to add new sales order line items using a portal in the Sales Order layout. We therefore need to modify the relationship between the SOrder and SOrder_SOrderItem table occurrences to allow creation of records with the relationship.

Figure 16.22: The SOrder TOG.

3.5: The DespatchOut TOG

When a sales order is fulfilled by the business, a new dispatch record needs to be created for the DespatchOut table. For a dispatch record to display and print correctly, a relationship must be established to the DespatchOutItem table and to the associated sales order in the SOrder table. The DespatchOut TOG is displayed in Figure 16.23.

The database operator will need the ability to add new line items to a dispatch record, so the relationship between DespatchOut and DespatchOut_DespatchOutItem will need modifying to allow creation of records in the latter table.

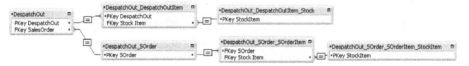

Figure 16.23: The DespatchOut TOG.

3.6: The SOrderItem TOG

A lookup is needed to establish the correct price for an item at the time that a sales order is created. A simple TOG that relates the SOrderItem table occurrence to the StockItem table occurrence is needed for the correct price to be added when new sales order lines are created.

The SOrderItem TOG can be seen in Figure 16.24.

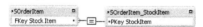

Figure 16.24: The SOrderItem TOG.

3.7: Stand-alone Table Occurrences in the StockMgt File

The completed StockMgt file will need layouts based on the line items for deliveries, purchase orders, and dispatches. Three stand-alone table occurrences for each of these line item tables need to be included in the StockMgt relationships graph and are shown in Figure 16.25.

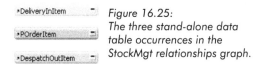

Figure 16.25:
The three stand-alone data
table occurrences in the
StockMgt relationships graph.

Step 4: Adding Calculation and Lookup Fields to the StockMgt File Tables

Now that a set of TOGs has been included in the StockMgt file, the use of calculation and lookup fields will be critical in making the database into a dynamic stock management system.

If the Define Database dialog box is not open, select the **File>Define> Database** menu option. Click the **Fields** tab to return to the fields list for each of the tables in the Stock Management database. The following fields need to be added to the existing file tables.

4.1: Additional Fields for the StockItem Table

Several calculation fields and one summary field, for total stock valuation, can be added to the StockItem table. These fields make use of the relationships in the StockItem TOG and are shown in Figure 16.26.

Field Name	Type	Options / Comments (Click to toggle)
Total Sales Order Qty	Calculation	Unstored, from StockItem, = Sum (StockItem_SOrderItem::Qty)
Total Purchase Order Qty	Calculation	Unstored, from StockItem, = Sum (StockItem_POrderItem::Qty)
Total DeliveryIn Qty	Calculation	Unstored, from StockItem, = Sum (StockItem_DeliveryInItem::Qty Received)
Total DespatchOut Qty	Calculation	Unstored, from StockItem, = Sum (StockItem_DespatchOutItem::Qty Despatched)
Current Stock on Hand Level	Calculation	Unstored, from StockItem, = Initial Qty + Total DeliveryIn Qty - Total DespatchOut Qty
Stock Awaiting Despatch	Calculation	Unstored, from StockItem, = Total Sales Order Qty - Total DespatchOut Qty
Stock Awaiting Delivery	Calculation	Unstored, from StockItem, = Total Purchase Order Qty - Total DeliveryIn Qty
Theoretical Stock Level	Calculation	Unstored, from StockItem, = Current Stock on Hand Level + Stock Awaiting Delivery
Reorder Flag	Calculation	Unstored, from StockItem, = Case (Theoretical Stock Level ≤ Minimum Reorder Level; "Reorder" ; "")
Theoretical Stock Level Value	Calculation	Unstored, from StockItem, = Theoretical Stock Level * Unit Price
Theoretical Stock Level Value Sum	Summary	= Total of Theoretical Stock Level Value
Stock Level Colour	Calculation	Unstored, from StockItem, = Case (Theoretical Stock Level ≤ Minimum Reorder Level and Theore...
Stock Code_Stock Item	Calculation	Indexed, from StockItem, = Stock Code & "_" & Stock Item

Figure 16.26: Additional fields for the StockItem table.

The calculation field called **Stock Level Colour** makes use of the global repeating container field from the StockMgt table, and changes the result of the calculation based on the theoretical stock level for a record.

The formula for the Stock Level Colour field is shown in Figure 16.27. If the theoretical stock level for an item is less than the preset minimum reorder level but there is still some of the item in stock, the field will display the fourth repetition of the gColours repeating field. If the theoretical stock level indicates that the item is out of stock, then the field will display the third repetition of the gColours repeating field. If neither situation is the case for a stock item, the field will display the first repetition of the gColours field. For this field to display correctly, the calculation result must be set to **Container**.

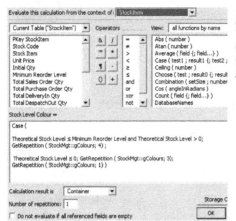

Figure 16.27:
The Stock Level
Colour calculation
field formula in the
StockItem table.

4.2: Additional Fields for the POrder Table

The POrder_POrderItem relationship can be used to create a new calculation field in the POrder table called **PO Total Price**. This field's formula uses the Sum function to add up the line price for any related POrderItem records. A summary field called **PO Total Price Sum** can also be added to the POrder table. These fields are shown in Figure 16.28.

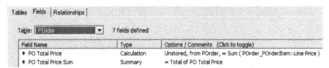

Figure 16.28: Additional fields for the POrder table.

4.3: An Additional Field for the SOrder Table

The value of related line items for a sales order record can now be calculated using the SOrder_SOrderItem relationship. Add the **Total Price** field as shown in Figure 16.29.

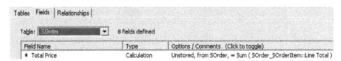

Figure 16.29: The Total Price field added to the SOrder table.

Step 5: Designing Data Entry and Report Layouts for the StockMgt File

A welcome screen or main menu layout would be a useful starting point in designing layouts for the stock management solution. From this screen that appears when the file is opened, the business manager will want the ability to open a stock list, or associated purchases, sales, delivery, or dispatch lists.

It is good practice to base all of the data entry and record list layouts on an anchor table occurrence, which is the table occurrence to the far left of all the TOGs in the relationships graph.

5.1: The Stock Management Welcome Menu

1. A default layout for the StockMgt file will already exist. Switch to **Layout** mode and select the **StockMgt** layout. We do not need a header or footer part in a menu layout, so these parts can be removed from the layout by highlighting the part label and pressing the **Backspace** or **Delete** key.

2. Give the body part a background color by using the **Fill Color** palette in the Status area.

3. Draw a set of buttons on the Welcome Menu, as shown in Figure 16.30, using the **Button** tool. These can be labeled to indicate which data list layout will be viewed when the button is clicked. A series of scripts will be written for each of these buttons shortly.

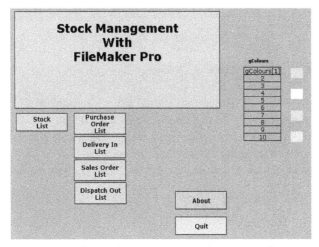

Figure 16.30: The Stock Management Welcome Menu layout.

While scripts will be described in detail later in this chapter, two scripts that are directly linked to the Stock Management Welcome Menu layout are described in this section.

4. The green About button is designed to provide more information on the solution and details about the author. The **About...** script, which is triggered by this button, is a good example of a conditional script. The Show Custom Dialog script step can display up to three buttons and, when combined with the LastMessageChoice function, the user's choice can be monitored by the script with a different outcome depending on which button is selected. In this case, the user can choose to open one of two websites. The About... script is shown in Figure 16.31.

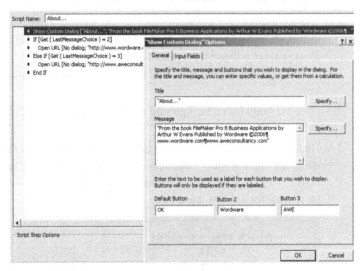

Figure 16.31: The About... script.

5. The red button labeled Quit is used to run a script with the same name. The **Quit** script also uses the Show Custom Dialog script step to create a conditional script. Depending on which button is selected, the user can choose to close the StockMgt file or quit FileMaker. The Quit script is shown along with the Show Custom Dialog Options dialog box in Figure 16.32.

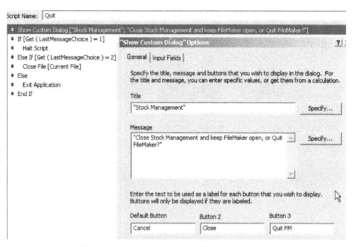

Figure 16.32: The Quit script is triggered by the button of the same name in the Welcome Menu layout.

6. The **gColours** field is included in the Welcome Menu layout. The field has been set to display all 10 repetitions using the **Field/Control>Setup** menu option. The gColours container field now needs to be populated with varying colors that will be used in the Stock Level Colour field. While still in **Layout** mode, draw a small rectangle on the layout and color it using the **Fill Color** palette. The rectangle can be duplicated by pressing **Ctrl+D** or by using the **Edit>Duplicate** menu option. Give each copy of the rectangle a new color. The final rectangle in Figure 16.33 has been given a striped pattern, which will be used to show stock items whose present quantity is below the reorder level.

7. Copy each of these colored rectangles to the clipboard in turn, switch to **Browse** mode, and paste the rectangle into the next repetition of the gColours field.

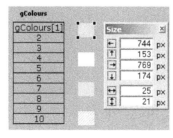

Figure 16.33: Drawing a series of rectangles to populate the gColours global container field in the StockMgt table.

8. Once the gColours repeating field has been populated, it can be removed from the Welcome Menu layout.

5.2: The Stock List Layout

All of the information on stock movements needs to be compiled and displayed in the Stock List layout.

Every stock item should be displayed with its initial stock quantity, and the total quantity allocated to sales, purchases, delivery in, and dispatch out. The stock on hand level multiplied by the unit price will display the stock value. The total value for all stock can be displayed in a trailing grand summary part on the Stock List layout.

1. A background field called Stock Level Colour has been sent to the back of the layout by using the **Arrange>Send to Back** menu option. The Field Behavior dialog box has been used to prevent users from selecting the Stock Level Colour field in Browse or Find mode. While the **Stock Level Colour** field is highlighted, choose the **Format>Graphic** menu option. Select the **Reduce or Enlarge** image to fit frame option, as shown in Figure 16.34. This will make the contents of a container field expand or shrink to the size of the field on a layout.

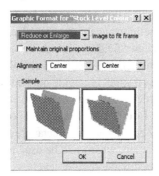

Figure 16.34:
The Graphic
Format dialog
box set to Reduce
or Enlarge, which
will make the
contents of a
container field
expand to the
field's object size.

2. As can be seen in Figure 16.35, a small gray button labeled with "<" next to each stock quantity switches the user to any related stock records in each of the four movement tables. These buttons make use of the Go to Related Record button command.

Based on the order in which the gColours repeating field was populated, a color key has been drawn in the header of the Stock List layout to indicate what the background color means, based on an item's current stock level.

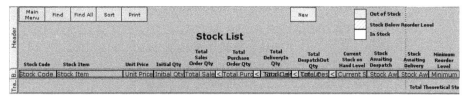

Figure 16.35: The Stock List layout (left side).

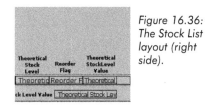

Figure 16.36: The Stock List layout (right side).

The background color changes can be tested with sample data, as shown in Figure 16.37.

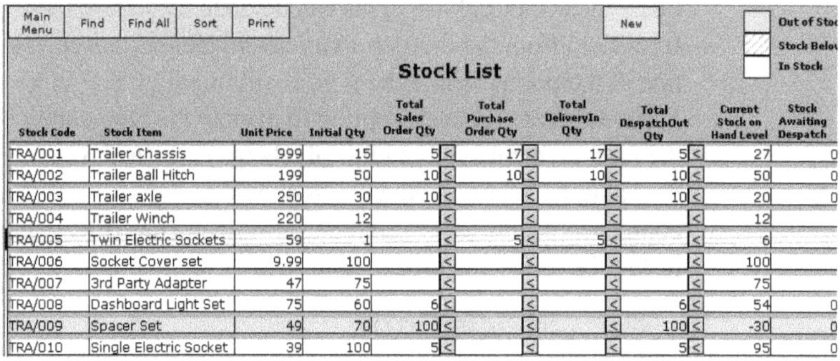

Stock Code	Stock Item	Unit Price	Initial Qty	Total Sales Order Qty		Total Purchase Order Qty		Total DeliveryIn Qty		Total DespatchOut Qty		Current Stock on Hand Level	Stock Awaiting Despatch
TRA/001	Trailer Chassis	999	15	5	<	17	<	17	<	5	<	27	0
TRA/002	Trailer Ball Hitch	199	50	10	<	10	<	10	<	10	<	50	0
TRA/003	Trailer axle	250	30	10	<		<		<	10	<	20	0
TRA/004	Trailer Winch	220	12		<		<		<		<	12	
TRA/005	Twin Electric Sockets	59	1		<	5	<	5	<		<	6	
TRA/006	Socket Cover set	9.99	100		<		<		<		<	100	
TRA/007	3rd Party Adapter	47	75		<		<		<		<	75	
TRA/008	Dashboard Light Set	75	60	6	<		<		<	6	<	54	0
TRA/009	Spacer Set	49	70	100	<		<		<	100	<	-30	0
TRA/010	Single Electric Socket	39	100	5	<		<		<	5	<	95	0

Figure 16.37: Sample data in the Stock List layout.

5.3: The Purchase Order Details Layout

The Purchase Order Details layout is based on the underlying POrder table occurrence.

1. A portal is needed in the layout to show related purchase order lines using the POrder_POrderItem table occurrence. Purchase orders are the starting point for increasing stock quantity. The relevant stock item must be selected as a new line item in the Purchase Order portal with the appropriate quantity for each item indicated.

The Purchase Order Details layout is shown in Figure 16.38.

Main Menu	Find	Find All	POrder Details	POrder List	Sort	Print		New

Purchase Order Details

POrder No `POrder No`   POrder Date `POrder Dat`

Supplier `Supplier`   PO Total Price `PO Total Pri`

Stock Code	Stock Item	Qty	Unit Price	Line Price
►	::Stock Code	::Stock Item	::Qty	::Unit Price	::Line Price

POrder_POrderItem [1..21+]

Figure 16.38: The Purchase Order Details layout.

As with the other solutions in this book, we want to save the database user the trouble of having to remember primary key values for records. We need to create a value list of stock items that can be selected every time a new portal record is added.

2. To avoid the confusion of displaying a meaningless foreign key field and the risk of a value being accidentally modified, we want to "hide" the FKey in each portal row. This can be done by adding the **FKey Stock Item** field from the POrder_POrderItem table occurrence into the first line of the portal. While the field is still highlighted, select the **View>Object Size** menu option to display the Size dialog box. Click on the measurement symbol until **pixels** (px) are displayed, and then type the value **1** into the width box, as shown in Figure 16.39. Use the keyboard arrow keys to position the "almost-hidden" FKey Stock Item field just to the left of the Stock Code field.

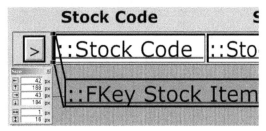

Figure 16.39: Setting the FKey Stock Item field to be one pixel wide (the field is drawn out in dark gray to highlight its position to the left of the Stock Code field).

3. While the FKey Stock Item field is still selected, choose the menu option **Format>Field/Control>Setup**. Create a new value list called **Stock Code_Item** using values from fields in the StockItem table. Use the fields as shown in Figure 16.40, and click the **Show values only from second field** check box.

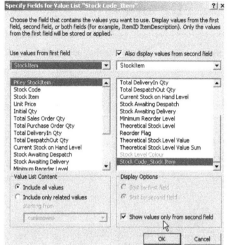

Figure 16.40:
"Hiding" the PKey
StockItem field
from the Stock
Code_Item value
list.

4. The **Stock Code** field in the portal can be defined as a button to run a script that selects the "hidden" FKey Stock Item field. The Go to Field script step will override field behavior settings that prevent a field from being selected.

    The result of this work is a drop-down list of recognizable stock items that appear every time the Stock Code field is clicked on in each portal row of the Purchase Order Details layout, as demonstrated in Figure 16.41. The user need not know that the FKey Stock Item field is being selected or that the value list is not defined for the Stock Code field.

Stock Code	Stock Item
TRA/001	Trailer Chassis
TRA/001_Trailer Chassis	
TRA/002_Trailer Ball Hitch	
TRA/003_Trailer axle	
TRA/004_Trailer Winch	
TRA/005_Twin Electric Sockets	
TRA/006_Socket Cover set	
TRA/007_3rd Party Adapter	
TRA/008_Dashboard Light Set	
TRA/009_Spacer Set	
TRA/010_Single Electric Socket	

Figure 16.41:
Triggering the
Stock Code Item
drop-down list
when the Stock
Code field is
clicked on in the
Purchase Order
Details layout.

The small gray button labeled with ">" to the left of each portal row uses the Go to Related Record button command to switch to the related stock item record.

5.4: The Purchase Order List Layout

1. Create the Purchase Order List layout that uses the header, body, and trailing grand summary parts to show basic information on each purchase order, with a summary of the total price displayed below a record set. The Purchase Order List layout is shown in Figure 16.42.

2. Copy the navigation buttons in the header from the Purchase Order Details layout.

   Along with the POrder Details button in the header, the gray ">" button to the left of the POrder No field will switch the user to the Purchase Order Details layout.

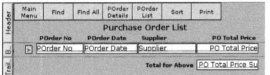

Figure 16.42:
The Purchase
Order List layout.

5.5: The Sales Order Details Layout

The quantity of a stock item is depleted if the item is selected as a line item in a new sales order. The Sales Order Details layout is very similar to the Purchase Order Details layout in that it includes a portal with a "hidden" value list for selecting stock items for each sales order item.

The Sales Order Details layout is displayed in Figure 16.43.

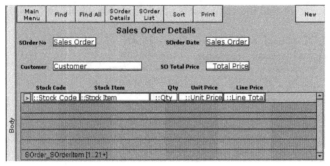

Figure 16.43:
The Sales Order
Details layout.

As with the Purchase Order List layout, the small gray button labeled with ">" to the left of each portal row uses the Go to Related Record button command to switch to the related stock item record.

5.6: The Sales Order List Layout

A list layout can be used to display basic information on several sales order records. The navigation buttons are copied from the Sales Order Details layout. An additional small gray ">" button in the body part can also switch to the Sales Order Details layout. The Sales Order List layout is shown in Figure 16.44.

*Figure 16.44:
The Sales Order
List layout.*

5.7: The Delivery In Details Layout

As any business owner knows, what is requested from a supplier is not always what turns up. The Delivery In Details layout is shown in Figure 16.45, and is used to record the quantity of stock items that are actually delivered as part of an original purchase order record.

1. In an ideal world, with great suppliers, all items requested in a purchase order will all arrive together on one delivery note. If that is the case, a script can be written that will automatically populate the DeliveryIn_DeliveryIn Item portal with the relevant stock item quantities, based on the POrder No typed into the delivery record. The button labeled Auto Fill will be set to run this script in due course.

    It is also possible to manually fill in the portal records with whatever items have been delivered this time. As in the real world, a purchase order record in the StockMgt file can have one or more related delivery records.

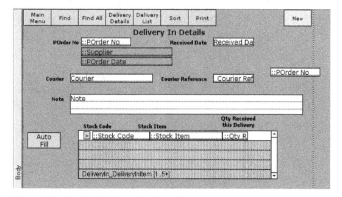

Figure 16.45: The Delivery In Details Layout.

2. The Delivery In Details layout, shown in Figure 16.45, includes an almost-hidden **FKey POrder** field adjacent to the POrder No field, the latter taken from the related DeliveryIn_POrder table occurrence. The same technique used to display stock codes in the Purchase Order Details and Sales Order Details layouts is applied to display a drop-down list of purchase orders in the FKey POrder field.

The "hidden" FKey POrder field is displayed and drawn in dark gray in Figure 16.46.

Figure 16.46: The FKey POrder field is shrunk to a width of one pixel using the Size dialog box.

5.8: The Delivery In List Layout

A Delivery In List layout, shown in Figure 16.47, is used to track several delivery records on screen.

The Delivery In List layout has the same navigation buttons as the Delivery In Details layout.

Main Menu	Find	Find All	Delivery Details	Delivery List	Sort	Print

Delivery In List

P.Order	Received Date	Courier	Courier Ref	Note
::POrder No	Received Date	Courier	Courier Ref	Note

Figure 16.47: The Delivery In List layout.

5.9: The Despatch Out Details Layout

When the business is ready to fill all or part of a sales order by sending goods out to a client, a new dispatch out record should be created using the Despatch Out Details layout.

1. The Despatch Out Details layout, shown in Figure 16.48, contains an almost-hidden **FKey SalesOrder** field adjacent to the Sales Order field, the latter taken from the related DespatchOut_SOrder table occurrence. The same technique used to display stock codes in the Purchase Order Details and Sales Order Details layouts is applied to display a drop-down list of sales orders in the "hidden" FKey SalesOrder field.

2. The FKey SalesOrder field is set to display a drop-down list of sales orders by using the Field/Control Setup dialog box.

3. The button labeled Auto Fill will, at a later stage, be set to run a script that automatically populates the Despatch Out portal with all items in the related sales order to save the operator from having to populate this list manually.

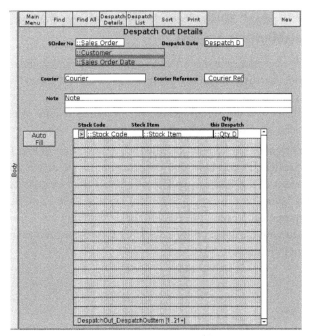

Figure 16.48: The Despatch Out Details layout.

5.10: The Despatch Out List Layout

A list layout can be created to display several dispatch records on screen, based on the underlying DespatchOut table occurrence. The navigation buttons in the header layout part are copied from the Despatch Out Details layout. To assist the user with record navigation, the small gray ">" button on the left side of the body part is set to switch to the Despatch Out Details layout.

The Despatch Out List layout is shown in Figure 16.49.

Figure 16.49: The Despatch Out List layout.

5.11: The "Hidden" SOrderItem, DeliveryInItem, POrderItem, and DespatchOutItem Layouts

As with other case studies in this book, FileMaker may require the use of a layout to isolate a subset of records when using the Go to Related Record script step as part of an automated task.

This is the case in the StockMgt solution with the line item records for purchase orders, sales orders, deliveries, and dispatch records.

1. Use the original four layouts that FileMaker created for SOrderItem, DeliveryInItem, POrderItem, and DespatchOutItem to create hidden layouts the user of the database never needs to see. Start by deleting all but the body layout part in each of these four layouts. Delete any fields that have automatically been inserted onto the layout body. Each layout can be labeled with the name of the underlying table for reference purposes, as shown in Figures 16.50 to 16.53.

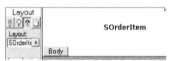

Figure 16.50: The SOrderItem layout.

Figure 16.51: The DeliveryInItem layout.

Figure 16.52: The POrderItem layout.

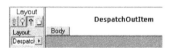

Figure 16.53: The DespatchOutItem layout.

2. Finally, for each of these layouts, open the Layout Setup dialog box using the **Layouts>Layout Setup** menu option and clear the "Include in layout menus" check box, as shown in Figure 16.54. This will prevent these layouts from being accidentally selected from the Layout menu in the Status area.

*Figure 16.54:
Removing the
DespatchOutItem
layout from the
layout menus.*

Step 6: Automating the StockMgt Solution with Scripts

There are three areas in the StockMgt file that would be ideal for automation using FileMaker's built-in ScriptMaker feature. These are the ability to make sure that the file always opens in the Welcome Menu layout, populating a new delivery record with all the items in a related purchase order, and automatically adding all sales order line items into the portal of a new dispatch note. Additionally, scripts can be used to go to the foreign key field in layouts where the field cannot normally be selected. Finally, a series of navigation scripts can be used to view the Status area and switch to the correct data entry or list layout.

6.1: The Opening Script

A simple script is required to switch to the Welcome Menu, maximize the window on screen, and hide the Status area. The Opening script is shown in Figure 16.55.

*Figure 16.55:
The Opening
script for the
StockMgt file.*

The menu option **File>File Options** should be selected and the **Perform Script** check box selected to run the Opening script.

6.2: The Auto Fill Delivery In From PO Script

To avoid the risk of error and save the database user the trouble of remembering to include all purchase order items in a new delivery in record, a script can be created that automatically populates a delivery's line items if the entire purchase order has been received in one delivery.

The Auto Fill Delivery In From PO script is shown in Figure 16.56. The script first checks whether or not the delivery in record has a valid related purchase order record. Then it checks whether the delivery in record already has line items in its portal. If this is the case, there is a risk that items could be double counted and the script is halted. The script then makes use of a Show Custom Dialog message to ask the user to confirm the wish to go ahead and if all PO line items are in this delivery. If the database user proceeds, the script sets the global field gPKey DeliveryIn to be equal to the current record's unique primary key field, PKey DeliveryIn.

The script then jumps to the related purchase order record and from there isolates any related purchase order items, switching to the "hidden" POrderItem layout. The script then moves to the "hidden" DeliveryInItem layout and imports the found set of purchase order line items. Finally, the contents of the FKey DeliveryIn field for the new set of DeliveryInItem records is set to be the same as the primary key field for the new delivery in record and the script switches back to the original layout where the script was run using the green Auto Fill button in the Delivery In layout.

Figure 16.56: The Auto Fill Delivery In From PO script.

6.3: The Auto Fill DespatchOut From SO Script

With a method very similar to the previous script, the business owner would like the database to provide the option of automatically populating a new dispatch out record with all the line items from a related sales order record.

The Auto Fill DespatchOut From SO script is displayed in Figure 16.57. The script first checks that a related sales order record does exist for the current dispatch out record. Then, if any line items already exist for the record, the script will notify the user that items are already allocated and the script will halt to avoid the risk of double counting stock items.

The database user will then be presented with a custom dialog box to confirm the wish to go ahead and include all the sales order line items in this dispatch record. The user can still cancel the script at this stage. Otherwise, the script will now set the global field gPKey DespatchOut to be equal to the primary key of this dispatch record. The script then jumps to the related sales order record and from there isolates all sales order line items in the "hidden" field SOrderItem. The script then switches to the "hidden" DespatchOutItem layout and imports the found set of sales order line items. Finally, the FKey DespatchOut field is set to the same value as the primary field of the new dispatch out record, and the script returns to the original layout where the script was run using the green Auto Fill button in the Despatch Out Details layout.

```
Script Name:    Auto Fill DespatchOut From SO

  ✷ Set Error Capture [On]
  ✷ If [Count (DespatchOut_SOrder::PKey SOrder) ≠ 1]
  ✷    Halt Script
  ✷ End If
  ✷ If [Count ( DespatchOut_DespatchOutItem::FKey DespatchOut ) > 0]
  ✷    Show Custom Dialog ["ERROR"; "ERROR: This DespatchOut Already has Items allocated..."]
  ✷    Halt Script
  ✷ End If
  ✷ Show Custom Dialog ["AUTO FILL"; "Can we assume all Sales Order Line Items are in this Despatch?"]
  ✷ If [Get ( LastMessageChoice ) = 1]
  ✷    Halt Script
  ✷ End If
  ✷ Set Field [DespatchOut::gPKey DespatchOut; DespatchOut::PKey DespatchOut]
  ✷ Go to Related Record [Show only related records; From table: "DespatchOut_SOrder"; Using layout: "SOrder" (SOrder)]
  ✷ Go to Related Record [Show only related records; From table: "SOrder_SOrderItem"; Using layout: "SOrderItem" (SOrderItem)]
  ✷ Go to Layout ["DespatchOutItem" (DespatchOutItem)]
  ✷ Import Records [No dialog; "StockMgt.fp7"; Add; Windows ANSI]
  ✷ Replace Field Contents [No dialog; DespatchOutItem::FKey DespatchOut; DespatchOut::gPKey DespatchOut]
  ✷ Go to Layout [original layout]
```

Figure 16.57: The Auto Fill DespatchOut From SO script.

6.4: The Navigation Scripts to Open the Data Layouts

Since the Opening script hides the Status area, a series of navigation scripts is needed to open the various data entry layouts and display the Status area, so that the number of records in each table or the current found count can be displayed correctly.

An example of one of the navigation scripts, to open the Stock List layout from the Welcome Menu, is shown in Figure 16.58.

```
Script Name:    Open Stock List

  ✷ Go to Layout ["Stock List" (StockItem)]
  ✷ Enter Browse Mode []
  ✷ Show All Records
  ✷ Sort Records [Restore; No dialog]
  ✷ Show/Hide Status Area [Show]
```

*Figure 16.58:
The Open Stock
List navigation
script.*

6.5: The Display Value List Scripts

To avoid accidental data deletion or overtyping errors, the foreign key field is "hidden" from the user in all the layouts of the StockMgt file. The menu option **Format>Field/Control>Behavior** has been used to prevent any of the FKey fields from being tabbed or clicked into in Browse or Find mode. Despite this, the script step Go to Field will override this field setting and select an FKey field in a layout. A series of scripts have been written that are triggered when the field adjacent to the FKey field is clicked. As an example, the Display Stock Code in PO script, which selects the FKey Stock Item field and makes the Stock Code_Item value list appear, is shown in Figure 16.59.

Script Name: Display Stock Code in PO

✦ Go to Field [POrder_POrderItem::FKey Stock Item]

Figure 16.59: The Display Stock Code in PO script is one of several value list scripts in the StockMgt file.

Taking the Solution Further

The basic stock management file built in this case study can be extended to provide further management information for a small business. The Purchase Order and Sales Order tables within the stock management database could be improved to provide accounting reports for sales and purchase ledgers.

The solution does not have a supplier table to improve the management of purchase orders or a client table to link to sales orders. Purchase order line items are only identified against items of stock, but could be linked to jobs or projects. This could enable the business owner to start calculating gross profit on orders and jobs.

Hopefully, the StockMgt database solution will provide you with some ideas on how your company's stock management requirements can be managed with FileMaker.

Chapter 17

Event Management

Introduction

Many businesses have, to some degree, a requirement for event management, while for others, event management is their business. The need to organize professional training events for staff members or perhaps an annual party for favored clients and suppliers is a common requirement for many businesses. A FileMaker database is capable of managing an event of any size. The almost limitless storage capabilities of a FileMaker Pro 8 file means that FileMaker is also perfectly capable of handling the requirements of a professional event management company or a conference center whose business model is the organization and management of many high-profile events throughout the year, involving thousands of invitees, delegates, courses, and invoices.

Event and training management is an excellent example of how FileMaker is able to tackle many-to-many relationships as part of a relational database structure. A large number of individuals may be invited to attend any number of courses or events over a period of time. A FileMaker database manages this information by creating a join table between individuals and courses. Of course, busy event organizers in the real world don't tend to get too concerned about join tables or what to call the entity that links people to courses; they merely think of individuals assigned to a course as delegates or booking records.

For those who have previously had to track invited individuals for an event, with provisional and confirmed bookings all on the same spreadsheet, FileMaker's ability to lay out event and delegate information in a series of easy-to-read layouts can make event management a whole lot easier.

The basic event management database example presented in this chapter can be enhanced further to include additional booking elements, seminars, or breakout sessions. These items are a level deeper than a simple booking record.

As with the other case studies in this book, a copy of the completed FileMaker Pro 8 database file, **Event Management**, is available to download from the publisher's website at www.wordware.com/files/fmapps and the author's website at www.aweconsultancy.com. You may find it easier to examine some of the FileMaker features and techniques discussed in this chapter in a copy of the completed file.

The default database password for the Admin account is **EVENTER** (all capitals).

The database file options have been preset to open with the active Guest account (with read-only access to the file). To open the file with full access privileges, hold down the Shift key (Windows) or Option key (Mac OS) while the file is opening. Type the word **Admin** in the Account Name box and type in the password in the box below. You can change the default password at a later stage. More information on database security issues, passwords, accounts, and privileges is given in Chapter 24.

The example Event Management template is based on the requirements of a fictitious educational event organization that wishes to target teachers and education professionals for specialized educational courses. The value lists and other example data can, of course, be modified and adapted for any event and subject area.

The Event Management Entity Relationship Diagram

A good way to think about how an event management database could be put together and what tables are required is to describe in basic terms how the business manager currently processes bookings for a new event.

While some events are unique, such as Bob's retirement bash or your parents' 25th wedding anniversary party, most commercial events and courses are repeated on a seasonal or annual basis. If your task is to organize the annual national equine veterinary conference, as an example, it is likely that last year's delegate list is the best starting point to target invitations for this year's event. A good event management database should let you keep a pool of target contacts who may be interested in attending future events that you are organizing. We can start with this **Target** group of individual contacts. The contact records can be queried based on areas of interest. Selected individuals can be **Invited** to attend an upcoming **Event** or course. If the individual responds to the invitation and confirms his or her attendance, a new **Registration** record is created. The individual may qualify for an "early bird," student, or other discounted **Registration Type** for the event. The Registration needs to be billed as a new **Invoice Line Item**, which forms all or part of an **Invoice** sent to the individual.

The Event Management ER diagram is shown in Figure 17.1. The circle and perpendicular line (|) symbols between the Invite and Registration tables in Figure 17.1 indicate that although not all invitees will proceed to registration and confirm they wish to attend an event, any submitted registration can be linked back to a targeted invite. Some events are happy to accept last-minute attendees who arrive, register, and perhaps pay for the event on the day it begins.

Event Management ER Diagram

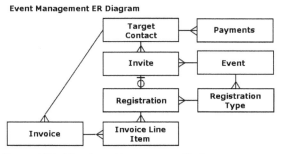

Figure 17.1: The Event Management ER diagram.

Building the Event Management File

Step 1: Adding Tables to the Event Management File

1. Launch FileMaker and create a new file called **Event Management**.

   FileMaker will automatically open the Define Database dialog box with the Fields tab selected for the default Event Management table, as shown in Figure 17.2.

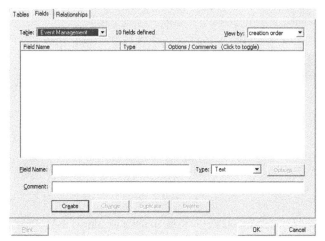

Figure 17.2: The Define Database dialog box for a new Event Management file with the Fields tab selected for the default table.

2. Click on the **Tables** tab at the top of the Define Database dialog box and add the additional eight tables listed in Figure 17.3.

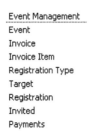

Event Management
Event
Invoice
Invoice Item
Registration Type
Target
Registration
Invited
Payments

Figure 17.3: The tables needed for the Event Management file.

Step 2: Adding Initial Fields to the Event Management File Tables

As with the other case studies in this book, we need to add a primary key field to each of our tables using FileMaker's ability to automatically assign a unique serial number to each record in each table. In addition, we will need to add foreign key fields to any of the tables to which we need to establish a relationship.

1. To add fields to each of the tables within the file, choose the **File>Define>Database** menu option and the **Fields** tab of the Define Database dialog box. It is important to ensure that the correct table is selected prior to adding new fields. Each of the tables can be selected from the drop-down list near the top of the dialog box, as shown in Figure 17.4.

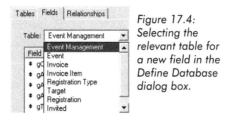

Figure 17.4: Selecting the relevant table for a new field in the Define Database dialog box.

We will add initial fields to each table as shown in Figures 17.5 to 17.15. Later, when we have established relationships between these tables using table occurrences in the relationships graph, we will add additional fields to the tables to improve the functionality of the file.

We will want to customize the solution business details for an event management company. We can do this by creating a series of global text fields in the Event Management table.

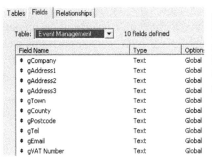

Figure 17.5:
The global fields used to customize the file for an event management company.

2. Add the text fields shown in Figure 17.5 to the **Event Management** table. For each text field, click the **Options** button to open the Options for Field dialog box. Click the **Storage** tab at the top of the dialog box and select the check box labeled **Use global storage**, as shown in Figure 17.6.

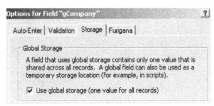

Figure 17.6:
Selecting the global storage option for a field.

Setting the global storage option means that the text fields that describe an event company can be displayed in any layout, for invoices or correspondence records, without the need to create a relationship from that layout's underlying base table to the table that holds the global fields.

In this solution, we will also make use of global number fields to temporarily store the contents of a record's primary key field when we create new related records in another table. As an example, a global number field will be used to store a target's primary key field value, which can then be placed as the target foreign key field value in a new related event invite record.

3. FileMaker can allocate a unique serial number for each record's primary key, or PKey, field, which is required for all the data tables in the solution. For example, in the **Event** table, after creating a new number field called **PKey Event**, click the **Options** button in the Define Fields dialog box. Select the **Auto-Enter** tab, click on the **Serial Number** check box,

and choose an initial value of **1** and an increment of **1**. Do the same for each of the tables' primary key field.

4. By careful use of value lists in conjunction with foreign key fields, there is no reason to display the primary key field in any of the layouts in our solution. This means that there is little chance of the unique serial number field value being modified, duplicated, or erased by a user accidentally clicking into the field in a layout. Despite this, it is good practice to also check the **Prohibit modification of value during data entry** option, shown in Figure 17.7.

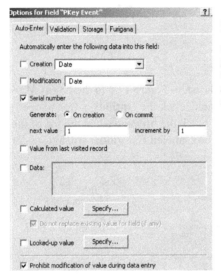

Figure 17.7:
The Auto-Enter options for all primary key (PKey) fields in the Event Management solution.

5. Create the initial fields required for the **Event** table as shown in Figure 17.8. The **Duration** calculation field is a simple subtraction of the Start Date from the End Date. As the result of this would be zero for a one-day event, 1 is added to the formula. As most events are one day in duration, the **End Date** field has been set to auto-enter the Start Date value. This can be overwritten if the event is longer.

The contents of the calculation field called **Event Title_Start Date** will be used to create a value list for the Target layout, on which upcoming events can be selected.

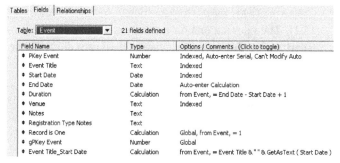

Figure 17.8: The initial fields for the Event table.

6. Create the initial fields for the **Invoice** table listed in Figure 17.9. While the **PKey Invoice No** field never needs to be seen and can start with an initial value of 1, the **Invoice No** field, which is also set to be a serial number, can be given any initial value for the first invoice record.

Tables Fields | Relationships |

Table: Invoice ▼   12 fields defined

Field Name	Type	Options / Comments (Click to toggle)
PKey Invoice No	Number	Auto-enter Serial, Can't Modify Auto
Invoice No	Number	Indexed, Auto-enter Serial, Always Validate, Unique
Invoice Date	Date	Creation Date
Fkey Registration	Number	Indexed
Fkey Target	Number	Indexed
gPKey Invoice No	Number	Global

Figure 17.9: The initial fields for the Invoice table.

7. The **Invoice Item** table will act as a line item for invoices and each record should represent a registration. The fields for the Invoice Item table are shown in Figure 17.10. Once relationships have been established in the file, the **Registration Net Fee Lookup** and **Qty** field lookups can be defined at a later stage.

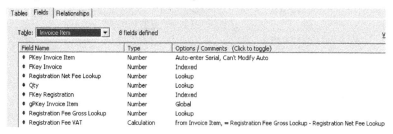

Figure 17.10: The fields for the Invoice Item table.

8. The **Registration Type** table will be used to hold records on the description and applicable fee for an event's set of registration types. These are the various categories by which an individual can register for an event.

Create the fields for the Registration Type table as shown in Figure 17.11. The sales tax or VAT rate may vary for certain events and the **Registration Fee Gross** calculation field uses the VAT rate to derive a total fee for each record.

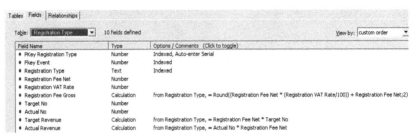

Figure 17.11 The fields for the Registration Type table.

9. The **Target** table will be used to hold information about individuals who will be invited to various events. To maximize the benefit of the target records, a fair amount of descriptive information can be held. In addition to contact details, which has similarities to a customer relationship management file, additional fields for specialized subject areas of interest are needed to identify specific groups and maximize the number of invites that turn into registrations. The initial fields for the Target table are shown in Figure 17.12.

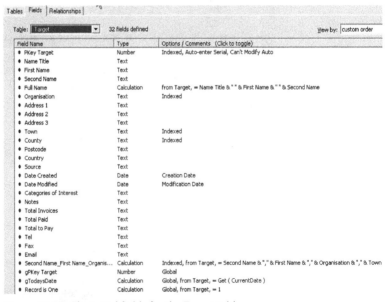

Figure 17.12: The initial fields for the Target table.

10. The **Registration** table will be used as a join table between the Target and Event tables. A registration record will also be related to one specific registration type record and, at a later stage, an invoice record. The initial fields for the Registration table are shown in Figure 17.13.

Tables Fields Relationships

Table: Registration 12 fields defined

Field Name	Type	Options / Comments (Click to toggle)
PKey Registration	Number	Indexed, Auto-enter Serial, Can't Modify Auto
Fkey Target	Number	Indexed
Fkey Event	Number	Indexed
FKey Registration Type	Number	
Qty	Number	Auto-enter Data
FKey Invoice	Number	Indexed
FKey Event_Fkey Invoice	Calculation	Indexed, from Registration, = Fkey Event & FKey Invoice
gPKey Registration	Number	Global

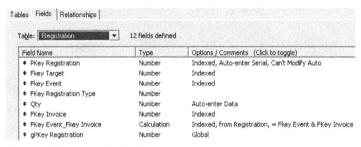

Figure 17.13: The initial fields for the Registration table.

11. The **Invited** table is another join table between the Target and Event tables. The fields for the Invited table are shown in Figure 17.14.

Tables Fields Relationships

Table: Invited 4 fields defined

Field Name	Type	Options / Comments (Click to toggle
PKey Invited	Number	Auto-enter Serial, Can't Modify Auto
FKey Event	Number	Indexed
FKey Target	Number	Indexed
Invite Date	Date	Creation Date

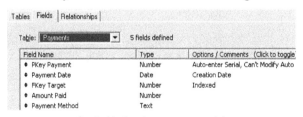

Figure 17.14: The fields for the Invited table.

12. The **Payments** table is used to log payments or remittance by individuals. The Payments table fields are shown in Figure 17.15.

Tables Fields Relationships

Table: Payments 5 fields defined

Field Name	Type	Options / Comments (Click to toggle
PKey Payment	Number	Auto-enter Serial, Can't Modify Auto
Payment Date	Date	Creation Date
FKey Target	Number	Indexed
Amount Paid	Number	
Payment Method	Text	

Figure 17.15: The fields for the Payments table.

We are now at the stage where we can create relationships between table occurrences representing each of these base tables. Additional calculation and lookup fields can then be added to these tables once the relationships have been established.

Step 3: Adding Relationships within the Event Management File

A series of relationships now needs to be designed between the tables in the Event Management database. This will enable related information to be displayed in data entry and list layouts and help to automate many of the procedures for creating new event bookings and invoices.

To assist the database designer with any future changes or revisions to the database, we will arrange the relationships between the various tables into a series of table occurrence groups, or TOGs. FileMaker's relationships graph needs to be opened to start creating relationships between table occurrences in the Event Management file.

1. If the Define Database dialog box is not open, select the menu option **File>Define>Database** and click the **Relationships** tab at the top of the dialog box. The nine base tables that we have created for the Event Management file will be visible as table occurrences, as shown in Figure 17.16.

Figure 17.16: The initial relationships graph for the Event Management file showing the nine base tables.

As with the other case study FileMaker solutions, we do not link the underlying base tables directly in the relationships graph. Instead, relationships are built up between table occurrences, which are representations of the base tables in the relationships graph. It is possible to have any number of table occurrences on the relationships graph for the same underlying base table.

As introduced in Chapter 7, our aim is to refine the relationships graph into a series of discrete TOGs. Each TOG should have a main or "anchor" table occurrence on its left-hand side, with any number of linked "buoy" tables related to the anchor table spread out on the right-hand side. To ease relationship design at the outset and to assist you or any colleagues who may work on the file at a later stage, a number of fundamental rules should be followed when using relationships in any FileMaker solution:

■   As a general rule, any relationships graph will have one anchor table occurrence for every base table in the file.

- All data entry layouts should only be based on an underlying anchor table occurrence.
- Any portals on layouts should be based on buoy table occurrences.
- To assist with documenting a complex FileMaker project, it is a good idea to limit the dimensions of any TOGs in the relationships graph to a single page in width but any number of pages in length.

To get the required functionality from our Event Management solution, we now need to add some TOGs to the relationships graph.

2. For the sake of reference, it is a good idea to preserve at least one table occurrence for each base table within the file displayed at the top of the relationships graph. To reduce the space used, click the button on the table header to toggle the display of the table and collapse it to its title only, as shown in Figure 17.17.

3. Note that an underscore (_) has been added to the base table occurrences so that the original table name can be used as an anchor table occurrence. Each table occurrence must have a unique name in the graph. A table occurrence can be renamed by double-clicking on it to open the Specify Table dialog box, or by highlighting the table occurrence and clicking the **Edit** button at the bottom of the graph (the button with a yellow pencil icon).

Figure 17.17: The reference base tables collapsed to display only the table titles.

3.1: The Event TOG

The business owner wants the event management system to be as flexible as possible in registering new delegates for an event. She wants to be able to create new registration records in a Target Contact Details layout and also in an Event Details layout. To avoid errors in registrations, the owner wants a warning message to appear before a new registration is added to an event. However, the owner is happy for new invitations and new registration types to be created through a portal in the Event Details layout.

Careful design of the relationships between the table occurrences can accommodate this level of flexibility.

1. The Event TOG is shown in Figure 17.18.

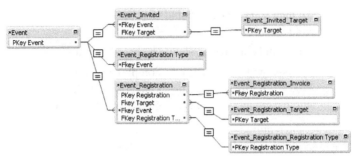

Figure 17.18: The Event TOG.

2. An event record needs to be related to many invited, registration type, and registration records using the **PKey Event** primary key field. Each of these new table occurrences should be added to the relationships graph and linked to the Event table occurrence with relationship lines.

3. The relationships between Event and Event_Invited and Event and Event_Registration Type need to be modified to allow the creation of related records. To modify the relationship, double-click anywhere on the relationship line to open the Edit Relationship dialog box. Check the **Allow creation of records in this table via this relationship** option, as shown in Figure 17.19

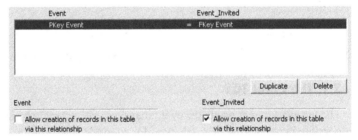

Figure 17.19: The "Allow creation of records in this table via this relationship" option in the Edit Relationship dialog box.

3.2: The Invoice TOG

An invoice record will be related to one or more invoice items and the target or recipient of the invoice.

In order for specific information to display correctly in the Invoice layout, a further set of relationships is needed to other table occurrences stemming from the Invoice table, as indicated in Figure 17.20.

Figure 17.20: The Invoice TOG.

3.3: The Target TOG

A data entry layout for targeted individuals will need to include portals to
show registration history, payments received, invitations to events, and any
related invoices.

The Target TOG is shown in Figure 17.21.

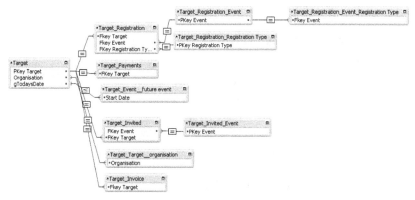

Figure 17.21: The Target TOG.

The relationships from the Target table occurrence to the Registration, Pay-
ments, and Invited tables are all set to allow new records via the relationship.
This means that new related records can be added through portals in a Target
Contact Details layout.

To help the database user, it would be sensible if events that have already
occurred were removed from any event invitation value list. This can be managed by including the global field **gTodaysDate** in a relationship to the Start
Date field in the Event table. This relationship will only be valid if the start
date of an event is greater than or equal to today's date. The relationship is
shown in Figure 17.22.

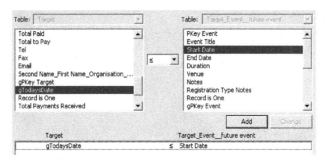

Figure 17.22: The relationship between the Target and Event tables to test whether an event's start date has occurred.

A value list will be defined that uses the result of this relationship to only display upcoming events.

3.4: The Invoice Item TOG

A simple TOG to include a relationship between the Invoice Item and Registration tables will be used so that the correct information is displayed in an Invoice Details layout. The Invoice Item TOG is shown in Figure 17.23.

Figure 17.23: The Invoice Item TOG.

3.5: The Registration TOG

The Registration TOG is used to manage related information for a registration record. The Registration TOG can be seen in Figure 17.24.

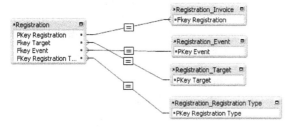

Figure 17.24: The Registration TOG.

3.6: The Invited TOG

A relationship between the Invited table and table occurrences for the Event and Target tables will be needed to display related information in the Target Contact Details and Event Details layouts. The Invited TOG is shown in Figure 17.25.

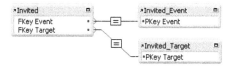

Figure 17.25: The Invited TOG.

A series of additional calculation and lookup fields can now be added to the base tables of the Event Management file, using these relationships.

Step 4: Additional Calculation and Lookup Fields for the Event Management File Tables

In order to display related information in data entry and list report layouts, a series of additional calculation, summary, and lookup fields can now be added to the Event Management file tables.

If the Define Database dialog box is not open, select the menu option **File>Define>Database** and click the **Fields** tab at the top of the dialog box.

4.1: Additional Fields for the Event Table

Add the calculation fields and the summary field shown in Figure 17.26 to the Event table.

Tables Fields | Relationships |

Table: | Event ▼ | 21 fields defined   View by: | custom order

Field Name	Type	Options / Comments (Click to toggle)
◆ Total Target No	Calculation	Unstored, from Event, = Sum (Event_Registration Type::Target No)
◆ Total Actual No	Calculation	Unstored, from Event, = Sum (Event_Registration Type::Actual No)
◆ Total Target Revenue	Calculation	Unstored, from Event, = Sum (Event_Registration Type::Target Revenue)
◆ Total Actual Revenue	Calculation	Unstored, from Event, = Sum (Event_Registration Type::Actual Revenue)
◆ Total Net Fee	Calculation	Unstored, from Event, = Sum (Event_Registration::Registration Fee Net Total)
◆ Total Gross Fee	Calculation	Unstored, from Event, = Sum (Event_Registration::Registration Fee Gross Total)
◆ Count Invited	Calculation	Unstored, from Event, = Count (Event_Invited::FKey Event)
◆ Count Registered	Calculation	Unstored, from Event, = Count (Event_Registration::FKey Event)
◆ Total Net Fee Sum	Summary	= Total of Total Net Fee
◆ Total Registered	Calculation	Unstored, from Event, = Sum (Event_Registration::Qty)

Figure 17.26: Additional fields for the Event table.

4.2: Additional Fields for the Invoice Table

A set of three calculation and three summary fields to display invoice totals can be added to the Invoice table. The new fields are listed in Figure 17.27.

Tables Fields | Relationships |

Table: | Invoice ▼ | 12 fields defined

Field Name	Type	Options / Comments (Click to toggle)
◆ Total Net	Calculation	Unstored, from Invoice, = Sum (Invoice_Invoice Item_Registration::Registration Fee Net Total)
◆ Total VAT	Calculation	Unstored, from Invoice, = Total Gross - Total Net
◆ Total Gross	Calculation	Unstored, from Invoice, = Sum (Invoice_Invoice Item_Registration::Registration Fee Gross Total)
◆ Total Net Sum	Summary	= Total of Total Net
◆ Total VAT Sum	Summary	= Total of Total VAT
◆ Total Gross Sum	Summary	= Total of Total Gross

Figure 17.27: Additional fields for the Invoice table.

4.3: Defining Lookups for Fields in the Invoice Item Table

The relationships in the Invoice Item TOG can be used to create a lookup for the **Registration Net Fee Lookup, Qty**, and **Registration Fee Gross Lookup** fields within the Invoice Item table.

Highlight each of these fields and click the **Options** button. Select the **Auto-Enter** tab and, starting with the **Invoice Item** table, select lookup values from the related **Invoice Item_Registration** table. A lookup example for the Registration Net Fee Lookup field is shown in Figure 17.28.

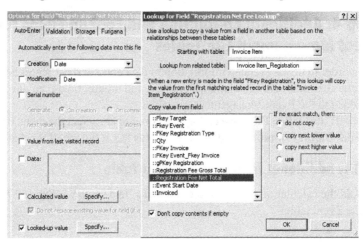

Figure 17.28: Creating a lookup for fields in the Invoice Item table.

4.4: Additional Fields for the Target Table

In the Target table, create calculation fields called **Total Invoiced**, **Total Payments Received**, and **Owing**, together with a summary field called **Owing Sum**. These new fields are shown in Figure 17.29.

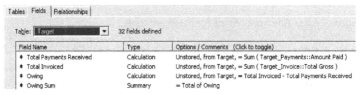

Figure 17.29: The additional fields for the Target table.

4.5: Additional Fields for the Registration Table

Four new calculation fields can now be added to the Registration table. These are needed to display related information correctly when a portal or list layout is created based on the underlying Registration base table. The new calculation fields for the Registration table are shown in Figure 17.30.

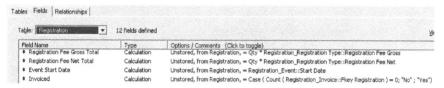

Figure 17.30: The new calculation fields for the Registration table.

Step 5: Designing Data Entry and List Layouts for the Event Management File

Regardless of how well designed the tables and relationships are within a FileMaker file, the concern of the database user and the business manager is that the data entry and list report layouts make sense and are easy to work with.

As discussed in Chapter 7, with FileMaker it is a good idea to base any data entry and report layouts on anchor table occurrences, which are the table occurrences to the far left of the table occurrence groups in our relationships graphs.

5.1: Creating a Wizard Layout to Capture Event Management Company Information

We need to create a layout to capture the business details of the event management company. This information will be used to customize invoice and letter layouts with the company's contact details. As this information is captured in global fields within the Event Management table, the information can be used in any layout, regardless of any underlying relationships.

1. Open the Event Management file, if it is not already open, select the menu option **View>Layout Mode** to switch to Layout mode, and create a new layout. Choose the menu option **Layouts>New Layout/Report** to open the New Layout/Report dialog box. Choose to show records from **Event Management**, type **Wizard** in the Layout Name box, and select **Blank layout**, as shown in Figure 17.31.

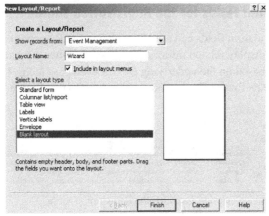

*Figure 17.31:
The New Layout/
Report dialog box
with the Show
records from,
Layout Name, and
Select a layout type
boxes.*

2. Delete the layout header and footer parts in the Wizard layout by high-lighting the part label for each and pressing the **Backspace** or **Delete** key.

3. As shown in Figure 17.32, give the layout body a fill color and use the **Button** tool to display the global fields on a background tile.

4. Add a button to link the Wizard layout back to the main menu at the top-left corner of the layout.

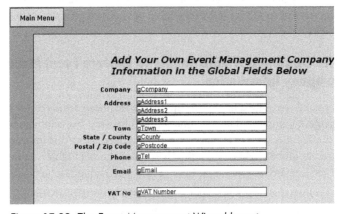

Figure 17.32: The Event Management Wizard layout.

5.2: The Main Menu Layout

The event management team will gain confidence in using the database software if the same main menu or welcome screen appears every time the file is launched.

1. The Main Menu layout should include a set of navigation buttons to open the various data entry and list layouts. In addition, buttons can be included to provide technical support, open the Wizard layout, and safely close the database or quit FileMaker. The Main Menu layout is shown in Figure 17.33.

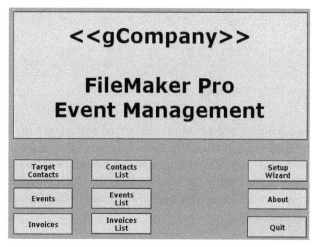

Figure 17.33: The Main Menu layout.

While scripts will be described in detail later in this chapter, two scripts that are directly linked to the Main Menu layout are described in this section.

2. The green About button is designed to provide more information on the solution and details about the author. The **About...** script, which is triggered by this button, is a good example of a conditional script. The Show Custom Dialog script step can display up to three buttons and, when combined with the LastMessageChoice function, the user's choice can be monitored by the script with a different outcome depending on which button is selected. In this case, the user can choose to open one of two websites. The About... script is shown in Figure 17.34.

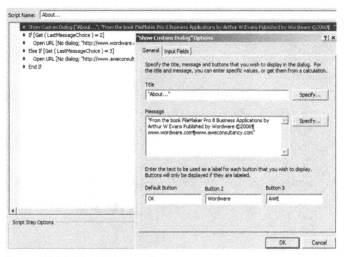

Figure 17.34: The About... script.

3. The red button labeled Quit is used to run a script with the same name.
    The **Quit** script also uses the Show Custom Dialog script step to create a
    conditional script. Depending on which button is selected, the user can
    choose to close the Event Management file or quit FileMaker. The Quit
    script is shown along with the Show Custom Dialog Options dialog box
    in Figure 17.35.

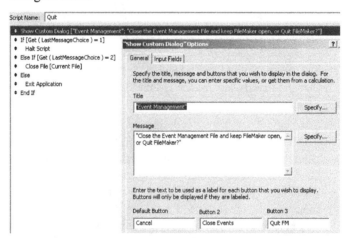

*Figure 17.35: The Quit script is triggered by the button of the same
name in the Main Menu layout.*

5.3: The Event Details Layout

From a single Event Details layout, the business owner wishes to see details about an event including the registration rates in a portal, together with a list of invited names and confirmed registrations attending. Prior to FileMaker Pro 8, this much related information would probably have had to be split into separate layouts, with a series of navigation buttons or tabs added to each so that the user could jump between an event's related data. With FileMaker Pro 8 it is possible to place each set of related data as portals in several tab panels by using the Tab Control tool in Layout mode.

1. We need to create a new blank layout called **Event Details** based on the Event table, or modify the default Event layout that FileMaker created when we first added the Event table to the file.

2. In order to display related registration types, invitees, and registrations, we need to add a tab control with three panels to the layout, as shown in Figure 17.36.

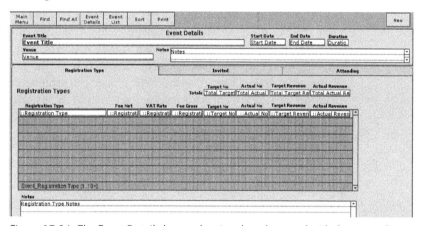

Figure 17.36: The Event Details layout showing the tab control with three panels.

3. The top section of the Event Details layout shows information on the event such as the dates and the venue. To include related information in the layout, click on the tab panel and drag the tab control rectangle to the size required on the layout. In the Tab Control Setup dialog box, add three tab names for the related record sets. On each of the tab panels in turn, add a portal to show records from the related Event_Registration Type, Event_Registration, and Event_Invited table occurrences.

    The event manager requested that new registration types be added through the Event_Registration Type portal. The user can therefore add new registration type records through the portal in this tab panel.

4. Set up the Event Details layout Invited tab panel as shown in Figure 17.37.

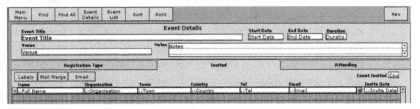

Figure 17.37: The Event Details layout Invited tab panel.

It was also requested that new invite records could be added through this portal within the Event Details layout. To assist the user in selecting the correct name from the Target database, a value list can be created that does not need to show the primary key value for each target, only the individual's name and company.

5. A new value list called **Surname First Target Pop Up** can be created using the **File>Define>Value Lists** menu option. The value list will make use of the "Use Values from Field" values option by using the **Target** table occurrence to select the **PKey Target** field and the **Second Name_First Name_Organisation** concatenated calculation field. This field was created to display a sorted surname names list that included an individual's company name. The settings for the Specify Fields for Value List dialog box are shown in Figure 17.38.

Figure 17.38: The value list settings for Surname First Target Pop Up.

6. Event managers deal with people's names rather than unique serial numbers, so to avoid any confusion or data errors, we can "hide" the FKey Target field from the Invite table. In the first row of the Event_Invited

portal, add the **FKey Target** field from the Event_Invited table occurrence and the **Full Name** field from the Event_Invited_Target table occurrence. Select the **FKey Target** field and, with the right-click menu option **Field/Control>Setup** or the menu option **Format>Field/Control>Setup**, choose the control style to display the field as a drop-down list using the **Surname First Target Pop Up**.

7. While the FKey Target field is still selected, select the menu option **View>Object Size**. Click on the unit of measurement until **px** appears in the Size dialog box as shown in Figure 17.39. Type **1** into the width box to shrink the field to a width of one pixel. Use the arrow keys to position the one-pixel wide field just to the left of the Full Name field. This is best done after setting FileMaker's zoom level to 400. (The Zoom In button is located at the bottom left of the FileMaker window.)

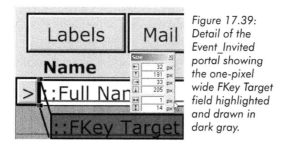

Figure 17.39: Detail of the Event_Invited portal showing the one-pixel wide FKey Target field highlighted and drawn in dark gray.

8. The user cannot be expected to select the "hidden" field, so define the **Full Name** field as a button that, when clicked on, will select the FKey Target field. The button settings for the Full Name field are displayed in Figure 17.40.

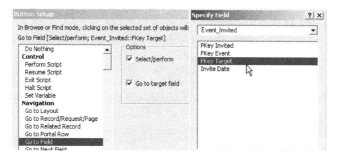

Figure 17.40: The Full Name field in the Invited portal is set to be a button that selects the almost-hidden FKey Target field.

The result of all this work is an easy-to-read value list for targets, displaying the full name and company and sorted by surname. The list appears to be linked to the Full Name field and the user does not need to be aware of the existence of the FKey Target field in the portal row.

This technique will be used throughout the Event Management file and in the other case studies in this book to hide, whenever possible, the primary and foreign key fields in all data entry layouts.

The Event_Registration portal uses the same technique as the Event_Invited portal to display a list of target names. However, the business owner has requested that a confirmation message appear before a new registration record is added to an event to avoid blank records or data errors.

9. Set the green button labeled **Add Registration** in the Attending tab panel to run a script asking the user to confirm the wish to add a new registration.

10. Set up a second green button in the Attending tab panel labeled **Inv** to run another script, in this case to convert an event registration into a new invoice.

11. Create the navigation buttons at the top of the Event Details layout to assist the users of the database.

12. The Invited and Attending tab panels also have three buttons that will be set to run scripts for creating labels, a mail merge text file, and an email for the selected group of individuals.

The Event Details layout Attending tab panel is shown in Figure 17.41.

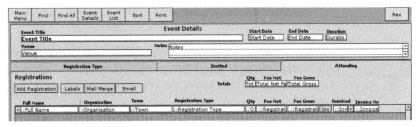

Figure 17.41: The Event Details layout Attending tab panel.

5.4: The Event List Layout

A list layout based on the Event table can be used to display a set of events on screen. A summary field, to display the total net fee for a selection of events, can be added to the trailing grand summary part of the list layout. The Event List layout is shown in Figure 17.42.

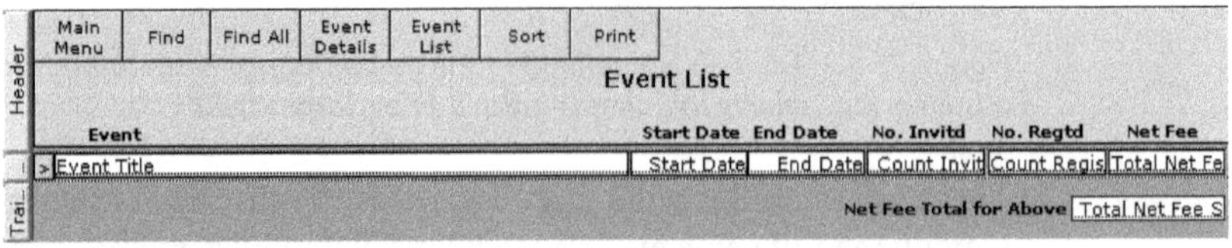

Figure 17.42: The Event List layout.

5.5: The Invoice Details Layout

The database is required to create new invoice records for event registrations. The Invoice Details layout, shown in Figure 17.43, includes a portal to display related invoice item records.

Merge fields are used to display the event management company's contact details and the target recipients' details.

The two navigation buttons at the top right of the Invoice Details layout make use of the Go to Related Record button command to switch to the related contact or event record details.

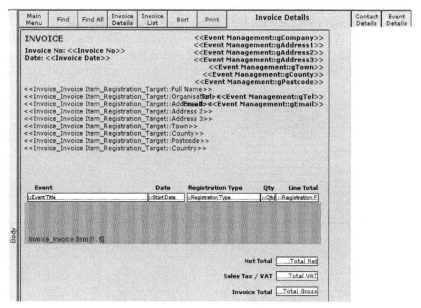

Figure 17.43: The Invoice Details layout.

5.6: The Invoice List Layout

A set of invoice records, showing summary totals for the net, VAT, and gross amount, can be displayed using a list layout based on the Invoice table occurrence.

The Invoice List layout is shown in Figure 17.44.

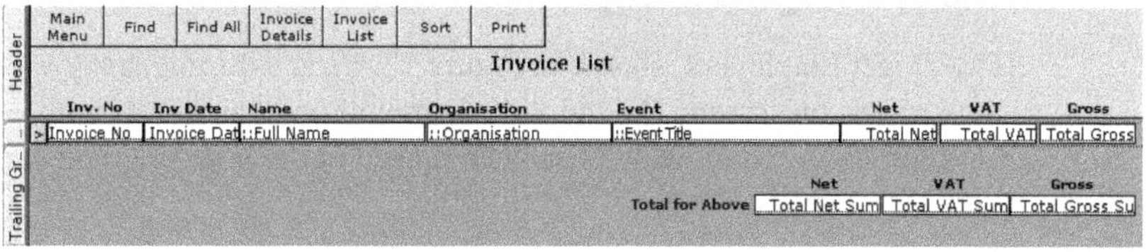

Figure 17.44: The Invoice List layout.

5.7: The Target Contact Details Layout

The business owner has requested that new event invitation and registration records also be created in a Target Contact Details layout. The Target Contact Details layout is shown in Figure 17.45 and includes four portals to display related invite, registration, invoice, and payment records.

A separate table for organizations has not been included in the solution. However, a small button to the right of the Organisation field uses the Go to Related Record button command to assist the user in querying whether any other records exist for the same organization name. FileMaker Pro 8 includes a menu option called Find Matching Records. This can be used to select records with the same field value when a field is selected.

Value lists are used to assist with data entry for the Name and the Source fields, and the auto-complete field option is used to display existing values in the Town and County fields.

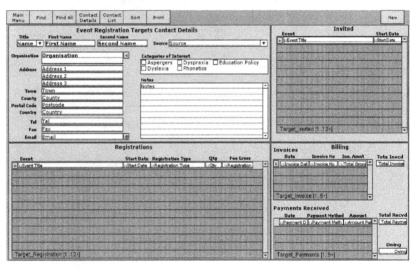

Figure 17.45: The Target Contact Details layout.

The same technique described earlier for "hiding" the foreign key field is used for selecting an event title in the Invited and Registration portals.

5.8: The Target List Layout

The Target List layout, shown in Figure 17.46, is used to display a set of contact records on screen. The individual amount owed is shown with a summary field for Owing Sum, which has been placed in the trailing grand summary part.

Figure 17.46: The Target List layout.

5.9: The Invited Labels Layout

The new layout assistant can be used to create a label layout for a preferred printer and label sheet size. The Invited Labels layout is based on the underlying Invited table occurrence and is used to display contact details for every targeted individual.

The label sheet includes the title, date, and venue for the event in the layout header to assist with putting the correct event details in the invite envelopes.

The Invited Labels layout is shown in Figure 17.47.

Figure 17.47: The Invited Labels layout.

5.10: The Registration Labels Layout

Once a label layout has been designed that fits the label sheets and the office printer, it is usually easier to duplicate this label layout than to design new layouts from scratch. The Registration Labels layout has been duplicated from the Invited Labels layout. In Layout mode, choose the **Layouts>Layout Setup** menu option to open the Layout Setup dialog box, them choose to show records from the **Registration** table.

The navigation buttons are designed to assist the user with returning to the Event Details layout or print the labels.

As with the invite labels, the event details are shown in the header layout part using merge fields.

```
H    <<Registration_Event::Event Title>> <<Registration_Event::StartDate>> <<Registration_Event::Venue>>

     <<Registration_Target::Full Name>>
     <<Registration_Target::Organisation>>                              Event
Body <<Registration_Target::Address 1>> <<Registration_Target::Address 2>>
     <<Registration_Target::Address 3>>
     <<Registration_Target::Town>> <<Registration_Target::County>>     Print
     <<Registration_Target::Postcode>>
```

Figure 17.48: The Registration Labels layout.

Step 6: Automating the Event Management Solution with Scripts

Before the event organization team begins to use the Event Management solution, a series of scripts would be of great benefit to aid with navigation around the file and to automate the creation of new invoices based on registration records.

6.1: The Opening Script

An opening script can be created to ensure that the database always opens on the Event Management Main Menu, with the FileMaker window maximized and the Status area hidden.

The Opening script is shown in Figure 17.49.

Script Name: Opening Script/Open Menu

- Go to Layout ["Event Management" (Event Management)]
- Show/Hide Status Area [Hide]
- Adjust Window [Maximize]
- Enter Browse Mode []

Figure 17.49: The Opening Script/Open Menu script.

6.2: Navigation Scripts to Open Data Entry and List Layouts

We will want to view the Status area in each of the data entry and list layouts.

A series of scripts can be created to open the various data entry layouts. As an example, the Open Event Details script is shown in Figure 17.50.

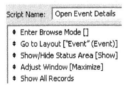

Script Name: Open Event Details

- Enter Browse Mode []
- Go to Layout ["Event" (Event)]
- Show/Hide Status Area [Show]
- Adjust Window [Maximize]
- Show All Records

Figure 17.50: The Open Event Details script.

6.3: Creating a New Invoice Record from within the Registration Details Layout

A script is an ideal method for automating the task of creating new invoice records when a new registration is booked for an event.

The script is shown in Figure 17.51 and its structure can be described as follows:

The script first uses a Count function to check that the current registration record has not already been invoiced. If it has, the script will be halted. Otherwise, a custom dialog message is displayed, asking the user to confirm the creation of a new invoice for the current registration. The user can halt the script or continue, depending on the button selected. If the script is continued, the global field gPKey Registration is set to be the same as the registration record's primary key value, PKey Registration. The global gPKey Target field in the related target record is set to be the same as the target's primary key value, PKey Target. The script then creates a new invoice item record, which has its FKey Registration field set to be the same as the Registration primary key value.

The script then creates a new invoice record that has its foreign key field values set equal to the relevant target and registration record. The global field gPKey Invoice is set to be the same as the invoice record's primary key value, PKey Invoice. The new invoice item record has its FKey Invoice field value set to be the same as the new invoice record. The registration record also has its FKey Invoice field value set to be the same as the new invoice record. Finally, the script displays the new invoice record in the Invoice layout.

Figure 17.51: The Invoice Registration from Event script.

The green button labeled Inv in each Event_Registration portal will be set to run the Invoice Registration from Event script.

6.4: Adding a New Registration in the Event Details Layout

The event manager has requested that a confirmation message be displayed before a new registration is captured for an event in the Event Details layout. The script to manage this is shown in Figure 17.52.

The structure of the script can be described as follows:

The script starts by displaying a custom dialog box that includes the name of the event in the message to minimize registration errors. If the user continues with the script, the global field gPKey Event is set to be the same value as the event's primary key, PKey Event. The script then creates a new record in the Registration layout and sets the FKey Event field value to be equal to the current event's PKey value. A new registration record has now been created that is related to the current event. A target individual has not yet been selected for the new registration record. This can be done back in the Event Details layout. To navigate to the correct new blank portal row, the script goes to the Event_Registration::FKey Target field. This ensures that the correct portal is selected. The script then goes to the last portal row. Since neither the relationship nor the portal row is set to be sorted by any particular field order, the last portal row must be the most recent registration record created. This is the new blank record awaiting an FKey Target value to be selected from the value list.

Figure 17.52: The Add Registration in Event script.

6.5: The BCC Email Registered Script

FileMaker Pro 8 contains some powerful email management features. Two scripts have been written to take advantage of the Send Mail script step feature. These scripts are designed to assist the event organizer in communicating with those invited and registered for an event. The BCC Email Registered script is shown in Figure 17.53.

The script steps can be described as follows:

The script starts by displaying a custom dialog box asking the user to confirm the wish to send a new BCC email to all registrations for the event. The event title appears in the dialog message to minimize errors. If the user goes ahead, the related set of registrations is selected. A warning message is displayed, reminding the user to make sure that the BCC box is selected in the new email header.

The Send Mail script step has some important features for ensuring that recipients do not see other email addresses. The Send Mail Options dialog box is also shown in Figure 17.53. The "For each message, collect addresses across found set" check box should be selected to place all registration email addresses in the BCC field for a new email. The email is also set to have the event details placed in the Subject field.

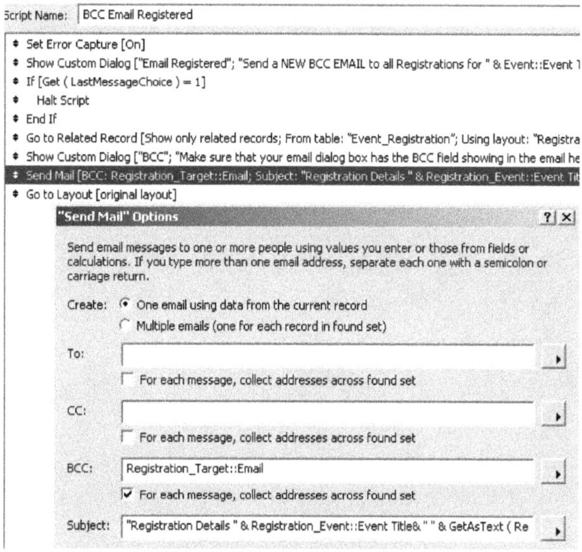

Figure 17.53: The BCC Email Registered script.

Taking the Solution Further

This event management solution only considers the main registration fee. In reality, you may wish to include additional chargeable items such as accommodation, seminars, or tours that a delegate may also wish to sign up for. These would become additional invoice line items. An additional table with a portal in the Event Details layout might then be needed to capture additional invoice line items.

In addition to the administrative elements of handling an event, such as capturing registration details and generating invoices, FileMaker is also ideal for generating registration badges. With the use of container fields in label layouts, it is possible for FileMaker to create photo ID badges for an event.

On the day of an event, FileMaker is capable of recording registration attendance using a barcode reader to capture preprinted registration badges. These can be sent out to the delegates prior to the event. To print barcodes with FileMaker you will need a barcode font and a barcode generator plug-in for FileMaker.

Attendance records can be captured directly into a copy of the database taken to the event location, or FileMaker Mobile can be used to capture attendance records using a PDA linked to a barcode reader. The attendance records can be synchronized with the main event database at a later stage. Delegates could also be booked in with a web browser at the event reception desk, meaning attendance records could be automatically updated using Instant Web Publishing.

Chapter 18

Asset and Facilities Management

Introduction

This case study examines how a FileMaker database can be used for the management of a building, its functional areas, and a company's physical assets within those areas. Some organizations, particularly those that operate in the media or software business sectors, might consider asset management to include the tracking and controlled use of intellectual property. These might include such items as a company's logo, an icon, a signature tune, or software development files and code. With FileMaker Pro 8's capability to store almost any binary code file in a container field, up to a theoretical maximum of 4 gigabytes, an asset management project of this type could easily be managed by a FileMaker solution. This case study concentrates more on the management of buildings and the work environment.

A facilities management solution is an excellent example of how FileMaker can record and present data at different levels of detail. The same FileMaker database can hold and report on building-wide information, such as when a lease is due for renewal, while being able to store technical support information for a software application running on one laptop in an office on the fourth floor. This scalability is achieved by designing a series of related data tables to manage each component of a building's costs and a company's assets.

This case study addresses the needs of a fictitious business center owner who manages several multistory buildings across the city and rents out rooms within the buildings to clients. As clients grow, they may wish to rent more rooms in the same building or at other locations.

As with the other case studies in this book, a copy of the completed FileMaker Pro 8 database file, **FMRooms**, is available to download from the publisher's website at www.wordware.com/files/fmapps and the author's website at www.aweconsultancy.com. You may find it easier to examine some of the FileMaker features and techniques discussed in this chapter in a copy of the completed file.

The default database password for the Admin account is **PICCADILLY** (all capitals).

The database file options have been preset to open with the active Guest account (with read-only access to the file). To open the file with full access privileges, hold down the Shift key (Windows) or Option key (Mac OS) while the file is opening. Type the word **Admin** in the Account Name box and type the password in the box below. You can change the default password at a later stage. More information on database security issues, passwords, accounts, and privileges is given in Chapter 24.

We can start by defining what tables we will need in the database, based on the entities needed to manage the facility and asset data.

The Asset and Facilities Management Entity Relationship Diagram

The business center owner requires a database to track who is based where in what building and which assets are linked to each room.

The table structure of the facility and asset management database should be based on the management requirements of the business center owner.

A database is required to hold commercial details on one or more **Buildings**. Each building will contain a number of **Rooms**. A room will either be vacant or have an **Occupier**. Each room will have several items of **Equipment**. A room will also have various **Telecommunications** connection points. Over time a room may need maintenance or **Refurbishment**. A room may include one or more computer **Workstations**. Each workstation will have several **Software** applications that need to be tracked for version numbers and for technical support contracts. Items of equipment and refurbishment work are both undertaken by **Suppliers**, and may be under warranty for a period of time, which should be flagged in a field.

The way in which these items are related can be drawn as an ER diagram, which is shown in Figure 18.1.

Asset & Facilities Management ER Diagram

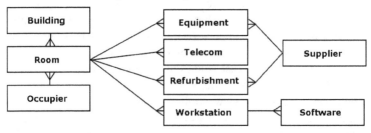

Figure 18.1: The Asset and Facilities Management ER diagram.

Building the Asset and Facilities Management File

Step 1: Adding Tables to the FMRooms File

1. Launch FileMaker and create a new file called **FMRooms**.

   FileMaker will automatically open the Define Database dialog box with the Fields tab selected for the default FMRooms table, as shown in Figure 18.2.

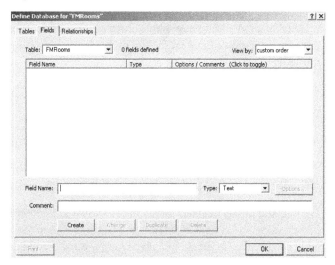

Figure 18.2: The Define Database dialog box for a new FMRooms file with the Fields tab selected for the default table.

2. Click on the **Tables** tab at the top of the Define Database dialog box and add the additional nine tables listed in Figure 18.3.

FMRooms
Building
Room
Equipment
Phone
Refurb
Occupier
Workstation
Software
Supplier

Figure 18.3: The tables needed for the FMRooms file.

Step 2: Adding Initial Fields to the FMRooms File Tables

As with the other case studies in this book, we need to add a primary key field to each of our tables using FileMaker's ability to automatically assign a unique serial number to each record in a table. In addition, we will need to add foreign key fields to any of the tables to which we need to establish a relationship.

1. To add fields to each of the tables within the file, choose the **File>Define>Database** menu option and the **Fields** tab of the Define Database dialog box. It is important to ensure that the correct table is selected prior to adding new fields. Each of the tables can be selected from the drop-down list near the top of the dialog box, as shown in Figure 18.4.

Figure 18.4: Selecting the relevant table for new fields in the Define Database dialog box.

We will add initial fields to each table as shown in Figures 18.6 to 18.17. Later, when we have established relationships between these tables using table occurrences in the relationships graph, we will add additional fields to the tables to improve the functionality of the file.

2. FileMaker can allocate a unique serial number for each record's primary key, or PKey, field which is required for all the data tables in the solution. For example, in the **Building** table, after creating a new number field called **PKey Building**, click the **Options** button in the Define Fields dialog box. Select the **Auto-Enter** tab, check the **Serial number** option, and set an initial value of **1** and an increment of **1**.

3. By careful use of value lists in conjunction with foreign key fields, there is no reason to display the primary key field in any of the layouts in our solution. This means that there is little chance of the unique serial number field value being modified, duplicated, or erased by a user accidentally clicking into the field in a layout. Despite this, it is good practice to also check the **Prohibit modification of value during data entry** option, as shown in Figure 18.5.

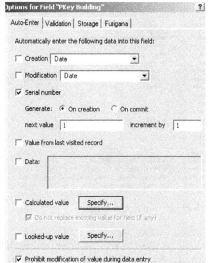

*Figure 18.5:
The auto-enter
options for all
primary key (PKey)
fields in the Asset
and Facilities
Management
solution.*

4. The initial fields required for the **Building** table are shown in Figure
    18.6. Later, when we have created relationships between table occur-
    rences in the FMRooms file, additional calculation fields can be added.

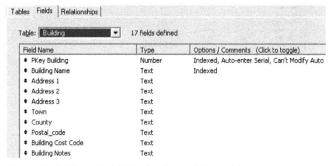

Figure 18.6: The initial fields for the Building table.

5. The fields required at this stage for the **Room** table are displayed in Fig-
    ure 18.7.

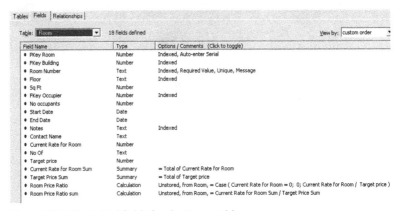

Figure 18.7: The initial fields for the Room table.

6. The **Equipment** table will be used to record asset information for items within rooms and buildings. Create the fields required to describe an item of equipment as shown in Figure 18.8.

Figure 18.8: The fields for the Equipment table.

The calculation field called **Remaining Life** is used to display the residual life of an item, based on its purchase date and the assigned depreciation life in years. The calculation result is a number and the formula is shown in Figure 18.9.

```
Remaining Life =
Round(

If((Date Purchased + (Depreciation Life * 365) - GetAsNumber((Get(CurrentDate)))) / 365 > 0 and
not(Depreciation Life<2);
(Date Purchased + (Depreciation Life * 365) - GetAsNumber((Get(CurrentDate)))) / 365;
0)

;4)
```

Figure 18.9: The Remaining Life calculation field formula in the Equipment table.

The **Book Value** calculation field is used to derive a current value for an item of equipment, based on the division of the item's **Remaining Life** by its **Depreciation Life**, multiplied by the original cost. The formula is shown in Figure 18.10.

```
Book Value =
If(GetAsNumber(Depreciation Life) <> 0;
Round( Remaining Life / Depreciation Life * Cost ; 2 );
0)
```

Figure 18.10: The Book Value calculation field formula.

The calculation field called **Next Test Date Calc** is a simple date formula designed to work out the next test date for an item of equipment, based on the text contents of the **Test Frequency** field. The calculation result is a date and the formula is shown in Figure 18.11.

```
Next Test Date Calc =
Case(
Test Frequency = "Daily"; Date( Month(Test Date); Day(Test Date) + 1; Year(Test Date));
Test Frequency = "Weekly"; Date( Month(Test Date); Day(Test Date) + 7; Year(Test Date));
Test Frequency = "Monthly"; Date( Month(Test Date) + 1; Day(Test Date) ; Year(Test Date));
Test Frequency = "Yearly"; Date( Month(Test Date); Day(Test Date) ; Year(Test Date) + 1))
```

Figure 18.11: The Next Test Date Calc field.

7. The **Phone** table is designed to hold records on telecommunication sockets and associated descriptive information. The calculation field **Next Test Date Calc** uses the same formula as the one in the Equipment table. The Phone table fields are shown in Figure 18.12.

Field Name	Type	Options / Comments (Click to toggle)
PKey Phone	Number	Indexed, Auto-enter Serial, Can't Modify Auto
FKey Room	Number	Indexed
Phone Ext	Number	Indexed
Test Date	Date	
Comment	Text	Indexed
Line Type	Text	Indexed
Live	Text	Auto-enter Data
Test Frequency	Text	
Next Test Date	Date	
User Name	Text	Indexed
Patch Panel No	Text	Indexed
Socket No	Text	Indexed
Next Test Date Calc	Calculation	Indexed, from Phone, = Case(Test Frequency

Figure 18.12: The fields for the Phone table.

8. The **Refurb** table is used to capture records on room redecoration and planned maintenance. The fields required for the Refurb table are shown in Figure 18.13.

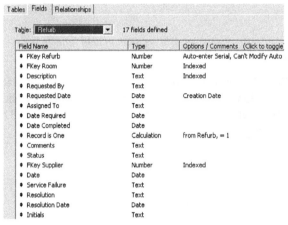

Field Name	Type	Options / Comments (Click to toggle
PKey Refurb	Number	Auto-enter Serial, Can't Modify Auto
FKey Room	Number	Indexed
Description	Text	Indexed
Requested By	Text	
Requested Date	Date	Creation Date
Assigned To	Text	
Date Required	Date	
Date Completed	Date	
Record is One	Calculation	from Refurb, = 1
Comments	Text	
Status	Text	
FKey Supplier	Number	Indexed
Date	Date	
Service Failure	Text	
Resolution	Text	
Resolution Date	Date	
Initials	Text	

Figure 18.13: The fields for the Refurb table.

9. Details on tenants will be held in the **Occupier** table. The initial fields for the Occupier table are displayed in Figure 18.14.

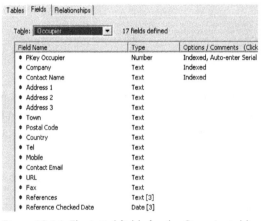

Field Name	Type	Options / Comments (Click
PKey Occupier	Number	Indexed, Auto-enter Serial
Company	Text	Indexed
Contact Name	Text	Indexed
Address 1	Text	
Address 2	Text	
Address 3	Text	
Town	Text	
Postal Code	Text	
Country	Text	
Tel	Text	
Mobile	Text	
Contact Email	Text	
URL	Text	
Fax	Text	
References	Text [3]	
Reference Checked Date	Date [3]	

Figure 18.14: The initial fields for the Occupier table.

10. The **Workstation** table will be used to record computer equipment. The initial fields for the Workstation table are listed in Figure 18.15.

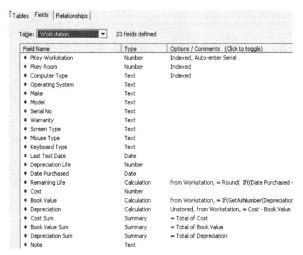

Figure 18.15: The initial fields for the Workstation table.

The **Remaining Life**, **Book Value**, and **Depreciation** calculation fields in the Workstation table each have the same formula as the similar named fields in the Equipment table.

11. The **Software** table is designed to hold details on software applications installed on workstations. The field list for the Software table is shown in Figure 18.16.

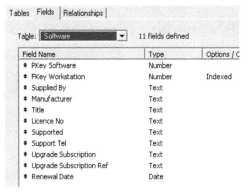

18.16: The fields for the Software table.

12. The **Supplier** table is used to store details on suppliers of equipment and office refurbishment or maintenance. The Supplier table is shown in Figure 18.17.

The **Supplier_Supplier Type** calculation field is a concatenation of the Supplier Name and Supplier Type fields and will be used to create a value list to display a list of suppliers in the Equipment and Refurb layouts.

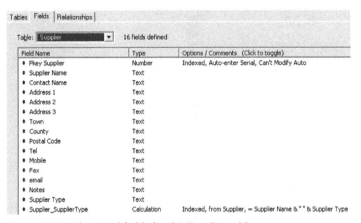

Figure 18.17: The initial fields for the Supplier table.

We now need to use the relationships graph to link up table occurrences based on these tables, using the PKey and FKey fields. We will then be able to make use of the relationships to create some additional calculation fields in our tables.

Step 3: Adding Relationships within the FMRooms File

The building owner or business manager will want to query the data at different levels of scale. At one stage, the amount of equipment in a single room may be required for a report; later, the manager may want to compare the total target price of two separate building records.

This can be achieved by good design of the table occurrence groups, or TOGs, in the relationships graph.

1. If the Define Database dialog box is not open, select the menu option **File>Define>Database** and click the **Relationships** tab at the top of the dialog box. The 10 base tables that we have created for the FMRooms file will be visible as table occurrences, as shown in Figure 18.18.

Figure 18.18: The initial relationships graph for the FMRooms file showing the 10 base tables.

As with the other case study FileMaker solutions, we do not link the underlying base tables directly in the relationships graph. Instead, relationships are built up between table occurrences, which are representations of the base tables in the relationships graph. It is possible to have any number of table occurrences on the relationships graph for the same underlying base table.

As introduced in Chapter 7, our aim is to refine the relationships graph into a series of discrete TOGs. Each TOG should have a main or "anchor" table occurrence on its left-hand side, with any number of linked "buoy" tables related to the anchor table spread out on the right-hand side. To ease relationship design at the outset and to assist you or any colleagues who may work on the file at a later stage, a number of fundamental rules should be followed when using relationships in any FileMaker solution:

- As a general rule, any relationships graph will have one anchor table occurrence for every base table in the file.

- All data entry layouts should only be based on an underlying anchor table occurrence.

- Any portals on layouts should be based on buoy table occurrences.

- To assist with documenting a complex FileMaker project, it is a good idea to limit the dimensions of any TOGs in the relationships graph to a single page in width but any number of pages in length.

To get the required functionality from our asset management solution, we now need to add some TOGs to the relationships graph.

2. For the sake of reference, it is a good idea to preserve at least one table occurrence for each base table within the file, displayed at the top of the relationships graph. To reduce the space used, click the button on the table header to toggle the display of the table and collapse it to its title only, as shown in Figure 18.19.

3. Note that an underscore (_) has been added to the base table occurrences so that the original table name can be used as an anchor table occurrence. Each table occurrence must have a unique name in the graph. A table occurrence can be renamed by double-clicking on it to open the Specify Table dialog box, or by highlighting the table occurrence and clicking the **Edit** button at the bottom of the graph (the button with a yellow pencil icon).

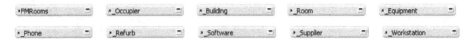

Figure 18.19: The reference base tables collapsed to display only the table titles.

3.1: The Building TOG

A Building Details layout is likely to be a good starting point when using the FMRooms database. The facilities manager will want to get an overview of all related rooms for a building record with a count of how many asset records are held for each room.

To provide the business manager with this level of detail when we design a Building Details layout, we need to create a Building TOG that relates the Building table to the Room table. Going a level deeper to report at least a count of related asset data, we need to add further relationships to link to table occurrences for the Phone, Equipment, Workstation, Refurb, and Occupier tables.

The Building TOG is shown in Figure 18.20.

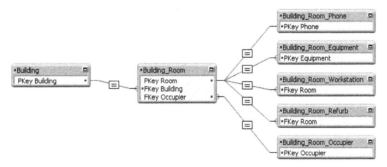

Figure 18.20: The Building TOG.

The facilities manager wants to be able to add new room records for a building using a portal in the Building Details layout. To make this possible, double-click anywhere along the relationship line between the Building and Building_Room table occurrences to open the Edit Relationship dialog box. On the Building_Room side of the dialog box, check the **Allow creation of records in this table via this relationship** option, as shown in Figure 18.21.

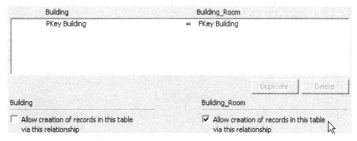

Figure 18.21: Use the Edit Relationship dialog box to create new records via a relationship.

3.2: The Room TOG

The head of facilities has decided the best way to update occupier details and create new related records is directly from a Room Details layout. The relationship between the Room table occurrence and the table occurrences for Equipment, Workstation, Phone, and Refurb all need to be modified to allow the creation of related records.

The Room TOG is shown in Figure 18.22.

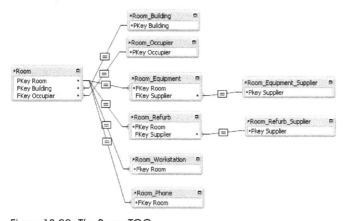

Figure 18.22: The Room TOG.

3.3: The Occupier TOG

It is possible to display what rooms a business occupies by relating an Occupier table occurrence to ones for the Room and Building. The Occupier TOG can be seen in Figure 18.23.

Figure 18.23: The Occupier TOG.

3.4: The Equipment TOG

An Equipment List layout will be able to display details on the room and building location of an item using the Equipment TOG, shown in Figure 18.24.

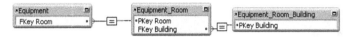

Figure 18.24: The Equipment TOG.

3.5: The Phone TOG

The Phone TOG is designed to enable the room and building location of a phone socket to be displayed in a layout based on the Phone table occurrence. The Phone TOG is shown in Figure 18.25.

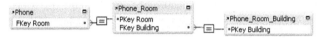

Figure 18.25: The Phone TOG.

3.6: The Software TOG

A list layout showing information on software titles should ideally include information on the workstation, the room location, and the building. This can be handled using fields across the Software TOG, which is displayed in Figure 18.26.

Figure 18.26: The Software TOG.

3.7: The Refurb TOG

A report or list layout giving details on maintenance, redecoration, or refurbishment should include details on the supplier who carried out the work, the relevant room location, and the building. Descriptive fields from each of the table occurrences in the Refurb TOG, shown in Figure 18.27, are needed to create a Refurb List layout.

Figure 18.27: The Refurb TOG.

3.8: The Supplier TOG

In order to display what refurbishment work has been done or what equipment has been provided by a supplier, the Supplier TOG has relationships to table occurrences for the Refurb and Equipment tables. The facilities manager wishes to create new refurbishment and equipment records from a Rooms Details layout, so none of the relationships in the Supplier TOG need to be modified to create new records.

The Supplier TOG is shown in Figure 18.28.

Figure 18.28: The Supplier TOG.

3.9: The Workstation TOG

The Workstation TOG forms the underlying method by which new software titles will be added in a portal within a Workstation Details layout. The relationship between Workstation and Workstation_Software needs to be modified to allow new records to be created. A relationship to table occurrences for the Room and Building tables enables location details for a computer to be displayed.

The Workstation TOG is displayed in Figure 18.29.

Figure 18.29: The Workstation TOG.

Some additional calculation fields can now be added to the tables of the FMRooms file. These will make use of some of these related field values in the calculation formula.

Step 4: Additional Calculation Fields for the FMRooms Tables

The job of managing building facilities can be made easier by letting FileMaker do much of the work in summarizing and reporting on related data.

If the Define Database dialog box is not open, select the **File>Define> Database** menu option. Click the **Fields** tab to return to the fields list for each of the tables in the FMRooms database.

4.1: Additional Fields for the Building Table

In the Building table, we can add a set of calculation and summary fields that count how many related room records exist for a building, and a calculation field total of the related room's area, target, and actual price. New summary fields for each of these new calculation fields can also be added to the table. These new fields for the Building table are displayed in Figure 18.30.

Field Name	Type	Options / Comments (Click to toggle)
✦ Count Rooms	Calculation	Unstored, from Building, = Count (Building_Room::FKey Building)
✦ Total Sq Ft	Calculation	Unstored, from Building, = Sum (Building_Room::Sq Ft)
✦ Total Target Price	Calculation	Unstored, from Building, = Sum (Building_Room::Target price)
✦ Total Sq Ft Sum	Summary	= Total of Total Sq Ft
✦ Total Actual Price	Calculation	Unstored, from Building, = Sum (Building_Room::Current Rate for Room)
✦ Total Target Price Sum	Summary	= Total of Total Target Price
✦ Total Actual Price Sum	Summary	= Total of Total Actual Price

Tables   Fields   Relationships

Table: [Building ▼]   17 fields defined

Figure 18.30: Additional calculation and summary fields for the Building table.

4.2: Additional Fields for the Room Table

A series of four new calculation fields can now be added to the Room table to count related records. These new fields are listed in Figure 18.31.

Tables   Fields   Relationships

Table: [Room ▼]   22 fields defined

Field Name	Type	Options / Comments (Click to toggle)
✦ No Computers	Calculation	Unstored, from Room, = Count (Room_Workstation::Fkey Room)
✦ No Equipment	Calculation	Unstored, from Room, = Count (Room_Equipment::FKey Room)
✦ No Maintenance	Calculation	Unstored, from Room, = Count (Room_Refurb::FKey Room)
✦ No Phones	Calculation	Unstored, from Room, = Count (Room_Phone::FKey Room)

Figure 18.31: Additional calculation fields for the Room table.

4.3: An Additional Field for the Occupier Table

The Occupier TOG can be used to display how many rooms a company is occupying. The **No Rooms Occupied** calculation field formula is shown in Figure 18.32.

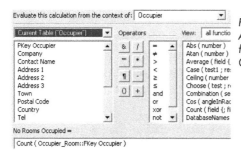

Figure 18.32:
A new calculation
field for the
Occupier table.

4.4: An Additional Field for the Workstation Table

The Workstation TOG can be used to create a new calculation field called
Count Software for the Workstation table. The calculation field formula is
shown in Figure 18.33.

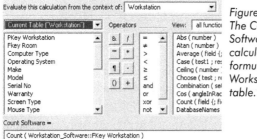

Figure 18.33:
The Count
Software
calculation field
formula in the
Workstation
table.

Step 5: Designing Data Entry and Report Layouts for the FMRooms File

A series of data entry and list layouts can now be added to the database to
assist the asset and facilities manager.

As discussed in Chapter 7, with FileMaker it is a good idea to base any
data entry and report layouts on anchor table occurrences, which are the table
occurrences to the far left of the table occurrence groups in our relationships
graph.

5.1: The FMRooms Welcome Menu

As the asset and facilities management team members are learning to use
their new database, it might be reassuring to them if the same welcome menu
appears every time the file is launched.

1.   The Welcome Menu layout should include a set of navigation buttons to
     open the various data entry and list layouts. In addition, buttons can be
     included to provide technical support, open the Wizard layout, and safely
     close the database or quit FileMaker.

The Welcome Menu layout is shown in Figure 18.34.

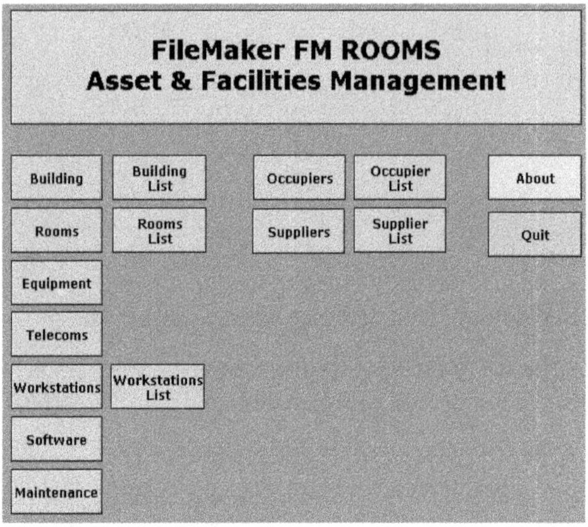

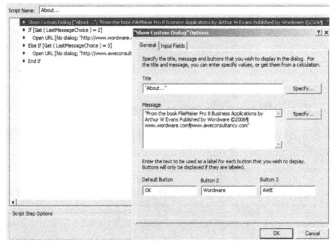

Figure 18.34: The Welcome Menu layout.

While scripts will be described in detail later in this chapter, two scripts that are directly linked to the Welcome Menu layout are described in this section.

2. The green About button is designed to provide more information on the solution and details on the author. The **About...** script, which is triggered by this button, is a good example of a conditional script. The Show Custom Dialog script step can display up to three buttons and, when combined with the LastMessageChoice function, the user's choice can be monitored by the script with a different outcome depending on which

Figure 18.35: The About... script.

button is selected. In this case, the user can choose to open one of two websites. The About... script is shown in Figure 18.35.

3.   The red button labeled Quit is used to run a script with the same name. The **Quit** script also uses the Show Custom Dialog script step to create a conditional script. Depending on which button is selected, the user can choose to close the FMRooms file or quit FileMaker. The Quit script is shown along with the Show Custom Dialog Options dialog box in Figure 18.36.

Figure 18.36: The Quit script is triggered by the button of the same name in the Welcome Menu layout.

5.2: The Building Details Layout

A building record is the largest scale of interest for the facilities manager. A building consists of a number of rooms or distinct areas. Related room records for a building can be created using a portal that is based on the Building_Room table occurrence. The Building Details layout is shown in Figure 18.37. Building records can be added using the New button. The navigation buttons at the top of the layout are designed to assist the user in working with the file.

In the Rooms portal, the small button labeled with a right arrow (>) on the left side makes use of the Go to Related Record function to switch to the selected room record. The other small buttons marked with a right arrow will switch to any related equipment, phone, workstation, or maintenance records for a specific room.

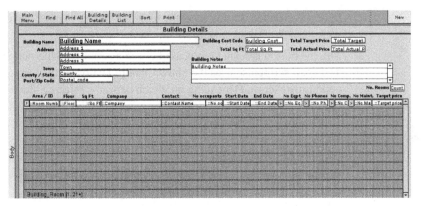

Figure 18.37: The Building Details layout.

5.3: The Building List Layout

The Building List layout uses the same navigation buttons as the Building Details layout. Summary field totals for area, target, and actual price are included in a trailing grand summary layout part. The Building List layout is shown in Figure 18.38.

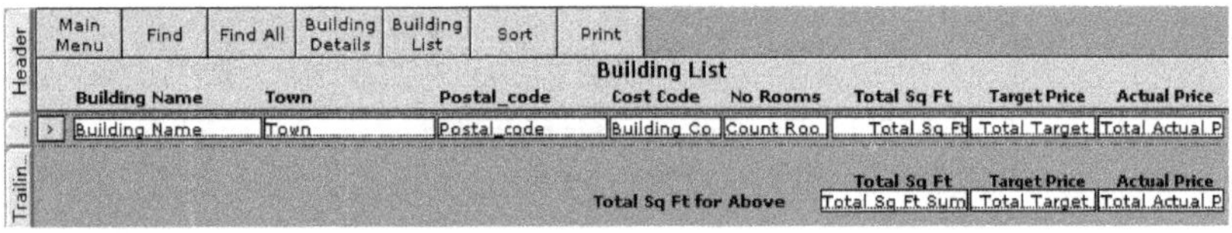

Figure 18.38: The Building List layout.

5.4: The Room Details Layout

The Room Details layout includes four portals to display the related records for a room. The relationship for each of the four portals has been set to allow the creation of related records.

Buttons at the top of the Room Details layout are defined to open the related occupier or client and building details using the Go to Related Record button command.

Whenever possible, value lists are used to assist with data entry in fields such as Equipment Type, Staff Initials, Computer Type, and Line Type for telecommunications.

The Room Details layout is shown in Figure 18.39.

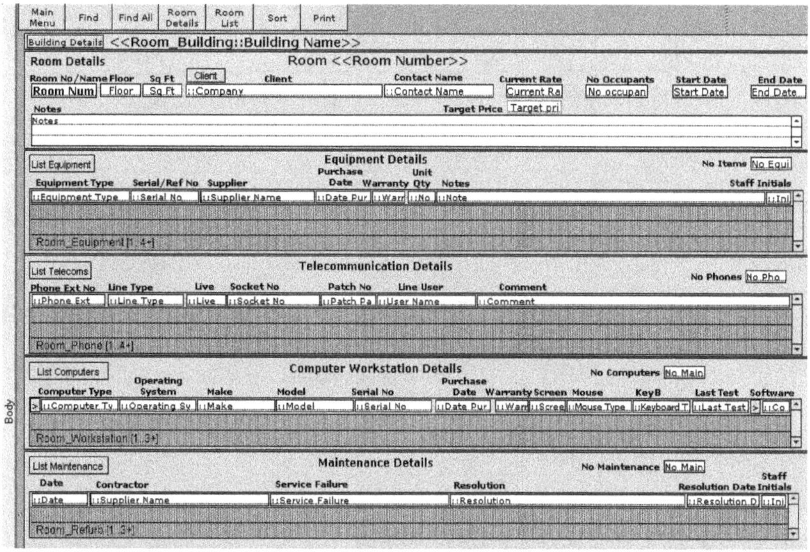

Figure 18.39: The Room Details layout.

5.5: The Room List Layout

The Room List layout is designed to display a series of room records on screen. Two buttons in the layout body are defined to open the Room Details layout or switch to the related occupier record. A summary total field to display the total of the Current Rate field is included in a trailing grand summary layout part.

The Room List layout is shown in Figure 18.40.

Figure 18.40: The Room List layout.

5.6: The Occupier Details Layout

The Occupier Details layout displays records for companies who lease rooms from the business center manager. The Occupier Details layout is shown in Figure 18.41. Included in the layout is a portal that displays records for each room occupied by a company. A company is assigned to a room from within the Room Details layout, so no related records are created using this portal.

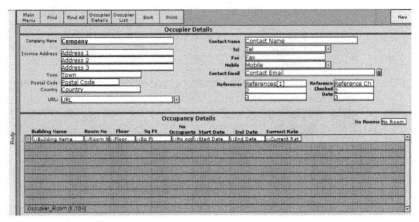

Figure 18.41: The Occupier Details layout.

5.7: The Occupier List Layout

A set of occupier records can be displayed on screen using the Occupier List layout, displayed in Figure 18.42. Two buttons in the layout body part are used to switch to the Occupier Details layout and to any related room records.

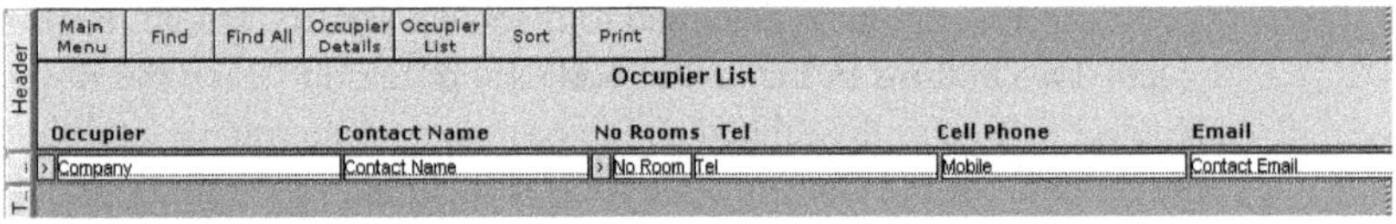

Figure 18.42: The Occupier List layout.

5.8: The Equipment List Layout

The asset manager is particularly interested in equipment items, which are displayed using an Equipment List layout. Buttons in the body layout part enable the user to view the related room and building records. Summary total fields for cost, book value, and depreciation are included in a trailing grand summary layout part.

The left side of the Equipment List layout is shown in Figure 18.43 and the right side in Figure 18.44.

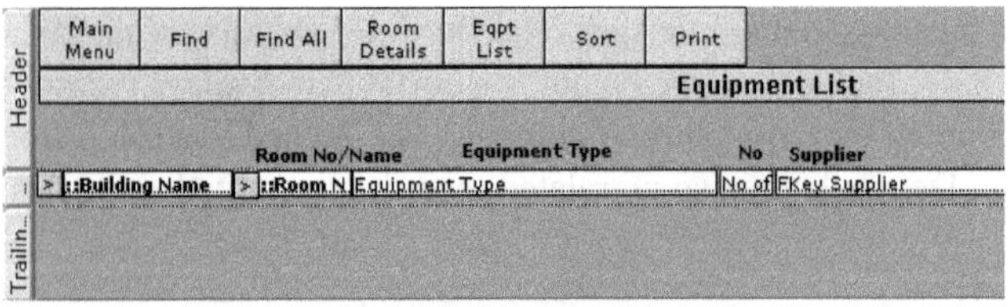

Figure 18.43: The Equipment List layout (left side).

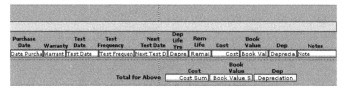

Figure 18.44: The Equipment List layout (right side).

5.9: The Workstation Details Layout

A Workstation Details layout is used to display information on computer equipment. The layout includes a portal to allow new related software records to be created. Two buttons are included in the layout to open the related room and building record from this layout using the Go to Related Record command. The Workstation Details layout is shown in Figure 18.45.

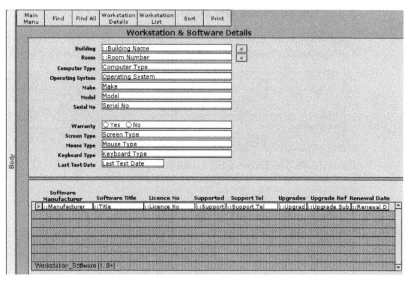

Figure 18.45: The Workstation Details layout.

5.10 The Workstation List Layout

Computer records can be displayed in a list layout using the same navigation buttons as the Workstation Details layout. The left side of the Workstation List layout is shown in Figure 18.46, and the right side of the layout is shown in Figure 18.47. Summary fields to display the total cost, book value, and depreciation for a set of workstation items are included in a trailing grand summary layout part.

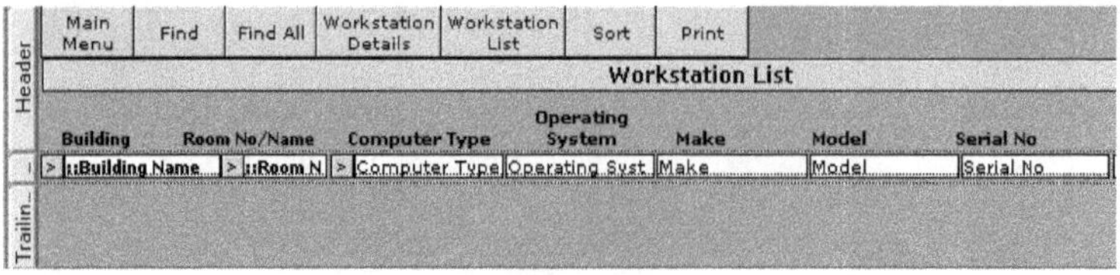

Figure 18.46: The Workstation List layout (left side).

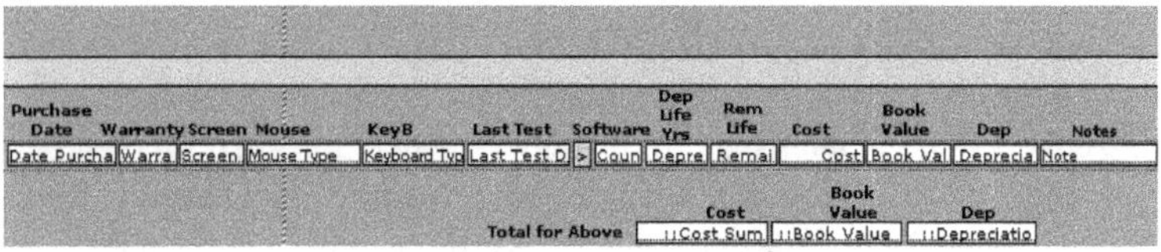

Figure 18.47: The Workstation List layout (right side).

5.11: The Software List Layout

In addition to the portal in the Workstation Details layout, software records can also be displayed in a list layout, as shown in Figures 18.48 and 18.49.

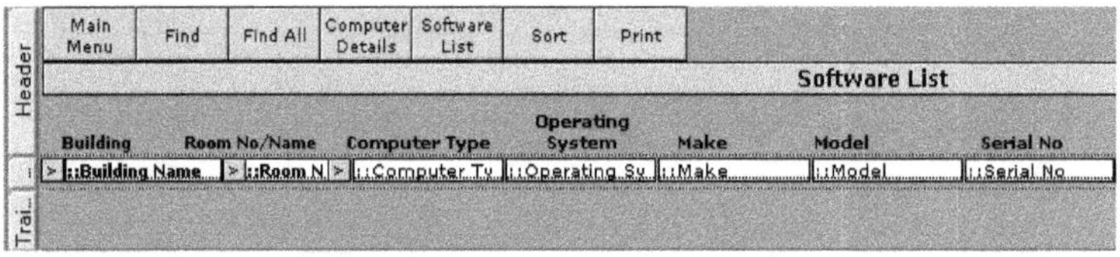

Figure 18.48: The Software List layout (left side).

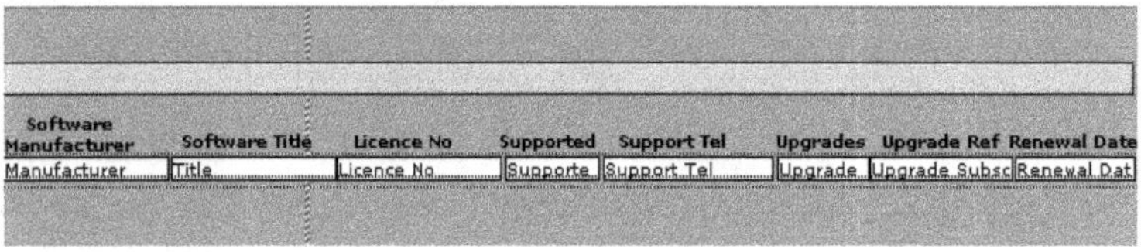

Figure 18.49: The Software List layout (right side).

5.12: The Supplier Details Layout

Information on equipment and refurbishment providers can be displayed in a Supplier Details layout, as shown in Figure 18.50. Two portals are included in the layout to display information on any related refurbishment or equipment records. As with portals in the other layouts, buttons are included to open the related room or equipment record.

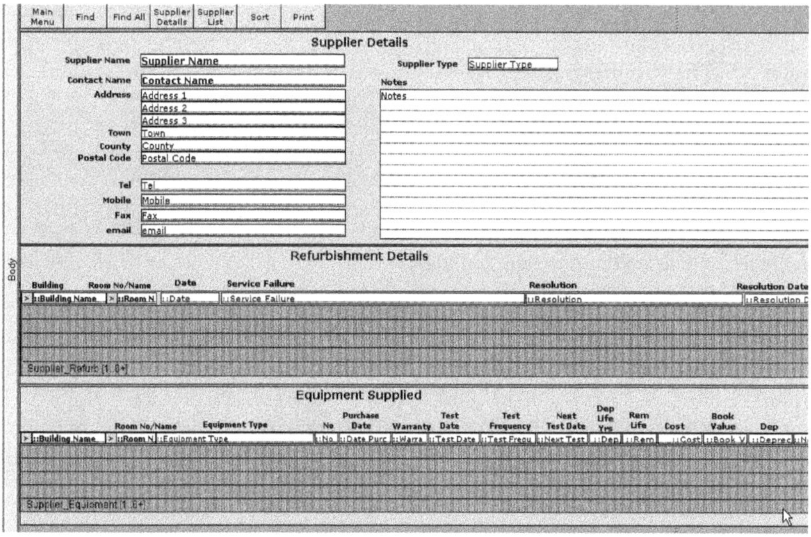

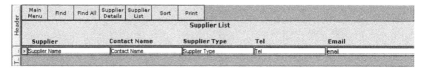

Figure 18.50: The Supplier Details layout.

5.13: The Supplier List Layout

A set of supplier records can be displayed on screen by creating a list layout based on the underlying Supplier table occurrence. The Supplier List layout is displayed in Figure 18.51.

Figure 18.51: The Supplier List layout.

5.14: The Telecoms List Layout

Records on phone connection points and line sockets can be displayed using a new list layout, as shown in Figure 18.52.

Figure 18.52: The Telecoms List layout.

5.15: The Refurbishment List

The Refurbishment List layout is shown in Figure 18.53.

Figure 18.53: The Refurbishment List layout.

Step 6: Automating the Asset and Facilities Management Solution with Scripts

Before the building manager starts to use the FMRooms file, a series of scripts would be of great benefit to assist with navigation around the file and for keeping records accurate and up to date.

6.1: The Opening Script

An opening script can be created to guarantee that the database always displays the FMRooms Welcome Menu when first opened, with the database window maximized and the Status area hidden.

The Opening script is shown in Figure 18.54.

Figure 18.54: The Opening script for the FMRooms file.

6.2: The Navigation Scripts to Open the Data Entry and List Layouts

The Opening script includes a script step that hides the Status area. It would be useful if the Status area could be displayed whenever a data entry or list layout is opened so that the number of records can be displayed. The Open Building script, shown in Figure 18.55, is used to open the Building Details layout from the Welcome Menu.

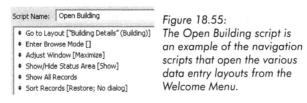

Figure 18.55: The Open Building script is an example of the navigation scripts that open the various data entry layouts from the Welcome Menu.

6.3: Displaying Value Lists in "Hidden" Fields — The Display Occupier List In Building Details Script

The Go to Field script step will select any field on a layout, even if the Field Behavior dialog box has been used to prevent a field from being entered in Browse or Find mode, as shown in Figure 18.56.

*Figure 18.56:
The Field Behavior
dialog box settings can
be overwritten by the
Go to Field script step.*

Several scripts have been written consisting solely of the Go to Field script step to select a "hidden" FKey field on a layout and trigger the display of a value list to select an FKey value for a related record. The script shown in Figure 18.57 is used to display the occupier list in the Building Details layout.

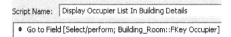

*Figure 18.57: The Display Occupier List In
Building Details script.*

Taking the Solution Further

A good database solution should be capable of evolving. More features can be added to the basic asset and facilities management database as data reporting requirements change and new business management techniques are adopted.

The Occupier table could be expanded to incorporate CRM functionality. A history of room rates could be included to log when the rate was last revised and by what percentage change. The database also does not include an accounting module to manage monthly rental invoices.

If a building provides shared conference and meeting rooms, FileMaker could be used to create a booking module. This could also be linked to an invoice file to charge for additional business center services.

Purchase orders and expenses for the business center are not currently recorded. With careful field design, it would be possible to record a summary cost per unit of area and cost per full-time staff equivalent to provide the facilities manager with information for benchmarking the building against industry standard indices.

Chapter 19

Subscription Management

Introduction

There are many magazine houses and publishers that use FileMaker to manage subscriptions for trade and consumer journals and publications. A FileMaker subscription solution is scalable and has the ability to grow with a new publishing business. A new magazine may have the initial requirement to print distribution labels or packaging in house. As the business grows, the publisher may decide to export subscriber details as delimited text or an XML file for an outside fulfillment house, while still retaining ownership of the subscription details.

If a publication office is using FileMaker to manage subscriptions, it is often the case that ancillary business requirements, such as article tracking, photo libraries, reviewer details, and competition entries, are also managed with FileMaker. Calculation fields in FileMaker can be used to prepare text for page layout software style sheets. Whenever text has a structured format in a magazine article, such as in a review guide, a price list, or a "what's showing" calendar, FileMaker is perfect for sorting and marking up the article text for a text frame in the page layout software.

Beyond the scope of this subscription case study, a publisher may also wish to adapt FileMaker to manage advertisement targets, placement, and revenue.

This case study concentrates on the needs of a small business called The Great Magazine Group, which has launched several magazines such as *Which Car* and *Which MP3*. The publisher wants to track and manage subscribers, invoice revenues, and subscription renewals.

As with the other case studies in this book, a copy of the completed FileMaker Pro 8 database file, **FMSubs**, is available to download from the publisher's website at www.wordware.com/files/fmapps and the author's website at www.aweconsultancy.com. You may find it easier to examine some of the FileMaker features and techniques discussed in this chapter in a copy of the completed file.

The default database password for the Admin account is **MAGAZINE** (all capitals).

The database file options have been preset to open with the active Guest account (with read-only access to the file). To open the file with full access privileges, hold down the Shift key (Windows) or Option key (Mac OS) while the file is opening. Type the word **Admin** in the Account Name box and type the password in the box below. You can change the default password at a later stage. More information on database security issues, passwords, accounts, and privileges is given in Chapter 24.

First we need to determine what entities the publishing team needs to manage as separate tables in the database.

The Subscription Management Entity Relationship Diagram

The publication business owner needs to think about how best the magazine and subscriber information should be managed in order to create a series of tables for the FileMaker subscription solution.

The business wishes to manage information on **Contacts** who currently have, or had in the past, a **Subscription** to at least one magazine **Title**. A varying **Rate** of subscription will be charged depending on the contact type or when the contact signed up for the subscription. The magazine title aims to get revenue for subscriptions by raising **Invoices**. Each **Invoice Item** should represent one subscription to one magazine title.

The Subscription Management entity relationship diagram is shown in Figure 19.1.

Subscription Management ER Diagram

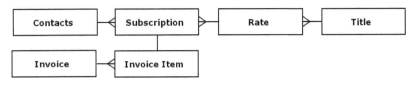

Figure 19.1: The Subscription Management entity relationship diagram.

Building the Subscription Management File

Step 1: Adding Tables to the FMSubs File

1.   Launch FileMaker and create a new file called **FMSubs**.

FileMaker will automatically open the Define Database dialog box with the Fields tab selected for the default FMSubs table, as shown in Figure 19.2.

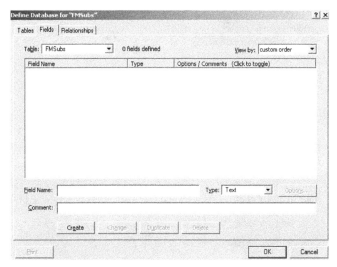

Figure 19.2: The Define Database dialog box for the new FMSubs file with the Fields tab selected.

2. Click the **Tables** tab at the top of the Define Database dialog box and add the six additional tables shown in Figure 19.3 to the FMSubs file.

FMSubs
Contact
Title
Rate
Subscription
Invoice
InvoiceItem

Figure 19.3: The tables needed for the FMSubs file.

Step 2: Adding Initial Fields to the FMSubs File Tables

As with the other case studies in this book, we need to add a primary key field to each of our tables using FileMaker's ability to automatically assign a unique serial number to each record in each table. In addition, we will need to add foreign key fields to any of the tables to which we need to establish a relationship.

1. To add fields to each of the tables within the file, choose the **File> Define>Database** menu option and the **Fields** tab of the Define Database dialog box. It is important to ensure that the correct table is selected

prior to adding new fields. Each of the tables can be selected from the drop-down list near the top of the dialog box, as shown in Figure 19.4.

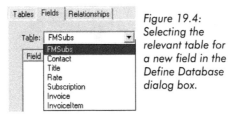

Figure 19.4: Selecting the relevant table for a new field in the Define Database dialog box.

We will add initial fields to each table as shown in Figures 19.5 to 19.11. Later, when we have established relationships between these tables using table occurrences in the relationships graph, we will add additional fields to the tables to improve the functionality of the file.

2.   The initial fields required for the **Contact** table are listed in Figure 19.5.

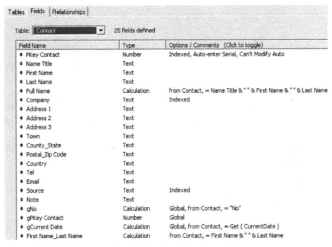

Figure 19.5: The initial fields for the Contact table.

3.   FileMaker can allocate a unique serial number for each record's primary key, or PKey field, which is required for all the data tables in the solution. For example, after creating a new number field called **PKey Contact** in the Contact table, click the **Options** button in the Define Fields dialog box. Select the **Auto-Enter** tab, click the **Serial number** option, and set an initial value of **1** and an increment of **1**.

4.   By careful use of value lists in conjunction with foreign key fields, there is no reason to display the primary key field in any of the layouts in our solution. This means that there is little chance of the unique serial number field value being modified, duplicated, or erased by a user

accidentally clicking into the field in a layout. Despite this, it is good practice to also check the **Prohibit modification of value during data entry** option, as shown in Figure 19.6.

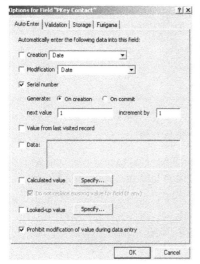

Figure 19.6: The auto-enter options for all primary key fields in the FMSubs solution.

5. Several of the fields in the FMSubs tables, such as **gPKey Contact**, are set to be global. This is set by highlighting the field and clicking the **Options** button, selecting the **Storage** tab, and checking the **Use global storage** option.

    In this solution, we will make use of global number fields to temporarily store the contents of a record's primary key field when we create new related records in another table. As an example, a global number field will be used to store a contact's primary key field value, which can then be placed as a subscription record's foreign key field value for the contact in a new related invoice record.

6. The initial fields needed for the **Title** table are displayed in Figure 19.7.

Tables   Fields   Relationships

Table: Title   15 fields defined

Field Name	Type	Options / Comments (Click to toggle)
✦ PKey Title	Number	Indexed, Auto-enter Serial, Can't Modify Auto
✦ Title	Text	Indexed
✦ Target Subscription No	Text	Indexed
✦ Target Subs Revenue	Text	Indexed
✦ Non Renewed Subs	Text	
✦ Notes	Text	
✦ gTitle	Text	Global
✦ gActive	Calculation	Global, from Title, = "Active"

Figure 19.7: The initial fields for the Title table.

7. Each title will have a number of different rates to describe each type of subscription fee. The fields for the **Rate** table are shown in Figure 19.8.

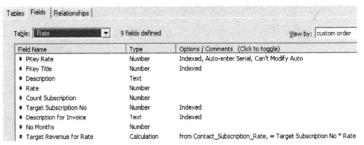

Figure 19.8: The fields for the Rate table.

8. The **Subscription** table will be used to link contacts with titles. The initial fields for the Subscription table are shown in Figure 19.9.

Figure 19.9: The initial fields for the Subscription table.

9. The **Invoice** table's initial fields are displayed in Figure 19.10. More fields will be added once relationships have been created using table occurrences in the relationships graph.

Figure 19.10: The initial fields for the Invoice table.

10. Each record in the **InvoiceItem** table will represent a subscription. The fields for the InvoiceItem table are shown in Figure 19.11.

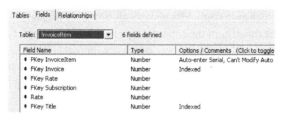

Figure 19.11: The fields for the InvoiceItem table.

To add the required functionality to the subscription file, we can now use the primary and foreign key fields to create relationships between table occurrences representing these tables. We do this with the relationships graph.

Step 3: Adding Relationships within the FMSubs File

An indispensable subscription management tool can be designed with FileMaker once relationships are established between the underlying tables in a file. Later, a series of scripts can be added to the file to automate various tasks.

First, we need to build a series of table occurrence groups, or TOGs, using the relationships graph. Once these TOGs are completed, we can add some additional calculation and lookup fields to the tables that make use of the new table relationships, then add these fields to a series of data entry and report layouts.

1. If the Define Database dialog box is not open, select the menu option **File>Define>Database** and click the **Relationships** tab at the top of the dialog box. The seven base tables that we have created for the FMSubs file will be visible as table occurrences as shown in Figure 19.12.

Figure 19.12: The initial relationships graph for the FMSubs file showing the seven base tables.

As with the other case study FileMaker solutions, we do not link the underlying base tables directly in the relationships graph. Instead, relationships are built up between table occurrences, which are representations of the base tables in the relationships graph. It is possible to have any number of table occurrences on the relationships graph for the same underlying base table.

As introduced in Chapter 7, our aim is to refine the relationships graph into a series of discrete TOGs. Each TOG should have a main or "anchor" table occurrence on its left-hand side, with any number of linked "buoy" tables related to the anchor table spread out on the right-hand side. To ease relationship design at the outset and to assist you or any colleagues who may work on the file at a later stage, a number of fundamental rules should be followed when using relationships in any FileMaker solution:

- As a general rule, any relationships graph will have one anchor table occurrence for every base table in the file.
- All data entry layouts should only be based on an underlying anchor table occurrence.
- Any portals on layouts should be based on buoy table occurrences.
- To assist with documenting a complex FileMaker project, it is a good idea to limit the dimensions of any TOGs in the relationships graph to a single page in width but any number of pages in length.

To get the required functionality from our FMSubs solution, we now need to add some TOGs to the relationships graph.

2. For the sake of reference, it is good practice to display a table occurrence for each table in a file at the top of the relationships graph as a key to the graph. To reduce the space used, click the button on the table header to toggle the display of these reference tables and collapse them to a title only, as shown in Figure 19.13.

3. Note that an underscore (_) has been added to some of the base table occurrences so that the original table name can be used as an anchor table occurrence. Each table occurrence must have a unique name in the graph. A table occurrence can be renamed by double-clicking on it to open the Specify Table dialog box, or by highlighting the table occurrence and clicking the **Edit** button at the bottom of the graph (the button with a yellow pencil icon).

Figure 19.13: The reference base tables collapsed to display only the table titles.

3.1: The Contact TOG

For any contact record, the publisher wants to be able to view all related details on all subscriptions taken out, a subtotal of active subscriptions, and invoices generated. To provide this level of information in a Contact Details layout, a number of table occurrences must be created and related to the Contact table occurrence.

The Contact TOG is shown in Figure 19.14. Nearly all of the Contact TOG relationships are fairly simple *equijoins*, where one field value must be equal to the contents of a field value in the other table for the relationship to be valid.

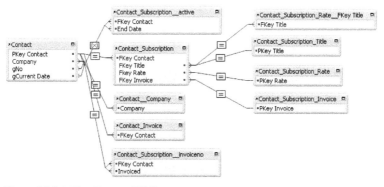

Figure 19.14: The Contact TOG.

Slightly more complex relationships have been built to manage subscriptions that have not yet been invoiced and subscriptions that are still active.

1. The table occurrence named **Contact_Subscription__invoiceno** uses its title to remind the database designer that the status of the invoice field value is crucial to the relationship being valid. The global field called **gNo** in the Contact table forms part of the relationship, so that only those invoice records for the same contact that have not yet been invoiced (with the contents of the invoiced field set to "No") are valid related records. The relationship for the Contact_Subscription__invoiceno table occurrence is shown in detail in Figure 19.15.

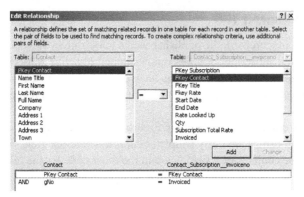

Figure 19.15: The relationship between Contact and
Contact_Subscription__invoiceno.

2. The relationship between **Contact** and **Contact_Subscription__active**
uses the global date field **gCurrent Date** from the Contact table to test
whether a subscription has run out or is still active. The relationship formula is shown in Figure 19.16.

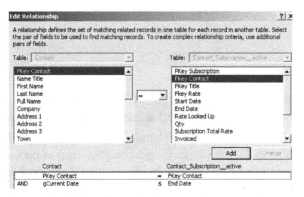

Figure 19.16: The relationship between Contact and
Contact_Subscription__active.

3. As the magazines are aimed at consumer rather than commercial subscribers, this solution does not need to capture company details, since the
magazine and invoices are mainly sent to private addresses. A self-join
relationship that links the **Contact** table occurrence to another table
occurrence based on the Contact table called **Contact__company** is used
to help isolate any contacts with the same company name. The Go to
Related Record function will later be used to enable the database user to
see whether or not a company name is unique in the database.

4. The relationship between **Contact** and **Contact_Subscription** needs to
be modified so that new subscription records can be created through a

portal in the Contact Details layout. To modify the relationship, double-click anywhere on the relationship line and check the **Allow creation of records in this table via this relationship** option in the Contact_Subscription table occurrence, as shown in Figure 19.17.

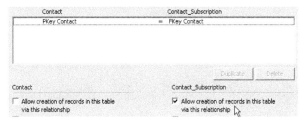

Figure 19.17: New subscription records can be created via the Contact to Contact_Subscription relationship.

3.2: The Subscription TOG

The Subscription TOG is used to relate subscription records to the magazine title, the contact, and the relevant rate record to a price for the subscription.

The Subscription TOG is shown in Figure 19.18.

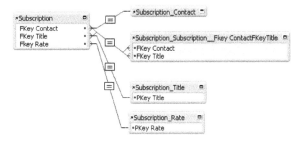

Figure 19.18: The Subscription TOG.

All but one of the relationships in the Subscription TOG are equijoins, with one field used on both sides of the relationship. The exception is a self-join relationship based on the underlying Subscription table: The relationship between the **Subscription** and the (admittedly rather long-winded) **Subscription_Subscription__FKey ContactFKeyTitle** table occurrence. This relationship is designed to check if a record is related by both the contact and title records being the same. It will later be used to test whether a contact has renewed a subscription or let it lapse. The relationship formula is shown in Figure 19.19.

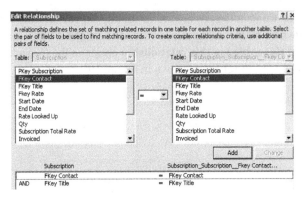

Figure 19.19: The relationship between Subscription and
Subscription_Subscription__Fkey ContactFKeyTitle.

3.3: The Title TOG

From a Title Details layout, the business manager want to get a snapshot of
all subscriptions for a selected magazine title, whether lapsed or active, all
invoices which at least in part include a subscription for the magazine, and a
list of rates or prices for subscriptions.

The Title TOG is shown in Figure 19.20.

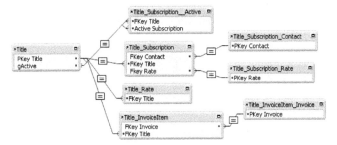

Figure 19.20: The Title TOG.

1.   The relationship between **Title** and **Title_Rate** will need to be modified
     so that new rate records can be created through this relationship.
     Double-click anywhere along the relationship line in order to open the
     Edit Relationship dialog box. Then check the **Allow creation of new
     records in this table via this relationship** option in the Title_Rate table
     via this relationship.

2.   All but one of the Title TOG relationships are equijoins, with a single
     field forming each side of the relationship. The exception is the relation-
     ship between the **Title** and **Title_Subscription__Active** table occur-
     rences. This relationship is designed to flag only active subscriptions to a
     title. The formula for this relationship is detailed in Figure 19.21.

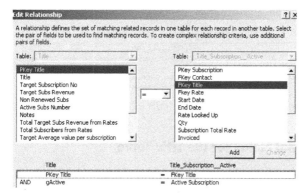

Figure 19.21: The relationship between Title and
Title_Subscription__Active.

3.4: The Invoice TOG

In order to create and print an invoice for subscriptions, the Invoice TOG will
need to include relationships to invoice items and the contact to whom the
invoice is addressed. To display subscription information on the invoice, further relationships will need to be established to table occurrences for the
Rate, **Subscription**, and **Title** tables.

The Invoice TOG is shown below in Figure 19.22.

Figure 19.22: The Invoice TOG.

Step 4: Adding Calculation and Lookup Fields to the FMSubs File Tables

The new TOGs in the relationships graph can be used to add some calculation
and lookup fields to the tables in order to maximize the effectiveness of the
subscription management software.

4.1: Additional Fields for the Contact Table

In order to display total subscription values for an individual along with a
count of related records in a Contact Details layout, the fields listed in Figure
19.23 need to be added to the Contact table.

Tables | Fields | Relationships

Table: Contact — 25 fields defined

Field Name	Type	Options / Comments (Click to toggle)
Total Subscription Fee	Calculation	Unstored, from Contact, = Sum (Contact_Subscription::Subscription Total Rate)
Count Subscriptions	Calculation	Unstored, from Contact, = Count (Contact_Subscription::FKey Contact)
Count Active Subscriptions	Calculation	Unstored, from Contact, = Count (Contact_Subscription__active::FKey Contact)
Count Invoices	Calculation	Unstored, from Contact, = Count (Contact_Invoice::FKey Contact)

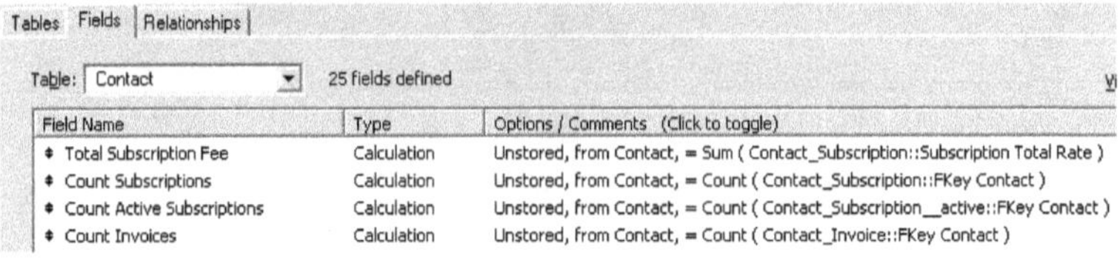

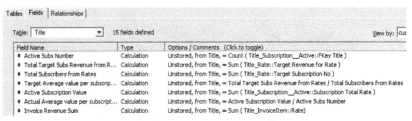

Figure 19.23: Additional fields for the Contact table.

4.2: Additional Fields for the Title Table

A layout based on the Title table occurrence will need to display the relative value of active and lapsed subscriptions for a magazine title. The fields shown in Figure 19.24 need to be added to the Title table.

Tables | Fields | Relationships

Table: Title — 15 fields defined — View by: cus

Field Name	Type	Options / Comments (Click to toggle)
Active Subs Number	Calculation	Unstored, from Title, = Count (Title_Subscription__Active::FKey Title)
Total Target Subs Revenue from R...	Calculation	Unstored, from Title, = Sum (Title_Rate::Target Revenue for Rate)
Total Subscribers from Rates	Calculation	Unstored, from Title, = Sum (Title_Rate::Target Subscription No)
Target Average value per subscrip...	Calculation	Unstored, from Title, = Total Target Subs Revenue from Rates / Total Subscribers from Rates
Active Subscription Value	Calculation	Unstored, from Title, = Sum (Title_Subscription__Active::Subscription Total Rate)
Actual Average value per subscript...	Calculation	Unstored, from Title, = Active Subscription Value / Active Subs Number
Invoice Revenue Sum	Calculation	Unstored, from Title, = Sum (Title_InvoiceItem::Rate)

Figure 19.24: Additional fields for the Title table.

4.3: An Additional Field and Lookup Definition for the Subscription Table

The **Rate Looked Up** field in the Subscription table can now be correctly defined using the Subscription_Rate relationship. The rate in the Subscription table is, of course, a looked-up value in case prices go up during the course of a subscription period. With a lookup value, the applicable rate at the time that

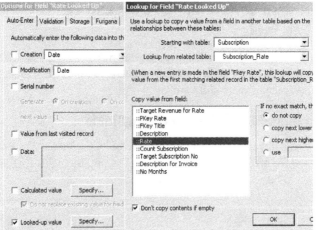

Figure 19.25: The lookup settings for the Rate Looked Up field in the Subscription table.

a subscription was taken out is the value used. The lookup settings are shown in Figure 19.25.

A new calculation field called **Subscription Status** can be added to the Subscription table. The formula for this calculation field, which uses the Case function to test whether a subscription is non-renewed, lapsed, or active, is shown in Figure 19.26.

Subscription Status =

```
Case ( End Date = Max ( Subscription_Subscription__Fkey ContactFKeyTitle::End Date ) and
End Date ≤ Get ( CurrentDate );
"Non Renewed" ;
End Date ≠ Max ( Subscription_Subscription__Fkey ContactFKeyTitle::End Date ) and
End Date ≤ Get ( CurrentDate) ;
"Lapsed" ;
"Active")
```

Figure 19.26: The formula for the Subscription Status calculation field.

4.4: Additional Fields for the Invoice Table

The total for all invoice items can now be calculated in the Invoice table, and a summary field for all invoice totals can be included. A count of how many invoice items exist is also added to the table. These three additional fields are listed in Figure 19.27.

Tables Fields Relationships

Table: Invoice   8 fields defined

Field Name	Type	Options / Comments (Click to toggle)
◆ Invoice Total	Calculation	Unstored, from Invoice, = Sum (Invoice_InvoiceItem::Rate)
◆ Invoice Total Sum	Summary	= Total of Invoice Total
◆ Count Items	Calculation	Unstored, from Invoice, = Count (Invoice_InvoiceItem::FKey Invoice)

Figure 19.27: Additional fields for the Invoice table.

Step 5: Designing Data Entry and Report Layouts for the FMSubs File

The FMSubs subscription management database will need to include data entry layouts for contacts, magazine titles, and invoices. A good starting point to assist with navigating around these layouts is the creation of an FMSubs Main Menu, which will include navigation buttons to the subscription data layouts. Ideally, we want this layout to appear each time the FMSubs file is opened.

5.1: The FMSubs Main Menu Layout

When the FMSubs file was created, FileMaker created a default layout based on the FMSubs default table.

1.   With the **FMSubs** file open, if we switch to **Layout** mode, the default FMSubs layout should be the first layout in the database.

2. As we are going to make the FMSubs layout into a navigation menu and not display any record data, the header and footer layout parts can be dispensed with. Highlight the header and footer part labels in turn and press the **Backspace** or **Delete** key on the keyboard to delete them.

3. Give the remaining body part a background fill color by selecting the body part label and selecting a fill color in the **Color Palette** tool in the Status area.

4. Use the **Button** tool to create a background tile for the database title. The Duplicate menu option has been used to create a set of standard size buttons with labels to open the various data entry layouts or run reports. These buttons will be set to run specific scripts in due course.

5. Give the FMSubs Main Menu a layout title by using the **Layouts>Layout Setup** menu option. The layout is shown in Figure 19.28.

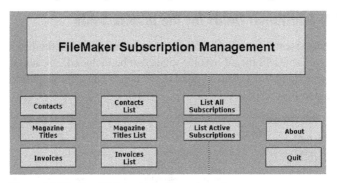

Figure 19.28: The FMSubs Main Menu layout.

The majority of the scripts for the solution will be discussed later in this chapter; however, two scripts that are directly linked to the Main Menu layout are described in this section.

6. The green About button is designed to provide more information on the solution and details about the author. The **About...** script, which is triggered by this button, is a good example of a conditional script. The Show Custom Dialog script step can display up to three buttons and, when combined with the LastMessageChoice function, the user's choice can be monitored by the script with a different outcome depending on which button is selected. In this case, the user can choose to open one of two websites. The About... script is shown in Figure 19.29.

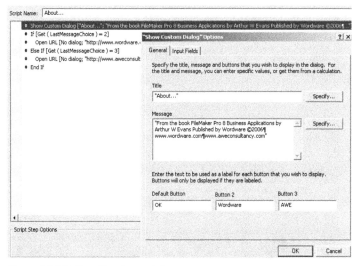

Figure 19.29: The About... script.

7. The red button labeled Quit is used to run a script of the same name. The **Quit** script also uses the Show Custom Dialog script step to create a conditional script. Depending on which button is selected, the user can choose to close the Subscription Management file or quit FileMaker. The Quit script is shown along with the Show Custom Dialog Options dialog box in Figure 19.30.

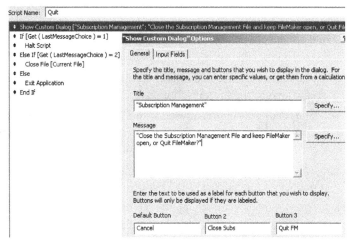

Figure 19.30: The Quit script is triggered by the button of the same name in the Main Menu layout.

5.2: The Contact Details Layout

The layout that FileMaker automatically created to display records for the Contact table can be used as the basis for the Contact Details layout, shown in Figure 19.31.

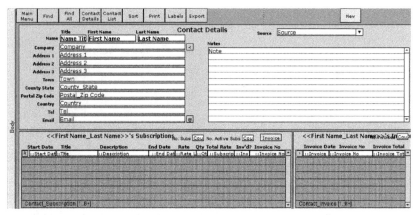

Figure 19.31: The Contact Details layout.

1. The **Button** tool has been used to divide the layout into three parts to show details on an individual, any related subscriptions using a portal to the Contact_Subscription table occurrence, and any invoices linked to the contact using a portal to the Contact_Invoice table occurrence.

2. The business manager wants to be able to renew subscriptions on an individual basis. The small green button labeled **R** to the left of each subscription will be linked to a script to do this.

3. The green button labeled **Invoice** will be set to run a script that creates a new invoice for any subscriptions that have not yet been invoiced.

4. The small gray button labeled with a left arrow (<) to the right of the Company field uses the Go to Related Record function to show if the company name is the same in any other contact records.

5. The button labeled with @ to the right of the Email field has been defined to run the Send Mail button command.

6. A series of standard navigation buttons across the top of the layout is designed to assist the database user in using the file.

7. Value lists are used for the contact's **Title** field and the **Source** field to indicate how the contact details were first acquired and the relative success of marketing campaigns.

8. The business manager wants to create new subscriptions using the portal in the Contact Details layout. To assist the database user, a drop-down

list using a preset value list will be set to appear when the Title field is clicked on in each Contact_Subscription portal row. To avoid any confusion by viewing the FKey Title field from the Contact_Subscription table, set this field to a width of only one pixel by using the Size dialog box. Use the keyboard arrow keys to position the FKey Title field just to the left of the Title field in the portal row. The field is shown and called out in dark gray in Figure 19.32.

Figure 19.32:
The "hidden"
FKey Title field in
the subscription
portal.

9. While the FKey Title field is still highlighted, use the menu option **Format>Field/Control>Setup** to allow the FKey Title field to display a drop-down list of magazine titles. A new value list will need to be defined. With FileMaker Pro 8, it is possible to hide a table's primary key field to help with clarity in picking an item from a value list. This is shown in Figure 19.33 for the definition of the PKey Title value list.

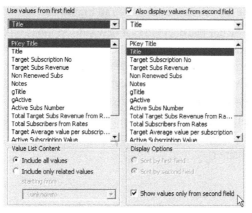

Figure 19.33:
The PKey Title
value list is set to
only show a
magazine title.

A script will be written that makes use of the Go to Field script step to select the FKey Title field. The Title field can be formatted as a button to run this script. The end result of all this effort is that when the Title field is clicked on in the subscription portal, a simple list of magazine titles will appear, making it easy to choose the correct title without the confusion of displaying an otherwise meaningless foreign key value on the layout.

The PKey Title value list, displayed as a drop-down list from the "hidden" FKey Title field, is shown in Figure 19.34.

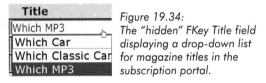

Figure 19.34:
The "hidden" FKey Title field
displaying a drop-down list
for magazine titles in the
subscription portal.

5.3: The Contact List Layout

A new list layout based on the Contact table occurrence can be used to give the business manager a view of several contacts and a count of related subscriptions, active subscriptions, and invoices.

The Contact List layout is shown in Figure 19.35.

Figure 19.35: The Contact List layout.

5.4: The Title Details Layout

The default Title layout can be adapted and used to display details on a magazine title. The Title Details layout is shown in Figure 19.36.

1. The business owner has decided that new subscriptions will be created from the Contact Details layout, so the portals for subscriptions and invoices do not need to create new related records. However, new and existing subscription rates can be created and modified through the Title_Rate portal in this layout.

2. A button labeled **New** is used to create a new magazine title record. The **Label** and **Export** buttons are linked to scripts that will be introduced later in this chapter.

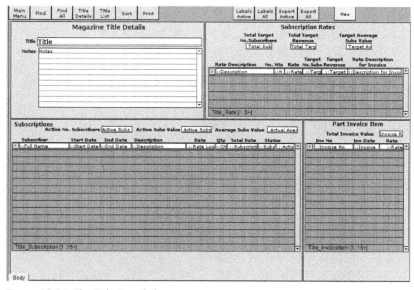

Figure 19.36: The Title Details layout.

5.5: The Magazine Title List Layout

A financial "heads up" can be given to the business manager using a new list layout based on the Title table occurrence.

The Magazine Title List layout, shown in Figure 19.37, includes calculation fields to show the totals for subscribers, together with target and actual revenue figures for each magazine.

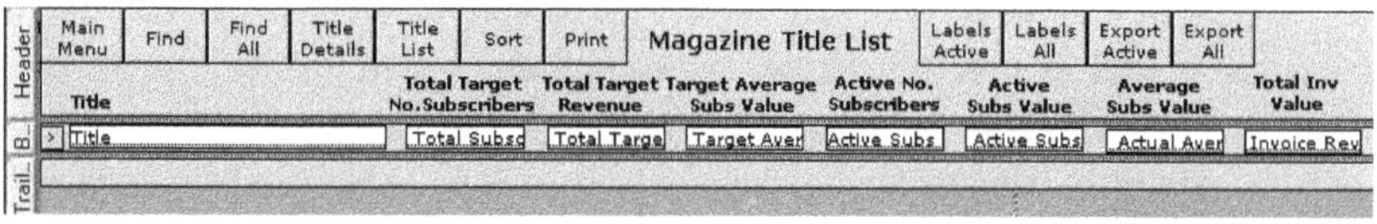

Figure 19.37: The Magazine Title List layout.

5.6 The Invoice Layout

Each invoice record is linked to a contact and should display the relevant subscriptions that go to make up the invoice total. The Invoice layout is shown in Figure 19.38.

A portal showing related records from the Invoice_InvoiceItem table occurrence is included in the layout, and merge fields are used to place the contact's address details in the correct position for window envelopes.

A non-printing button makes use of the Go to Related Record function to switch to the contact record using the Contact Details layout.

The Invoice total is displayed at the bottom of the portal. In this basic subscription example, sales tax is not included in consumer magazine subscription invoices.

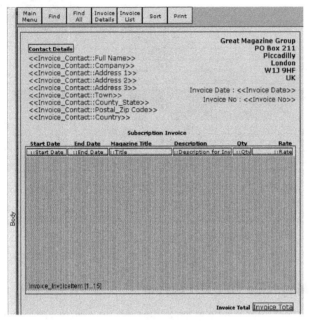

Figure 19.38: The Invoice layout.

5.7: The Invoice List Layout

A List view layout based on the Invoice table occurrence is used to display several invoices on screen, with a summary total for the found set displayed in a trailing grand summary layout part. The Invoice List layout is displayed in Figure 19.39.

Figure 19.39: The Invoice List layout.

5.8: The Subscription List Layout

A list layout based on the Subscription table occurrence is useful for allowing searches to be made of active and historic magazine subscriptions. A trailing grand summary layout part is used to display a record count and the summary subscription total.

The Subscription List layout is shown in Figure 19.40.

Figure 19.40: The Subscription List layout.

5.9: Contact and Subscription Labels

A newly established magazine firm is usually faced with the problem of printing subscription labels. FileMaker's Layout wizard can be used to create two new label layouts, one based on the Contact table occurrence, as shown in Figure 19.41, and a second based on the Subscription table occurrence, as shown in Figure 19.42. Once the dimensions have been fine-tuned for a specific printer, the dimensions of the layout can be repeated for any label layout. Two buttons have been set to not print using the **Format>Set Sliding/Printing** menu option. These buttons are set to return to the Contact or Subscription layouts, or to print the label sheets for the found set of records. In the case of the Subscription Labels layout, the magazine title is included in the layout.

Figure 19.41: The Contact Labels layout.

Figure 19.42: The Subscription Labels layout.

A set of scripts are now needed to automate the management of subscription records using the FMSubs database.

Step 6: Automating the FMSubs File with Scripts

The business manager can expect FileMaker to manage the creation of new invoices based on subscription records. An effective subscription management database should also be able to automate a selected subscription renewal.

At some stage the business manager may want to export subscription details for printers or fulfillment houses. ScriptMaker is ideal for automating and managing data exports.

6.1: The Opening and Navigation Scripts

As with all the solutions in this book, an opening script will be written that ensures the Main Menu layout is always selected when the file is first opened. As there is no reason to show the Status area with the Main Menu layout, since it does not relate to any particular record set, a script step will hide it. The downside of this is that a series of navigation scripts will be needed to switch to the correct data layout and make the Status area visible again.

The Opening script for the FMSubs file is shown in Figure 19.43.

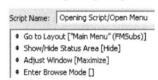

Figure 19.43: The Opening script.

An example of one of the navigation scripts to open a data entry layout is shown in Figure 19.44. The Show/Hide Status Area step is now set to [Show].

The buttons in the Main Menu layout are set to run a corresponding navigation script.

Figure 19.44: The Open Subscribers navigation script.

6.2: The Invoice Outstanding Subscriptions for Contact Script

It is good business practice to want to invoice any subscriptions as and when they are requested. A script needs to be triggered by a button in the Contact Details layout that creates a new invoice for any new subscriptions.

This script needs some checks to make sure that a subscription is never invoiced twice, and is shown in Figure 19.45.

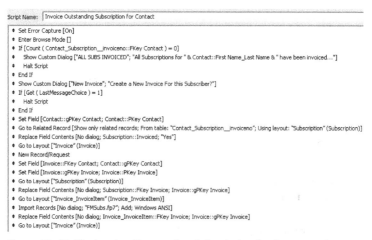

Script Name: Invoice Outstanding Subscription for Contact

- Set Error Capture [On]
- Enter Browse Mode []
- If [Count (Contact_Subscription__invoiceno::FKey Contact) = 0]
-     Show Custom Dialog ["ALL SUBS INVOICED"; "All Subscriptions for " & Contact::First Name_Last Name & " have been invoiced..."]
-     Halt Script
- End If
- Show Custom Dialog ["New Invoice"; "Create a New Invoice For this Subscriber?"]
- If [Get (LastMessageChoice) = 1]
-     Halt Script
- End If
- Set Field [Contact::gPKey Contact; Contact::PKey Contact]
- Go to Related Record [Show only related records; From table: "Contact_Subscription__invoiceno"; Using layout: "Subscription" (Subscription)]
- Replace Field Contents [No dialog; Subscription::Invoiced; "Yes"]
- Go to Layout ["Invoice" (Invoice)]
- New Record/Request
- Set Field [Invoice::FKey Contact; Contact::gPKey Contact]
- Set Field [Invoice::gPKey Invoice; Invoice::PKey Invoice]
- Go to Layout ["Subscription" (Subscription)]
- Replace Field Contents [No dialog; Subscription::FKey Invoice; Invoice::gPKey Invoice]
- Go to Layout ["Invoice_InvoiceItem" (Invoice_InvoiceItem)]
- Import Records [No dialog; "FMSubs.fp7"; Add; Windows ANSI]
- Replace Field Contents [No dialog; Invoice_InvoiceItem::FKey Invoice; Invoice::gPKey Invoice]
- Go to Layout ["Invoice" (Invoice)]

Figure 19.45: The Invoice Outstanding Subscription for Contact script.

The script steps can be described as follows:

If no related subscriptions that have not yet been invoiced are found, a custom dialog message will appear and the script will be halted. If there are related subscription records that have not yet been invoiced, a custom dialog message will ask the user to confirm the wish to go ahead and create a new invoice. If the user confirms this, the global field gPKey Contact is set to be equal to the current contact's primary key field value. The related subscription records that have not yet been invoiced are isolated using the Go to Related Record script step. The subset of records then have their invoice status changed to "Yes". A new invoice record is then created and related to the contact by setting the FKey Contact field to be the same as the global gPKey Contact field. The global field gPKey Invoice is set to be the same as the primary key for the new invoice. The isolated set of subscription records have the contents of their FKey Invoice field set to the new invoice primary key value. The script then switches to the InvoiceItem layout and imports the isolated set of subscriptions. Finally, the FKey Invoice field in these new InvoiceItem records are replaced with the new invoice's primary key field value. The script then ends back in the new invoice record.

6.3: The Renew Single Subscription Script

The green R button in each subscription portal row in the Contact Details layout will be set to perform a script that renews the chosen magazine. The Renew Single Subscription script is displayed in Figure 19.46.

Script Name: Renew Single Subscription

- Set Error Capture [On]
- If [Count (Contact_Subscription::FKey Contact) = 0]
-     Show Custom Dialog ["No Subscriptions"; "No Subscriptions held for this Contact!..."]
-     Halt Script
- End If
- Show Custom Dialog ["Renewals"; "Renew Selected Subscription for this Contact?"]
- If [Get (LastMessageChoice) = 1]
-     Exit Script []
- End If
- Go to Related Record [Show only related records; From table: "Contact_Subscription"; Using layout: "Subscription" (Subscription)]
- Set Field [Subscription::gEnd Date; Subscription::End Date]
- Duplicate Record/Request
- Set Field [Subscription::Fkey Rate; "" & Subscription::Fkey Rate]
- Set Field [Subscription::Start Date; Date (Month (Subscription::gEnd Date) + 1; Day (Subscription::gEnd Date); Year (Subscription::gEnd Date))]
- Go to Layout [original layout]

Figure 19.46: The Renew Single Subscription script.

The script steps can be described as follows:

The script checks to see if any subscriptions are held for the current contact record. If no related subscriptions exist, the script will be halted. The database user is then presented with a custom dialog box asking to confirm the renewal of the selected subscription for this contact. If the user chooses to continue, the script isolates the related subscription record using the Go to Related Record script step. A global date field is then set to be the same as the subscription record's end date. A new subscription for the same title and contact is then created and the start date is set to be equal to the global end date plus one month. The current subscription rate is looked up for the new subscription record using the Set Field script step in the FKey Rate field. Finally, the script returns to the original Contact Details layout.

6.4: The Export Contacts Script

FileMaker can export records in a variety of file formats. These can be automated using variations of the Export Record script step. The Export Contacts script is shown in Figure 19.47.

Script Name: | Export Contacts

- ✦ Show Custom Dialog ["EXPORT CONTACTS"; "EXPORT the current set of Contacts?"]
- ✦ If [Get (LastMessageChoice) = 1]
- ✦   Halt Script
- ✦ End If
- ✦ Sort Records [Restore; No dialog]
- ✦ Show Custom Dialog ["EXPORT FILE TYPE"; "Please select an EXPORT File Type for the Contact records...Tab, comma (CSV) or Merge"]
- ✦ If [Get (LastMessageChoice) = 1]
- ✦   Export Records ["Subcontacts.tab"; Windows (ANSI)]
- ✦ Else If [Get (LastMessageChoice) = 2]
- ✦   Export Records ["Subcontacts.csv"; Windows (ANSI)]
- ✦ Else
- ✦   Export Records ["Subcontacts.mer"; Windows (ANSI)]
- ✦ End If
- ✦ Show Custom Dialog ["EXPORT FILE COMPLETE"; "A new exported Subcontacts text file has now been created..."]

Figure 19.47: The Export Contacts script.

The script can be described as follows:

A custom dialog prompts the user to confirm the wish to export the current found set of contact records. The records are then sorted by last name, first name, and company. A further custom dialog box shown in Figure 19.48 gives the database user the choice of selecting a tab delimited, comma separated, or merge text field format export file. The Export Records script step has been customized three times for each of these text format options. Finally, a confirmation message informs the user that a new text file called Subcontacts has been created.

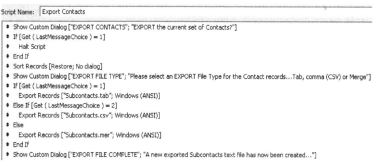

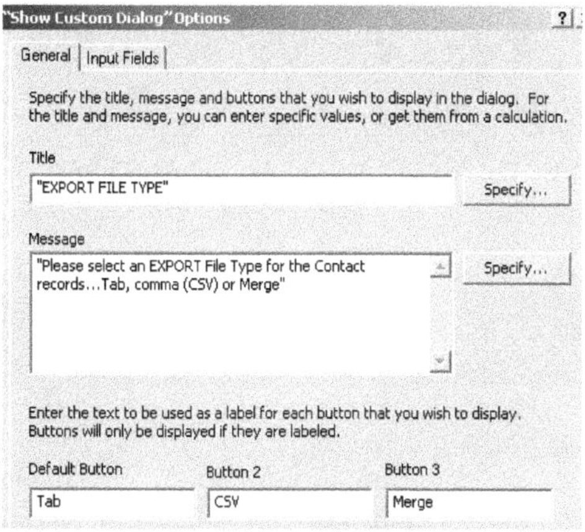

Figure 19.48: The custom dialog box that gives the user the option to choose from three different text formats for the exported contact records.

The Export Contacts script can also be used for a selected set of subscription records.

Taking the Solution Further

A natural progression for a subscription management solution is to encourage subscribers to keep their own details up to date and manage their own renewals via a web page. In a basic format, this is possible using the Instant Web Publishing capabilities of FileMaker Pro. The method for publishing a FileMaker database with Instant Web Publishing is discussed in Chapter 27.

The business owner may wish to use email marketing techniques to remind subscribers that their renewal date is approaching or generate reminder letters each week as a renewal date approaches. This could be done on a "three strikes and you're out" basis, with a reminder letter automatically generated 30 days before renewal, another letter on the renewal date if there has been no response, and a third and final letter sent 30 days after the subscription has lapsed. FileMaker is ideal for designing letter layouts and writing scripts that automate the process of finding renewals over a period of time.

Chapter 20

Patient and Treatment Management

Introduction

Accurate data management is crucial to anyone involved in health care and patient record management. FileMaker is used by many hospitals and physicians to record details on patients; the name of the specialist, general practitioner, or consultant who referred a patient in the first place; details on a patient's condition at the time of consultation; and ongoing treatment details. FileMaker is also capable of managing the administrative element of private patient health care by processing bills on behalf of the care provider for treatment of the patient.

Records of procedural history, or what has been done to whom and when, is of course a requirement across many business sectors. When I recently took my car in for major service, I was struck by how similar the data management element of logging the car service was to recording medical details for a patient. Both procedures require accurate recording of the subject's details, for both the car and the person. A record is created of what work is to be done using standard codes and procedure descriptions, with a standard pricing structure for the work. While I don't want to take the comparison between surgery and other service industries too far, even if you are not involved in the health sector, hopefully you may find that some of the techniques used in this case study could be applied for your own database design requirements.

Health insurance providers are increasingly requesting that physicians and dentists provide details on treatment in an electronic format. The capability of FileMaker to export records in delimited text format and Extensible Markup Language (XML) means that FileMaker is ideal for managing patient records within a practice, while being compatible with larger hospital or insurance database systems.

Private physicians and their staff need to record contact details on individuals, their ages, and state of health at the time they first became patients of the doctor. The contact details of the patient's primary care physician and specialists will be important, and it is likely that reports to fellow doctors on a patient's condition or the success of treatment will be needed. Specific details on treatment provided and at what location needs to be logged. Some private health plans or government departments have standard codes and applicable fees for procedures and it would be a good idea to keep this in a database table. The private surgeon needs to create a bill for treatment and present this either to the patient or to the health insurance company.

As with the other case studies in this book, a copy of the completed FileMaker Pro 8 database file, **Patient Management**, is available to download from the publisher's website at www.wordware.com/files/fmapps and the author's website at www.aweconsultancy.com. You may find it easier to examine some of the FileMaker features and techniques discussed in this chapter in a copy of the completed file.

The default database password for the Admin account is **DOCTOR** (all capitals). The database file options have been preset to open with the active Guest account (with read-only access to the file). To open the file with full access privileges, hold down the Shift key (Windows) or Option key (Mac OS) while the file is opening. Type the word **Admin** in the Account Name box and type the password in the box below. You can change the default password at a later stage. More information on database security issues, passwords, accounts, and privileges is given in Chapter 24.

Let's start by considering what tables we need to manage patient, treatment, and billing records.

The Patient Management Entity Relationship Diagram

The surgeon needs to keep details on a **Patient**. It is likely that the patient will have been referred to the surgeon through a general practitioner or **Doctor**. In many cases the patient will already have seen a **Consultant**, who may also have made the original patient referral. The surgeon is going to want to record what happened when the patient was seen during a course of **Treatment**. Several procedures may be carried out while the patient is being seen. Each procedure can be considered as a **Treatment Item**. There are likely to be standard codes and prices in place for procedures. These may change over time, so it would be best to hold them in a lookup table for **Procedures**. After treatment, the surgeon will want to be paid for his services by processing a bill or **Invoice**. The invoice should represent the various procedures carried out. Each treatment item should therefore have an equivalent **InvoiceItem**.

The basic way in which these tables are related can be viewed in the entity relationship diagram shown in Figure 20.1.

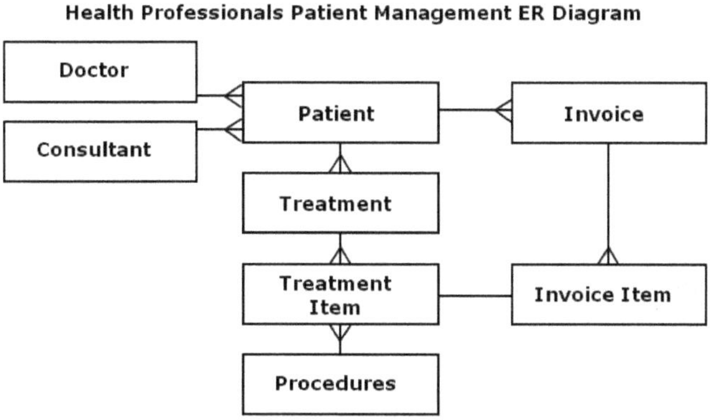

Health Professionals Patient Management ER Diagram

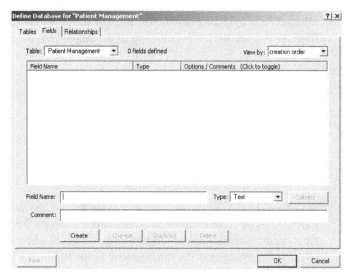

Figure 20.1: The Patient Management entity relationship diagram.

Building the Patient Management File

Step 1: Adding Tables to the Patient Management File

1. Launch FileMaker and create a new file called **Patient Management**.

   FileMaker will automatically open the Define Database dialog box with the Fields tab selected for the default Patient Management table, as shown in Figure 20.2.

Figure 20.2: The Define Database dialog box for a new file with the Fields tab selected for the default table.

2. Click on the **Tables** tab at the top of the Define Database dialog box and add the additional eight tables listed in Figure 20.3.

Patient Management
Patient
Treatment
Treatment Item
Procedures
Invoice
InvoiceItem
Doctor
Consultant

Figure 20.3: The tables needed for the Patient Management file.

Step 2: Adding Fields to the Patient Management File Tables

As with the other case studies in this book, we need to add a primary key field to each of our tables using FileMaker's ability to automatically assign a unique serial number to each record in each table. In addition, we will need to add foreign key fields to any of the tables to which we need to establish a relationship.

1. To add fields to each of the tables within the file, choose the **File>Define>Database** menu option and the **Fields** tab of the Define Database dialog box. It is important to ensure that the correct table is selected prior to adding new fields. Each of the tables can be selected from the drop-down list near the top of the dialog box, as shown in Figure 20.4.

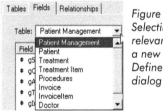

Figure 20.4: Selecting the relevant table for a new field in the Define Database dialog box.

We will add initial fields to each table as shown in Figures 20.5 to 20.16. Later, when we have established relationships between these tables using table occurrences in the relationships graph, we will add additional fields to the tables to improve the functionality of the file.

We will want to customize the solution business details for an individual surgeon or health practice. We can do this by creating a series of global text fields in the Patient Management table.

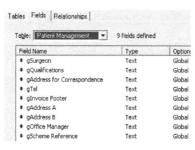

Figure 20.5:
The global fields
used to customize
the file for a patient
management
solution.

2. Add the text fields shown in Figure 20.5 to the Patient Management table. For each text field, click the **Options** button to open the Options for Field dialog box. Click the **Storage** tab at the top of the dialog box and click the **Use global storage** check box, as shown in Figure 20.6.

Figure 20.6:
Selecting the
global storage
option for a field.

Setting the global storage option means that the text fields for an individual surgeon can be displayed in any layout without the need to create a relationship from that layout's underlying base table to the table that holds the global fields.

In this solution, we will also make use of global number fields to temporarily store the contents of a record's primary key field when we create new related records in another table. As an example, a global number field will be used to store a treatment event's primary key field value, which can then be placed as the treatment event's foreign key field value in a new related invoice record.

3. FileMaker can allocate a unique serial number for each record's primary key, or PKey, field, which is required for each of the data tables in the solution. For example, after creating a new number field called **PKey Patient** in the Patient table, click the **Options** button in the Define Fields dialog box. Select the **Auto-Enter** tab, check the **Serial number** option, and set an initial value of **1** and an increment of **1**.

4. By careful use of value lists in conjunction with foreign key fields, there is no reason to display the primary key field in any of the layouts in our solution. This means that there is little chance of the unique serial number field value being modified, duplicated, or erased by a user accidentally clicking into the field in a layout. Despite this, it is good

practice to also check the **Prohibit modification of value during data entry** option, as shown in Figure 20.7.

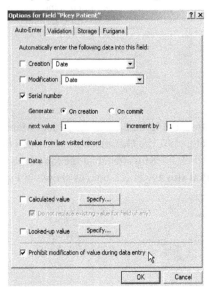

Figure 20.7: The auto-enter options for all primary key fields in the Patient Management solution.

5. The initial fields required for the **Patient** table are shown in Figure 20.8.

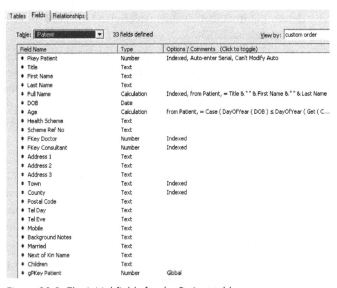

Figure 20.8: The initial fields for the Patient table.

The Patient table includes two calculation fields for an individual's full name and age. The formulas in these calculation fields are based on the contents of other fields. The **Full Name** formula is a concatenation of the Title, First Name, and Last Name fields. The Age formula makes use of the date given in the DOB (date of birth) date field. The formula for the **Age** field is shown in Figure 20.9 and is based on a test to see whether or not an individual's birthday has been reached during the present year. If it has, the formula simply has to subtract the year the patient was born from the current year. If the birthday is yet to occur in the current year, then 1 must be subtracted from the year difference.

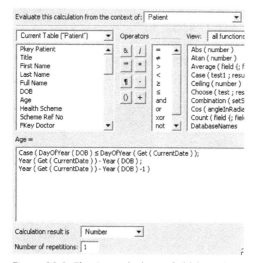

Figure 20.9: The Age calculation field formula.

6. The initial fields for the **Treatment** table are shown in Figure 20.10. Later, when we have created a relationship between the Patient and Treatment tables using the PKey Patient field, we can set the Age at time of Treatment field to look up the current age of an individual.

At the time the record is created, a treatment event will not have been invoiced, so the Treatment Invoiced text field has an auto-entered value of "N". The contents of this field value can be automatically changed to "Y" with a script that creates a new invoice for a treatment event.

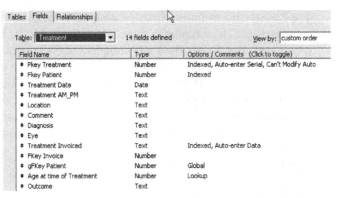

Figure 20.10: The initial fields for the Treatment table.

7. The fields for the **Treatment Item** table are shown in Figure 20.11. When a relationship between the Treatment Item and Procedures tables has been established, the Fee Looked Up field can be set to look up the fee for a specific treatment item based on the PKey Procedure field.

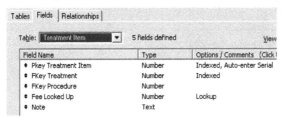

Figure 20.11: The fields for the Treatment Item table.

8. The **Procedures** table is designed to hold records for all billable services that a surgeon may undertake and the associated fees for the services. The fields for the Procedures table are shown in Figure 20.12.

To assist with the selection of the correct procedure in the Treatment Details layout that we will design, we will want to include the medical code and the procedure description in a value list alongside the PKey Procedure serial number field. To enable more than two fields to be displayed in a value list, we use a calculation field, which in this case concatenates the Medical Code and Procedure text fields.

Field Name	Type	Options / Comments (Click to toggle)
PKey Procedure	Number	Indexed, Auto-enter Serial, Can't Modify Auto
Medical Code	Text	
Procedure	Text	Indexed
Last Updated	Date	Modification Date
Fee	Number	
Medical Code_Procedure	Calculation	Indexed, from Procedures, = Medical Code & " " & Procedure

Figure 20.12: The fields for the Procedures table.

9. The **Invoice** table will be related to the Patient, Treatment, and
   InvoiceItem tables. The initial fields for the Invoice table are shown in
   Figure 20.13. The Amount Paid and Amount Paid Date fields are
   designed to record the amount and date of payments received from the
   patient for an invoice. These fields are defined to be repeating fields with
   three repetitions to capture partial payments. The Total Paid calculation
   field totals the Amount Paid repeating field using the Sum function.

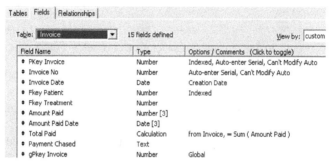

Figure 20.13: The initial fields for the Invoice table.

10. The **InvoiceItem** table holds details on the fees charged for each treat-
    ment item at the time of treatment. The InvoiceItem table can be seen in
    Figure 20.14.

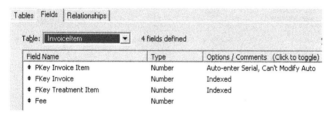

Figure 20.14: The fields for the InvoiceItem table.

11. The **Doctor** table will hold records on doctors or general practitioners
    who refer patients to the surgeon. To assist in selecting the correct doctor
    record from a value list, a concatenated calculation field called Doc-
    tor_Address1_Town has been included, as shown in Figure 20.15.

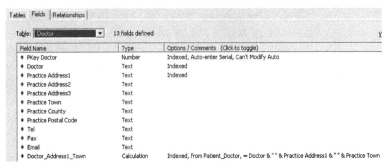

Figure 20.15: The initial fields for the Doctor table.

12. The **Consultant** table will also hold contact details on other surgeons or consultants who have referred patients. The surgeon may want to correspond with consultants on the outcome of patient treatment. A text field called Formal_Informal will display a value list with these values, and the Salutation calculation field can be used as a merge field in a letter layout with the correct level of formality. Note that in the Salutation formula, the default outcome is "formal." The Consultant table fields are shown in Figure 20.16.

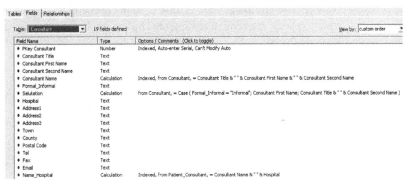

Figure 20.16: The initial fields for the Consultant table.

We can now use the primary and foreign key fields from the tables to create a series of relationships using FileMaker's relationships graph. We will then be able to add some additional calculation fields to the tables that use related tables in their formulas and redefine some text and number fields to use lookup values.

Step 3: Adding Relationships within the Patient Management File

The surgeon or the practice manager will want to be able to trust FileMaker to manage the creation of new treatment records and generate accurate invoices.

This can be achieved by good design of several table occurrence groups, or TOGs, in the relationships graph, and data entry layouts that match the method by which the surgeon wishes to record patient and treatment information.

1. If the Define Database dialog box is not open, select the menu option **File>Define>Database** and click the **Relationships** tab at the top of the dialog box. The nine base tables that we have created for the Patient Management file will be visible as table occurrences, as shown in Figure 20.17.

Figure 20.17: The initial relationships graph for the Patient Management file showing the nine base tables.

As with the other case study FileMaker solutions, we do not link the underlying base tables directly in the relationships graph. Instead, relationships are built up between table occurrences, which are representations of the base tables in the relationships graph. It is possible to have any number of table occurrences on the relationships graph for the same underlying base table.

As introduced in Chapter 7, our aim is to refine the relationships graph into a series of discrete TOGs. Each TOG should have a main or "anchor" table occurrence on its left-hand side, with any number of linked "buoy" tables related to the anchor table spread out on the right-hand side. To ease relationship design at the outset and to assist you or any colleagues who may work on the file at a later stage, a number of fundamental rules should be followed when using relationships in any FileMaker solution:

■ As a general rule, any relationships graph will have one anchor table occurrence for every base table in the file.

■ All data entry layouts should only be based on an underlying anchor table occurrence.

■ Any portals on layouts should be based on buoy table occurrences.

■ To assist with documenting a complex FileMaker project, it is a good idea to limit the dimensions of any TOGs in the relationships graph to a single page in width but any number of pages in length.

To get the required functionality from our Patient Management solution, we now need to add some TOGs to the relationships graph.

2. For the sake of reference, it is a good idea to preserve at least one table occurrence for each base table within the file displayed at the top of the relationships graph. To reduce the space used, click on the button on the table header to toggle the display of the table and collapse it to its title only, as shown in Figure 20.18.

3. Note that an underscore (_) has been added to each of the base table occurrences so that the original table name can be used as an anchor table occurrence. Each table occurrence must have a unique name in the graph. A table occurrence can be renamed by double-clicking on it to open the Specify Table dialog box, or by highlighting the table occurrence and clicking the **Edit** button at the bottom of the graph (the button with a yellow pencil icon).

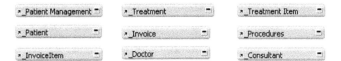

Figure 20.18: The reference base tables collapsed to display only the table titles.

3.1: The Patient TOG

The surgeon has decided that a Patient Details layout will form the central information "hub" of the database. New patients will be added to the database in the Patent Details layout, and new treatment records can be created for existing patient records. The surgeon or practice manager will also want to view summary details on invoices generated for each patient and details of payments received. The name of the doctor or consultant who referred the patient also needs to be displayed.

The Patient TOG will therefore be used to manage the relationships between patients, referring doctors and consultants, treatment history, invoices generated, and payments received.

The Patient TOG is shown with the Patient table occurrence as the anchor table on the left-hand side in Figure 20.19.

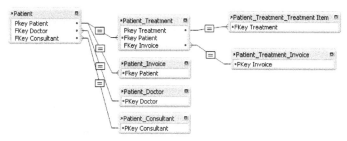

Figure 20.19: The Patient table occurrence group.

The surgeon wants to create new treatment records by means of a script with a custom warning message. As related records will not be created through portals in the Patient Details layout, we do not need to modify any of the relationships in the Patient TOG to allow creation of records via the relationship.

3.2: The Treatment TOG

Once a new treatment record has been created for a patient, the surgeon will want to add new related treatment item records via a portal in the Treatment Details layout. In order to select the correct procedure from a value list, we will need a relationship between Treatment, Treatment Item, and Procedures in this TOG, as shown in Figure 20.20. Each treatment record is also related to a patient and an invoice record.

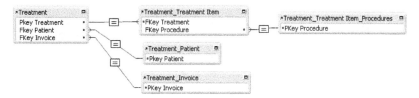

Figure 20.20: The Treatment table occurrence group.

3.3: The Invoice TOG

Once created, an invoice record is related to more than one invoice item record. For these to display correctly in an invoice on screen and on paper, each treatment item must also be related to a procedure to show the correct procedure name and treatment record, which in turn is related to a patient. A direct relationship between the Invoice and Patient tables can also be established. The Invoice TOG is shown in Figure 20.21.

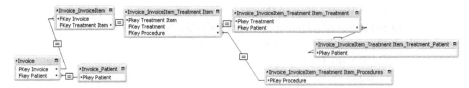

Figure 20.21: The Invoice table occurrence group.

3.4: The Doctor TOG

The surgeon decides that in a list layout displaying records about doctors, it would be of benefit to display a count of how many patients each doctor has referred. A Count Patients calculation field needs to make use of a relationship between the Doctor and Patient tables using the Doctor primary and foreign key fields. The Doctor TOG is displayed in Figure 20.22.

Figure 20.22: The Doctor table occurrence group.

3.5: The Consultant TOG

In a similar manner to the Doctor TOG, a relationship between the Consultant and Patient tables will enable the surgeon to see which consultants are referring the most patients, based on a count of the Consultant foreign key field in the Patient table. The Consultant TOG can be seen in Figure 20.23.

Figure 20.23: The Consultant table occurrence group.

3.6: The Treatment Item TOG

A relationship is needed between the Treatment Item and Procedures tables so that the correct fee can be looked up at the time of treatment. The Treatment Item TOG is shown in Figure 20.24.

Figure 20.24: The Treatment Item table occurrence group.

3.7: Stand-alone Table Occurrences in the Patient Management File

Layouts will be needed to capture global field details on the surgeon's practice and display tables of procedures and invoice items in order for a script to convert treatment events into invoices. Three isolated or stand-alone table occurrences are therefore needed in the relationships graph based on the InvoiceItem, Procedures, and Patient Management tables. These are shown in Figure 20.25.

Figure 20.25: The three stand-alone table occurrences in the Patient Management file.

Additional calculation and lookup fields that make use of these table occurrences in their definitions can now be added to the Patient Management tables.

Step 4: Adding Calculation and Lookup Fields to the Patient Management Tables

We can maximize the effectiveness of the Patient Management file to manage a surgeon's practice by using calculation fields to add up an invoice for treatment or look up the current fee for an item of treatment.

If the Define Database dialog box is not open, select the **File>Define>Database** menu option. Click the **Fields** tab to return to the fields list for each of the tables in the Patient Management database.

4.1: Additional Fields for the Patient Table

In the Patient table, we can add a set of calculation and summary fields that count how many related records exist for a patient in the Treatment and Invoice tables, how much the patient has been invoiced, how much has been paid, and what is still owing. These new fields for the Patient table are displayed in Figure 20.26.

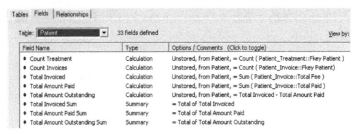

Figure 20.26: Additional fields for the Patient table.

4.2: Additional Fields for the Treatment Table

The Treatment table requires the addition of a calculation field to add up the fee for all related treatment items. The formula for the new Treatment Fee Total field is displayed in Figure 20.27.

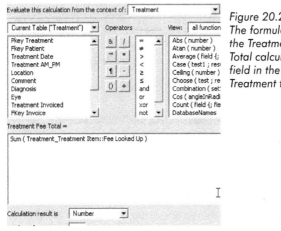

Figure 20.27: The formula for the Treatment Fee Total calculation field in the Treatment table.

The Age at time of Treatment field can now be set to be a looked-up value using the Treatment_Patient relationship to copy a patient's age when seen by the surgeon. The lookup setting is shown in Figure 20.28.

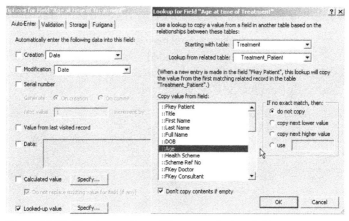

Figure 20.28: The Age at time of Treatment lookup field.

4.3: A Lookup Definition for a Field in the Treatment Item Table

In the Treatment Item table, the number field called Fee Looked Up can now
be set to be a lookup value based on the Treatment Item TOG. The lookup
settings for Fee Looked Up are shown in Figure 20.29.

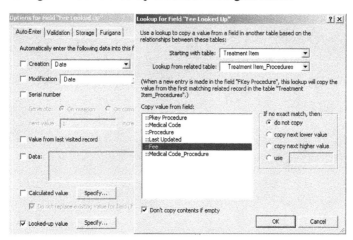

Figure 20.29: The Fee Looked Up field settings in the Treatment Item
table.

4.4: Additional Fields for the Doctor and Consultant Tables

To display how many patients are related to doctor and consultant records, a field called Count Patients must be added to both the Doctor and Consultant tables. The formula for the Count Patients field is shown for the Doctor table in Figure 20.30 and for the Consultant table in Figure 20.31.

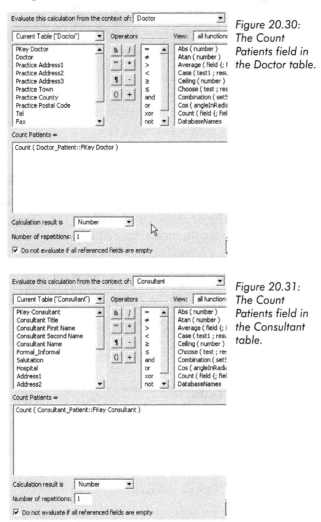

Figure 20.30: The Count Patients field in the Doctor table.

Figure 20.31: The Count Patients field in the Consultant table.

4.5: Additional Fields for the Invoice Table

We can add fields to the Invoice table that can display totals for the amount outstanding. We can then create summary fields for total fees, total paid, and amount outstanding. Figure 20.32 shows the additional Invoice table fields.

Tables   Fields   Relationships

Table: Invoice ▼   15 fields defined

Field Name	Type	Options / Comments (Click to toggle)
Total Fee	Calculation	Unstored, from Invoice, = Sum (Invoice_InvoiceItem::Fee)
Amount Outstanding	Calculation	Unstored, from Invoice, = Total Fee - Total Paid
Total Fee Sum	Summary	= Total of Total Fee
Total Paid Sum	Summary	= Total of Total Paid
Amount Outstanding Sum	Summary	= Total of Amount Outstanding

Figure 20.32: The additional fields needed for the Invoice table.

We are now ready to design a series of data entry and report layouts for the Patient Management solution.

Step 5: Designing Data Entry and Report Layouts for the Patient Management File

We need to design the most important part of our database solution, namely the data input and reporting screens that users of the software will spend the most time using. As discussed in Chapter 7, with FileMaker it is a good idea to base any data entry and report layouts on anchor table occurrences, which are the table occurrences to the far left of the table occurrence groups in our relationships graph.

5.1: Creating a Wizard Layout to Capture Surgeon Information

We need to create a layout that the surgeon can use to capture contact details on the practice. As this information is captured in global fields within the Patient Management table, the information can be used in any layout, regardless of any underlying relationships.

1. Open the Patient Management file, if it is not already open, and select the menu option **View>Layout Mode** to switch to Layout mode and create a new layout.

2. Choose the menu option **Layouts>New Layout/Report** to open the New Layout/Report dialog box. Choose to show records from the **Patient Management** table, type **Wizard** in the Layout Name box, and select **Blank layout**, as shown in Figure 20.33.

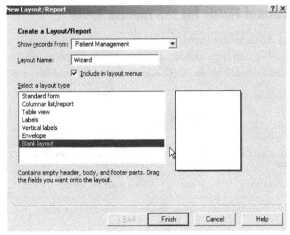

Figure 20.33: The New Layout/Report dialog box with the Show records from, Layout Name, and Select a layout type boxes filled in.

3. Delete the layout header and footer parts in the Wizard layout by highlighting the part label for each and pressing the **Backspace** or **Delete** key.

4. As shown in Figure 20.34, give the layout body a fill color, and use the **Button** tool to display the global fields on a background tile.

5. Add a button in the upper-left corner of the layout to link the Wizard layout back to a Main Menu layout.

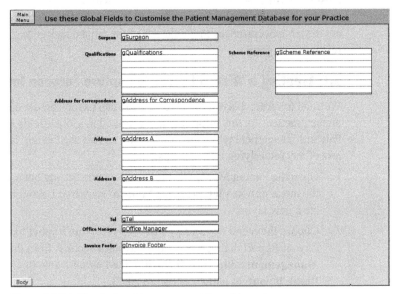

Figure 20.34: The Patient Management Wizard layout.

5.2: The Main Menu Layout

The surgeon and any colleagues using the database in the practice will gain confidence in the software if the same main menu or welcome screen appears every time the file is launched.

1. The Main Menu layout should include a set of navigation buttons to open the various data entry and list layouts. In addition, buttons can be included to provide technical support, open the Wizard layout, and safely close the database or quit FileMaker. The Main Menu layout is shown in Figure 20.35.

2. At the top of the layout, a "brass plate" is created that even has "screws" created with the **Circle** and **Line** tools. Merge fields for the surgeon name, qualifications, and mailing address are placed on the plate.

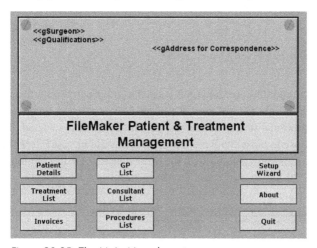

Figure 20.35: The Main Menu layout.

While scripts will be described in detail later in this chapter, two scripts that are directly linked to the Main Menu layout are described in this section.

3. The green About button is designed to provide more information on the solution and details about the author. The **About...** script, which is triggered by this button, is a good example of a conditional script. The Show Custom Dialog script step can display up to three buttons and, when combined with the LastMessageChoice function, the user's choice can be monitored by the script with a different outcome depending on which button is selected. In this case, the user can choose to open one of two websites. The About... script is shown in Figure 20.36.

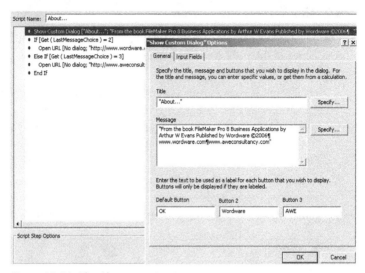

Figure 20.36: The About... script.

4. The red button labeled Quit is used to run a script with the same name.
    The **Quit** script also uses the Show Custom Dialog script step to create a
    conditional script. Depending on which button is selected, the user can
    choose to close the Patient Management file or quit FileMaker. The Quit
    script is shown along with the Show Custom Dialog Options box in Fig-
    ure 20.37.

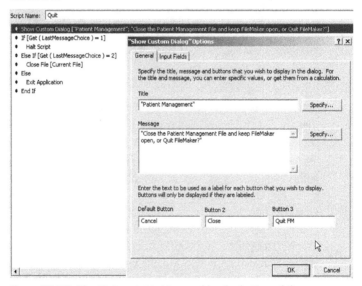

Figure 20.37: The Quit script is triggered by the button of the same
name in the Main Menu layout.

5.3: The Patient Details Layout

The Patient Details layout is designed to act as an information "hub" for the surgeon and the practice to view contact details for a patient, together with related treatment history, invoices, and payments received, all in one screen view.

1. The Patient Details layout makes use of two portals to show any related treatment and invoice records for the patient currently being viewed. The layout is displayed in Figure 20.38.

2. A series of standard navigation buttons at the top of the Patient Details layout will be copied and used in a similar form in most of the file's layouts to help users work with the file. The small gray buttons to the left of both portals make use of the Go to Related Record button command to switch to any related treatment or invoice records and display them using the correct Treatment or Invoice Details layouts.

3. Two green buttons can be seen in the Patient Details layout. The button labeled **New** is set to create a new record. The other green button, which is labeled **New Treatment**, will be set to run a script that creates a new related treatment record for the current patient.

4. Several value lists are displayed as drop-down lists in the Patient Details layout. The fields for Title, Health Scheme, and Married (status) are all defined to display as drop-down lists.

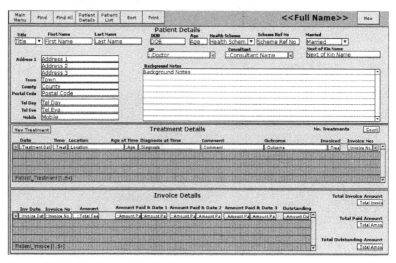

Figure 20.38: The Patient Details layout.

5. The surgeon wants to be able to select which doctor or consultant referred the currently viewed patient by using a value list of doctor and consultant records. As with the other case study solutions in this book,

the primary key for a related record is hidden in the value list to avoid confusion in selecting the correct value. Also whenever possible, the foreign key field is camouflaged or "hidden" on the layout to avoid this field being selected by the user, with the risk of accidental modification or deletion of the field's contents.

6. The user is "tricked" into thinking that the value list for doctors is actually linked to the Doctor field in the Patient Details layout. The Doctor field that is placed on the Patient Details layout is taken from the related Patient_Doctor table occurrence. To select the correct referring doctor, FileMaker expects the operator to type a valid Doctor primary key (PKey) value into the foreign key (FKey) Doctor field in the Patient Details layout. The procedure for selecting a valid FKey Doctor field value can be simplified for the user.

7. Most of us like to work with names rather than serial numbers. With FileMaker Pro 8 there is no need to include a table's unique primary key number in a value list. For example, to create a value list for doctors using the record set in the Doctor table, start by selecting the menu option **File>Define>Value Lists**. In the Define Value Lists dialog box, click the **New** button and name the new value list **Doctor List**. Click the **Use Values from Field** radio button and, in the Specify Fields dialog box, select the **Doctor** table. Choose **PKey Doctor** for the first field value and **Doctor_Address1_Town** for the second field, as shown in Figure 20.39. To hide the primary key for each value in the list, check the **Show values only from second field** option.

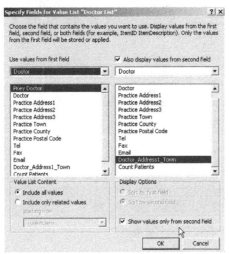

Figure 20.39: Hiding the PKey from the Doctor value list.

8. In the Patient Details layout, we want to make the Doctor value list appear when the FKey Doctor field is selected; however, for clarity on the layout we don't want the FKey Doctor field to be visible. This can be achieved by making the FKey Doctor field only one pixel wide by using the menu option **View>Object Size**. Before shrinking the field, highlight it and use the menu option **Format>Field/Control>Setup** to make the FKey Doctor field display the Doctor list as a drop-down list.

9. When the FKey Doctor field is one pixel wide, use the keyboard arrow keys to move the field just to the left of the Doctor field. The FKey Doctor field is shown in its correct position and called out in dark gray to illustrate its location in Figure 20.40.

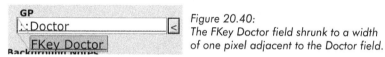

Figure 20.40:
The FKey Doctor field shrunk to a width of one pixel adjacent to the Doctor field.

10. We want the FKey Doctor field to be momentarily selected and display the Doctor value list every time the Doctor field is selected. This can be achieved by writing a new script called Display Doctor List, as shown in Figure 20.41. The Display Doctor List script consists of a single line that uses the Go to Field script step to jump to the FKey Doctor field. Note that even though a user can be prevented from selecting a field in Browse or Find mode by using the menu option **Format>File/Control/Behavior**, the Go to Field script step will still overwrite this behavior setting and select the target field when the script is run.

Figure 20.41: The Display Doctor List script.

11. To avoid the user accidentally changing the contents of the FKey Doctor field by tabbing or clicking the field, choose the menu option **Format> Field/Control>Behavior** to open the Field Behavior dialog box. To prevent a field from being selected in either Browse or Find mode, uncheck those options in the Field Behavior dialog box, as shown in Figure 20.42.

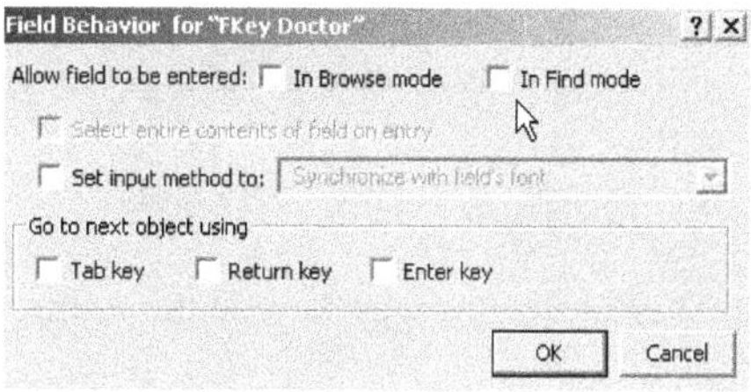

Figure 20.42:
The Field Behavior dialog box.

12. Finally, we need to select the Doctor field in Layout mode and use the menu option **Format>Button Setup** to define the field as a button that runs the Display Doctor List script.

A similar list of consultants can be created with a hidden FKey Consultant field for the Patient Details layout.

5.4: The Patient List Layout

A Patient List layout can be used to display several records on screen at once with a snapshot count of how many related treatment and invoice records exist for each patient. The left-hand side of the Patient List layout is shown in Figure 20.43, and the right-hand side, with summary fields for patient invoice amounts, payments received, and amount outstanding is shown in Figure 20.44.

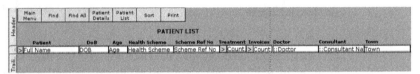

Figure 20.43: The Patient List layout (left side).

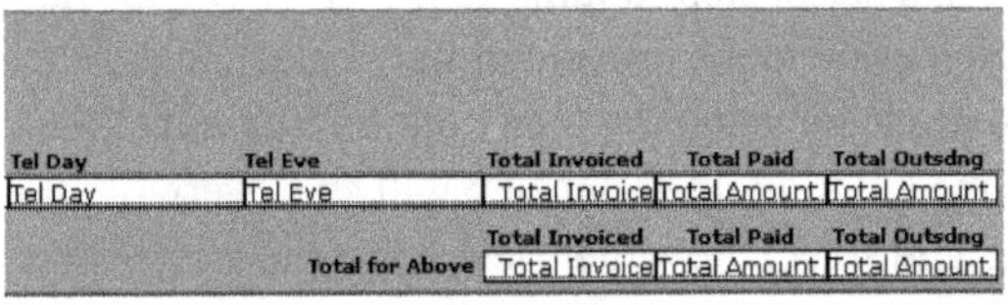

Figure 20.44: The right-hand side of the Patient List layout with summary fields for invoices, payments received, and amount outstanding.

5.5: The Doctor and Consultant List Layouts

Basic details on doctors and consultants need to be held in the Patient Management file. The surgeon is likely to want to store sufficient contact information to be able to create emails or letters to fellow health professionals.

New list layouts can be created to display records from the Doctor and Consultant table occurrences. Both tables have a calculation field that counts the number of related patients. The Count Patient field can be included in both list layouts, with a button that uses the Go to Related Record function to display any related patient records.

The Doctor List layout is shown in Figure 20.45 and the Consultant List layout in Figure 20.46.

There is no reason to display the primary key field in either list layout for doctors or consultants.

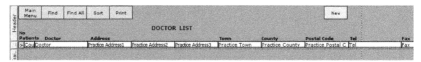

Figure 20.45: The Doctor List layout.

Figure 20.46: The Consultant List layout.

5.6: The Procedure Layout

A layout is needed to display a list of surgery procedures. FileMaker's Table view is an ideal method for displaying procedure records on screen.

We will want to adapt FileMaker's default Table view so that we can make use of the header layout part to include some navigation buttons to return to the Main Menu layout and a New button for creating new procedure records.

The Procedure layout is shown in Figure 20.47. Each field included in the layout will be displayed as a column when the layout is viewed in Browse mode.

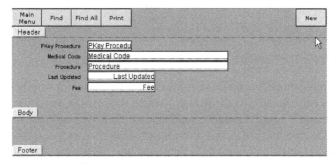

Figure 20.47: The Procedure layout.

Before switching to Browse mode to test how the layout looks, some changes to the Table view settings are required. In Layout mode, select the menu option **Layouts>Layout Setup** and click the **Views** tab in the Layout Setup dialog box. Check the **Table View** option and click the **Properties** button. In the Table View Properties dialog that appears, as shown in Figure 20.48, click the **Include header part** check box.

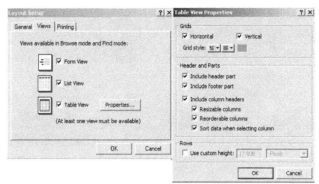

Figure 20.48: The Layout Setup and Table View Properties dialog boxes.

When Browse mode is selected for the Procedure layout, the list of procedure records should be clearly visible, with the navigation buttons and New button available in the header part. The Procedure layout in Browse mode is shown in Figure 20.49.

Main Menu	Find	Find All	Print		New

PKey Procedure	Medical Code	Procedure	Last Updated	Fee
109	C/06/001	Short Consultation	05/12/2005	£99.00
110	C/06/002	Long Consultation	05/12/2005	£150.00
1	E/06/001	Exenteration of orbit	12/12/2005	£2500.00
2	E/06/002	Enucleation of eyeball	12/12/2005	£2500.00
3	E/06/003	Excision of lesion of orbit	12/12/2005	£2500.00
4	E/06/004	Reconstruction of cavity of orbit	12/12/2005	£2500.00
5	E/06/005	Biopsy of lesion of orbit	12/12/2005	£2500.00
6	E/06/006	Drainage of orbit	12/12/2005	£2500.00

Figure 20.49: The Procedure layout in Browse mode.

The example procedure codes shown in Figure 20.49 are for demonstration purposes only. In the UK, the British Medical Association and some of the private medical health insurance companies will provide surgeons with procedure descriptions, codes, and recommended fee charges as a spreadsheet file. This information can easily be imported into FileMaker. Methods for importing and exporting data with FileMaker are detailed in Chapter 25.

5.7: The Treatment List Layout

The Treatment List layout should display the name of the related patient, a portal showing what treatment items were provided at the time of treatment, comments on the procedure and outcome notes, and details on whether an invoice has been generated for the treatment record.

The Treatment List layout is shown in Figure 20.50.

Figure 20.50: The Treatment List layout.

With a technique similar to that used for displaying doctor and consultant names in the Patient Details layout, a drop-down list of medical codes and procedures needs to be designed for the Treatment Item portal within the Treatment Details layout.

Figure 20.51 shows the FKey Procedure field within the first line of the Treatment_Treatment Item portal, immediately to the left of the Medical Code_Procedure field. The field dimension has been set to a width of one pixel using the Object Size menu option and is called out in dark gray for display purposes.

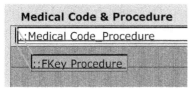

Figure 20.51: The FKey Procedure field is "hidden" in the Treatment Item portal.

A new script can be created that uses the Go to Field script step to select the "hidden" FKey Procedure field when the Medical Code_Procedure field is clicked. The FKey Procedure field can be formatted to display a procedure list, but does not need to display PKey Procedure field values.

The value list settings for the Procedure Codes list are shown in Figure 20.52.

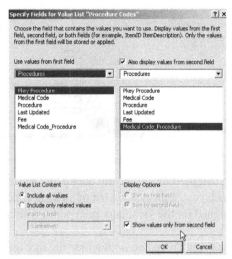

Figure 20.52:
The Procedure
Codes value list
settings.

5.8: The "Hidden" Treatment Item and Invoice Item Layouts

A FileMaker solution may often require a layout that is referenced by a script but is not used for data entry or record reporting. In the Patient Management database, this situation occurs with two simple layouts that are based on the Treatment Item and InvoiceItem table occurrences.

Create a new blank layout called **Treatment Item** to show records from Treatment Item table occurrence. The header and footer layout parts can be deleted and the body part shrunk to a minimum size. For reference, the name of the underlying table occurrence can be written on the layout, as shown in Figure 20.53.

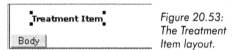

Figure 20.53:
The Treatment
Item layout.

The same procedure can be repeated to create a layout for the **InvoiceItem** table occurrence, as shown in Figure 20.54.

Figure 20.54:
The Invoice Item
layout.

The database user does not need to view these layouts or know of their existence. To prevent a layout from being displayed in the Status area's Layout menu, select the menu option **Layouts>Layout Setup** and uncheck the **Include in layout menus** option. The Layout Setup dialog box is shown in Figure 20.55.

*Figure 20.55:
The Layout Setup
dialog box with
the "Include in
layout menus"
option
unchecked.*

5.9: The Invoice Layout

The database generates printable invoices using the Invoice layout. The Invoice layout includes a portal to show related line items from the Invoice_ InvoiceItem table occurrence. Merge fields can be used to display contact details for the surgeon's practice and for the patient's contact details. Merge fields have the advantage of automatically shrinking or expanding based on the amount of text in the field for each record. They also prevent gaps between fields in address blocks. Another benefit of using merge fields is that a user cannot accidentally change a patient's details by clicking into the address fields.

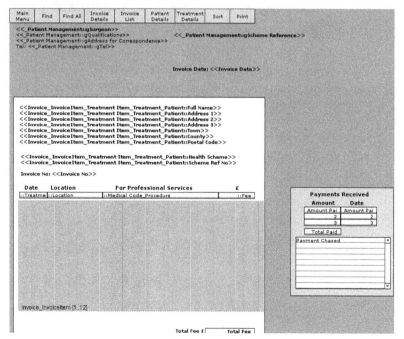

Figure 20.56: The Invoice layout.

The Invoice layout is shown in Figure 20.56. Included in the layout are the repeating fields to record remittance amounts and the dates payments are received. A series of navigation buttons at the top of the layout enable the user to view the related treatment and patient records.

5.10: The Invoice List Layout

The Invoice List layout consists of three layout parts: a header, which includes navigation buttons to view the Invoice layout or the related patient or treatment event; a body with basic details on each invoice; and a footer with summary fields to show the totals for invoice fee, amount paid, and amount outstanding. A small gray button to the left side of the body is set to switch to the Invoice Details layout.

The Invoice List layout is shown in Figure 20.57.

	Main Menu	Find	Find All	Invoice Details	Invoice List	Patient Details	Treatment Details	Sort	Print	
					INVOICE LIST					
	Invoice No	**Date**	**Patient**			**Total Fee**	**Total Paid**		**Amount Outstanding**	
	> Invoice No	Invoice Dat	::Full Name			Total Fee	Total Paid		Amount Out	
				Total for Above		Total Fee Su	Total Paid S		Amount Out	

Figure 20.57: The Invoice List layout.

Step 6: Automating the Patient Management Solution with Scripts

Before the surgeon or the practice management team start using the Patient Management solution, a series of scripts would be of great benefit to aid with navigation around the file, automate new treatment records, and create new invoices based on treatment events.

6.1: The Opening Script

An Opening script can be created to guarantee that the database always opens on the Welcome Menu with the database window maximized and the Status area hidden.

The Opening script is shown in Figure 20.58.

Script Name: Opening Script/Open Menu

- Go to Layout ["Welcome Menu" (Patient Management)]
- Show/Hide Status Area [Hide]
- Adjust Window [Maximize]
- Enter Browse Mode []

Figure 20.58: The Opening Script/Open Menu script.

6.2: Navigation Scripts to Open Data Entry and List Layouts

We will want to view the Status area in each of the data entry and list layouts.

A series of scripts can be created to open the various data entry layouts. As an example, the Open Patient Details script is shown in Figure 20.59.

Script Name: Open Patient Details

- Go to Layout ["Patient Details" (Patient)]
- Enter Browse Mode []
- Show/Hide Status Area [Show]
- Adjust Window [Maximize]
- Show All Records

Figure 20.59: The Open Patient Details script.

6.3: Creating a New Treatment Record from within the Patient Details Layout

The surgeon has decided that creating a new treatment record by being able to add new records through the treatment portal is too prone to data error and would like a warning message to appear before a new treatment record is created for any patient.

This level of automation can be achieved with a script. The New Treatment From Patient script is shown in Figure 20.60.

The formula for the Show Custom Dialog script step includes the patient name in the message question to minimize errors before creating a new treatment record. If the user goes ahead and requests a new treatment record for the currently viewed patient, the global field gPKey Patient is used to store the PKey Patient field value, and the database switches to the Treatment layout, creates a new record, and sets the FKey Patient field as being equal to the global gPKey Patient field. The script then finishes by leaving the cursor in the Treatment Date field, ready for the user to start filling in details on the date, location, and type of treatment provided.

Script Name: New Treatment From Patient

- Set Error Capture [On]
- Show Custom Dialog ["Add Treatment"; "Add a NEW TREATMENT record for " & Patient::Full Name & "?"]
- If [Get (LastMessageChoice) = 2]
-   Halt Script
- End If
- Set Field [Patient::gPKey Patient; Patient::Pkey Patient]
- Go to Layout ["Treatment" (Treatment)]
- New Record/Request
- Set Field [Treatment::Fkey Patient; Patient::gPKey Patient]
- Go to Field [Treatment::Treatment Date]

Figure 20.60: The New Treatment From Patient script.

6.4: Creating a New Invoice for a Treatment Record

After a treatment record is completed, FileMaker needs to create a new invoice record that displays all the treatment items that occurred as part of the treatment record. To do this, treatment item records will need to be transferred, or imported, into the InvoiceItem table and the invoice record needs to be related to the original treatment record.

This can be automated with a script, as shown in Figure 20.61. The script begins by setting FileMaker's Error Capture on and checking to see whether this treatment record has already been invoiced. This test involves counting whether a related record already exists in the Treatment_Invoice table occurrence. If the count of PKey Invoice in the related Treatment_Invoice table is greater than 0, the script will be halted. This avoids the error of a treatment record being invoiced twice.

As with the New Treatment From Patient script, to avoid any confusion the custom dialog box includes the patient's name in the message asking if the user wishes to go ahead and create an invoice for this treatment.

The global gFKey Patient field in the Treatment table is used to capture the foreign key FKey Patient. Then the related Treatment_Treatment Item records are isolated as a found set using the Go to Related Record script step. The script then jumps to the Invoice layout before creating a new invoice record. The global gPKey Invoice field is then used to capture the primary key field PKey Invoice. The script switches to the Invoice Item layout (which the database user never needs to see) and imports the previously isolated found set of treatment item records. The Replace script step is then used to set the foreign key field FKey Invoice in the new invoice item records to be the same as the primary key field of the new invoice record, PKey Invoice. The script then returns to the original treatment record, sets the Treatment Invoiced field to "Y", and sets the foreign key field FKey Invoice to be the same as the new invoice record's PKey Invoice field value.

Finally, the script returns to the new invoice record and sets the foreign key field FKey Patient to be the same as the global gFKey Patient field from the treatment record in order to establish a direct relationship between this invoice and the patient record.

Script Name: New Invoice for Treatment

```
● Set Error Capture [On]
● If [Count ( Treatment_Invoice::PKey Invoice ) > 0]
●    Show Custom Dialog ["Invoice Treatment"; "Treatment ALREADY Invoiced…"]
●    Halt Script
● End IF
● Show Custom Dialog ["Invoice Treatment"; "Create an Invoice for " & Treatment_Patient::Full Name & " for treatment at " & Treatment::Locatio…"]
● If [Get ( LastMessageChoice ) = 1]
●    Halt Script
● End IF
● Set Field [Treatment::gFKey Patient; Treatment::Fkey Patient]
● Go to Related Record [Show only related records; From table: "Treatment_Treatment Item"; Using layout: "Treatment Item" (Treatment Item)]
● Go to Layout ["Invoice" (Invoice)]
● New Record/Request
● Set Field [Invoice::gPkey Invoice; Invoice::PKey Invoice]
● Go to Layout ["Invoice Item" (InvoiceItem)]
● Import Records [No dialog; "Patient Management.fp7"; Add; Windows ANSI]
● Replace Field Contents [No dialog; InvoiceItem::FKey Invoice; Invoice::gPkey Invoice]
● Go to Layout ["Treatment" (Treatment)]
● Set Field [Treatment::Treatment Invoiced; "Y"]
● Set Field [Treatment::FKey Invoice; Invoice::gPkey Invoice]
● Go to Layout ["Invoice" (Invoice)]
● Set Field [Invoice::Fkey Patient; Treatment::gFKey Patient]
```

Figure 20.61: The New Invoice for Treatment script.

While this last script is quite convoluted and may not be easy to follow on first reading, it is a great example of how FileMaker can help eliminate data errors and give the database user the ability to create a cascade of related records at the click of a button.

Taking the Solution Further

The surgeon now has an effective database that manages the treatment history of patients and generates invoices for consultations and surgical procedures.

Over time, the surgeon might like to extend the capabilities of the database by adding a communication table to manage letters to consultants, general practitioners, and patients. All health workers have a duty of care, and the surgeon might like to use FileMaker to assist with this by creating an action table. An action table could be related to patients and have critical dates and activities logged, such as a callback or new appointment reminder for an acute or critical condition. If a patient fails to make a scheduled appointment, the surgeon may in the future wish to refer to the database records to prove that several appointment reminder letters or phone calls were generated by the database.

Chapter 21

Veterinary/Professional Practice Management

Introduction

FileMaker is ideal for managing a veterinary practice. As in the previous chapter, where similarities were noted between the structure of databases to manage patient treatment and automotive servicing, the business data management requirements of a veterinary surgeon are analogous to most professional service providers, including lawyers and accountants. A series of tables are required to hold information on clients, what pets are owned by clients, what treatment has been carried out on a pet for a client, and what fees are to be charged as part of an invoice.

The veterinary database solution developed in this chapter varies slightly from the health professionals example in that treatment records are associated with a pet or animal, which in turn is linked to an owner, rather than treatment being performed on the contact record directly (although my veterinarian wife has threatened me with this from time to time).

For simplicity, the veterinary case study solution is based on a small animal practice. That is a practice that predominantly sees household pets rather than a large animal or mixed practice, which would also serve the veterinary needs of horses and livestock. Large animal and agricultural vets may also be interested in groups of animals as herds for the sake of disease testing or conducting clinical trials. This data management requirement can easily be tackled with FileMaker if an additional table is included in the solution to hold records for herds or equine yards between tables to hold details on the farmer or owner and to describe the individual animal.

In some countries and states, as a professional practitioner, a vet may be required to charge varying rates of sales tax depending on whether consultancy advice is being given or drugs dispensed. This situation occurs in Ireland and also affects other service industries such as IT, with a different rate of value-added tax (VAT) charged for a training course than the rate for software development or sales.

The following example is based on the database requirements of a small animal veterinary surgeon in Ireland. To manage multiple rates of VAT, a Fees table in the solution includes a field for the relevant VAT rate percentage that must be charged for services or dispensed drugs.

As with the other case studies in this book, a copy of the completed FileMaker Pro 8 database file, **VetPractice**, is available to download from the publisher's website at www.wordware.com/files/fmapps and the author's website at www.aweconsultancy.com. You may find it easier to examine some of the FileMaker features and techniques discussed in this chapter in a copy of the completed file.

The default database password for the Admin account is **ANIMAL** (all capitals). The database file options have been preset to open with the active Guest account (with read-only access to the file). To open the file with full access privileges, hold down the Shift key (Windows) or Option key (Mac OS) while the file is opening. Type the word **Admin** in the Account Name box and type the password in the box below. You can change the default password at a later stage. More information on database security issues, passwords, accounts, and privileges is given in Chapter 24.

The Veterinary Practice Management Entity Relationship Diagram

A veterinary surgeon makes a living by treating animals and receiving fees from the owners for these treatments. Our FileMaker solution will need an **Animal** table with details on each pet. Each animal is linked to a single record in an **Owner** table. When an animal is seen by the vet, a new record needs to be created in a **Treatment** table. Several professional services may be rendered by the vet during the consultation that need to be recorded in a **Treatment Item** table. For consistency, the vet needs to know how much to charge for a treatment item and the currently applicable rate of tax. This information can be held in a **Fees** table. After the consultation is concluded, the owner needs to be presented with a bill from an **Invoice** table. Each treatment item needs to be included as part of an invoice, each one being an **Invoice Item.**

The vet may also wish to use FileMaker to create an expenses database to manage the costs of running the practice. An example of how an **Expenses** table can be used to manage and report on professional costs incurred is included in the solution.

The Veterinary Practice entity relationship diagram is shown in Figure 21.1. The crow's-foot symbol is used to denote a "one-to-many" relationship. As an example, an owner can have several animals as pets. The line with a circle at one end and a perpendicular line at the other, such as the one between the Treatment and Invoice tables and between the Treatment Item and Invoice Item tables, is used to demonstrate that not all treatment items must be invoiced, while any invoice and invoice items records will have one associated treatment event and treatment item record, respectively. The veterinary practice may choose not to create a new invoice for every treatment event if, for example, the animal is from a rescue organization. However, all invoices that are created will be linked to a treatment event, while all corresponding invoice item records are directly imported from the Treatment Item table.

Health Professionals
Veterinary Practice ER Diagram

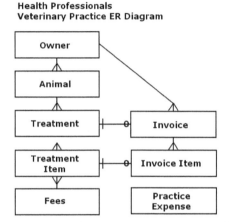

Figure 21.1: The Veterinary Practice entity relationship diagram.

Building the Veterinary Practice Management File

Step 1: Adding Tables to the Veterinary Practice Management File

1. Launch FileMaker, if it is not already open, and create a new file called **VetPractice**. FileMaker will automatically open the Define Database dialog box with the Fields tab selected for the default VetPractice table, as shown in Figure 21.2.

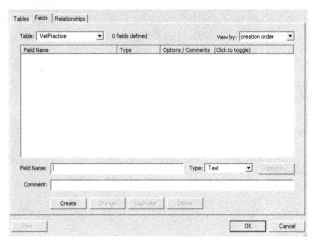

Figure 21.2: The Define Database dialog box for a new file with the Fields tab selected for the default table.

2. Click on the **Tables** tab at the top of the Define Database dialog box and add the additional eight tables listed in Figure 21.3.

VetPractice
Owner
Treatment
Fees
Expenses
Animal
TreatmentItem
Invoice
InvoiceItem

Figure 21.3: The tables needed for the VetPractice file.

Step 2: Adding Fields to the VetPractice File Tables

As in the other case studies in this book, we need to add a primary key field to each of our tables using FileMaker's ability to automatically assign a unique serial number to each record in each table. In addition, we will need to add foreign key fields to any of the tables to which we need to establish a relationship.

1. To add fields to each of the tables within the file, choose the **File>Define>Database** menu item and the **Fields** tab of the Define Database dialog box. It is important to ensure that the correct table is selected prior to adding new fields. Each of the tables can be selected from the drop-down list near the top of the dialog box, as shown in Figure 21.4.

Figure 21.4:
Selecting the
relevant table for
a new field in the
Define Database
dialog box.

We will add initial fields to each table as shown in Figures 21.5 to 21.18. Later, when we have established relationships between these tables using table occurrences in the relationships graph, we will add additional fields to the tables to improve the functionality of the file.

We will want to customize the solution business details for a specific professional practice. We can do this by creating a series of global text fields in the VetPractice table.

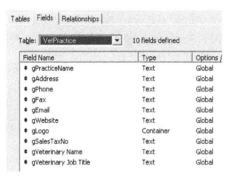

Figure 21.5:
The global fields
used to customize
the file for a
veterinary
practice.

2. Add the text fields shown in Figure 21.5 to the **VetPractice** table. For each text field, click the **Options** button to open the Options for Field dialog box. Click the **Storage** tab at the top of the dialog box and select the **Use global storage** option, as shown in Figure 21.6.

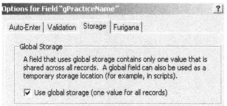

Figure 21.6:
Selecting the
global storage
option for a field.

Setting the global storage option means that the text fields that describe a practice can be displayed in any layout, without the need to create a relationship from that layout's underlying base table to the table that holds the global fields.

In this solution, we will also make use of global number fields to temporarily store the contents of a record's primary key field when we create new related records in another table. As an example, a global number field will be used to store a treatment event's primary key field value, which can then be placed as the treatment event's foreign key field value in a new related invoice record.

Container fields can also be set to have a global value. In our VetPractice table a container field called gLogo is designed to hold a company logo, which can be used on letterhead or an invoice layout.

3. FileMaker can allocate a unique serial number for each record's primary key, or PKey, field, which is required for each of the data tables in the solution. For example, after creating a new number field called **PKey Owner** in the Owner table, click the **Options** button in the Define Fields dialog box. Select the **Auto-Enter** tab, check the **Serial number** option, and set an initial value of **1** and an increment of **1**.

4. By careful use of value lists in conjunction with foreign key fields, there is no reason to include the primary key field in any of the layouts in our solution. This means that there is little chance of the unique serial number field value being modified, duplicated, or erased by a user accidentally clicking into the field in a layout. Despite this, it is good practice to also check the **Prohibit modification of value during data entry** option, as shown in Figure 21.7.

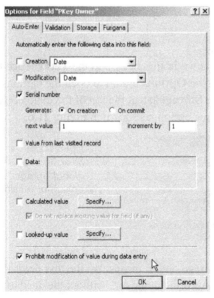

Figure 21.7:
The auto-enter options for all primary key fields in the VetPractice solution.

5. The initial fields required for the **Owner** table are shown in Figure 21.8.

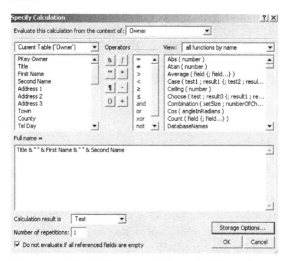

Figure 21.8 The initial fields for the Owner table.

The Owner table includes a calculation field called **Full name**, the formula for which is shown in Figure 21.9, with the calculation result of **Text**.

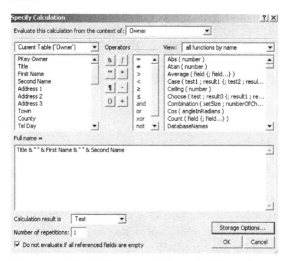

Figure 21.9: The Full name calculation field formula.

6. The initial fields needed for the **Animal** table are shown in Figure 21.10.

Field Name	Type	Options / Comments (Click to toggle)
● FKey Owner	Number	Indexed
● Animal Name	Text	Indexed
● Animal Type	Text	Indexed
● Sex	Text	By Value List, Allow Override
● DOB	Date	
● Age	Calculation	from Animal, = Case (IsEmpty (DOB) ; 0 ; DayOfYear (DOB) ≤...
● Date Entered	Date	Creation Date
● Insured	Text	Lookup, By Value List, Allow Override
● Scheme Name	Text	Lookup
● Scheme Ref	Text	Lookup
● Notes	Text	
● Breed	Text	
● Neutered	Text	
● Colour	Text	Indexed
● PKey Animal	Number	Indexed, Auto-enter Serial, Can't Modify Auto
● Status	Text	
● gPKey Animal	Number	Global

Table: Animal   18 fields defined   View by: custom order

Tables Fields Relationships

Figure 21.10: The initial fields for the Animal table.

Not all owners are likely to know the exact date of birth of their pets. However, the vet can make use of FileMaker's drop-down calendar in the **DOB** date field to select an approximate birth date for an animal in order to get an approximate age. The calculation formula for the **Age** field makes use of FileMaker's DayOfYear formula to test whether or not a pet's birthday in the current year has been reached. If it has, then the formula only needs to subtract the year that the animal was born from the current year. If the birthday is yet to fall this year, then 1 is subtracted from the result. The formula, whose result is a number, is shown in Figure 21.11.

```
Case (
IsEmpty ( DOB ) ; 0 ;
DayOfYear ( DOB ) ≤ DayOfYear ( Get ( CurrentDate ) ); Year ( Get ( CurrentDate )) - Year ( DOB)
; Year ( Get ( CurrentDate )) - Year ( DOB ) - 1 )
```

Figure 21.11: The Age formula.

7. The initial fields for the **Treatment** table are shown in Figure 21.12. It is assumed that most consulting takes place at the clinic, or surgery in the UK, so the Treatment location field has "surgery" automatically entered into the field for new records. Similarly, at the time that the record is created, a treatment record has not been invoiced, so "N" for "no" is automatically entered in the Treatment Invoiced field. When we have established a relationship in the VetPractice file between the Treatment and Animal tables, we will be able to define a lookup for an animal's Age at Treatment field.

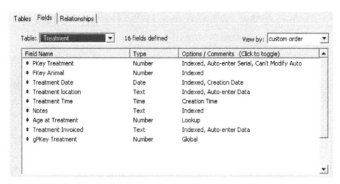

Figure 21.12: The initial fields for the Treatment table.

8. The **Fees** table is used to record the prices and the sales tax, or VAT rate applicable, for professional services. The fields needed for the Fees table are shown in Figure 21.13. The calculation field called **Drugs Code_Drugs Description** is a concatenation of the Fee Code and Fee Description fields, and is used to display the contents of more than one field in a drop-down list. The **Net Price** and **VAT Amount** calculation fields apply the relevant VAT rate to the basic net price for each record. This information will be looked up by corresponding fields in the Treatment Item table once we have established a relationship between the TreatmentItem and Fees tables in the file based on the PKey Fee field.

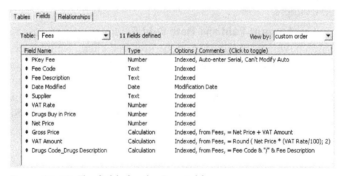

Figure 21.13: The fields for the Fees table.

9. The **TreatmentItem** table is used to record individual fee items that are created at the time of a consultation or treatment event. The TreatmentItem table is shown in Figure 21.14. When we have established a relationship between the TreatmentItem and Fees tables, we can create lookups between the **Gross Price Looked Up**, **VAT Rate Looked Up**, and **Net Price Looked Up** fields. The three calculation fields, **Line VAT Amount**, **Line Net Amount**, and **Line Gross Amount**, all multiply the fee rate by the Qty field in their formula to derive a total line price

for the net VAT and gross item price. The Qty field is defined to auto-enter a default value of 1.

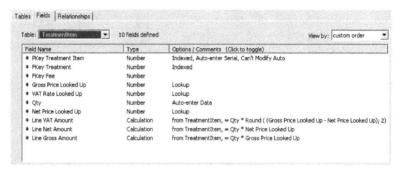

Figure 21.14: The fields for the TreatmentItem table.

10. The initial fields for the **Invoice** table are shown in Figure 21.15. Both the **PKey Invoice** and the **Invoice No** fields make use of FileMaker's auto-enter feature to automatically assign a unique serial number and a unique invoice number at the time that a new invoice record is created. These two values can, of course, be completely different. A business advisor once told me never to start trading with an invoice number 0001 because "it will worry your first client!" You might want to include the year in the Invoice No auto-enter option, starting with 06/1001 as an example.

The **Amount Paid** and **Date Paid** fields are used to capture information on payments received from the invoiced client. Remittance fields could also be placed in a new table that is related to the Invoice table; however, for this solution, by using repeating fields it is likely that three repetitions will be enough to capture partial payments and total what has been paid using the **Amount Paid Total** calculation field. The Sum formula, when used to reference a repeating field in the same table, will evaluate a total for the repeating field.

Tables   Fields   Relationships

Table: Invoice   19 fields defined   View by: custom order

Field Name	Type	Options / Comments (Click to toggle)
• Pkey Invoice	Number	Indexed, Auto-enter Serial, Can't Modify Auto
• Invoice No	Text	Auto-enter Serial, Can't Modify Auto
• Invoice Date	Date	Creation Date
• FKey Treatment	Number	Indexed
• Amount Paid	Number [3]	
• Date Paid	Date [3]	
• Credit Control Notes	Text	
• VAT12_5	Calculation	Global, from Invoice, = 12.5
• VAT21	Calculation	Global, from Invoice, = 21
• VAT0	Calculation	Global, from Invoice, = 0
• gPKey Invoice	Number	Global
• Amount Paid Total	Calculation	from Invoice, = Sum(Amount Paid)

Figure 21.15: The initial fields for the Invoice table.

Three global calculation fields have been included in the Invoice table: **VAT12_5**, **VAT21**, and **VAT0**. For the present example of an Irish veterinary practice solution, these global fields will be used via relationships to the InvoiceItem table to summarize the total VAT payable at each of these rates for this invoice. The calculation formula for VAT12_5 is shown in Figure 21.16. The **Storage Options** button has been clicked to access the **Use global storage** option.

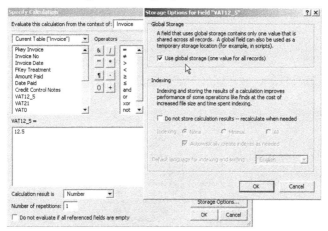

Figure 21.16: The calculation formula for VAT12_5 in the Invoice table.

11. The **InvoiceItem** table is relatively straightforward with just eight number fields needed, as shown in Figure 21.17.

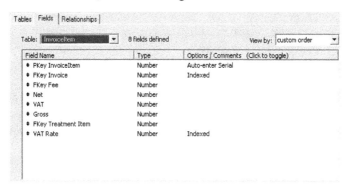

Figure 21.17: The fields for the InvoiceItem table.

12. Finally the **Expenses** table is going to be used to record expenses incurred by the practice. In order to report accurately on practice overhead by category and proportion claimed, the Expenses table is relatively large with 40 fields. The Expenses fields are shown in Figure 21.18.

Figure 21.18:
The fields for the
Expenses table.

We now need to create relationships between these tables in order to design the input and reporting screens in our veterinary practice solution, and to finalize some of the field definitions and formulas in the tables.

The reality for most FileMaker solutions is that a complete relationships graph is only achieved after a period of time, during which feedback is given to the database designer from key users of the system. The effectiveness and functionality of a solution can only be assessed once records have been added to the tables using the base data input layouts.

Step 3: Adding Relationships within the Practice Management File

The busy veterinary surgeon will want FileMaker to do as much of the work as possible in capturing new owner and pet details, logging consultations, and generating accurate invoices based on the items dispensed during a treatment event. This is particularly the case if the vet does not have a practice manager or assistant to take care of record management in FileMaker. Ideally, the vet will want to create and print out invoices that can be presented to the owner and paid before he or she leaves the office.

Careful design of the table occurrence groups, or TOGs, in the relationships graph coupled with good design of layouts at a later stage should provide the vet with an effective practice management tool.

1. If the Define Database dialog box is not open, select the menu option **File>Define>Database** and click the **Relationships** tab at the top of the dialog box. The nine base tables that we have created in the VetPractice file will be visible as table occurrences, as shown in Figure 21.19.

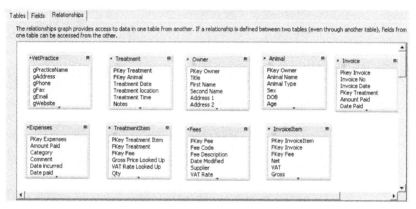

Tables | Fields | Relationships |

The relationships graph provides access to data in one table from another. If a relationship is defined between two tables (even through another table), fields from one table can be accessed from the other.

VetPractice	Treatment	Owner	Animal	Invoice
gPracticeName	PKey Treatment	PKey Owner	FKey Owner	Pkey Invoice
gAddress	FKey Animal	Title	Animal Name	Invoice No
gPhone	Treatment Date	First Name	Animal Type	Invoice Date
gFax	Treatment location	Second Name	Sex	FKey Treatment
gEmail	Treatment Time	Address 1	DOB	Amount Paid
gWebsite	Notes	Address 2	Age	Date Paid

Expenses	TreatmentItem	Fees	InvoiceItem
PKey Expenses	PKey Treatment Item	PKey Fee	PKey InvoiceItem
Amount Paid	FKey Treatment	Fee Code	FKey Invoice
Category	FKey Fee	Fee Description	FKey Fee
Comment	Gross Price Looked Up	Date Modified	Net
Date incurred	VAT Rate Looked Up	Supplier	VAT
Date paid	Qty	VAT Rate	Gross

Figure 21.19: The initial relationships graph for the VetPractice file showing the nine base tables.

As with the other case study FileMaker solutions, we do not link the underlying base tables directly in the relationships graph. Instead, relationships are built up between table occurrences, which are representations of the base tables in the relationships graph. It is possible to have any number of table occurrences on the relationships graph for the same underlying base table.

As introduced in Chapter 7, our aim is to refine the relationships graph into a series of discrete TOGs. Each TOG should have a main or "anchor" table occurrence on its left-hand side, with any number of linked "buoy" tables related to the anchor table spread out on the right-hand side. To ease relationship design at the outset and to assist you or any colleagues who may work on the file at a later stage, a number of fundamental rules should be followed when using relationships in any FileMaker solution:

- As a general rule, any relationships graph will have one anchor table occurrence for every base table in the file.
- All data entry layouts should only be based on an underlying anchor table occurrence.
- Any portals on layouts should be based on buoy table occurrences.

■ To assist with documenting a complex FileMaker project, it is a good idea to limit the dimensions of any TOGs in the relationships graph to a single page in width but any number of pages in length.

To get the required functionality from our Veterinary Practice solution, we now need to add some TOGs to the relationships graph.

2. For the sake of reference, it is a good idea to preserve at least one table occurrence for each base table within the file, displayed at the top of the relationships graph. To reduce the space used, click on the button on the table header to toggle the display of the table and collapse it to its title only, as shown in Figure 21.20.

3. Note that an underscore (_) has been added to some of the base table occurrences so that the original table name can be used as an anchor table occurrence. (The VetPractice, Expenses, and Fees tables are not used as the main table occurrence in any TOGs, so they have not been renamed.) Each table occurrence must have a unique name in the graph. A table occurrence can be renamed by double-clicking on it to open the Specify Table dialog box, or by highlighting the table occurrence and clicking the **Edit** button at the bottom of the graph (the button with a yellow pencil icon).

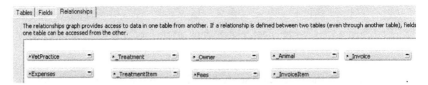

Figure 21.20: The reference base tables collapsed to display only the table titles.

3.1: The Owner TOG

As with any FileMaker solution, the fundamental business rules within a workgroup or company should dictate how records are captured in the database. For this example, the vet decides that no animal details will be captured until a related owner's details are captured first. This means that the owner's record is the first to be created in our solution. The Owner TOG is used to manage the relationships between owners and their pets, together with any treatment given and subsequent invoices.

The Owner TOG is shown with the Owner table occurrence as the anchor table on the left-hand side in Figure 21.21.

Figure 21.21 The Owner table occurrence group.

The vet decides it would be a good idea to add animal details for an owner, using a portal within an Owner Details layout. To enable this, we need to make sure that the relationship between the Owner and the Owner_Animal table occurrences is set to allow creation of records in the Owner_Animal table. Double-click anywhere on the relationship line and click the **Allow creation of records in this table via this relationship** check box on the Owner_Animal side of the relationship, as illustrated in Figure 21.22.

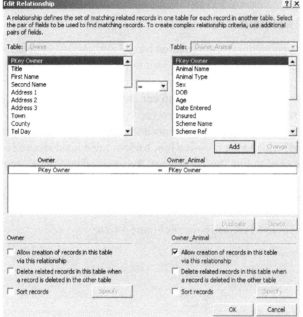

Figure 21.22:
The "Allow creation of records in this table via this relationship" option is selected for the Owner_Animal table.

The vet decides that it would be best to add new treatment records from within the Animal Details layout, so we do not need to worry about creating records via a relationship in any of the other tables in the Owner TOG.

3.2: The Animal TOG

The Animal TOG consists of three table occurrences linked to the Animal table occurrence on the left-hand side. The vet decides that she would like a warning button in the finished solution that asks the user to confirm whether a new treatment record is needed, rather than automatically letting the user create treatment records via a relationship. None of the Animal TOG relationships need to allow creation of related records via a relationship.

The Animal TOG is shown in Figure 21.23.

Figure 21.23: The Animal table occurrence group.

3.3: The Treatment TOG

Once a new treatment record is created for an animal, the vet decides that it would be most effective if new treatment items could be automatically added via a portal to treatment item records within the Treatment Details layout. In order for this to work, we will need to edit the relationship between **Treatment** and **TreatmentItem** so that new records in the latter table can be created via the relationship. We will need to include table occurrences based on the Animal and Owner tables to link back to the related record in each. In addition, we need to link the **Treatment_TreatmentItem** table occurrence to the **Fees** table so that the current price and applicable VAT rate for a treatment item is looked up, and to populate values in a drop-down list of fee item descriptions.

The Treatment TOG is shown in Figure 21.24.

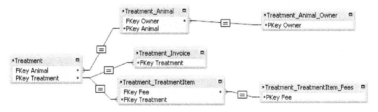

Figure 21.24: The Treatment table occurrence group.

3.4: The TreatmentItem TOG

It is good practice to base any lookups within a field's definition on an anchor table occurrence in the relationships graph. As the solution is developed, we will also want to switch to a TreatmentItem layout within a script that isolates all the relevant treatment item records for a treatment record in order to enable the InvoiceItem table to import the correct treatment item records and convert them into invoice item records.

The TreatmentItem TOG consists of a single relationship between the TreatmentItem and the Fees underlying tables and is shown in Figure 21.25.

Figure 21.25: The TreatmentItem table occurrence group.

3.5: The Stand-alone InvoiceItem Table Occurrence

In order to make our solution convert treatment item records into invoice item records without the vet having to retype any existing information, we will need to reference a layout based on the InvoiceItem table. As one of our fundamental rules for good relational database design using FileMaker, which is detailed in Chapter 7, is to base any layouts on anchor table occurrences, the InvoiceItem table can be placed in isolation on our relationships graph, as shown in Figure 21.26.

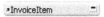

Figure 21.26: The InvoiceItem stand-alone table occurrence.

3.6: The Invoice TOG

The vet will want to call up the correct treatment event, animal details, and owner information when viewing an invoice on screen. The invoice will also need to display details on a fee procedure in each invoice line item. Further, the vet wishes to display the proportion of the invoice made up of VAT at three specific rates: 12.5%, 21%, and 0%. We will need to use the three VAT global fields in the Invoice table to do this.

The Invoice TOG is shown in Figure 21.27.

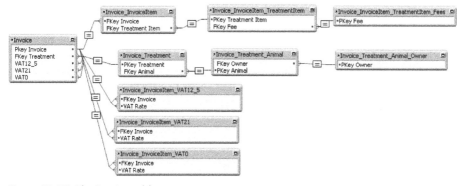

Figure 21.27: The Invoice table occurrence group.

Now that we have finished building the relationships graphs, there are some additional calculation fields, based on the relationships we have built, that we need to add to our existing tables.

Step 4: Adding Calculation and Lookup Fields to the Veterinary Practice Tables

4.1: Additional Fields for the Owner Table

There are several calculation and lookup fields that we can now add to the database tables to maximize the solution's effectiveness. As examples, we can now get FileMaker to add up all the invoice line item values for an invoice to get the grand total, display a count of how many pets an owner has in the database, or count how many times a dog has been for treatment.

1.   If the Define Database dialog box is not open, select the **File>Define> Database** menu item. Click the **Fields** tab to return to the fields list for each of the tables in the VetPractice database.

2.   In the Owner table, we can now add a set of calculation and summary fields to count how many related records exist for an owner in the Animal, Treatment, and Invoice tables, and total how much the owner has been invoiced, how much has been paid, and what is still owing. These new fields are displayed in Figure 21.28.

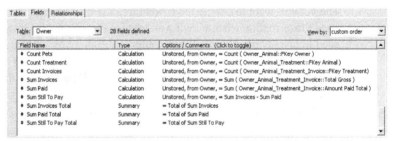

Figure 21.28: Additional calculation and summary fields added to the Owner table.

4.2: An Additional Field for the Animal Table

The vet may wish to display on screen a count of how many times a pet has been in for treatment. We only need to add one field to the Animal table, named **Count Treatments**, which is shown in Figure 21.29. As with all calculation fields, care should be taken that the calculation is being evaluated from the context of the anchor table, in this case Animal, as shown at the top of the Specify Calculation dialog box.

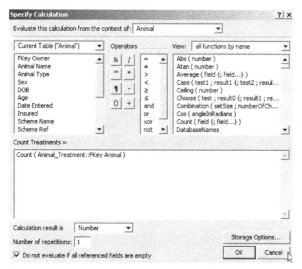

Figure 21.29: The new Count Treatments field in the Animal table.

4.3: Additional Fields for the Treatment Table

In the Treatment table, we can create calculation fields to display the total net, VAT, and gross fee that will be due for all related treatment line items held in the TreatmentItem table. Additionally, if we create three summary fields for the net, VAT, and gross totals, we can display summary values in a treatment list report. We are also going to add a new number field to hold the foreign key field for a related invoice record. The additional fields for the Treatment table are shown in Figure 21.30.

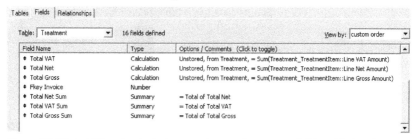

Figure 21.30: Additional calculation, number, and summary fields added to the Treatment table.

4.4: Additional Fields for the Invoice Table

Finally, we can add additional fields to the Invoice table to display the total value for all related invoice line items held in the InvoiceItem table. We can display the proportional VAT total at 0%, 12.5%, and 21% by making use of the relationships that use the VAT global calculation fields. We can have FileMaker calculate if any money is still owed for an invoice with the new calculation field called **Amount to Pay**. All of these calculation fields can also be summarized so that an invoice list report can show the total values for a selected set of invoice records.

The additional fields for the Invoice table are shown in Figure 21.31.

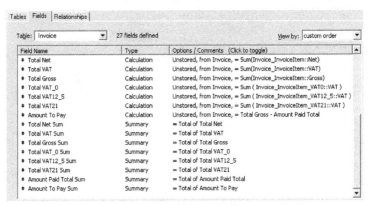

Figure 21.31: The additional calculation and summary fields added to the Invoice table.

We are now ready to design a series of data entry and report layouts for the VetPractice solution.

Step 5: Designing Data Entry and Report Layouts for the VetPractice File

As discussed in Chapter 7, with FileMaker it is a good idea to base any data entry and report layouts on anchor table occurrences, which are the table occurrences to the far left of the table occurrence groups in our relationships graphs.

We are now at the stage with our VetPractice project where we need to design layouts to assist us with capturing, managing, and reporting on our business data.

5.1: Creating a Wizard Layout to Capture Veterinary Practice Information

Let's start by creating a new layout to capture business information on the practice that is going to use the solution by using the global text and container fields in the VetPractice table.

1. Open the **VetPractice** file, if it is not already open, and select the menu option **View>Layout Mode** to switch to Layout mode and create a new layout.

2. Choose the menu option **Layouts>New Layout/Report** to open the New Layout/Report dialog box. Choose to show records from **VetPractice**, type **Wizard** in the Layout Name box, and select **Blank layout**, as shown in Figure 21.32.

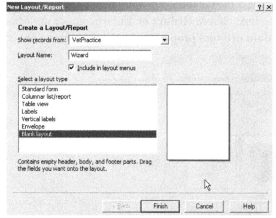

Figure 21.32: The New Layout/Report dialog box with the Show records from, Layout Name, and Select a layout type boxes filled in.

3. Click the **Finish** button. The blank layout can now be customized to our requirements. As the Wizard layout is not a report and will only be used to capture global field values for the practice, delete the header and footer parts by clicking on the header and footer labels and pressing the **Backspace** or **Delete** key.

4. Give the body a background color by clicking on the body label and selecting a fill color from the Status area.

5. Create a background tile effect by using the **Button** tool to draw a large rectangle, and drag the global fields onto this colored area using the **Field** tool. The finished Wizard layout is shown in Figure 21.33.

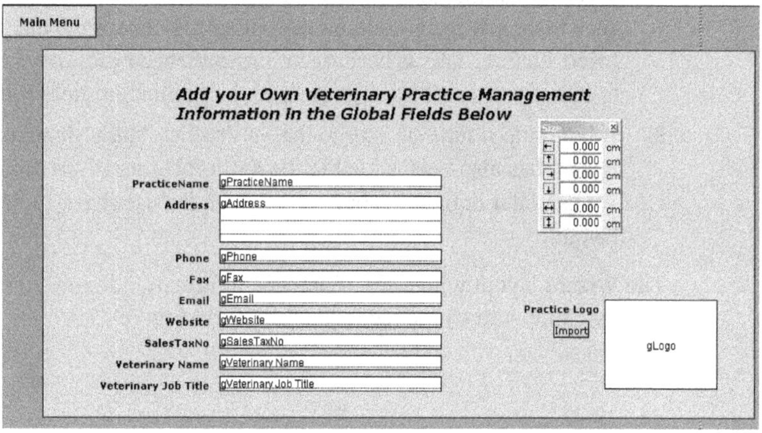

Figure 21.33: The Wizard layout.

6. The global container field for the practice logo, gLogo, has been added to the Wizard layout. It is important to highlight the container field in Layout mode and ensure that any graphic held in the container field is displayed correctly. In Layout mode, right-click on the **gLogo** container field and select the **Graphic Format** menu option. In the Graphic Format dialog box, choose **Reduce or Enlarge** image to fit frame and click the **Maintain original proportions** option, as shown in Figure 21.34.

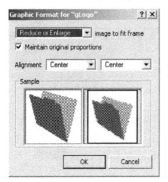

Figure 21.34: The Graphic Format dialog box for the gLogo container field.

7. To assist the user of the finished solution, a small button labeled **Import** has been placed next to the gLogo container field. This button can be set to perform a script that will select the gLogo global container field and open the Insert Picture dialog box. The Insert Logo script is shown in Figure 21.35.

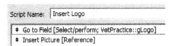

Figure 21.35: The Insert Logo script.

A script that includes the Go to Field command has been used in preference to simply programming the button to perform the menu command Insert Picture. This is because an inexperienced user may have forgotten to initially select the gLogo field as the destination field for the image.

8. A button to return the user to the VetPractice Main Menu, or welcome layout, has also been added to the top-left corner of the Wizard layout. We can later define this button to switch the user back to the Main Menu layout.

The Wizard layout with a set of practice information for an example Irish veterinary clinic with a practice logo is shown in Figure 21.36.

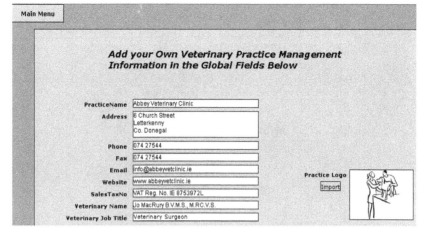

Figure 21.36: The Wizard layout with practice information added to the global fields.

5.2: The Main Menu Layout

As with any FileMaker solution, a welcome screen or main menu layout is a useful starting point for the practice management software. The user can decide which information to work with from this screen. By including a button to return to the main menu from any of the other layouts, the user can always return to this screen.

1. Create a new blank layout based on the VetPractice table and, as with the Wizard layout, delete the header and footer.

2. Highlight the body label and select a fill color from the Status area's **Fill** tool.

3. As shown in Figure 21.37, use the **Button** tool to create a box that looks like a brass plaque, then place the practice information fields on top as merge fields by using the **Insert>Merge Field** menu option, as well as the **gLogo** container field. Screws in the corners of the plaque were created using the **Circle** and **Line** tools. A series of standard size buttons were created using the **Edit>Duplicate** menu option, which will shortly be defined to run scripts to open the various data entry screens.

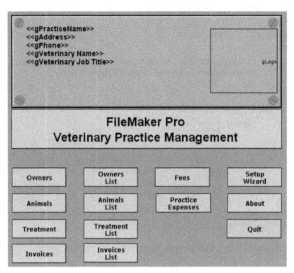

Figure 21.37: The VetPractice Main Menu screen.

While most of the scripts needed for the file are discussed in Step 6 of this case study, two standard scripts that are added to the file and form part of the functionality of the Main Menu layout are discussed here.

4. The red button labeled Quit is defined to run the **Quit** script, and the green button labeled About runs a script that provides contact details for the publisher and author of the solution. Both scripts make use of the Show Custom Dialog script step to create a conditional script, where the user decides which message choice to select. The Quit script is shown below in Figure 21.38, with the Show Custom Dialog script step highlighted.

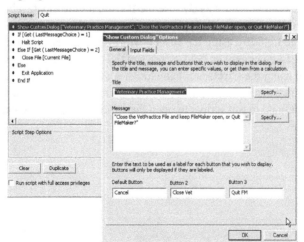

Figure 21.38: The Quit script is performed when the red Quit button is selected from the Main Menu screen.

5. The **About...** script, which is triggered by the green About button, is an example of how web addresses can be opened through a script step, as shown in Figure 21.39.

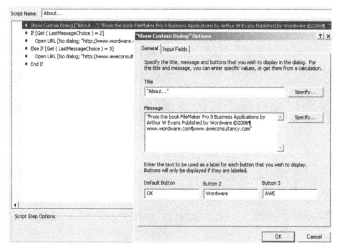

Figure 21.39: The About... script step.

The remaining buttons in the Main Menu layout can be set up to open the various data entry screens once the layouts are ready.

5.3: The Owner Details Layout

In our example, the vet has made the decision that owner details should be captured in the database before collecting information on pets and treatment events. An Owner Details layout is therefore needed to display information about pet owners, their animals, treatment events, invoices already generated, and, to assist the practice with cash flow, any payments outstanding. The Owner Details layout is based on the Owner table.

1. As with most of the solutions in this book, a series of standard navigation buttons is added to the Owner Details layout. As these buttons are consistent through most of the solution layouts, users of the practice software should rapidly become familiar with working through the data entry and report screens.

2. Three portals are used in the Owner Details layout to display related record information on animals, treatment, and invoices. The finished Owner Details layout is shown in Figure 21.40.

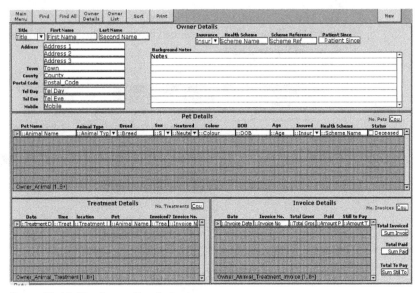

Figure 21.40: The Owner Details layout.

3. The green button labeled **New** is defined to create a new owner record. Pet records are added through the portal based on the relationship Owner_Animal.

4. Value lists are used to assist the vet in selecting insurance plans, the type of animal, and closed response (yes or no) questions on each animal. The Deceased value in the **Status** field is designed to avoid embarrassment, such as sending out an immunization reminder for a dog that has passed away. FileMaker Pro 8's auto-complete field control is a useful feature to help complete the name of the town and other fields where clients are generally local to a practice.

5. Treatment and invoice records cannot be created in the Owner Details layout as the business flow is based on clicking to the Pet Details layout next before creating a new treatment record and subsequent invoice. The small buttons on the left side of the pet, treatment, and invoice portals will switch the user to the correct related record by using the Go to Related Record button command once layouts are completed for these records.

5.4: The Owner List Layout

An Owner List layout is designed to make it easy for the user to view all clients and get a snapshot view of related pets, treatment events, and the level of invoices generated. The Owner List layout is based on the Owner table. Navigation buttons to the left side of each record in the list, and adjacent to the related record count fields, will be used to assist navigation around the file. The Owner List layout is shown in Figure 21.41.

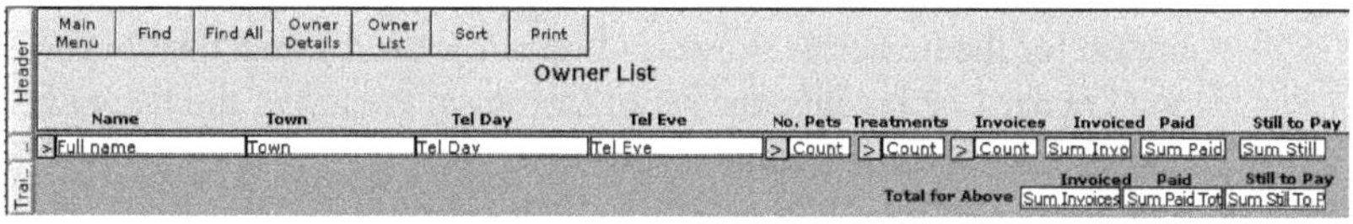

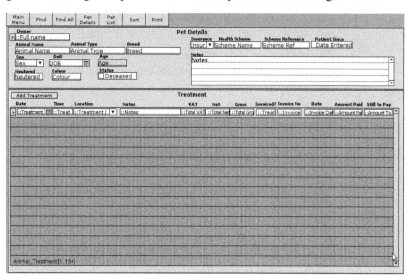

Figure 21.41: The Owner List layout.

5.5: The Pet Details Layout

The Pet Details layout is based on the Animal table and is designed to display details on a single pet, the owner's name (with a button to switch back to the related owner record), and a portal showing the treatment history for the animal.

As new pets can already be created in the Owner Details layout, the green Add Treatment button in the Pet Details layout is defined to run a script that checks whether the user wants to create a new treatment record. This could be simplified by defining the relationship to the Animal_Treatment table occurrence to allow the creation of related records. The vet has decided that a "trigger guard" on the creation of new treatment records would be a good idea, using a script. The Pet Details layout is shown in Figure 21.42.

Figure 21.42: The Pet Details layout.

5.6: The Pet List Layout

A Pet List layout, based on the Animal table, with a Go to Related Record button for the owner, is shown in Figure 21.43. As with the Owner Details and Owner List layouts, the set of buttons at the top of the layout header is copied from the Pet Details layout.

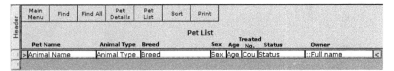

Figure 21.43: The Pet List layout.

5.7: The Treatment Details Layout

A new treatment record will be created by the user in the Pet Details layout.

1. The Treatment Details layout has a green **Create Invoice** button for creating a new invoice once the treatment details have been captured.

2. The Treatment Details layout includes a portal using the **Treatment_ TreatmentItem** table occurrence. This portal is used to record the treatment items that were provided during the treatment event. Three calculation fields in the Treatment table are used to total the net, sales tax, and gross total fees for the treatment record.

3. Two buttons are used to switch back to the related owner and pet records from the Treatment Details screen. Figure 21.44 shows the Treatment Details layout.

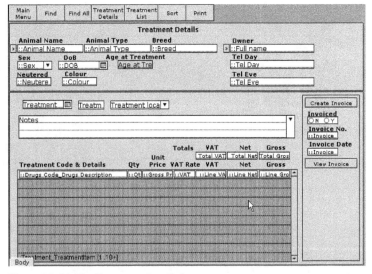

Figure 21.44: The Treatment Details layout.

4. To assist the database user in adding related treatment items to the treatment record, a value list will be used to display a list of fee items. To avoid the risk of error and confusion in choosing a fee item based on the item's primary key field value, it is decided not to include the primary field's contents in the value list.

5. With FileMaker Pro 8, it is also possible to virtually "hide" the foreign key field in a layout by shrinking the field's width to one pixel. To do this, add the **FKey Fee** field from the TreatmentItem table into the first line of the **Treatment_TreatmentItem** portal. Do not give the field a fill color, and make the field text the same color as the background color. As a further method of disguise, you can also choose the menu option **Format>Set Sliding/Printing** and choose not to print the field. While the field is highlighted, select the menu option **View>Object Size**. In the Size dialog box, change the size unit of measurement to pixels by clicking on the unit of measurement display just to the right of the size measurements until the **px** unit of measurement appears. Change the width to **1** pixel and press **Enter** on the keyboard.

The Size dialog box is shown in Figure 21.45, and the FKey Fee field is shown just to the left of the Treatment_TreatmentItem portal.

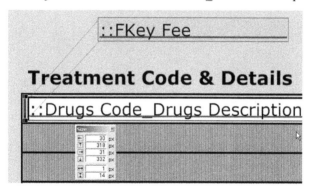

Figure 21.45: Adjusting the FKey Fee field in the Treatment_
TreatmentItem portal to be only one pixel wide. The FKey Fee
field is called out here for clarity.

6. Use the keyboard arrow keys to "nudge" the FKey Fee field just to the left edge of the Drugs Code_Drugs Description field.

7. While the almost-hidden FKey Fee field is still selected, make the field display a new value list by using the **Format>Field/Control>Setup** menu option. A value list is needed that only displays the fee code and details, and not the primary field values. FileMaker Pro 8 makes this easy to do. When the value list is being defined, in the Specify Fields dialog box, select the **PKey Fee** and **Drugs Code_Drugs Description**

fields. Check the **Show values only from second field** option in the bottom right of the Specify Fields dialog box.

Now, when the value list is displayed there should be no confusion over practice fee codes and descriptions and FileMaker's key field values.

8. The value list needs to be made up of all records in the Fees table. The Specify Fields for Value List dialog box is shown in Figure 21.46.

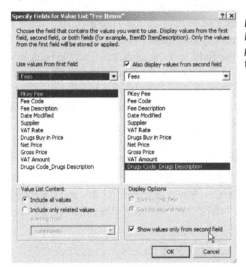

Figure 21.46: Hiding the primary key value for a value list.

9. We have almost made the FKey Fee field invisible, so the user will have a hard time selecting it to trigger the value list display. We can "fool" the user into thinking that the value list is actually appearing in another field. This is done by writing a script that goes to the FKey Fee field, which has already been set to display the drop-down value list of fee items. The script is shown in Figure 21.47.

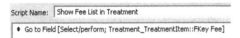

Script Name: Show Fee List in Treatment

✦ Go to Field [Select/perform; Treatment_TreatmentItem::FKey Fee]

Figure 21.47: The Show Fee List in Treatment script.

10. We now need to define the Drugs Code_Drugs Description field as a button that will trigger the Show Fee List in Treatment script when clicked. In Layout mode, highlight the **Drugs Code_Drugs Description** field and select the menu option **Format>Button Setup**.

We could have used a Go to Field button step to avoid going to the trouble of writing the script; however, the Go to Field button command will not select a field that has had its field behavior set so that it cannot be

entered in Browse mode. By contrast, the Go to Field command in a
script will.

The menu option Format>Field/Control>Behavior opens the Field
Behavior dialog box shown in Figure 21.48. The designer has deliber-
ately switched off the option to enter the field in Browse mode to avoid
data entry errors.

*Figure 21.48:
The Field
Behavior dialog
box.*

If the disguised FKey Fee field is placed just to the left of the Drugs
Code_Drugs Description field, the user may think the value list is based
in this field and not in FKey Fee.

The triggered value list can be seen in Figure 21.49, with no sign of
the FileMaker's primary key values from the Fees table.

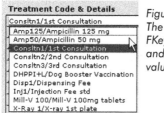

*Figure 21.49:
The "hidden"
FKey Fee field
and its fee items
value list.*

5.8: The Treatment List Layout

A second layout based on the underlying Treatment table occurrence is used
to display a Treatment List layout.

The Treatment List layout can be used to display the treatment history of
a single animal or the total fees generated for all animals over a searched
range of dates. Summary fields called Total Net, Total VAT, and Total Gross
can be placed in a trailing grand summary layout part.

The Treatment List layout is shown in Figure 21.50.

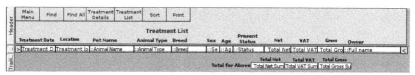

Figure 21.50: The Treatment List layout.

5.9: The Treatment Item Layout

When working with TOGs in FileMaker to navigate to a related record, there is sometimes a requirement to create a layout based on a table that the user will never have need to view for data entry or reporting. The layout can be hidden from the Layout menu by selecting the menu option **Layouts>Layout Setup**.

The Treatment Item layout is based on the underlying TreatmentItem anchor table and is an example of such a "hidden" layout. The layout will be needed shortly in a script that isolates only the relevant treatment items in order to import them into the InvoiceItem table as part of the procedure for creating a new invoice for a treatment event.

The layout is only needed as the target layout for a Go to Related Record script step command. No user interface or fields are required on the layout, which is shown in Figure 21.51.

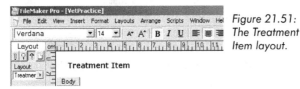

Figure 21.51: The Treatment Item layout.

5.10: The Invoice Details Layout

The Invoice Details layout will be used to print out an invoice for an animal's owner and will collect its information from a related treatment event. A portal on the Invoice layout, based on the related Invoice_InvoiceItem table occurrence, is used to display details on individual fee procedure line items that make up the invoice total.

Rather than have a separate table to manage remittance payments or payments on account, the vet has decided to include fields for credit control within each individual invoice record. Repeating fields have been used for Amount Paid and Date Paid, with three lines to record any partial payments. Calculation fields for Amount Paid and Still to Pay for each invoice record are also displayed.

Merge fields are used to place the practice letterhead in the top-right corner of the printed area of the layout, with additional merge fields from the related Invoice_Treatment_Animal_Owner table occurrence.

The Invoice Details layout is shown in Figure 21.52.

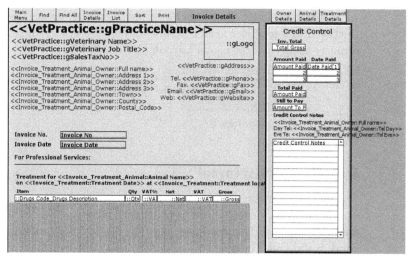

Figure 21.52: The Invoice Details layout.

5.11: The Invoice List Layout

A list of invoices generated will be useful for the practice in reporting on the amount invoiced over a selected period of time.

A series of small buttons in the body part of the Invoice List layout can be used to take the user to the related owner or animal record, while the button to the far left of the Invoice List layout will switch to the Invoice Details layout. The buttons in the header part of the Invoice List layout are the same as those in Invoice Details.

The Invoice List layout is shown in Figure 21.53 below.

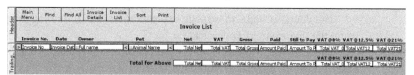

Figure 21.53: The Invoice List layout.

5.12: The Invoice Item Layout

As with the previous Treatment Item layout, the Invoice Item layout does not form part of the user interface of the VetPractice solution. An Invoice Item layout is merely required as part of a script to create invoices from treatment events. The Invoice Item layout is based on the underlying InvoiceItem table and is shown in Figure 21.54.

Like the Treatment Item layout, to avoid an operator getting "lost" in the solution, it is a good idea to hide the Invoice Item layout from the Layout menu by using the menu option **Layouts>Layout Setup**.

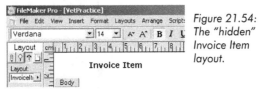

*Figure 21.54:
The "hidden"
Invoice Item
layout.*

5.13: The Fees List Layout

The vet practice wants to store standard procedures, such as consultancy charges, x-ray fees, or the cost of injections and other medications, in a Fees table. The Fees List layout, which is based on the Fees table and displays fee items, is shown in Figure 21.55.

The applicable VAT rate for each procedure can be selected from a drop-down list.

Figure 21.55: The Fees List layout.

5.14: The Expenses Details Layout

We have now completed all the layouts needed to mange owner, pet, treatment, and invoice details for the practice.

The vet now wants to manage expenses incurred in running the practice using the underlying Expenses table.

The Expenses Details layout is used to record the category and item descriptions for expenses. Additional calculation fields are used to work out an expense item's net VAT and gross figures based on the applicable VAT rate and the proportion claimed, which is 100% or less.

A global text field called gVAT PERIOD is used as the header for a set of expense subsummary reports.

The Expenses Details layout is shown in Figure 21.56. A text block on the right side of the layout is a copy of the category drop-down list and is used for reference. The vet's accountant should be able to advise the practice on expenses and capital equipment categories, which may change over time.

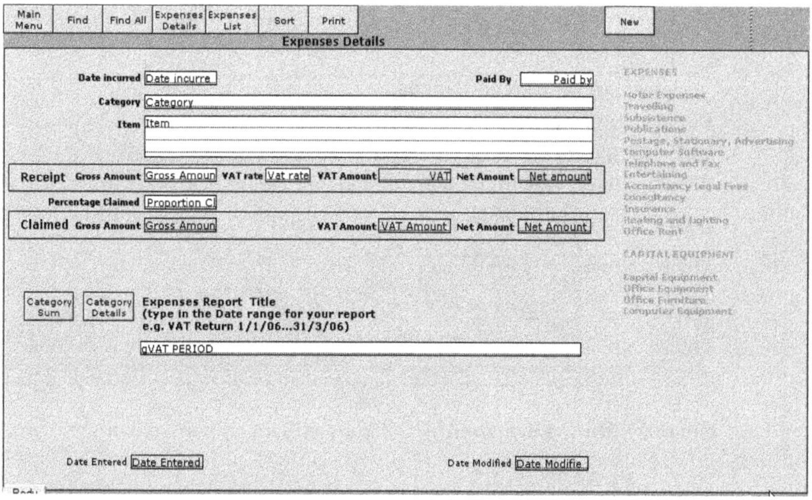

Figure 21.56: The Expenses Details layout.

5.15: The Expenses List Layout

We are going to create three list layouts using the Expenses table: a simple Expenses List report and two subsummary reports, sorted by category and date incurred.

A simple Expenses List layout, made up of header, body, and trailing grand summary layout parts, can be seen in Figure 21.57.

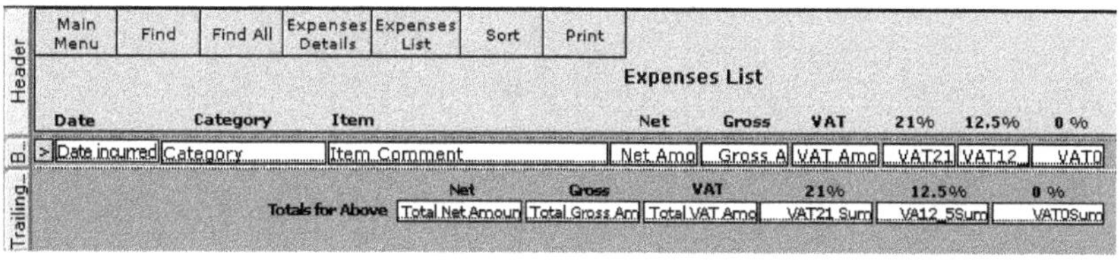

Figure 21.57: The Expenses List layout.

The decision to include summary fields under a list report in a trailing grand summary, in preference to a footer part, is based on the fact that FileMaker displays a trailing grand summary directly after the last record in a list.

5.16: The Expenses by Category in Detail Report

The vet's accountant has promised to reduce the fee for producing an annual set of accounts if the practice can provide expense reports broken down into category subsummaries. We can do this by creating a new layout using FileMaker's Layout wizard. The aim is to produce a report layout consisting of header, leading grand summary, sub summary when sorted by category, body, and footer layout parts.

A set of buttons in the header is set not to print by using the menu option **Format>Set Sliding/Printing**. The page number and date symbols have been added to the footer using the options in the FileMaker **Insert** menu.

The Expenses by Category in Detail report is shown in Layout mode in Figure 21.58, with a closeup of the layout parts shown in Figure 21.59.

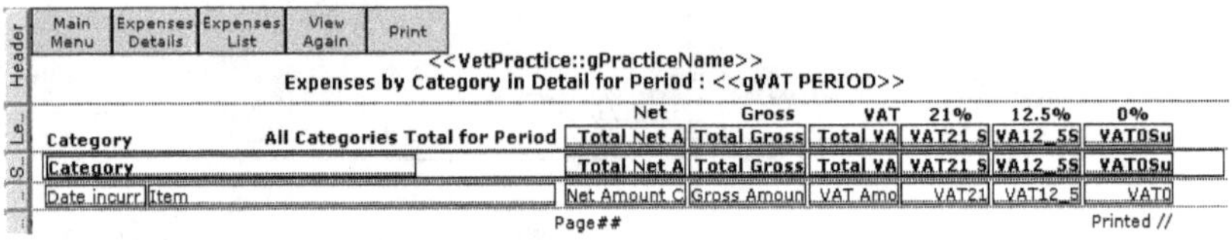

Figure 21.58: The Expenses by Category in Detail report layout.

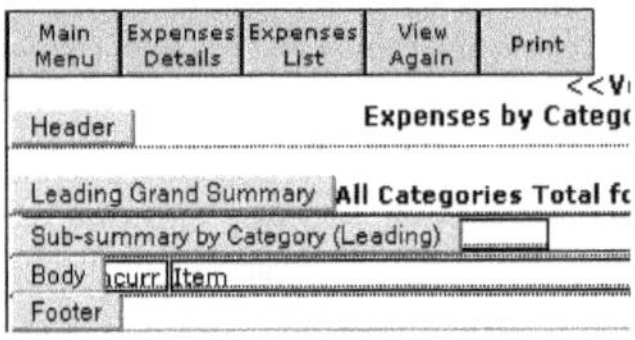

Figure 21.59:
Closeup view of the layout parts required for the Expenses by Category in Detail report layout.

We do need to write a script to run the report, as described in the next section. We can still test the report in the meantime by selecting a set of expense records and sorting the record set in ascending order by the expense category and date incurred. The report can be tested and viewed by switching to Preview mode. A sample of how the report will look is shown in Figure 21.60. The report title typed into the gVAT PERIOD global text field in the Expenses Details layout is displayed in the header of the report.

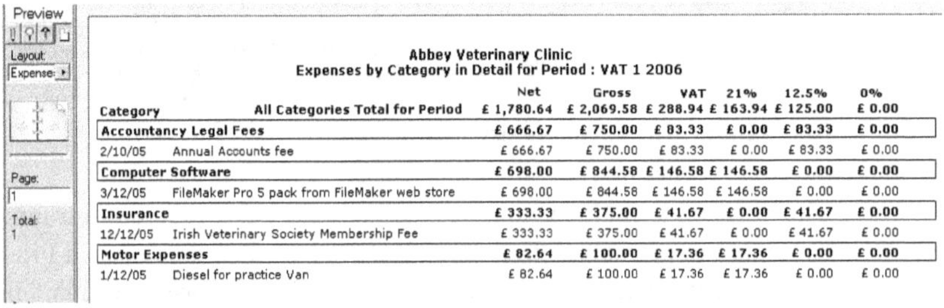

Figure 21.60: Example of the Expenses by Category in Detail report.

5.17: The Expenses by Category Summary Report

A summarized version of the report can be created by duplicating the previous report layout and deleting the body layout part.

The report layout created in Section 5.16 can be duplicated using the menu option **Layouts>Duplicate Layout** in Layout mode. Highlight the body part label and press the **Backspace** or **Delete** key.

The Expenses by Category Summary report is shown in Layout mode in Figure 21.61, with a closeup of the layout parts shown in Figure 21.62.

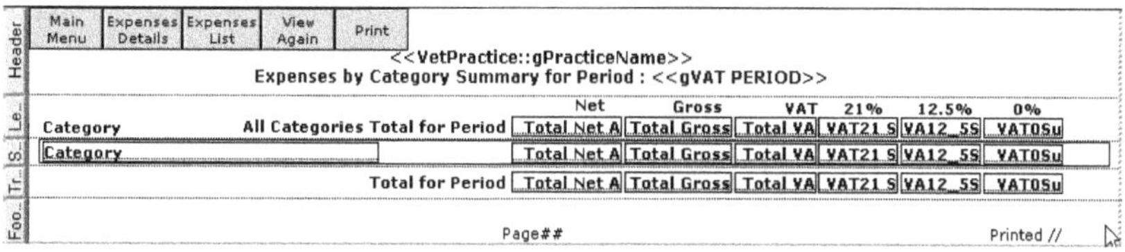

Figure 21.61: The Expenses by Category Summary report layout.

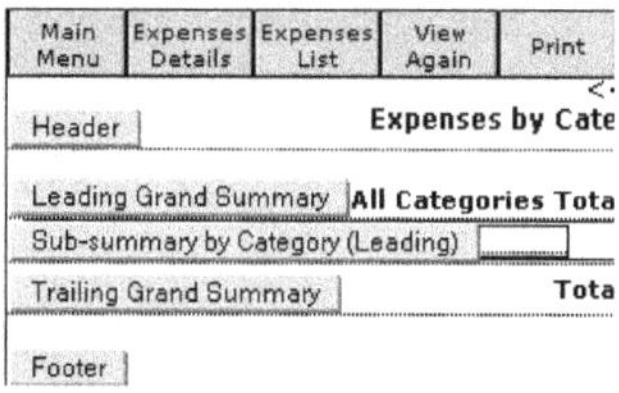

Figure 21.62: Closeup of the layout parts required for the Expenses by Category Summary report layout.

As before, if a set of expense records is found and sorted by category, the report can be tested by selecting **Preview** mode from the View menu. An example of the summary report is shown in Figure 21.63.

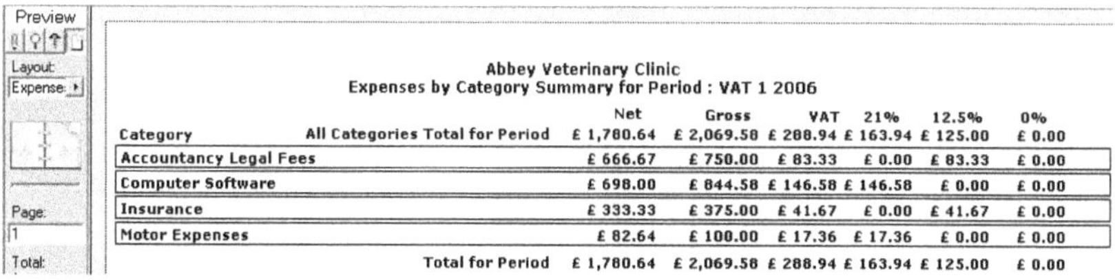

Figure 21.63: Example of the Expenses by Category Summary report.

These reports can be automated using the scripts that are described in the following section.

Step 6: Automating the VetPractice Solution with Scripts

A series of scripts would help to make the VetPractice database easy to use and would automate the process for adding a new treatment for a pet and converting a treatment event into a new invoice.

6.1: The Opening Script

As with any FileMaker solution, new user confidence is boosted if the same screen appears every time the file is opened. We want the file to switch to the Main Menu layout and hide FileMaker's Status area when the database is launched.

We can write an Opening script to do this, as shown in Figure 21.64. As this script is relatively simple and does not, for instance, open a series of related files each time it is run, we can also use it as a way of returning to the Main Menu. The same script is therefore used each time the Main Menu button is clicked on in any of the solution layouts.

Figure 21.64:
The Opening
Script/Open Menu
script.

To make the Opening script run every time the VetPractice database is opened, choose the menu option **File>File Options**. In the File Options dialog box, check the **Perform script** option and choose the **Opening Script/Open Menu** script, as shown in Figure 21.65.

Figure 21.65:
Customizing the file
options for the
database to run the
Opening script
when the file is
opened.

6.2: Navigation Scripts to Open Data Entry and List Layouts

Since the Status area is now hidden when the Main Menu layout is displayed, a series of scripts will be needed to show the Status area and switch to the correct data entry or list layouts. An example script that is used to switch to the Owner Details layout is shown in Figure 21.66.

Figure 21.66: The Open
Owner Details script.

6.3: The Add Treatment in Animal Details Script

While we could have changed the relationship between Animal and Animal_Treatment to enable new treatment records to be created via the portal in the Animal Details layout, the vet would like more control on when a new treatment record is created.

We need to make use of the global number field gPKey Animal in the Animal table in order to set the correct FKey Animal value in a new treatment record.

A Show Custom Dialog script step is used to ask the operator to confirm the creation of a new treatment record.

If the user goes ahead and a new treatment record is created, the operator will expect to "land" in the new treatment record using the Treatment Details layout, with the cursor positioned in the Treatment Notes field, as all the related information on the pet and the owner should be in place by this stage.

The Add Treatment in Animal Details script is shown in Figure 21.67.

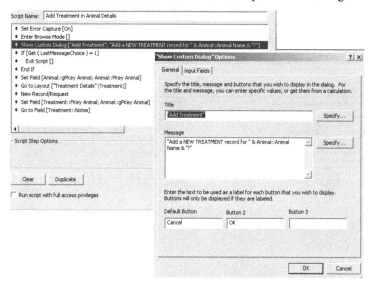

Figure 21.67: The Add Treatment in Animal Details script.

The green Add Treatment button in the Animal Details layout should be set to run this script.

6.4: The Create Invoice for Treatment Script

Once a treatment record is completed, the vet is likely to want to generate a new invoice so that the owner can settle up before leaving the clinic. A script is needed that converts all treatment items into invoice items and relates these to a new invoice.

As with the previous Add Treatment in Animal Details script, extensive use is made in this script of the global number field to temporarily hold the primary key value for a treatment record, an owner record, and an invoice record.

The Create Invoice for Treatment script, with the initial Show Custom Dialog script step expanded, is shown in Figure 21.68.

The operator will expect to "land" in the newly created invoice record, ready to print out the bill for the owner to pay.

The green Create Invoice button in the Treatment Details layout should be defined to run this script.

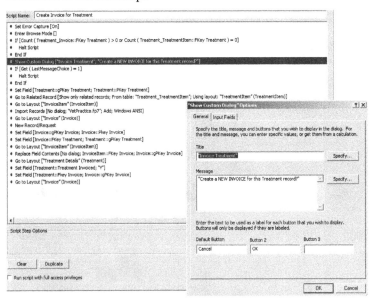

Figure 21.68: The Create Invoice for Treatment script.

6.5: The Expense Category for Period Detail and Summary Reports

In order for a subsummary report in FileMaker to work effectively, the found set of records must be sorted by the correct fields in the right order, and FileMaker must switch to Preview mode for the report to display correctly on screen. Ideally, the Print Setup option should also be set so that the report is oriented correctly for portrait or landscape viewing and printing.

For the practice expense reports, these procedural steps can be easily arranged in a script that can be triggered by clicking on a button in the Expenses Details layout. The script for the Category for Period Details report is shown in Figure 21.69.

Figure 21.69:
The Category for
Period Details
report script.

Note that when a script is being created to run a subsummary report, the Sort Records script step may only display the correct fields if the current layout references the table containing the same fields. It is good practice to "park" FileMaker in the report layout before designing a subsummary report script so that the correct fields for the sort order can be picked. This is shown in Figure 21.70.

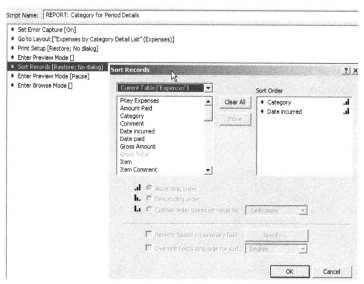

Figure 21.70: The Sort Records script step is influenced by the current layout's table when a script is defined.

The expense summary report is identical to the detailed report, with the exception that the target layout in the script needs to change. The previous script can be duplicated in the ScriptMaker Define Scripts dialog box. Rename the duplicated report script **Category for Period Summary** and change the Go to Layout script step's target layout to **Expenses by Category Summary List**, as shown in Figure 21.71.

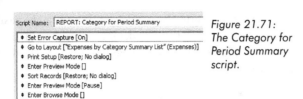

Figure 21.71:
The Category for
Period Summary
script.

Taking the Solution Further

Any effective FileMaker database solution should be able to evolve and keep up with the business data management requirements of a professional practice.

You might want to consider how the Fees table could be expanded to link to tables managing stock items, veterinary suppliers, and supplier purchase orders. The stock control solution in Chapter 16 might give you some ideas on how to do this.

The vet might want to record the cost of medications used in treatment item records in order to determine the gross profit made by the professional practice for each treatment record.

As mentioned at the start of this chapter, you might also want to think about how the solution could be adapted to manage large animal herds. FileMaker Mobile has the potential to capture treatment data away from the clinic on farms and in horse stables. This information can be synchronized with the main database in the clinic at a later stage.

Part III

Deploying Your Business Solution

Chapter 22

FileMaker Deployment Options

In this chapter:

- Introduction
- Sharing a FileMaker File
- Peer-to-Peer FileMaker Sharing
- Configuring a File for Network Sharing
- Peer-to-Peer Database Hosting Troubleshooting
- Sharing a Database with FileMaker Server
- Web Publishing
- Other Methods for Deploying a FileMaker Database

Introduction

You have written your own database solution using FileMaker Pro that does a great job of matching your business or workgroup data management requirements. It's time to share the fruits of your labor with colleagues! FileMaker enables several users to share your database at the same time.

Of course a database does not have to be shared. If your database is still at the testing stage or contains confidential information that you might not want staff to access, the same menu options and settings that enable FileMaker sharing over a network can also be used to prevent others from accessing your file.

A key factor in preparing a FileMaker database for sharing is security. Accounts and privileges, which are used to control and manage the accessibility of FileMaker files, are discussed in Chapter 24. Before trying out any of the sharing techniques introduced in this chapter with your real data, or hosting a database with FileMaker Pro 8 Server, which is discussed in the next chapter, you should consider the issue of who should have access to the database and to what extent.

Information contained in a FileMaker file can be shared using a variety of techniques, each of which is discussed in this chapter. Subsequent chapters provide a more detailed description of how to host a database with FileMaker Server, how to manage user access to a file, getting data in and out of FileMaker, and publishing a database on the web using FileMaker's Instant Web Publishing feature.

Sharing a FileMaker File

FileMaker has been designed to make sharing a custom database easy. If you never take the next step of configuring a database for multiple users, no matter how good your solution, the fact that it can only be used by one colleague at a time may cause a data access "bottleneck" that will prevent your business from deriving the maximum benefit from the file.

Peer-to-Peer FileMaker Sharing

Peer-to-peer sharing of a FileMaker database is the simplest way to enable a limited number of colleagues on the same computer network to use the same file. Before preparing a file for network sharing, you will need a licensed copy of FileMaker Pro for each computer that will open the database.

The built-in file sharing capabilities of FileMaker Pro restrict the number of concurrent users sharing the same file to five, with a maximum of 10 files available for sharing.

Before configuring a database file for network sharing it is worth considering where the file will be located in the business network, which colleagues are likely to want to use the file most during the course of a working day, and a procedure for backing up the file.

The network performance of a FileMaker database is maximized if the file resides on the computer that first opens the file. The person using that computer is known as the host, and any colleagues who subsequently open the database are client users of the file. While a database is shared over a network, any users of the file who have the correct access privileges can modify record data, change the underlying database structure, and modify scripts and layouts. The database host cannot close the database until all client users quit out of the file. If the host attempts to close a file that is currently being shared by clients, FileMaker will display a dialog box and offer to send a message to clients informing them that the named host wishes to close the file.

This method of sharing a FileMaker file is termed peer-to-peer, as both the host and the clients of a database are using the standard desktop version of FileMaker Pro 8 (or FileMaker Pro 8 Advanced).

The database does not have to reside on the computer hard disk of the file's most frequent user. The FileMaker file can be located on an allocated server. This may be of benefit if the server hard disk is frequently backed up. It is important to be aware that a FileMaker file cannot be easily copied or backed up when it is being used. FileMaker Server, which is discussed later, has built-in functionality to pause a database file while a scheduled backup takes place. However, when a database is being hosted across a network with the standard desktop version of FileMaker, the file must be closed first before creating a backup copy of the file.

In addition to being able to manage regular backups of the file, your choice of whether to locate a shared database on a server or on a local hard disk for the usual host user should also consider the reliability and power of the computer and whether other memory-intensive applications are used at the same time as FileMaker. These can affect the performance of a shared FileMaker file.

Configuring a File for Network Sharing

Any FileMaker file can be configured for network sharing. With the file open, select the **Edit>Sharing>FileMaker Network** menu option. The FileMaker Network Settings dialog box, shown in Figure 22.1, will appear.

At the top of the dialog box is a pair of buttons to switch on or off network sharing using TCP/IP. The Network Sharing setting should be switched on.

A list of currently open files will be displayed. Highlight the file or files that you want to configure for network access, then select one of the buttons to the right in the Network access to file section. As we have not yet started to discuss settings for file access privileges and privilege sets, you might want to select the "All users" button to test file sharing at this stage.

An additional check box labeled "Don't display in Open Remote File dialog" allows you to choose whether or not the file name will be displayed to the client user when attempting to open a hosted file. This can be of benefit if you only want a single "welcome" or "main menu" file to be displayed, with hidden files opened using scripts or related fields on a layout. Allowing clients to open files first can cause problems for peer-to-peer hosting, however, so it is recommended that the host open all related files for a solution at the start of a work session.

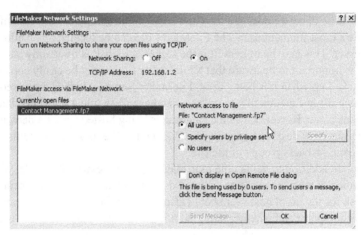

Figure 22.1: The FileMaker Network Settings dialog box.

Colleagues on the network who wish to open the hosted file must first launch FileMaker Pro and then select the menu option **File>Open Remote**, use the Windows keyboard shortcut **Ctrl+Shift+O**, or click the **Remote** button in the Open File dialog box.

The Open Remote File dialog box will then appear, as shown in Figure 22.2.

The window on the left side of the dialog box displays a list of hosts, and the one on the right displays a list of files available for network sharing. A drop-down list of database hosts can be displayed in the View box, at the top of the dialog box.

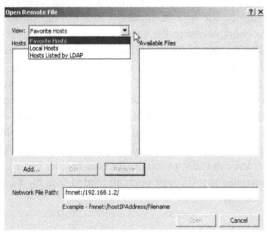

Figure 22.2: The Open Remote File dialog box.

If the allocated host computer does not show up in the Hosts window after having used the FileMaker Network Settings dialog to modify a file for network sharing, click the Add button to open the Edit Favorite Host dialog box and type the local network IP address for the host computer. The IP address can be found by going back to the host computer and choosing the **Edit> Sharing>FileMaker Network** menu option. As displayed in Figure 22.1, the allocated TCP/IP address for the host computer is shown in the FileMaker Network Settings dialog box. Type this IP address into the Host's Internet Address box, as shown in Figure 22.3, select the **Show all available files for this host** button, then click the **Save** button.

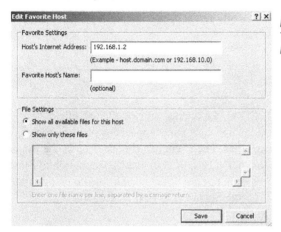

Figure 22.3:
The Edit Favorite
Host dialog box.

A host name, which is the same as the User Name in the FileMaker Preferences dialog box, should now appear in the Hosts window of the Open Remote File dialog box along with a list of available files, as displayed in Figure 22.4.

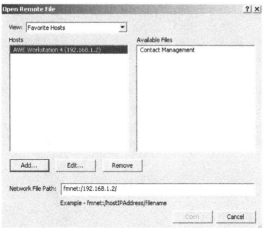

Figure 22.4:
The Open
Remote File
dialog box with a
host and a list of
available files
displayed.

The client user can now double-click on a selected file name or highlight a file from the list and click the **Open** button. Provided that the client user has a valid account with an extended privilege to enable access via FileMaker Network, which is discussed below, the user will be able to open the file.

The host user will not be alerted that a new client user has opened the database file. If the host attempts to close a file that currently has client users, a message will appear, as shown in Figure 22.5, with details on the clients.

Figure 22.5: The message that a host sees when attempting to close a file that has client users.

If the Ask button is clicked, the clients will see a Close File dialog box, as displayed in Figure 22.6. The host name appears as part of a message that lists the file or files to close. The client can choose to close the file now by using the button in the dialog box, or click the Cancel button to finish a task. If the client is away from his or her desk, an additional message states that an automatic close will be attempted in the next 30 seconds.

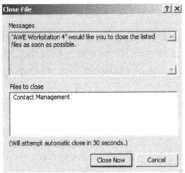

Figure 22.6: The Close File message that a client sees when the database host attempts to close a shared file.

The host can check to see if any clients are using the file at any stage by selecting the **Edit>Sharing>FileMaker Network** menu option. In the bottom right of the FileMaker Network Settings dialog box, the number of users for the selected database is displayed, as shown in Figure 22.7.

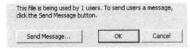

Figure 22.7: The FileMaker Network Settings dialog box shows the number of users in a shared file.

The host can communicate with the client users of a file by clicking the **Send Message** button. A Send Message dialog box will appear and a message can be composed and sent, as shown in Figure 22.8.

Figure 22.8:
The Send
Message dialog
box.

The host's message appears on the client computer as shown in Figure 22.9.

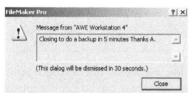

Figure 22.9:
A message sent
to clients from
the database
host.

Peer-to-Peer Database Hosting Troubleshooting

Peer-to-peer sharing of a FileMaker database is the easiest method for allowing more than one user to access a file concurrently. If a client can see the host computer in the Open Remote File dialog box but cannot see the required database listed, it is likely that the file has had its network access set to "All Users" by the host in the FileMaker Network Settings dialog box. It is also possible that the client's account and the associated privilege set does not include "Access via FileMaker Network." Accounts and privilege sets are discussed in Chapter 24. For now, if you want to test network sharing of a file that has an active Admin account with or without a password, click the **All Users** option in the FileMaker Network Settings dialog box to switch on Access via FileMaker Network in the account's privilege set.

Sharing a Database with FileMaker Server

If you need to share more than 10 database files or give more than five colleagues access to a FileMaker database, FileMaker Server 8 can address your needs.

FileMaker Server is a dedicated database server that opens FileMaker files and hosts them on your network. Database performance over a network is enhanced by the use of this advanced client-server technology that optimizes how the files are managed.

FileMaker Server 8 can host up to 125 database files for up to a maximum of 250 FileMaker Pro clients. In addition, FileMaker Server Advanced can support up to an additional 100 Custom Web Publishing or Instant Web Publishing sessions. This means that a significant number of users can also gain access to your FileMaker data via a web browser. FileMaker Server Advanced also enables data in a FileMaker file to be exchanged with or used by sources from other applications across the network by using open database connectivity (ODBC) and Java database connectivity (JDBC) data sources. Up to 50 ODBC and JDBC clients are also supported using FileMaker Server Advanced. FileMaker Server is discussed in more detail in Chapter 23.

Web Publishing

At the time of this book's publication, FileMaker is in a unique position among database applications in that a database can be easily published to the web using FileMaker's built-in Instant Web Publishing feature without any prior web programming experience on the part of the database designer. If your computer has an Internet connection and you open the appropriate port on your network firewall, you can publish a FileMaker database to the web for up to five concurrent web users by using the standard desktop copy of FileMaker Pro 8. Colleagues or associates who want to open one of your databases via a web browser need to know the IP address of your host computer. FileMaker Server Advanced increases the number of concurrent web clients to a potential maximum of 100. FileMaker's Instant Web Publishing feature is discussed in Chapter 27.

It is also possible to publish static data from FileMaker to the web using FileMaker's ability to export data as an HTML or XML formatted file. For example, you can add this file to your company's web page to publish an updated product price list.

While it is beyond the scope of a book that is primarily concerned with writing FileMaker databases for you and your colleagues working on an office or workgroup network, it is worth being aware that FileMaker Server Advanced can also support Custom Web Publishing (CWP). CWP may be of interest to you if your team expands and remote users, suppliers, and clients wish to share some of your company's data via a web page, or you wish to add data from a FileMaker file into an existing company website. Information from a FileMaker database can be published to, and updated by, a web page if the file is hosted by FileMaker Server Advanced. You must configure the supplied Web Publishing Engine and have an appropriate web server using Apache or Internet Information Server (IIS). CWP does require some web application development and programming experience. It is mentioned to reassure you, and any business colleagues or associates, that FileMaker will not put your business data into a blind alley as your data requirements and number of users expands. More information on CWP can be obtained from the FileMaker website at www.filemaker.com.

Other Methods for Deploying a FileMaker Database

In addition to hosting your business database on your network or publishing a file to the web, there are other methods by which authorized users can access data in your FileMaker file.

The standard Windows version of FileMaker Pro 8 can be used to exchange data with other applications and data sources using ODBC/JDBC (xDBC). Once xDBC data drivers have been configured, a FileMaker file can act as an xDBC data source, enabling other applications to interrogate the file and extract data via the xDBC driver.

An example of using the ODBC driver that ships with FileMaker Pro 8 to extract data in FileMaker into a Microsoft Excel worksheet is described in Chapter 26.

FileMaker Pro can work well with remote access software such as Citrix Metaframe and Terminal Services. A fair amount of configuration is required, in addition to the licensing costs to set up remote access to a database using Citrix or Terminal Services. More information on using FileMaker with remote access software is available from the company website.

FileMaker Pro 8 Advanced has all the features in the standard version of the application and includes several additional developer utilities. One of these is the ability to create a run-time solution from one or more FileMaker database files. A FileMaker run-time solution can be distributed to users who do not have a copy of FileMaker Pro installed on their computer. A run-time solution cannot be shared peer-to-peer; however, FileMaker Server can be configured to open run-time files over a network. A run-time solution is one method by which remote users can browse or update FileMaker records remotely in what are, in effect, copies of the original database file. This method of data exchange can be useful to collect records from sites that do not have a web connection or perhaps in a business franchise situation where a single user in a branch office could use a copy of your original business database template. You may want to later compile information from run-time copies of a file. To do this you will have to design an import procedure to capture records that were added to run-time versions of the file. Methods for importing and exporting FileMaker records are discussed in Chapter 25.

It is possible to exchange data between a FileMaker file and a handheld device using FileMaker Mobile. You can decide which fields should be available in the handheld device version of a database file and how the fields should appear (as check boxes, drop-down menus, and edit boxes) to assist with data capture. Any records that are edited, deleted, or added to the handheld device can be synchronized with the primary copy of the database at a later stage. To use FileMaker Mobile 8, the operating system of your handheld device or PDA needs to be Palm OS 4.1 to 5.4, or be a Windows Mobile 2003 or 5.0 based Pocket PC. Some examples of field-based data capture procedures involving FileMaker Mobile include veterinary data testing of herds and event management booking of delegates, often using a handheld device/barcode reader.

An example screen shot of how FileMaker Mobile can appear on a handheld device is shown in Figure 22.10.

Figure 22.10: Screen shot of the Contact Management starter solution that ships with FileMaker Mobile 8.

Previous version of FileMaker Mobile could only synchronize with a local copy of a FileMaker database, not one hosted by FileMaker Server. When a file was shared across a network, this meant that at least one copy of a database had to exist in order to get data in and out of a handheld. This has implications for data accuracy and the risk of two data sets being opened at the same time by accident over the network. With FileMaker Mobile 8, it is now possible to synchronize the data in a handheld device directly with a hosted database.

Chapter 23

FileMaker Server 8

In this chapter:

- Introduction
- Does My Business Need FileMaker Server 8?
- Minimum Computer Requirements to Run FileMaker Server 8
- FileMaker Server Installation
- Testing the Server Installation
- Preparing Your Database Files for Hosting with FileMaker Server 8
  - Preparing the File for Network Access
  - Where to Put the Hosted Files
- Scheduling Database Backups with FileMaker Server
- The Database Hosting Assistant
- The Client Connections Assistant
- Opening a File Hosted by FileMaker Server

Introduction

The most effective method for deploying your FileMaker business solution and enabling colleagues to work with your database is to host the file using FileMaker Server.

As briefly outlined in Chapter 2 when introducing the FileMaker product line, FileMaker Pro 8 offers three server products: FileMaker Server 8, FileMaker Server 8 Advanced, and the FileMaker Server 8 Option pack. The Option Pack is an add-on option that enables existing FileMaker Server 8 users to benefit from all the features of FileMaker Server 8 Advanced.

FileMaker Server 8 is used to provide concurrent access for up to 250 networked FileMaker clients. The Server application can host up to 125 FileMaker files. In addition to these hosting levels, FileMaker Server Advanced can make FileMaker data available for up to 100 Custom Web Publishing or Instant Web Publishing sessions, and up to 50 ODBC or JDBC clients.

This chapter provides an introduction to how FileMaker Server 8 can assist you in hosting your business database. Even if your current business database needs are fulfilled within the peer-to-peer limitation of five concurrent clients, it is hoped that this chapter will help you to plan how to use FileMaker Server as your business grows.

In remembering that you have a business or a workgroup to manage, this chapter is not a comprehensive guide to all the features available in FileMaker Server. If by now you have already added a "database developer" role in addition to your existing role as business manager, the basic functionality of FileMaker Server is fairly straightforward. Hopefully, you won't feel by the end of this chapter that you now have to cram a "server manager" hat on your overcrowded head!

Does My Business Need FileMaker Server 8?

FileMaker Server 8 is a dedicated database server application for hosting FileMaker Pro 8 (and 7) files. There are two main components to FileMaker Server: an administration application called FileMaker Server Admin, and the services (Windows) or daemons (Mac OS) that comprise FileMaker Server.

If you are a FileMaker user with a need to share databases among a growing number of users, you shouldn't think that the migration to FileMaker Server is just a method to overcome the five user peer-to-peer hosting limit. There are many benefits to hosting files with FileMaker Server. For example, in addition to the far larger client and file hosting limits, FileMaker Server uses advanced client-server technology to improve the performance of hosted files for clients. Also, file and client management, in addition to automated tasks such as backups, can all be managed using the Server Admin application.

Minimum Computer Requirements to Run FileMaker Server 8

Ideally, FileMaker Server should be installed and run on a dedicated computer that is not expected to perform any tasks for the business other than as a database server. If at all possible, you should not use the same computer as the firm's web server, mail server, or CAD or DTP design machine. The use of any other applications on the allocated FileMaker Server computer that are processor, memory, or hard disk intensive will slow down the performance of hosted databases.

For Windows, the minimum requirements to run FileMaker Server for 1 to 50 clients is as follows:

- Intel-compatible PC with a Pentium III 1 GHz or Xeon processor
- 256 MB of installed RAM (1 GB or more recommended)
- Windows Server 2003 Standard Edition (with Service Pack 1), Windows 2000 Server (with Service Pack 4), or Windows XP Professional SP 2 operating system
- A hard disk with at least 1 GB of available disk space. Allow additional space for the database files you intend to host, which must be located on the same disk as the FileMaker Server application.
- Login account with administrative privileges for installing FileMaker Server
- A CD or DVD drive

To host FileMaker databases for more than 50 clients on the Windows platform, the minimum requirements are:

- Intel-compatible PC with a Pentium 4 or Xeon processor
- 512 MB of installed RAM (1 GB or more recommended)
- Windows Server 2003 Standard Edition (with Service Pack 1) or Windows 2000 Server (with Service Pack 4) operating system
- A hard disk with at least 1 GB of available disk space. Allow additional space for the database files you intend to host, which must be located on the same disk as the FileMaker Server application.
- Login account with administrative privileges for installing FileMaker Server
- A CD or DVD drive

To host files for clients on a network, the allocated server computer will also need;

- A Windows-compatible network card
- The software driver for the network card
- TCP/IP network protocol

FileMaker Server Installation

Install FileMaker Server on the allocated computer. Unless you are very familiar with Windows XP or Windows Server 2000/2003 administration, it is recommended that the default installation settings for FileMaker Server be used. By default, a folder called Program Files\FileMaker\FileMaker Server is created. You can choose an automatic or manual option for FileMaker Server startup. Choose automatic if you want FileMaker Server to start whenever Windows starts. Choose manual if you want FileMaker Server to start only after you start the FileMaker Server service in the Services console. After installation, you should register the application with FileMaker if you have not already done so, then manually start FileMaker Server or restart the computer if you chose an automatic startup option.

If you have a firewall connected to your allocated FileMaker Server computer, you will need to configure the firewall settings to allow FileMaker to use its allocated ports. These port numbers are:

- 5003 — FileMaker Pro and FileMaker Server file hosting
- 50003 — FileMaker Server service
- 50006 — FileMaker Server Helper service

Testing the Server Installation

Before attempting to host your business database with FileMaker Server, it may be worth testing that the Server installation has been completed successfully.

Start FileMaker Server from the Services console, if it has not automatically started. The Services console is shown in Figure 23.1.

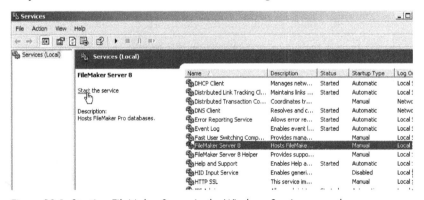

Figure 23.1: Starting FileMaker Server in the Windows Services console.

Now start the FileMaker Server Admin application from Windows by choosing the **Start>All Programs>FileMaker Server Admin** menu option. The FileMaker Server Admin window should appear, as shown in Figure 23.2.

Figure 23.2: The FileMaker Server Admin window.

Click on the yellow **FileMaker Server** icon and a dialog box titled Connect to FileMaker Server will appear, as shown in Figure 23.3.

Figure 23.3:
The Connect to
FileMaker Server
dialog box.

Highlight **localhost** in the Hostname list, and click the **Connect** button.

The FileMaker Server Admin window should now appear with a set of six icons, each with a brief description, as displayed in Figure 23.4.

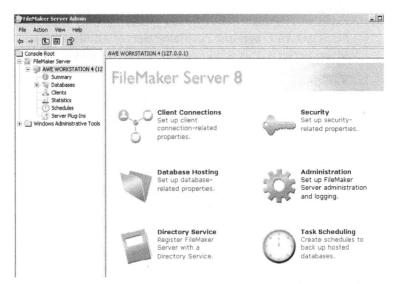

Figure 23.4: The FileMaker Server Admin window connected to a named FileMaker Server.

Click on the **Databases** item in the tree view on the left side of the window, then double-click **Files** as shown in Figure 23.5.

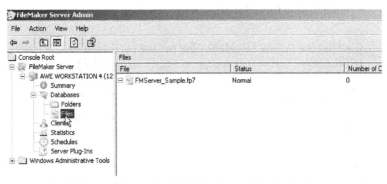

Figure 23.5: Selecting Files in the FileMaker Server Admin window to see what files are currently being hosted by FileMaker Server.

The default installation of FileMaker Server includes a sample database called FMServer_Sample.fp7, which can be used to test whether the application has been installed correctly and to see if clients can open a server-hosted file. If the file appears in the list, as shown in Figure 23.5, FileMaker Server has been successfully installed on the server.

You should now check that the file can be used from a client computer. Switch to another computer on the network and launch FileMaker Pro. Choose the menu option **File>Open Remote**. Select **Local Hosts** from the

View menu. The Open Remote File dialog box will appear, as shown in Figure 23.6. The FMServer_Sample file should appear in the Available Files list when the server computer is highlighted in the Hosts list.

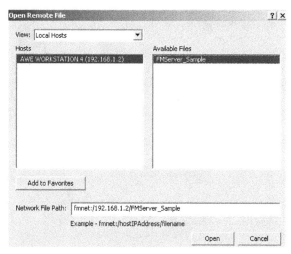

Figure 23.6: The Open Remote File dialog box should list the server in the Hosts box and any hosted files in the Available Files box.

Preparing Your Database Files for Hosting with FileMaker Server 8

It is important to check that your FileMaker database can be hosted by FileMaker Server before copying the file to the intended location on the server.

Preparing the File for Network Access

It is important to consider the issue of file security before your business solution is hosted using FileMaker Server or peer-to-peer network sharing. The ability to access a file via a FileMaker network is managed using an extended privilege set. Accounts and privilege sets are discussed in the next chapter. As we have not yet added a series of accounts and privileges, it is likely that our solution file includes a default Admin and Guest account. At least one of these accounts must be active with full access to the database file.

Open the database file with FileMaker Pro using the Admin account, with a password if required, to gain full access to the file.

Use the **Edit>Sharing>FileMaker Network** menu option to open the FileMaker Network Settings dialog box, as shown in Figure 23.7.

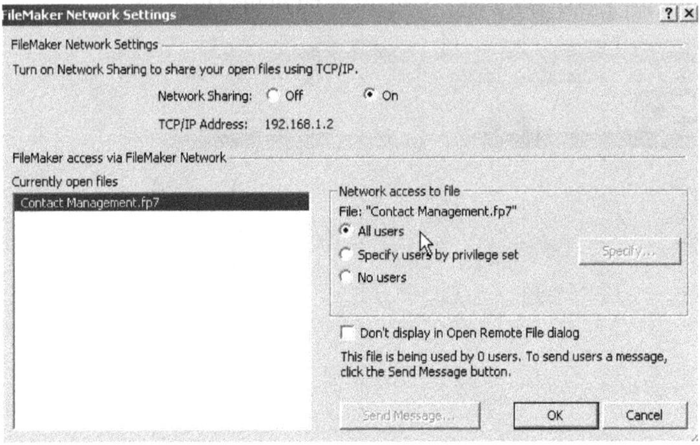

Figure 23.7: The FileMaker Network Settings dialog box.

In the Network access to file section, click the **All users** button. This will switch on the "Access via FileMaker Network" extended privilege option for the Admin and Guest accounts and enable us to test that FileMaker Server can host the business solution across the firm's network.

As we have not yet added accounts and privileges to the file at this stage, it is strongly recommended that you make a backup copy of the file and avoid including sensitive data in the hosted file for now. Anyone with a copy of FileMaker Pro installed on their computer can potentially gain full access to the file via the server.

Where to Put the Hosted Files

Any FileMaker files that you want FileMaker Server to host need to be placed in the following Windows directory:

Program Files\FileMaker\FileMaker Server\Data\Databases\

FileMaker Server will open any files in this folder when the service is launched.

In addition, FileMaker Server will also automatically open any database files that are located one folder level down from the Databases folder.

You can also specify a custom location to place database files for hosting with FileMaker Server. Open the FileMaker Server Admin window and highlight the **FileMaker Server** icon in the left side of the console window. Select the menu option **Action>Properties** to open the Server Properties dialog box and choose the **Default Folders** tab, as shown in Figure 23.8. You

can check the "Use additional database folder" option and type the folder's
path here.

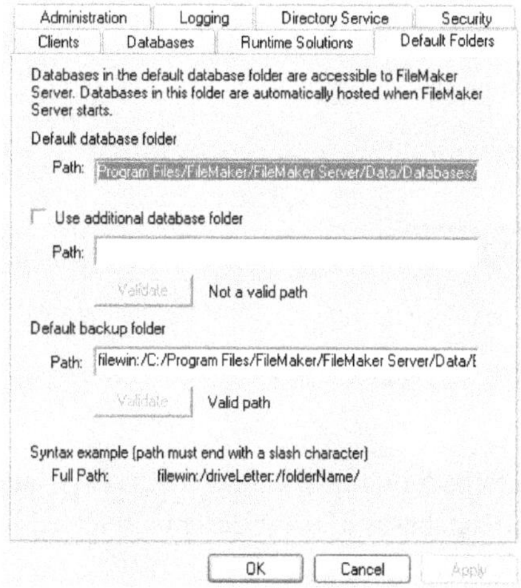

Figure 23.8: The FileMaker Server
Properties dialog box Default Folders tab.

Scheduling Database Backups with FileMaker Server

The Default Folders tab of the Server Properties dialog box shown in Figure
23.8 includes a box where you can type in a backup folder location.
FileMaker Server can back up hosted database files that are currently open or
that are in a selected folder.

FileMaker Server is able to back up files while they are open, and clients
can continue to use a file without interruption. The Server application is
designed so that on completion of the backup, the database is paused momentarily to synchronize the backed-up file with the hosted version. The service
then resumes. Any colleagues using a hosted database should be unaware that
a backup of the file is taking place.

Database backups can be managed by FileMaker Server as a scheduled
task. On the Windows platform, a set of six configuration assistant options
can be selected from the FileMaker Server Admin console. Click on the
Clock to launch the Task Scheduling Assistant and open a new dialog box.
Click the **Next** button and you will see three task buttons to choose from, as
shown in Figure 23.9.

Click the **Back Up Databases** button and then click the **Next** button.

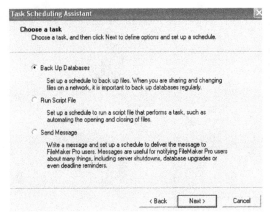

Figure 23.9:
The Task
Scheduling
Assistant dialog
box.

The next window in the Task Scheduling Assistant contains two buttons to allow you to back up either all databases or databases in a selected folder location, as shown in Figure 23.10.

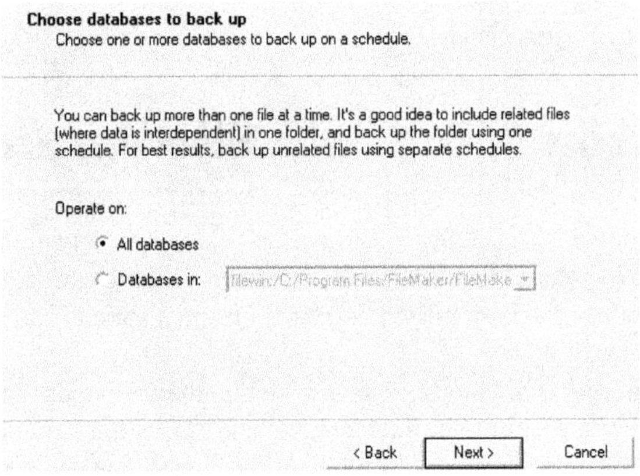

Figure 23.10:
Choosing which
databases to
back up with the
Task Scheduling
Assistant.

When the **Next** button is clicked again, the following window includes a box to type in a location destination for the backed-up databases, as shown in Figure 23.11.

You can check that FileMaker Server recognizes the path by clicking the **Validate** button. It is important to check that the destination volume has sufficient space for the backup files.

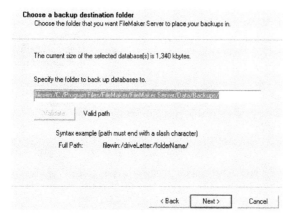

Figure 23.11:
Selecting a
destination path
for the database
backups.

The next window in the Task Scheduling Assistant includes a title box for naming the task and three buttons for the task frequency: Daily, Weekly, or One time only, as shown in Figure 23.12.

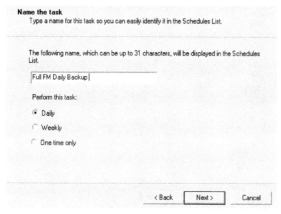

Figure 23.12:
Naming the
scheduled task
and setting a
repeat frequency.

If you click the **Daily** button, the window will change and enable you to choose a start time for the scheduled backup, the frequency of the daily backup, and a start date, as shown in Figure 23.13.

Figure 23.13:
Options for when
a daily scheduled
task should run.

If the **Weekly** button is clicked, the window will change and enable you to choose a start time for a weekly scheduled backup and which days of the week to perform the backup, as shown in Figure 23.14.

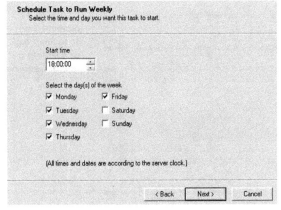

Figure 23.14:
Options for a
weekly scheduled
backup.

Finally, when the **Next** button is clicked the window will confirm that the new task schedule is complete, as shown in Figure 23.15.

*Figure 23.15:
The Task
Schedule
Complete
message.*

The new scheduled task will appear in the Schedules list in the console window of the FileMaker Server Admin application, as shown in Figure 23.16.

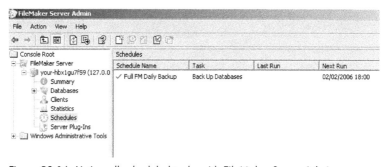

Figure 23.16: Listing all scheduled tasks with FileMaker Server Admin.

The properties of an existing scheduled task can be modified by highlighting the schedule name and right-clicking it, then selecting the **Properties** menu option. Scheduled tasks can also be removed with the **Delete** menu option.

The Database Hosting Assistant

Once installed, FileMaker Server 8 is a relatively easy application to administer. On the Windows platform a set of six configuration assistant options are displayed in the FileMaker Server Admin console. Each of these assistants is designed to make it easy to manage the settings for FileMaker Server.

Creating and scheduling a backup procedure for your business database is one of the most important configurations to put in place after FileMaker Server has been installed.

It is worth investigating the other five configuration assistants and understand how FileMaker Server can be customized for your database deployment needs. While a detailed guide to FileMaker Server administration is provided as a PDF document within the FileMaker Server application folder, an overview of the most important settings to help you host your business database is discussed here.

The Database Hosting Assistant is used to manage how many files FileMaker Server can host and includes settings for optimizing memory management.

Click on the **Database Hosting** option in the FileMaker Server Admin console. A dialog box will appear, introducing the Database Hosting Assistant. Click the **Next** button. The Assistant will display a window in which you can enter the maximum number of FileMaker files that you want FileMaker Server to host, as shown in Figure 23.17. While a maximum of 125 files is possible, specifying fewer files based on the number of databases being deployed in your business will free up more memory.

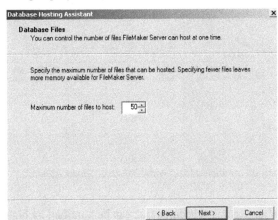

Figure 23.17: Setting the maximum number of files to host with the Database Hosting Assistant.

When you have set a value for the number of files to host, click the **Next** button. The next window that appears enables you to specify the amount of memory to reserve for FileMaker Server's database cache, as shown in Figure 23.18. A high value for the database cache can speed up performance, particularly if large files are hosted for a lot of clients.

The maximum setting is calculated for the server computer based on physical RAM. This maximum setting is a value equivalent to 70% of the amount of RAM available in the computer running FileMaker Server.

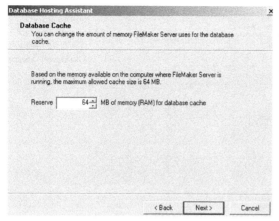

*Figure 23.18:
Setting the
database
memory cache
with the
Database
Hosting Assistant.*

If you click the **Next** button again, another window appears, enabling you to manage the interval in which the database cache is flushed to disk, as shown in Figure 23.19, with the default period set to one minute. You may discover that database hosting performance is marginally improved if the cache flush interval is increased; however, any performance benefit by increasing the period must be offset against the risk of losing unsaved changes to a database in the event of the server computer crashing.

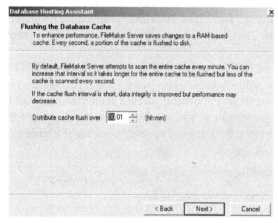

*Figure 23.19:
The database
cache flush
setting in the
Database
Hosting Assistant.*

The final window is used to make FileMaker Server recognize and host run-time database solutions. Runtime Solutions can only be created with FileMaker Pro Advanced. A run-time file will have the file type suffix ".fp7". The edit box, as shown in Figure 23.20, enables you to register run-time file types with FileMaker Server.

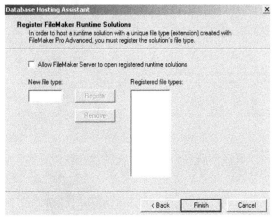

Figure 23.20:
Registering
run-time files with
FileMaker Server.

The Client Connections Assistant

The Client Connections Assistant is used to fine-tune how many colleagues can access a FileMaker Server hosted file using FileMaker client, ODBC/JDBC, or web connections.

Choose **Client Connections** from the FileMaker Server Admin window. When the **Next** button is clicked, the Client Connections Assistant presents edit boxes to control the number of FileMaker connections permitted for Server hosted files. The Client Connections Assistant window is shown in Figure 23.21.

With a standard FileMaker Server license, a maximum of 250 FileMaker client connections is possible. However, setting a number based on how many colleagues are likely to be using the files at any one time will improve server hosted file performance. You should increase the amount of RAM memory allocated using the Database Hosting Assistant if a large number of client connections is set.

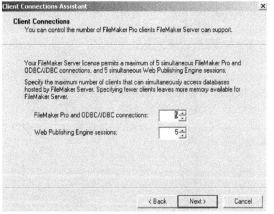

Figure 23.21:
The client
connections
settings for the
Client
Connections
Assistant.

If you click through the Client Connections Assistant panels you will also see a control box to manage idle FileMaker Pro clients, as shown in Figure 23.22. You can set a time limit that is used with the privilege sets in a file that will disconnect clients that have not been actively using a file within that period of time.

Figure 23.22: Managing idle client disconnections with the Client Connections Assistant.

The most important elements to consider after installing FileMaker Server and hosting files using the application have been introduced. It is worth spending some time becoming familiar with the other options available to manage databases with FileMaker Server. All of these features are discussed in the PDF document called FMS8_Admin_Guide, which is installed within the Electronic Documents folder when FileMaker Server is installed.

Opening a File Hosted by FileMaker Server

Any colleagues who wish to open a file hosted by FileMaker Server should select the menu option **File>Open Remote** or click the **Remote** button in the Open File dialog box.

The Open Remote File dialog box will appear as shown in Figure 23.23.

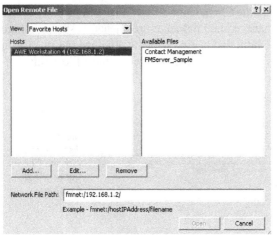

Figure 23.23:
The Open
Remote File
dialog box.

The host computer running FileMaker Server should appear in the left-hand box of the Open Remote File dialog box. If it is not visible, click the **Add** button and type in the IP address of the computer running FileMaker Server in the Edit Favorite Host dialog box, as shown in Figure 23.24.

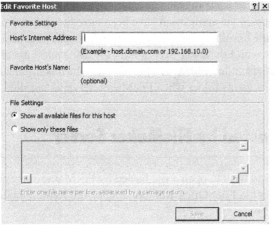

Figure 23.24:
Add the IP
address of the
FileMaker Server
in the Edit
Favorite Host
dialog box.

When the **Save** button is clicked, a list of available files that are being hosted should be displayed, as shown in Figure 23.25. It is possible to hide a file from the list by using the "Don't display in Open Remote File dialog" check box in the FileMaker Network Settings dialog box before a file is hosted using FileMaker Server.

Figure 23.25:
Detail of the Open Remote
File dialog box with the
server highlighted and
available files displayed.

An available file can now be opened, provided that a valid account and password is used.

Provided the IP address of the computer running FileMaker Server does not change in the interim, the next time the Open Remote File dialog box appears, the server should be listed.

The server administrator can send a message to connected clients. A message for selected clients or all clients can be created using the FileMaker Server Admin Action menu, shown in Figure 23.26, when the Client Connections icon is highlighted.

Figure 23.26:
The FileMaker Server
Admin Action menu
appears when the
Client Connections icon
is selected.

A sample message will appear on the screens of connected clients, as shown in Figure 23.27.

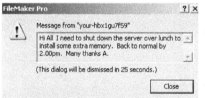

Figure 23.27:
A message to
connected clients
from the
FileMaker Server
Admin operator.

In addition to custom messages, standard messages will be sent to connected clients when a hosted file is closed using the FileMaker Server Admin application, as shown in Figure 23.28.

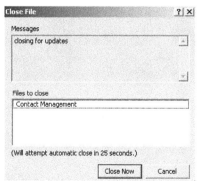

Figure 23.28:
The message
received by a
client when a
server hosted file
is about to be
closed.

If you decide to stop the FileMaker Server service or choose the Stop FileMaker Server option from the Server Admin Action menu, connected clients will receive the message shown in Figure 23.29.

Figure 23.29: A message sent to any connected clients when the FileMaker Server service is about to stop.

Even for a small number of users, your colleagues should see a marked increase in network performance hosting a file with FileMaker Server compared to peer-to-peer file sharing.

Chapter 24

Security Issues

In this chapter:

■ Introduction

■ Accounts, Privilege Sets, and Extended Privileges

■ Managing Accounts and Privileges in a File

■ Adding a New Account to a File and Assigning Privilege Sets

■ A Closer Look at Privilege Set Management

■ Security Checklist

Introduction

The business data that you add to a FileMaker database is usually confidential and often highly sensitive. FileMaker includes a set of powerful security tools to help you manage who has access to the information in a FileMaker file. A series of accounts can be created for a file, and each account has a set of privileges associated with it. The privilege set determines to what degree information within a file can be accessed. Each account is validated by a password at the time that a user opens a file.

It is important to draw up a security plan for a file before the database is made available for workgroup or business colleagues by sharing the file over the office network. The plan should consider how colleagues wish to interact with a file. With FileMaker Pro 8, it is possible to change existing accounts and privileges for a file while the database is being used by colleagues. Any changes that may affect the account and associated privileges of current users will take effect the next time the file is opened.

If you develop a FileMaker database solution that consists of more than one file, you will have to set up accounts and privileges for each file. Access to the data within a single file's tables is managed by the file's accounts and privileges.

Accounts, Privilege Sets, and Extended Privileges

A completely revised method for managing the security of FileMaker files was introduced with FileMaker Pro 7 and continued with version 8. Accounts, privilege sets, and extended privilege sets are used to control access to a database file.

Accounts are used to authenticate persons attempting to open a protected FileMaker file. An account name, with or without a password, is used to validate a user when the file is opened. Once validated, the extent to which the user can work with a database is determined by a predefined privilege set for the account used to open the file.

A privilege set determines the level of access to the file for an account user. A FileMaker database contains three standard privilege sets for the most common levels of file access required: Full Access, Data Entry Only, and Read-Only Access.

As the database designer, you can create new accounts and customize the privilege sets for each account to determine the level of access available for users. You might wish to create an account for every colleague, or have a limited number of accounts that are used by several staff members. The Edit Privilege Set dialog box contains many options to control file accessibility. These include the ability to hide selected layouts, tables, fields, and scripts and restrict printing and record exporting. Extended privileges control the file sharing options and network accessibility for a database, as an additional feature of a privilege set. The Extended Privileges box includes the ability to determine whether an account user can open a file over the network or view the file via a web browser using Instant Web Publishing.

Managing Accounts and Privileges in a File

When you create a FileMaker database, the new file by default contains two predefined accounts: Admin and Guest. The Admin account is not assigned a password when a file is created and the account is given the Full Access privilege set. The Admin account is set to be active. The Guest account is initially set to use the Read-Only Access privilege set and is not active.

The Contact Management database template that ships with FileMaker can be used to demonstrate how file security can be managed. Accounts and privileges for a file are managed using the menu option **File>Define> Accounts & Privileges**. The Define Accounts & Privileges dialog box will open, as shown in Figure 24.1.

The default Guest and Admin accounts are listed in the Accounts tab. A check mark is displayed to indicate that the Admin account is active. The Type column displays the word FileMaker. This indicates that the accounts used with this file are authenticated by the FileMaker file. If you plan to host files using FileMaker Server 8, it is also possible to create external server accounts that confirm an account is authorized using an authentication server such as Apple Open Directory or Windows Domain. This chapter concentrates on the procedures for account authorization using a FileMaker file.

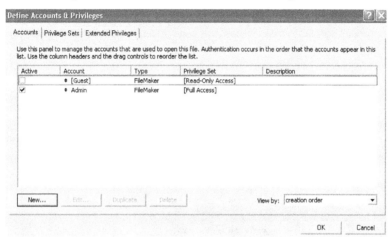

Figure 24.1: The Define Accounts & Privileges dialog box.

Double-click on the **Admin** account and the Edit Account dialog box will open, as shown in Figure 24.2.

As part of the security plan for the file, the Admin account should be given a password. Ideally your password should be eight or more characters in length and contain at least one numeric character. If you plan to publish the file to the web using FileMaker's built-in Instant Web Publishing, it is recommended that you use standard alphanumeric characters for passwords, as other characters may not be interpreted correctly in a browser.

It is very important that you keep a safe record of the account name and password that has the Full Access privilege set assigned. If you lose the full access password for a file, it is not possible for FileMaker or any other third party to recover it for you. Note that passwords in FileMaker Pro 8 are case specific.

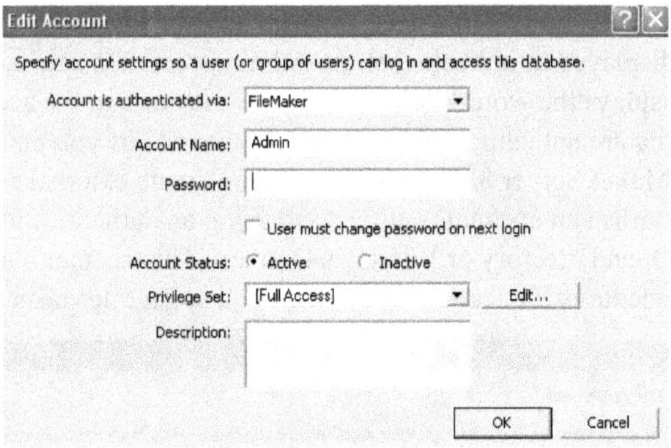

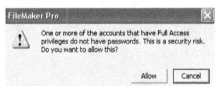

Figure 24.2: The Edit Account dialog box.

New accounts are created by clicking the **New** button in the Accounts tab of the Define Accounts & Privileges dialog box.

If the Admin account is left without a password, or if any other account with the Full Access privilege set assigned is left password free, when you attempt to close the Define Accounts & Privileges dialog box, FileMaker will display the warning message shown in Figure 24.3.

Figure 24.3: FileMaker's warning that at least one account with Full Access privileges does not have a password assigned.

Your security plan for the file may be undermined if you do not assign a password to all accounts that have Full Access privileges to a file.

By default, the Full Access and Read-Only Access privilege sets do not have extended privileges active. Extended privileges are used to manage data sharing options for a file. To modify the file settings and activate any of the extended privileges, click on the **Privilege Sets** tab of the Define Accounts & Privileges dialog box, highlight a privilege set, and click the **Edit** button. In Figure 24.4, the default Full Access privilege set has been customized to include the Access via FileMaker Network extended privilege.

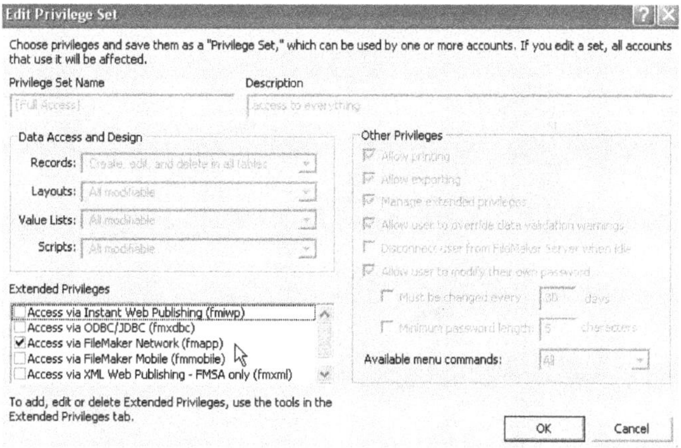

Figure 24.4: Adding extended privileges to a selected privilege set.

As briefly mentioned in Chapter 22, when preparing a file for network sharing, you can also activate the Access via FileMaker Network extended privilege using the Network access to file section within the FileMaker Network Settings dialog box.

Adding a New Account to a File and Assigning Privilege Sets

To create and manage accounts and privilege sets for a database, you need to have opened the file with an account that has the Full Access privileges assigned. Let's use the FileMaker's Contact Management template to experiment with adding new accounts and customizing privilege sets.

Let's suppose that you decide to add a new account to the file for the sales team. Open the Contact Management file and use the **File>Define>Accounts & Privileges** menu option to view the Define Accounts & Privileges dialog box. The Accounts tab should be selected. Click the **New** button, type **Sales** in the Account Name box, and give the new account a password. As shown in Figure 24.5, select the Privilege Set drop-down list, then select **New Privilege Set** from the list.

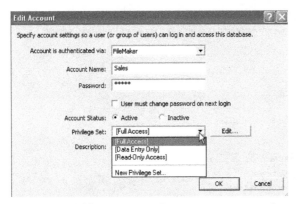

Figure 24.5: Adding a new privilege set to an account in the Edit Account dialog box.

When New Privilege Set is selected from the list, the Edit Privilege Set dialog box will appear, as shown in Figure 24.6. A unique name can be given to the new privilege set and an optional description added if required.

You now need to decide the level of data and design access available to accounts that are tied to this privilege set. You can check which extended privileges you wish to include for the privilege set. The Other Privileges section of the dialog box includes further privilege set customization check boxes. A drop-down list is also included to control what menu commands are available.

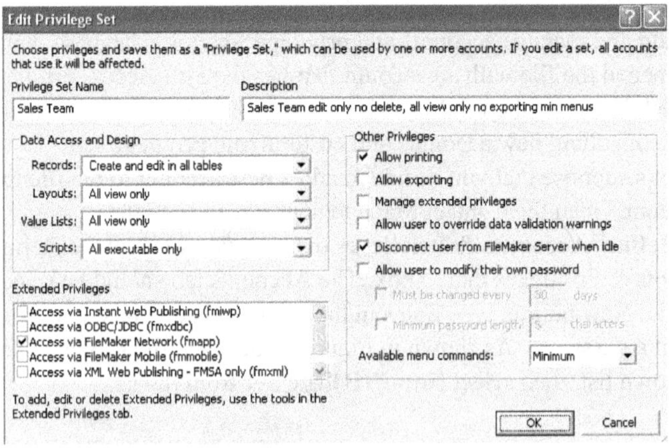

Figure 24.6: The Edit Privilege Set dialog box.

After you have finished customizing the settings, click the **OK** button to display the new Sales Team privilege set in the Privilege Sets tab of the Define Accounts & Privileges dialog box, as shown in Figure 24.7. With full access to the file, you can, of course, change the settings for the privilege set at any time.

The three default privilege sets that are included in a FileMaker database, shown in brackets in Figure 24.7, cannot be deleted. It is also only possible to change their extended privilege settings. They can, however, be duplicated and used as the basis for a new custom privilege set.

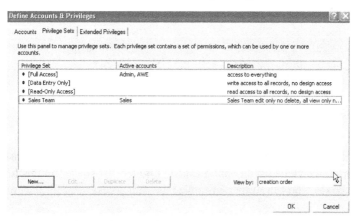

Figure 24.7: The privilege sets listed in the Define Accounts & Privileges dialog box.

A Closer Look at Privilege Set Management

As part of a security and data management plan for a file, it is worth spending some time experimenting with the available settings in the Data Access and Design section of the Edit Privilege Set dialog box.

As an example, with our new Sales Team privilege set selected in the Edit Privilege Set dialog box, select **Custom Privileges** from the Records drop-down list.

The Custom Record Privileges dialog box will open, as shown in Figure 24.8. In it will be listed all the tables in the database solution. You can use the drop-down lists at the bottom of the dialog box to decide which record privileges to activate for the set.

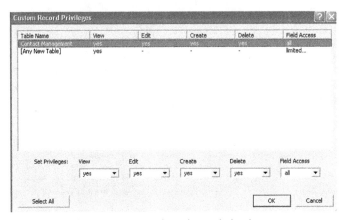

Figure 24.8: The Custom Record Privileges dialog box.

With the sole exception of Create, each of the Set Privilege boxes has in its drop-down value list an option called "Limited." If you select this for any of the boxes, you can further customize the data access rules for the privilege set.

As an example, select **Limited** in the Field Access box. A new dialog box appears called Custom Field Privileges, as displayed in Figure 24.9. Imagine that there is a list of people who have specified they not be called at their home phone numbers. You decide to prevent your sales team from being able to view data in the Phone 2 field by highlighting and clicking the **no access** button.

Figure 24.9: The Custom Field Privileges dialog box.

The same level of flexibility and customization is available for layouts. The Custom Layout Privileges dialog box that appears when **Custom Privileges** is selected from the Layouts drop-down (in the Data Access and Design section of the Edit Privilege Set dialog) is shown in Figure 24.10. All the layouts in the file are listed in the dialog box. You can decide whether or not to allow the layout or records in that layout to be viewed or modified by the currently selected privilege set user.

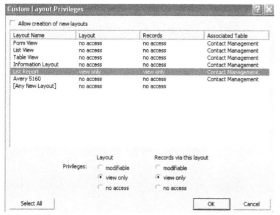

Figure 24.10:
The Custom
Layout Privileges
dialog box.

You can determine whether or not the privilege set can view or modify any of the value lists in the file after selecting **Custom Privileges** in the Value Lists drop-down in the Edit Privilege Set dialog. You can also decide whether users can create new value lists. The Custom Value List Privileges dialog box can be seen in Figure 24.11

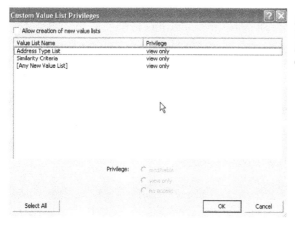

Figure 24.11:
The Custom Value
List Privileges
dialog box.

Scripts can be similarly managed in the Custom Script Privileges dialog box, as shown in Figure 24.12. You can decide whether to let users create new scripts, or if they can execute or modify any or all of the existing scripts in the file.

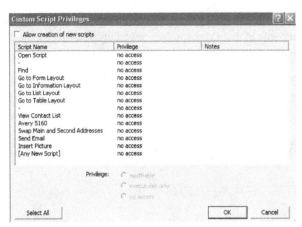

Figure 24.12:
The Custom
Script Privileges
dialog box.

Security Checklist

If you have expended considerable resources in developing an ideal relational database for your business, you should take steps to make sure that your file is secure by using accounts and privileges.

Before you deploy your solution across your office network, or on the web with Instant Web Publishing, it is advisable to assign a password for any accounts with Full Access privileges, decide if any of your colleagues need to access the file to this level, then create a series of accounts with associated privilege sets for colleagues to work with the file.

If you are lucky enough to have interns or students helping you to add new sales prospects to your database over the summer, you don't want them to accidentally delete all records on a Friday afternoon. Equally, if the brother of one of your interns happens to work for a rival company, don't make it easy for your intern to export all your sales records as part of his account's privilege set. I am not trying to instill "data paranoia" in you, but your two most important assets are your staff and your business information. Your FileMaker database is where they should both get along!

Chapter 25

Getting Data In and Out of FileMaker

In this chapter:

Introduction

FileMaker Pro supports an extensive list of file types for importing and exporting data into and out of a database file. In addition, you can also use new features in FileMaker Pro 8 to create a new Excel file or PDF document directly from the File menu. These new saving and sending file options are detailed in Chapter 26. This chapter introduces the data type formats that FileMaker can recognize for exchanging information with other applications.

The import and export capabilities of FileMaker mean that a business database can be populated with records from another application and the database in turn can create data files based on selected records, which can be used in other software packages. This capability means that FileMaker can match how information flows in your work environment. You may receive new price lists from a supplier as a spreadsheet, or an exhibit company might send you a text file containing details on all the delegates who visited your display booth. This information can be imported into a FileMaker table and arranged in the correct field order. On the "downstream" side of FileMaker, you may wish to export sales figures out of FileMaker for a spreadsheet or create a HTML table of standard goods and service prices for your company website.

FileMaker Pro 8 has extended the data exchange capabilities of the application by enabling XML and ODBC/JDBC data sources to be used as the basis for imported data. A detailed discussion of XML and ODBC data importing is beyond the scope of this book. FileMaker can import image or text files in a folder, and any subfolders, as separate records in a database.

The use of each of the import and export file types is discussed in this chapter.

If possible, it is worthwhile to investigate how data is structured and delimited, or separated, in a source file. Your FileMaker file may have organizations and contacts split into two separate tables. It is likely that any commercial data that you have rented or bought from a mailing house will have combined this information into a single flat file or table. You may have to fine-tune your FileMaker file to make the data import run smoothly, or create a script in your FileMaker file to manipulate the data once it is imported into the file. An example of how to do this with data from an Excel worksheet is presented at the end of this chapter.

FileMaker's Import and Export File Formats

Most software applications have their own proprietary file format, including FileMaker with its .fp7 file type, and many include options to enable data to be exported or imported in a standard format.

In addition to importing data into an existing FileMaker database, you can also create a new file using the file types described below. Rather than use the **File>Import Records** menu option, you can choose **File>Open** and select the file type from the drop-down list that matches the source document type.

As you might expect, FileMaker can import records into a table from another FileMaker file and create a new FileMaker database by exporting records using the FileMaker file format. You can only import into one FileMaker file table at a time. Similarly, a FileMaker file created by exporting data will only contain one table. However, you can select fields from more than one table to be included in the list of exported fields.

Most of the import and export file formats support data conversion only and do not import or export formatting such as font, size, style, and color.

FileMaker Pro recognizes and supports the following file formats for importing and exporting with the exception of an HTML table, which is only supported for exported data.

Note that the HTML Table Files and XML Files options are out of the scope of this book.

Tab-Separated Text

If a text file is described as including a tab separator, it should have a tab character separating each descriptive field, and a paragraph character or line return should separate each record in the file. Many applications support the ability to create tab-separated text files. You may want to open the file with a word processor application to check the field structure and to see if the first line in the file contains field names or a data record. The file type for a tab-separated text file is usually .tab or .txt.

Comma-Separated Text

Another very commonly supported data exchange format, a comma-separated text file uses a comma to separate each field value, and a paragraph character or line return should separate each record in the file. Each field value is usually contained within quote marks. The file extension for a comma-separated text file is usually .csv or .txt.

SYLK

SYLK stands for symbolic link format. This is a common spreadsheet format that is used to delimit columns (or fields) and rows (or records). If you are planning on exporting data from FileMaker as an SYLK file and your database includes repeating fields, only the first value in a repeating field will be included in the export file. The file extension for a symbolic link format file is usually .slk.

DIF

DIF stands for data interchange format. It is a legacy spreadsheet file format, where each field is a column and each row is a record. If the DIF file contains field names, FileMaker will recognize and use them for a new table if the source file is opened rather than imported by FileMaker. The file extension for a data interchange format file is .dif.

Lotus 1-2-3

WKS is a legacy spreadsheet format used by Lotus 1-2-3, where each field is a column and each row a record. WKS files are recognized by FileMaker on both the Mac OS and Windows platforms, while WK1 files are only recognized by FileMaker on the Windows platform. Only the first value in a repeating field can be exported as part of a WKS file, and only 240 characters per field are exported. The file extension for a Lotus 1-2-3 file is .wks or .wk1.

BASIC

A BASIC document is similar to a comma-separated text file and is designed for use with Microsoft's standard BASIC language. The file extension for a BASIC file is .bas.

Merge

A merge data file, when exported from FileMaker, can be used as the data source for a mail merge document using Microsoft Word. A merge example is demonstrated in the next chapter. FileMaker can also import the contents of a merge file. All fields are text fields and FileMaker can recognize field names that are included as the header record in the first line of the file. Each field is contained within quote marks, and repeating field contents can be preserved when a merge file is created. Microsoft Word does not at first recognize a merge file exported from FileMaker unless you choose the "All files" option from the File Type list when selecting a data source for a new mail merge. The file extension for a merge file is .mer.

Microsoft Excel

FileMaker can import data directly from an Excel worksheet and export records as a new Excel file. FileMaker cannot export to Excel versions earlier than Excel 97. When importing into Excel, you can choose whether to treat the first row of an Excel worksheet as field names or data. FileMaker Pro assigns an appropriate field type (text, number, date, or time) if all rows in an Excel column contain the same data type. Otherwise, a column's contents are imported into a text field. The file extension for Excel documents is .xls.

dBASE

DBF is the data format for dBASE III and dBASE IV. FileMaker does not support dBASE II file formats. FileMaker is able to include any field name data in a DBF file, which means that you can use the Open menu option to create a new FileMaker database from a DBF file and the field names will be automatically created. Field names, however, are truncated after 10 characters. A DBF file, when exported from FileMaker, is limited to a maximum of 128 fields, a maximum of 254 characters in a field, and a maximum record size of 4,000 bytes. The file extension for a dBASE file is .dbf.

Viewing the Source File before Importing into FileMaker

Before importing data into the destination FileMaker file, if you have the opportunity to do so, it is worth viewing the source file to check for a consistent data pattern. If you cannot open the file with its original application, a text editor should be able to open the file so you can view it. You should ideally make a copy of the source file to open. You can, of course, use FileMaker to check the format of the source data file, but don't use the destination file. Choose the Open menu option to create a new database using the source file data. If field names are supported with the selected file format, your new FileMaker file should include any descriptive field names that existed in the source document. You may then choose to import the new data directly from your new FileMaker file, which can make the import process easier.

It is also possible to view the source data from within FileMaker's Import Field Mapping dialog box. Additionally, imported records can be tidied up and manipulated using scripts once the source data is in FileMaker.

Importing Records into a FileMaker Table from a Source File

Open the destination FileMaker database in Browse mode and select the **File>Import Records>File** menu option. The Open File dialog box will appear, as shown in Figure 25.1. Select the location folder for the source file and choose the appropriate file type from the drop-down list. Then select the source data file and click the **Open** button.

*Figure 25.1:
The Open File
dialog box with
the Files of type
drop-down list
selected.*

The Import Field Mapping dialog box will then appear, as displayed in Figure 25.2. Some important settings are included in the Import Field Mapping dialog box. The target table, into which the source data will be imported as new records, is displayed in the top-right corner of the dialog box. The current table is dependent on which layout was active in the FileMaker file when the import procedure began. The underlying table linked to that layout is displayed as the current table.

The left side of the window in the dialog box shows data in the source file to be imported. The right side of the window lists the fields for the destination FileMaker table. The order in which data is displayed in the left side cannot be manipulated; however, it is possible to click the double vertical arrows to the left of a field's name and move the field up or down in the import target field list. A gray arrow between a source field and a target field indicates that data will be imported into this field. You can click the arrow to toggle it on or off. A red X over the field mapping arrow indicates that the chosen target field is unable to import data.

Figure 25.2:
The Import Field
Mapping dialog
box.

It is also possible to select a new table from the drop-down list that will have the same name as the source file. The new table will also include fields to match the source file field data if fields are included in the file. If field data is not available, FileMaker will create a default field naming convention for the new table of f1, f2, f3, etc., as shown in Figure 25.3.

If you find that your target table has a missing field, you can click the Define Database button to add a field, rename a field, or change the options for an existing field. When you click OK in the Define Database dialog box, the new field will be added to the target fields list.

Figure 25.3:
Creating a new
table to import
the source data
in the FileMaker
file.

The Arrange by drop-down list can be used to assist in deciding the order of the target fields. The "matching names" option is available if the source file has field information. If you are importing data from a FileMaker file or other target document that has the same field names as the target table, using matching names can greatly assist in aligning the target fields in the correct order. Although a calculation target field with the same name as a source file will align correctly, these fields are grayed out as you cannot import data into a calculation field.

The Arrange by drop-down list is shown in Figure 25.4.

Figure 25.4:
The Arrange by
drop-down list.

The three buttons in the Import Action panel of the Import Field Mapping dialog box affect how much of the source data is imported into the target table.

If this is the first time you are populating the FileMaker file target table with external data, you will want to select the "Add new records" import action. All records from the source file will be imported into the target table based on the target field order. Immediately after the new records have been imported into the target table, they will be separated as a found count. This is a big benefit. If you notice a mix-up or an omission in the import field order, you can delete just the imported records in the table and begin the import again.

The "Update existing records in found set" option can be used to update the same number of records that were in the current found set in the target table when the import began. Any records that were not selected in Browse mode when the import was started will be left unaffected. If a larger number of records exist in the source file, these will only be imported if you click the check box labeled "Add remaining data as new records."

The "Update matching records in found set" option can be used to select a match field between records in the source file and the current found set of records in the target table. This might be a part number or a social security number for a personnel database, for example. When this option is selected, clicking the field mapping arrow toggles it between importing data, not importing data, or acting as a match field to update records in the current found set based on source data values. An example to update address and contact details, based on the Company name being matched in the target found set and the source data, is displayed in Figure 25.5. It is important to remember that any records outside the current found count will not be tested for the match. To avoid errors from selecting the wrong group of records, it is important to check that all records in the target table are being browsed by using the Ctrl+J keyboard shortcut.

Figure 25.5:
Updating existing
records in
FileMaker's
found count with
data from the
source file when
the Company
field contents are
matched.

When new records are being added to the file and you are ready to begin,
click the Import button in the Import Field Mapping dialog box. If any of the
fields in the target table have auto-enter options set, an Import Options dialog
box will then appear, as shown in Figure 25.6. If you have a primary key field
in the target table that is based on a unique serial number being auto-entered,
you will want to click the check box so that the new records have a unique
value.

Figure 25.6:
The Import
Options dialog
box that appears
before data is
imported.

If the serial number is to be used, for example, as a unique invoice number,
and you subsequently notice a mistake in the imported records after deleting
the imported dataset, it is recommended that you reset the next serial number
value using the Define Database dialog box to avoid gaps in the number
sequence.

Importing Data into FileMaker from a Folder

FileMaker Pro 8 enables you to select a folder within which any files of a selected file type will be imported as new records into a FileMaker file target table.

Select the menu option **File>Import>Folder** to open the Folder of Files Import Options dialog box, as shown in Figure 25.7.

The dialog box enables you to specify the folder location and whether or not to include files from any subfolders in the data import. You can specify whether FileMaker should select picture or movie files and text files. If image files are to be imported, it is recommended that you click the "Import only a reference to each picture file" check box. This will prevent the FileMaker file size from becoming extremely large, if it has to contain a large number of image files, rather than only storing a reference to the file. You cannot, however, later change the location of the image files; otherwise, FileMaker may fail to display the image.

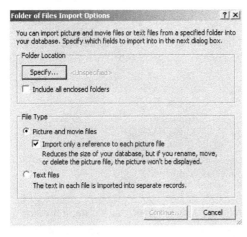

Figure 25.7: The Folder of Files Import Options dialog box.

If you choose to import picture files, FileMaker can import four fields for each image, as shown in Figure 25.8. These are the image itself, the file name, the file path, and an image thumbnail.

Figure 25.8: The four fields that can be imported for each picture file.

Exporting Data from FileMaker

You can choose which records to export from a FileMaker file by selecting all records or only a selection of records in the source FileMaker table. The source table is determined by which layout you are in when you choose the **File>Export Records** menu option.

The list of file types appears as a drop-down list in the Export Records to File dialog box, as shown in Figure 25.9. This list is identical to the list of import file types with the addition of HTML table files and XML files.

Figure 25.9:
The Export
Records to File
dialog box.

Type an appropriate name for the new export file, select a file type from the list, make a note of where you are going to create the new data file, then click the **Save** button. The Specify Field Order for Export dialog box will appear, as displayed in Figure 25.10.

A list of fields for the current layout is displayed on the left side of the dialog. You can add any of these fields to the field export order on the right side of the dialog by double-clicking on the field or highlighting it and clicking the **Move** button. You can also click the Move All button or start over by clicking the Clear All button. A table drop-down list is included in the dialog box. You can expand the list of available fields to include the current table or any fields in related tables. The order in which fields are listed in the export order can be changed by clicking on the vertical arrow to the left of the field name and dragging the field up or down.

If you click the "Apply current layout's data formatting to exported data" check box, the format style for fields in the current layout will be preserved in some of the exported data formats. For example, a custom date field format of 1 December 2004 can be preserved when a new tab-delimited, comma-delimited, BASIC, merge, HTML, XML, or FileMaker file is created.

The Group by window will display any fields included in the current sort order for the record set. It is possible to export summary data by a sort field.

You are now ready to create the new export data file by clicking the **Export** button.

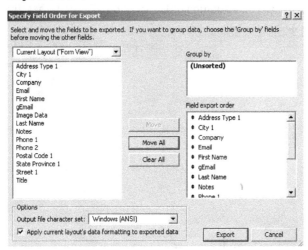

Figure 25.10:
The Specify Field
Order for Export
dialog box.

Your chosen settings for importing and exporting records in and out of FileMaker can be stored as part of a script. The script in turn could be triggered by a button or other layout object if periodic data import or export procedures are required for your business database.

Improving the Format of Imported Data with FileMaker

Most of the file formats that FileMaker can import are based on the column and row format, where each column is equivalent to a FileMaker field and each row equates to a single record. Regrettably, not all applications, particularly proprietary systems, can export report data in a consistent column and row pattern. If this is the case, you can use FileMaker to tidy up the data using ScriptMaker after the inconsistent data has been imported.

In the following example, the custom timesheet application used by a design company produces work done reports for each designer in the format displayed in Figure 25.11. The output data can be opened and saved as an Excel document, with each designer's hours reported in one worksheet. The report has gaps in the data, where the job number and job name are only displayed above the first row for any activities related to a job. Similarly, the client code is only displayed at the start of any job activity records.

	A	B		C	D	
1	The Design Studio Work Done Report 12/12/05					
2						
3	Designer: Jane Eames.	Period: 01/01/2005 to 31/11/2005				
4						
5	Job no	Job name		Client Code	Client Name	Client Ref
6	78956	Euro Bank Corporate Headquarters		CLG	Cross Group	3/65/7/8/9/0
7		24/04/2005	client brief			
8		02/05/2005	More client stuff			
9						
10						
11	46545	Cross Channel Ferry Group		CLG	Cross Group	3/65/7/4/2/3
12		01/10/2005	work work work			
13		07/10/2005	work work work			
14		18/11/2005	work work work			
15		04/12/2005	work work work			
16		06/12/2005	work work work			
17						
18						
19	45782	Megalith Stones Visitor Centre		CLG	Cross Group	4546545454
20		23/05/2005	work work work			
21		11/06/2005	work work work			
22		12/06/2005	work work work			
23		13/06/2005	work work work			
24		14/06/2005	work work work			
25		17/06/2005	work work work			
26		18/06/2005	work work work			
27		23/10/2005	work work work			
28		24/10/2005	work work work			
29						
30						
31	47623	London 2012 Olympic Visitor Maps		CLG	Cross Group	646464656

Figure 25.11: A timesheet system with inconsistent row and column data.

If you wanted to compile timesheet reports for all design staff using FileMaker, you could import all the worksheets; however, there would be large gaps in the data. The designer name, job number, client code, and client name will be blank for many records, but at least the data will have a consistent pattern. For the imported set of records, blank values in a field will need to be replaced by the previous record in the set that has a valid entry in that field. Field data omissions in the imported records can be corrected using a script.

Start by importing the Excel worksheet into a FileMaker destination table. The Import Field Mapping dialog box is shown in Figure 25.12. The import field arrows for all required columns in the source worksheet have been clicked on.

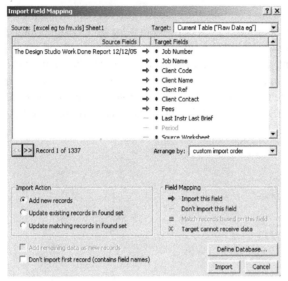

*Figure 25.12:
The Import Field
Mapping dialog
box set to import
the required
columns from the
source worksheet.*

It is apparent from Figure 25.11 that the column headings are always in the fifth row of each worksheet. You can check that the source data will be imported into the correct target fields by scanning through the source worksheet rows. This is done by clicking the left and right arrow buttons below the source data. When row five is displayed, it is easier to align the destination fields to the source rows. FileMaker also displays the total number of rows that will be imported next to the << and >> buttons, as shown in Figure 25.13.

*Figure 25.13:
The fifth row, or
record, of the
source data
displays the
column headings,
which makes field
alignment easier.*

After the **Import** button is clicked, the sample data will be displayed as a found set of records in the destination table, as displayed in Figure 25.14. Even though the data has large gaps and many of the records have missing field values, the same pattern that existed in the worksheet is repeated in FileMaker. The job number value of the third record contains the designer's name and the date period for the report. The fifth record contains the original column headings. Any blank values in the job number or client code fields should contain the same value as the most recent preceding record that has data in that field.

Browse	Job Number	Job Name	Client Code
	The Design Studio Work Done Report 12/12/05		
Layout:			
Layout #	Designer: Jane Eames. Period: 01/01/2005 to 31/11/2005		
	Job no	Job name	Client Contact
	78956	Euro Bank Corporate Headquarters	
		24/04/2005 client brief	
		02/05/2005 More client stuff	
Record:			
3			Case total:
Found:	46545	Cross Channel Ferry Group	Mr S Curtis
1337		01/10/2005 work work work	
Total:		07/10/2005 work work work	
1337		18/11/2005 work work work	
Unsorted		04/12/2005 work work work	
		06/12/2005 work work work	
			Case total:
	45782	Megalith Stones Visitor Centre	Mr. S Conway
		23/05/2005 work work work	
		11/06/2005 work work work	
		12/06/2005 work work work	
		13/06/2005 work work work	
		14/06/2005 work work work	
		17/06/2005 work work work	
		18/06/2005 work work work	
		23/10/2005 work work work	
		24/10/2005 work work work	
			Case total:
	47623	London 2012 Olympic Visitor Maps	Mr. G Dickinson
		25/04/2005 work work work	

Figure 25.14: The found count of newly imported records in FileMaker.

A script can be created to fill in the data gaps. We can use the Go to Record script step to make FileMaker move up and down the newly imported record set, and employ loops in the script to populate blank fields with the last valid entry in the record list for that field.

An example script called "clean up data" is shown in Figure 25.15. The relative order of records in the found count is important for the script and will be lost as soon as the Show All Records option is selected. It is therefore imperative that this script is run as soon as the worksheet data has been imported.

The script starts by going to the third record in the found count and uses the Set Field script step to make the Designer field equal to the Job Number field value in this record. The Replace Field Contents script step is then used to replicate the designer's name in the field for all records in the found count, without the Replace dialog box appearing. The script then returns to the first record and proceeds to delete the first four records, again with no dialog box appearing.

A global field called gJob Number is then used for temporary storage of any valid job number values and is combined with a loop to go through each record and test whether or not the Job Number field has a valid entry. If, when the next record is selected, the Job Number field is empty, the value the last valid job number held in the gJob Number field is inserted into the field. If the Job Number field already contains a value, then this value in turn is inserted into the global field gJob Number, ready to test whether or not the next record has a blank Job Number field.

It is important that any loops in a script can be exited when a condition is fulfilled. In this case, the Go to Record/Request Next script step sets the option to "Exit after last." This will force the loop to end at the last record.

The loop method is repeated to populate missing client code data. If the script is starting to appear too long, you may prefer to create a number of scripts to tidy up each missing field set and then chain them together in a master script that calls each in turn with the Perform Script step.

Figure 25.15:
An example of a
script to clean up
missing data with
values in previous
records.

The cleaned up record set is shown in Figure 25.16. Some work may still be required. A Perform Find can be scripted to search for any records with "Job no" in the Job Number field and delete these records. This will strip column header records out of the table. You can also speed things up by making dependent field contents, such as the client name, be a lookup to the same table based on the client code. You will need to add another table occurrence for this table in the relationships graph and create a relationship based on the client code to do this. It will, however, save adding a further looping script to copy the client name down the list.

Job Number	Job Name	Client Code	Designer
Job no	Job name	Client Code	Designer: Jane Eames. Period: 01/01/2005 to
78956	Euro Bank Corporate Headquartes	CLG	Designer: Jane Eames. Period: 01/01/2005 to
78956	24/04/2005 client brief	CLG	Designer: Jane Eames. Period: 01/01/2005 to
78956	02/05/2005 More client stuff	CLG	Designer: Jane Eames. Period: 01/01/2005 to
78956		CLG	Designer: Jane Eames. Period: 01/01/2005 to
78956		CLG	Designer: Jane Eames. Period: 01/01/2005 to
46545	Cross Channel Ferry Group	CLG	Designer: Jane Eames. Period: 01/01/2005 to
46545	01/10/2005 work work work	CLG	Designer: Jane Eames. Period: 01/01/2005 to
46545	07/10/2005 work work work	CLG	Designer: Jane Eames. Period: 01/01/2005 to
46545	18/11/2005 work work work	CLG	Designer: Jane Eames. Period: 01/01/2005 to
46545	04/12/2005 work work work	CLG	Designer: Jane Eames. Period: 01/01/2005 to
46545	06/12/2005 work work work	CLG	Designer: Jane Eames. Period: 01/01/2005 to
46545		CLG	Designer: Jane Eames. Period: 01/01/2005 to
46545		CLG	Designer: Jane Eames. Period: 01/01/2005 to
45782	Megalith Stones Visitor Centre	CLG	Designer: Jane Eames. Period: 01/01/2005 to
45782	23/05/2005 work work work	CLG	Designer: Jane Eames. Period: 01/01/2005 to
45782	11/06/2005 work work work	CLG	Designer: Jane Eames. Period: 01/01/2005 to
45782	12/06/2005 work work work	CLG	Designer: Jane Eames. Period: 01/01/2005 to
45782	13/06/2005 work work work	CLG	Designer: Jane Eames. Period: 01/01/2005 to
45782	14/06/2005 work work work	CLG	Designer: Jane Eames. Period: 01/01/2005 to
45782	17/06/2005 work work work	CLG	Designer: Jane Eames. Period: 01/01/2005 to
45782	18/06/2005 work work work	CLG	Designer: Jane Eames. Period: 01/01/2005 to
45782	23/10/2005 work work work	CLG	Designer: Jane Eames. Period: 01/01/2005 to
45782	24/10/2005 work work work	CLG	Designer: Jane Eames. Period: 01/01/2005 to
45782		CLG	Designer: Jane Eames. Period: 01/01/2005 to
45782		CLG	Designer: Jane Eames. Period: 01/01/2005 to
47623	London 2012 Olympic Visitor Maps	CLG	Designer: Jane Eames. Period: 01/01/2005 to
47623	25/04/2005 work work work	CLG	Designer: Jane Eames. Period: 01/01/2005 to
47623	02/05/2003 E Preparation for and	CLG	Designer: Jane Eames. Period: 01/01/2005 to
47623	17/10/2005 IR Instructions Received -	CLG	Designer: Jane Eames. Period: 01/01/2005 to
47623	20/10/2005 PREP Preparation for and	CLG	Designer: Jane Eames. Period: 01/01/2005 to
47623	18/11/2005 E Preparation for and	CLG	Designer: Jane Eames. Period: 01/01/2005 to
47623	21/11/2005 BOH Brief on Hearing	CLG	Designer: Jane Eames. Period: 01/01/2005 to
47623	23/11/2005 PREP Preparation for and	CLG	Designer: Jane Eames. Period: 01/01/2005 to
47623	30/11/2005 REF Refresher	CLG	Designer: Jane Eames. Period: 01/01/2005 to

Figure 25.16: After the cleanup script is run the data has a more consistent pattern.

Some script design and testing work is always necessary if you work with imported data that does not adhere to the simple column and row data format. If the source data at least has a consistent pattern to it, with a little thought and perseverance you should be able to tame the data in FileMaker with a script or two.

Chapter 26

FileMaker and Other Applications

In this chapter:

- Introduction
- Saving and Sending Data in Other Formats with FileMaker Pro 8
  - Excel Maker
  - PDF Maker
  - Fast Send
- Using FileMaker Records as Mail Merge Data Source with Microsoft Word
- Using ODBC to Capture FileMaker Data from Microsoft Excel
- Using a Looping Script in FileMaker to Send a BCC Email

Introduction

No matter how effective your FileMaker business database solution, the fact remains that you are going to want to use information that resides in your database with other applications. Clients and suppliers may need a copy of an invoice or purchase order created in FileMaker as a PDF document, or your company accountant might want you to provide an invoice list as a spreadsheet file.

New features built into FileMaker Pro 8 make getting information out of FileMaker and into other applications easier than ever. These features are presented in this chapter. Some of the most common reasons to get data out of FileMaker and into Microsoft Office are demonstrated, together with a basic example of accessing FileMaker data using an ODBC data query from Excel.

Saving and Sending Data in Other Formats with FileMaker Pro 8

FileMaker Pro 8 includes new features that make sending information from a database to Excel or a PDF document an almost one-click operation. You are no longer limited to using FileMaker's Export Records option to extract data from a database into Excel. The File menu now includes a **Save/Send Records As** option, which allows you to choose an **Excel** or **PDF** option. An example for both is described in this chapter using the Contact Management template file. You can also use the **Export Field Contents** option from the Edit menu to quickly send the contents of a field as an email attachment.

Excel Maker

With your FileMaker database open, select the **File>Save/Send Records As>Excel** menu option. A Save Records as Excel dialog box will appear. The file save part of the dialog box is detailed at the top of Figure 26.1. You now have the capability of naming a new Excel file from within FileMaker and choosing whether to add either the current record on screen or all records being browsed to the new spreadsheet file. The check boxes at the bottom of the dialog allow you to automatically open the Excel file, assuming you have Excel installed on your computer, or create an email with the new spreadsheet file included as an attachment.

If you click the **Options** button in the Save Records as Excel dialog box, the Excel Options dialog box will open. This dialog allows you to include FileMaker field names as column headers in the first row of the new spreadsheet and gives you the option to name the active worksheet and fill in standard file ownership fields.

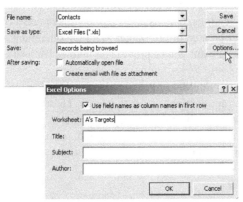

Figure 26.1: Detail from the Save Records as Excel dialog box and the dialog box that opens when you choose the Options button.

The new Excel file, shown with example data in Figure 26.2, will only include data for the record/records selected and will only include as columns in the worksheet the fields that were present on the selected FileMaker layout. Just as you cannot capture Excel cell formulas when you import data from a spreadsheet into FileMaker, only the contents of fields — not any underlying calculation field formulas — are transferred to Excel. For any container fields in the FileMaker layout, a text title for a container field's contents will be displayed in the Excel spreadsheet.

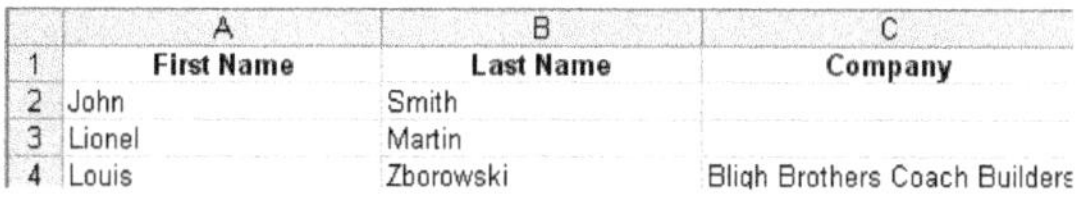

	A	B	C
	First Name	**Last Name**	**Company**
1			
2	John	Smith	
3	Lionel	Martin	
4	Louis	Zborowski	Bligh Brothers Coach Builders

Figure 26.2: Records sent from FileMaker to Excel using the Save/Send Records As Excel option.

PDF Maker

FileMaker Pro 8 contains the Adobe PDF Library, so you can also choose to save and send a FileMaker record or record set as a PDF document. While the Mac OS has included a built-in PDF printer driver for a while, this is a great new feature for Windows users of FileMaker.

Select the **File>Save/Send Records As>PDF** menu option. A Save Records as PDF dialog box will appear. The file options within the dialog are shown in Figure 26.3.

In a similar manner to saving an Excel file, you can specify a file name for the new PDF document and select whether to include all records being browsed or the current record only. In addition, if you click the **Options** button, you can also specify a range of PDF document settings in the PDF Options dialog box, as shown in the lower half of Figure 26.3.

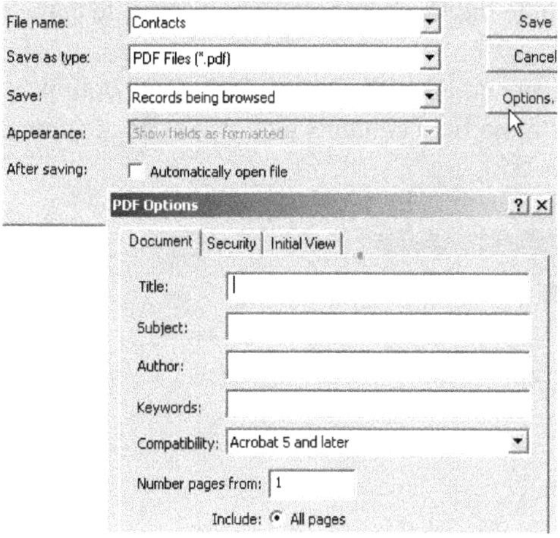

Figure 26.3: Detail of the Save Records as PDF dialog box with the PDF Options dialog box displayed.

After clicking the **Save** button, a new PDF document will be created that will have its page layout based on the selected FileMaker layout. An example document is shown in Figure 26.4.

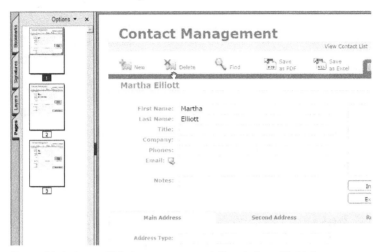

Figure 26.4: A new PDF document created directly from FileMaker.

Fast Send

With FileMaker Pro 8 you can now include the contents of any field as an email attachment directly from within the database. Click into any field in a layout and choose the menu option **Edit>Export Field Contents**, or select this option using the right-click menu. The Export Field to File dialog box will appear. The file name and save options of the dialog box are detailed in Figure 26.5.

You can export any binary data contained in a FileMaker field. It is recommended that you include the file type extension in the File name field for container field contents.

If you click the "Create email with file as attachment" option, a new email will be created with the field contents included as an attachment file.

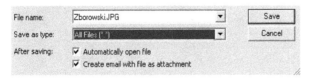

Figure 26.5: Detail of the Export Field to File dialog box.

Using FileMaker Records as Mail Merge Data Source with Microsoft Word

Several of the case studies in this book include examples of how to design a letter layout in FileMaker to write to contacts. FileMaker is a great database application, but inevitably in business you will probably have a reason to write to business contacts using Word. You may want to customize an incredibly complex document using Word that contains graphs, tables, and wrapped text frames, along with recipient information from FileMaker. The following steps describe the procedure to place fields from a FileMaker table in a Word document.

You may want to first sort the target records by a particular field or fields before exporting the records as a merge data file. If you are planning on including a large number of targets in the file, your postal service or fulfillment house may offer a discount if mail is presorted by a postal code or zip code.

1. With your FileMaker source database open, select the target records that you wish to include in the completed mail merge document. Choose the menu option **File>Export Records**. The Export Records to File dialog box will appear, as shown in Figure 26.6.

2. Type a name for the exported data file and choose **Merge Files (*.mer)** in the Save as type box. Make a note of where you are planning to save the new merge file on your computer.

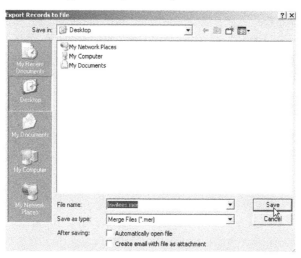

Figure 26.6: The Export Records to File dialog box.

3. Click the **Save** button. The Specify Field Order for Export dialog box appears, as shown in Figure 26.7.

   By default, FileMaker will only display fields from the current layout in the dialog box. You can expand your choice of fields to include in the export by selecting the drop-down list and picking the underlying table for the current layout, or you can select any other related table from the file. This means that fields from more than one table can be included in the merge data file.

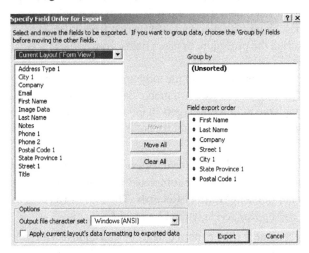

Figure 26.7: The Specify Field Order for Export dialog box.

4. Choose the desired fields and place them in the current sort order, then click the **Export** button to create the new merge data file.

5. We can now switch our activity to creating a letter for our merge document. Launch Microsoft Word and create a new letter document or open an existing file.

6. In Figure 26.8, an example invitation letter has been created and needs to have merge fields added to it for a target name and address. If you have not already done so, save the newly composed letter.

Tuesday, 31 January 2006

Dear

2006 European Car Design School Open Day

On behalf of all the team at the Booklands Car Design School, I would like to invite you to our Summer 2006 Design Exhibition.

I do hope you will be able to come along on the Day.

Yours sincerely

RG Parry Thomas

Figure 26.8: An example invitation letter that will be used to create a new merge document.

7. Your version of Microsoft Word may have the Mail Merge Wizard in a different menu location, although it is usually found in the **Tools** menu, under **Letters and Mailings>Mail Merge Wizard**. When selected, the Mail Merge menu bar will appear over the current Word document with the title Step 1 of 6, as shown in Figure 26.9.

8. In this example we are going to click the **Letters** button and then click the **Next: Starting document** hyperlink.

Figure 26.9: Step 1 of Microsoft Word's Mail Merge Wizard.

9. In the next Mail Merge step, shown in Figure 26.10, click the button labeled **Use the current document** and then click the **Next: Select recipients** hyperlink.

Figure 26.10: Step 2 of Microsoft Word's Mail Merge Wizard.

10. In the third step of the wizard, click the hyperlink labeled **Browse** under the "Use an existing list" heading, as shown in Figure 26.11.

Figure 26.11: Step 3 of Microsoft Word's Mail Merge Wizard.

11. A dialog box named Select Data Source will open. You need to select the merge data file that was created when we exported our chosen records from FileMaker. It is very important that **All Files** is selected in the Files of type drop-down list; otherwise, Microsoft Word will not recognize your merge document as a valid data source file type. This setting is shown in Figure 26.12.

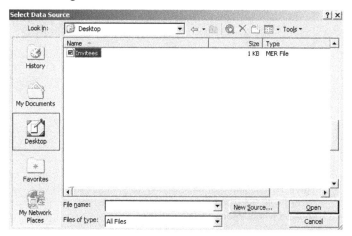

Figure 26.12: The Select Data Source dialog box.

12. With the merge file highlighted and selected, click the **Open** button.

13. In the fourth step of Microsoft Word's Mail Merge Wizard, the option to add merge fields to the document can be triggered by clicking the **More items** hyperlink. This will open the Insert Merge Field dialog box, as shown in Figure 26.13.

14. You may find it easiest to add all the database fields in the list to the document and rearrange the position of the fields once all the fields have been selected. Highlight each field in turn and click the **Insert** button to add it to the document.

Figure 26.13: Step 4 of Microsoft Word's Mail Merge Wizard with the Insert Merge Field dialog box that appears when "More items" is clicked.

15. Your own letter document, with the merge fields added, should look similar to the example shown in Figure 26.14. Click the hyperlink labeled **Next: Preview your letters**.

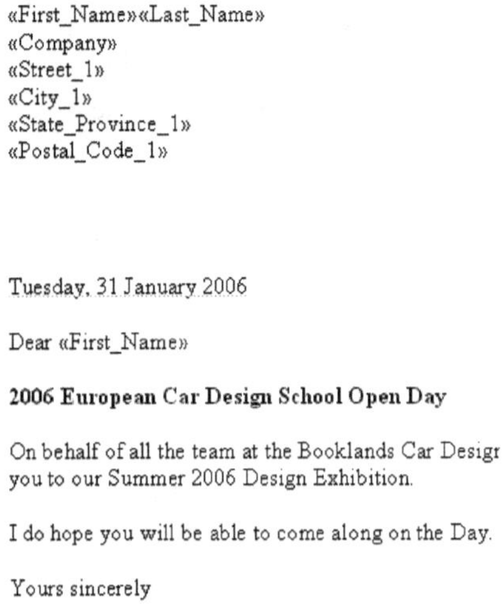

«First_Name»«Last_Name»
«Company»
«Street_1»
«City_1»
«State_Province_1»
«Postal_Code_1»

Tuesday, 31 January 2006

Dear «First_Name»

2006 European Car Design School Open Day

On behalf of all the team at the Booklands Car Desigr
you to our Summer 2006 Design Exhibition.

I do hope you will be able to come along on the Day.

Yours sincerely

Figure 26.14: The letter document with merge fields from the exported data file added.

The merged document can now be previewed on screen with recipient data derived from FileMaker merged with the letter that was designed using Microsoft Word.

An example letter is shown in Figure 26.15.

16. You can use the features available in Microsoft Word to exclude names at this stage, then click the hyperlink labeled **Next: Complete the merge**. You can customize text for selected letters in the merged set. Finally, the completed merge file, which reproduces the letter for every target recipient, can now be saved to disk and printed.

Figure 26.15: The merge letters can be previewed in Step 5 of Microsoft Word's Mail Merge Wizard.

Using ODBC to Capture FileMaker Data from Microsoft Excel

There are three ways to populate a Microsoft Excel worksheet with data that originates from a FileMaker Pro database. The first method is to use FileMaker's **File>Export Records** menu option to export selected data as an Excel file. The second method is to use the new Excel Maker feature to directly create and open a new Excel file using the **File>Save/Send Records As>Excel** menu option. The third method is slightly more complicated and utilizes FileMaker's ability to act as an ODBC data source for other ODBC-compliant applications.

You may have an existing Microsoft Excel file with data set at a particular position in a specific worksheet. This data may be used to populate a chart in Excel. If you have written a macro to create the chart, you are unlikely to want to create a new Excel file every time you want to get the latest sales data from a FileMaker database. Ideally, you will want Excel to capture the latest sales data from FileMaker and overwrite the previous sales data, starting at the same cell reference every time. FileMaker Pro 8's ability to act as an ODBC data source can be used to define a data source query from within Excel.

You will need to install an ODBC driver on your computer that is compatible with FileMaker Pro 8 in order to enable a database to act as the ODBC data source. On the Windows platform the DataDirect 32-BIT SequeLink 5.4 ODBC driver has been tested to work with FileMaker Pro 8.

You may also need to install the Microsoft Query application, which is included in the Microsoft Office suite, if it was not installed as part of a default Microsoft Office setup.

1. The database that will provide the data for the Excel-driven ODBC query needs to be open on your computer. The Excel user also needs to be in possession of a valid FileMaker account with an associated privilege set that has been edited to enable the **Access via ODDBC/JDBC** extended privilege set, as shown in Figure 26.16.

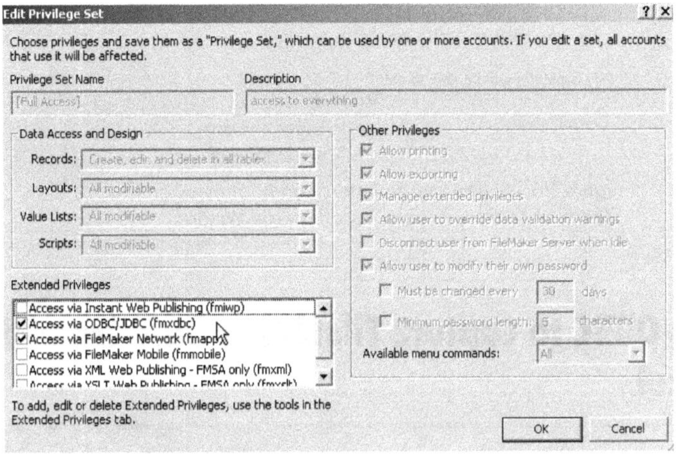

Figure 26.16: Editing a privilege set to include the Access via ODBC/JDBC extended privilege set.

2. You will also need to open the ODBC/JDBC Sharing Settings dialog box to enable access to the target database file. Select the menu option **Edit>Sharing>ODBC/JDBC** to open the dialog box, which is shown in Figure 26.17. You can choose to allow ODBC access to the file for all users or control access via a specific privilege set. If you are using

FileMaker Server 8 Advanced with multiple ODBC sessions supported, this is likely to present a security issue.

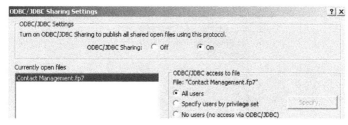

Figure 26.17: The ODBC/JDBC Sharing Settings dialog box with sharing switched on for all users.

3. Open the Excel file that is intended to capture data from FileMaker via an ODBC query, then select the starting cell where you wish to place the FileMaker sourced data. Select the menu option **Data>Import External Data>New Database Query**, as shown in Figure 26.18.

Figure 26.18: The New Database Query menu option.

The Choose Data Source dialog box will appear, as displayed in Figure 26.19.

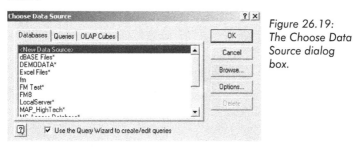

Figure 26.19: The Choose Data Source dialog box.

4. Select the **Databases** tab in the dialog box and highlight the **<New Data Source>** option at the top of the list. When you click the **OK** button, a new dialog box named Create New Data Source will appear, as shown in Figure 26.20.

5. Type a descriptive name for the new data source, such as **FileMaker to Excel** and, from the driver drop-down list, select **DataDirect 32-BIT SequeLink 5.4**.

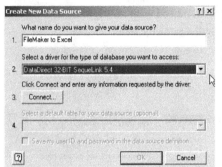

Figure 26.20:
The Create New
Data Source
dialog box.

6. Click the **Connect** button to open the Connect to the SequeLink Server dialog box. Type the IP address for the SequeLink Server Host, which is **127.0.0.1** for local hosting, and type **2399** for the Sequelink Server Port, as shown in Figure 26.21.

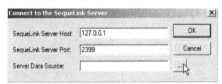

Figure 26.21:
The settings for connecting
to a FileMaker database
using the SequeLink Server
driver.

7. Click the **Browse** button labeled with three dots to test the connection and, if successful, display a list of data sources. In the example shown in Figure 26.22, the Contact Management database is displayed. The space in the file name has been replaced with the "%20" string.

Figure 26.22:
Open FileMaker
files are displayed
in the Server Data
Sources dialog
box.

8. Highlight the file that you want to connect to and click the **OK** button. The Logon to SequeLink Service dialog box will appear, as displayed in Figure 26.23.

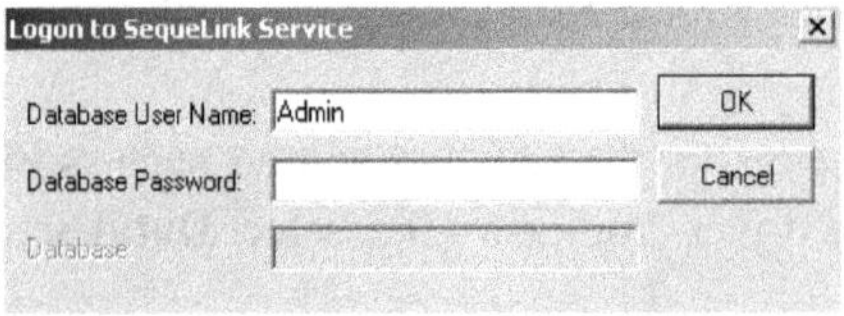

Figure 26.23:
The database account name
and password must be typed
into the Logon to SequeLink
Service dialog box.

9. After successfully making an ODBC connection to the database, back in the Create New Data Source dialog box you will notice a list of tables in the data source file displayed in a drop-down list, as shown in Figure 26.24. Select a table from the list and click the **OK** button.

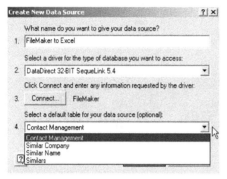

Figure 26.24: With a successful connection to a FileMaker file, a list of tables is displayed in the Create New Data Source dialog box.

The Query Wizard dialog box will then open and show a list of available tables, as shown in Figure 26.25.

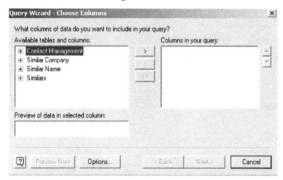

Figure 26.25: The Query Wizard dialog box showing available tables for the data query.

Each table can be expanded to show columns. These are equivalent to the fields in the tables and are shown for the Contact Management table in Figure 26.26.

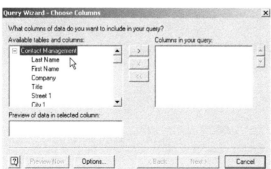

Figure 26.26: The Query Wizard can also display a list of columns in each table that can be used in the data query.

10. You can add all columns (or fields) that exist in a FileMaker table to the query by double-clicking on the table name, as shown in Figure 26.27.

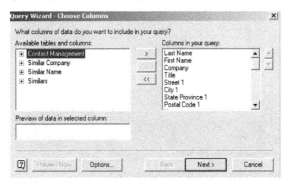

Figure 26.27: All columns in a table can be added to the query by double-clicking on a table name.

11. You can now use the Query Wizard to filter the data that will be extracted from the FileMaker file. This is equivalent to writing a SQL query. In Figure 26.28 the data is being filtered to only include rows (or records) where the City 1 column (or field) equals London.

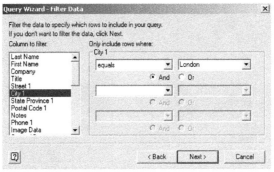

Figure 26.28: The Query Wizard - Filter Data dialog box.

12. If you click the **Next** button in the Query Wizard, a Sort Order dialog box will appear, as shown in Figure 26.29.

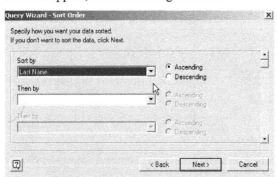

Figure 26.29: The filtered rows are to be sorted by the Last Name column.

13. Finally, when the **Next** button is clicked, the Query Wizard gives the option to return the data to the active Excel worksheet, open Microsoft Query, or create an OLAP Cube from the query. As shown in Figure 26.30, you can also click the Save Query button, which is particularly useful if you regularly want to capture and perhaps chart FileMaker data in the Excel file.

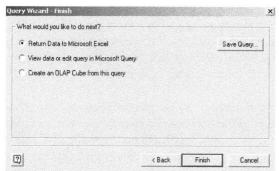

Figure 26.30: The Query Wizard dialog box with the option to return to Excel and save the query.

14. Back in Excel an Import Data dialog box will appear, as shown in Figure 26.31, asking the user to confirm that the data is to be placed in the active worksheet and to specify the reference cell to use.

Figure 26.31: Excel's Import Data dialog box.

For future data queries on your computer, the new FileMaker to Excel data source should be visible in the Databases tab of the Choose Data Source dialog box, as shown in Figure 26.32.

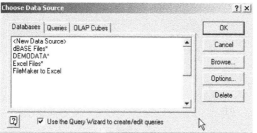

Figure 26.32: The newly created data source is saved for future data queries.

Using a Looping Script in FileMaker to Send a BCC Email

Many of the email workarounds used by FileMaker developers with earlier versions of the database application have been made obsolete by the improved email features of FileMaker Pro 8. The Send Mail menu option in the File menu means that an email can be composed from within FileMaker to include the current record or all records being browsed. The Send Mail option can also be included as a script step. A script can automate the generation of emails, for example, when an overdue invoice becomes over 30 days old.

You may still occasionally have a need to extract a large number of emails from a FileMaker database and have these emails available in a Word document or stored in the clipboard to paste into the BCC header field for an email. You may have composed a complex HTML email in Outlook or another email application and want to paste a set of email addresses from FileMaker into the BCC field.

One method of extracting the contents of a field for many records is to create a new export file consisting of just the Email field. This takes a little time to do. Although each email address is delimited by a tab, comma, or other separator, depending on which file type was chosen for the data export, your email application is likely to want a semicolon character (;) between each email address.

A method that was devised before the powerful Send Mail option became available in FileMaker is to create a looping script that copies all the emails in a found set to the clipboard. You will need to add a global text field to your solution, which will need to be included in one of your layouts.

An example of such a script is shown in Figure 26.33.

The script first clears the contents of the global text field gEmail, and then goes to the first record in the found set. A loop is then begun that will end on the last record in the found set (as part of the Go to Record/Request script step). The Set Field script step is used to update the contents of the gEmail field for each record with a separating semicolon, but only if the Email field is not empty. Some email applications will report an error if the contents of the BCC field starts with a semicolon. Finally, the script copies the contents of the gEmail field to the clipboard for use in the email application.

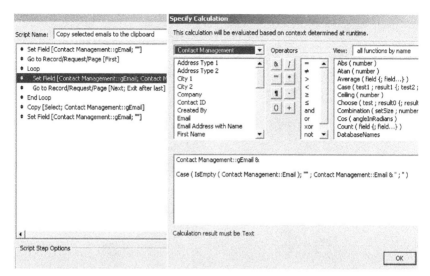

Figure 26.33: An example looping script to copy multiple email addresses to the clipboard to paste into the BCC field in an email header.

It is important to note that some versions of Microsoft Outlook will only accept up to 32 K of text in the BCC field. With semicolon separators, this is equivalent to approximately 750 to 1,000 email addresses.

Chapter 27

FileMaker and Instant Web Publishing

In this chapter:

- Introduction
- Instant Web Publishing Requirements
- Preparing a Database for IWP
- Testing the IWP Connection
- Working with a Database in IWP
- Adapting a Business Database for IWP

Introduction

With FileMaker Pro 8 you can enable others to open and work with your database using a web browser. FileMaker has included a feature called Instant Web Publishing (IWP) since version 4 of the application. Previously, some work was required to prepare a FileMaker file for web publishing. The latest edition of Instant Web Publishing enables anyone with a web browser to access your database, and with very little effort. If you are running your database on a computer with a permanent Internet connection, this potentially means that anyone across the globe can access your file. There are therefore some important security settings that should be considered before a file is shared over the web.

The productivity benefits that IWP can give your business include enabling you and your colleagues to access and update a database from remote sites or while on the move with ever improving wireless network protocols.

There are three ways in which FileMaker data can be published to the web. Besides using IWP, you can also publish fixed or static data from your file to a web page using FileMaker's ability to export HTML tables or XML data. This information, however, will not automatically be updated when records change back in the FileMaker file. The third method is to use the

Custom Web Publishing (CWP) technology that ships with FileMaker Server Advanced. CWP exchanges data using XML with XSLT style sheets to customize the appearance of FileMaker data on a website and capture data submitted via a browser. Ideally, some web development and XML experience is required before implementing CWP to publish a database. This method is beyond the scope of this book. This chapter concentrates on the steps required for FileMaker web publishing using IWP.

The settings required on your computer to start hosting a database on the web using IWP are described in this chapter. Some preparation and planning is required for the FileMaker database to assist web users of the file.

Instant Web Publishing Requirements

To publish a FileMaker file to the web so users can view your data via a browser, the computer on which you are running FileMaker Pro 8 and your business database needs to have a connection to the Internet or your office intranet.

You cannot web publish a FileMaker database that is being hosted by the standard version of FileMaker Server 8. Also, you cannot enable IWP on your computer if it is also running FileMaker Server. In contrast, FileMaker Server Advanced can publish a database for up to 100 web clients, using IWP (or CWP), in addition to hosting the same database for up to 250 FileMaker clients.

The database that you wish to publish with IWP must be open on your computer. Ideally, your computer should have a fixed IP address for colleagues to bookmark in their browser software so they know what address to type into the browser bar to access the file. It is not essential to have a fixed IP address, but you will need to inform any colleagues or associates who wish to view your FileMaker file with a browser of your current IP address before they can open the file. If you have a permanent DSL or T1 connection to the web, even if your ISP does not provide you with a fixed IP address, your IP value should only change if the connection is lost or service is interrupted for a significant period of time. You could even claim to other business acquaintances that your cheaper dynamic IP web service is an additional security feature as the IP address for the hosted FileMaker files keeps changing! For remote work colleagues, you may have to accept that you will receive phone calls from your sales team asking you today's IP address for the FileMaker files.

There are benefits to hosting a FileMaker file with FileMaker Server Advanced. The files can be backed up automatically as a scheduled task using the Server Advanced software, and more files can be hosted simultaneously for up to 100 browser clients in contrast to up to five concurrent users using IWP with FileMaker Pro 8. As an added security feature, FileMaker Server Advanced supports Secure Sockets Layer (SSL) data encryption for data transfer between the web server host computer and the web user's browser.

Not all browsers support IWP. On the Windows platform, IWP has been tested with Internet Explorer 6.0 and Firefox 1.0. For Mac OS X 10.4, IWP works with Safari 2.0 on and Firefox 1.0. Safari 1.1 is compatible with IWP on OS X 10.2, while Safari 1.2 and 1.3 are IWP compatible on OS X 10.3.

Preparing a Database for IWP

To publish your database on the web, you need to enable IWP in the file and determine which accounts can access the file via a browser by changing the extended privileges settings for the associated privilege set.

In this example, the settings for the Contact Management template will be modified to enable browser users to see the file using IWP.

1. Open the file that you wish to publish to the Web with an account that enables full access to the file.

2. Open the Instant Web Publishing dialog box by selecting the menu option **Edit>Sharing>Instant Web Publishing**.

3. With the selected file highlighted, click the **On** button to turn on Instant Web Publishing, as shown in Figure 27.1.

   By default, FileMaker uses port 80 for guest access to the file using IWP. This port may already be allocated on your computer, in which case an error message will appear, advising of the port number conflict and asking you to choose another port number.

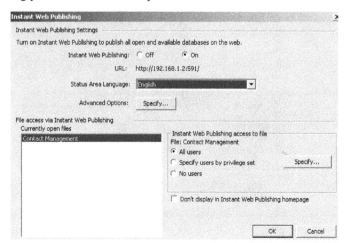

Figure 27.1: The Instant Web Publishing dialog box.

4.   You can specify a port number by clicking the **Specify** button next to
     Advanced Options. FileMaker Inc. has registered port 591 specifically
     for FileMaker web publishing. Type the number **591** into the port num-
     ber box as shown in Figure 27.2.

     There are some useful security features in the Advanced Web Publishing
     Options dialog box. If you want to restrict which computers can have
     browser access to the file over your office network, you can type in val-
     ues for the IP addresses that are permitted to access the file. This feature
     is not so useful for remote users whose IP address will be allocated by
     the service provider, but can prevent users in the workgroup downstairs
     from opening your file. You can separate named IP addresses with a
     comma. In addition, you can type a range of authorized IP addresses into
     the box by using an asterisk character in a section of the IP address, such
     as 192.34.5.* (but not in the first section of the address). You can also
     switch on web logs, which will collate login data in a web logs folder
     within the FileMaker Pro 8 application folder.

     When using IWP with FileMaker Pro 8, up to five simultaneous
     browser clients can access a file. To ensure that the file is available to a
     maximum number of browser clients, you can set a time period to dis-
     connect inactive browser clients. After the preset time period of up to
     one hour, the inactive user will be logged out of the file.

     The Advanced Web Publishing Options dialog box is shown in Fig-
     ure 27.2.

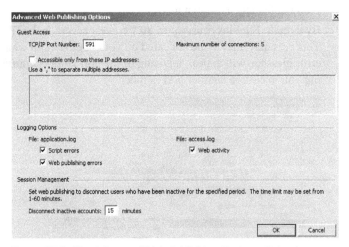

Figure 27.2: The Advanced Web Publishing Options dialog box.

5.   When you click the **OK** button and return to the Instant Web Publishing
     dialog box, you will see the IP address of your computer and, if you are
     not using port 80 for IWP, the suffix port number. Web clients need to

type the displayed URL into the browser address box to gain access to the database.

6. Check that the "Don't display in Instant Web Publishing homepage" option is unchecked at this stage. As you become more familiar with IWP you can experiment with using scripts to open files that are hidden to browser clients on the IWP homepage.

7. You now need to decide which accounts may have access via a browser to the file using IWP. You can click the "All users" button or choose which privilege sets can have IWP access to the file by clicking the "Specify users by privilege set" button.

Before allowing colleagues and associates to open the file, it is a good idea to test how the file performs with IWP.

Testing the IWP Connection

1. If you do not have an Internet or intranet connection on your computer and you merely want to test the interaction of your FileMaker file with IWP, you can open a browser on your computer and type **http://localhost/** or **http:://127.0.0.1/** and press **Return** or **Enter**.

If you already have Windows Internet Information Services (IIS) installed on your computer, or have an intranet or Internet connection to the host computer running the FileMaker file, type in the URL address that was displayed in the Instant Web Publishing dialog box. If you are not using port 80, you will need to ensure that the URL ends with a colon (:) and the allocated port number, such as http://192.167.1.3:591/ for example, and then press Return or Enter.

FileMaker's database homepage should appear in your browser, as shown in Figure 27.3.

2. Hosted files should be listed in the homepage. If you do not see the file you were expecting, go back to the host computer and check that the "Don't display in Instant Web Publishing homepage" option is unchecked. To avoid any display errors, the file name should also not contain any single or double quote marks.

Figure 27.3: The FileMaker IWP database homepage.

3. To open a file on the list, click the file name hyperlink. You will then be prompted to enter an account name and a password before you can login to the file, as shown in Figure 27.4.

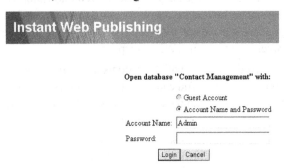

Figure 27.4: The Open database login page.

If the file does not open, you will need to go back to FileMaker and check that the account has been granted access to the file with its privilege set. If the account is accepted, the file will open in the browser window.

The similarity of the database when viewed using a browser, compared to a normal FileMaker client connection, is quite amazing, as shown in Figure 27.5.

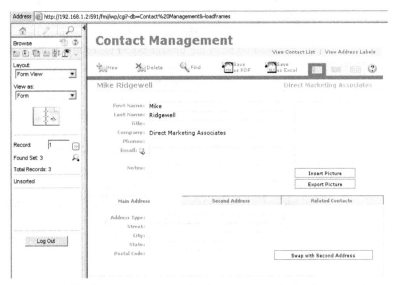

Figure 27.5: The browser presents a database in a very similar format to the way it looks in FileMaker.

Working with a Database in IWP

The IWP Status area that appears in the browser window has many similarities with the Status area in the desktop application. Browser clients can work with the database in Find and Browse modes, and a comprehensive set of buttons needed to work with the database is included in the Status area, provided the browser user's account has permission to do so. You can hold the cursor over a button to see its description.

If your business solution includes an opening script that hides the Status area, a browser user will not automatically see the Status area. Provided the opening script has not locked it, the Status area can be opened in the browser by clicking the left arrow in the Status area boundary bar.

The current mode is displayed in the Status area, as shown for Browse mode in Figure 27.6. The three buttons at the top of the Status area can be used to return to the database homepage or switch to Browse or Find mode. It is important to inform web clients that returning to the homepage with the "house" icon button will not end their session with the database. As far as FileMaker is concerned, that user is still logged into the file via a browser and is taking up one of the five available web client allocations. To make sure that web users quit out of a file, you should encourage them to click on a button in the database that is set to run the Exit Application command or a script that does the same. Alternatively, the browser user can click the Log Out button in the Status area to correctly end a session. As a third option, if the user is inactive for a period of time, your IWP settings can disconnect the web browser client session after the set time limit has elapsed.

Figure 27.6: The IWP Status area in Browse mode.

The browser user can select different layouts with which to view records from the Layout drop-down list in the Status area. It is also possible to alternate the layout view between Form, List, and Table view by using the View as drop-down list in the Status area. As the database designer, you can limit which layouts are visible in the menu and which views are permitted for each layout. With the accounts and privileges option settings, you can also control which records are visible to the browser client based on the client's account and associated privilege set.

If the web client has permission to edit a record and chooses to do so by clicking anywhere on the layout, the Status area will change for editing records, as shown in Figure 27.7.

After changing data in the record, the web client must click either the **Submit** button to save new or changed data to the host computer or the **Cancel** button to abandon any change. The Status area will then revert to Browse mode.

When the **Find** button is clicked, the Status area changes to Find mode, as shown in Figure 27.8.

The icons that are available in the desktop FileMaker application are included in the Status area in Find mode with IWP.

Figure 27.8: The IWP Status area in Find mode.

Figure 27.7: The IWP Status area when editing records.

Adapting a Business Database for IWP

FileMaker's ability to publish a database to the web using IWP with very little preparation and no web programming experience required is a great deployment feature. You may be keen to use IWP to enable one or two remote colleagues, home-based workers, or trusted suppliers and clients to have a controlled degree of access to your database.

Not all script steps that you may have used in the course of developing your business solution are compatible with IWP. Scripts that are linked to buttons and some buttons or other layout objects may not work or be displayed correctly when a database is published to the web using IWP.

You can check which scripts in your FileMaker file are likely to have problems. If you open a script in the Edit Script dialog box, you can check the "Indicate web compatibility" box in the lower-left corner, as shown in Figure 27.9.

Figure 27.9: The "Indicate web compatibility" check box in the Edit Script dialog box.

Script steps that are not web compatible will be grayed out. The Send Email script, which is included in the Contact Management template, is shown as an example in Figure 27.10.

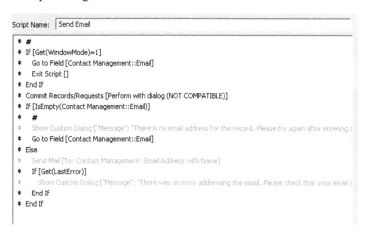

Figure 27.10: The Send Email script will not run for web users.

While it is apparent when publishing to the web with IWP that you may have to forego some of the functionality of your database that desktop FileMaker clients enjoy, FileMaker can give your business a great advantage in being able to make your data available to a limited number of remote workers.

The above has been intended to introduce to you how easily your business database can be published to the web. There is, of course, much more to web publishing with FileMaker than can be covered in this chapter. If you want to include images in container fields as part of your web published solution, for example, you must move the image files to the web folder of the FileMaker Pro 8 application folder on your computer. If you want to find out more about FileMaker web publishing, you can download FileMaker's guides to web publishing with FileMaker and a FileMaker Security white paper from the company's website.

If you decide to publish a database with IWP, be sure to make backups, check the web logs in the FileMaker folder, and pay close attention to accounts and privileges to control how users work with your business data.

Chapter 28

Taking It Further

It is hoped that this book has been able to demonstrate to you that writing a relational database to address your specific business needs is an easier task than you expected.

It is also hoped that the case study database projects, described in Chapters 11 to 21, have given you some practical ideas on how a FileMaker database can be adapted to match your data management requirements.

All the case studies presented in this book can be created using FileMaker Pro 8 or FileMaker Pro 8 Advanced. You may find the additional features and development tools included in FileMaker Pro 8 Advanced are of benefit to you in tackling new database development projects. These include the ability to customize the FileMaker menus that appear when layouts in a file are opened, adding tooltips to layout objects or fields to help colleagues use a database, or generating a comprehensive set of reports for a database using the Database Design Report feature.

If you enjoyed the challenge of designing your own business database, you might now be wondering where to go next. It is likely that as you learn new FileMaker tricks, additional calculation functions, or ScriptMaker script steps, you will find new ways of solving old data manipulation problems. There is probably no such thing as a "finished" database. A good database should be capable of evolving with your business. New ideas generated by you and your colleagues can be incorporated into the solution. You may be surprised how easily the latest management tools and methods for your business sector can be added as new reports for the file. Trade journals often publish benchmarking data for a specific industry. An example for the commercial property and facilities management sector is to compare the cost per square foot and cost per full-time equivalent to run a commercial building. If you know how these indices are derived and the functions and formulas in the equation, it is not too difficult to replicate a similar report with your business data.

As the business or workgroup manager, you may be pleasantly surprised when your FileMaker solutions indicate that the average gross profit on a design job or a print run is above your industry norm. Even if your FileMaker database is the bearer of bad business news, such as your timesheet file indicating that the team spent far longer on a job than previously thought, at least you now have that data to act on and ask why.

You may by now have the "FileMaker bug" if you enjoyed the exercise of defining your database needs, drawing ER diagrams, identifying your tables and fields, and adding relationships between them. Your sense of personal satisfaction can be reinforced whenever clients or supplier representatives visit your office and ask with a hint of envy, "Who wrote your software system?"

If you want to find out how far you can push a FileMaker database, join the FileMaker Solutions Alliance. Details on the FSA can be found on the FileMaker website at http://www.filemaker.com. You might also like to consider attending the FileMaker Developer's Conference that takes place every August. The tips, techniques, ideas, enthusiasm, and networking opportunity of being among nearly 2,000 delegates is incredible and far outweighs the cost of attending.

There may be a FileMaker user group based near you. The FileMaker office for your region or country should be able to provide you with a contact for the local FileMaker user group. Another good source with a list of group contacts on their website is the U.S.-based FMPUG (http://www.fmpug.com). Other FileMaker resources are mentioned in Appendix B.

Of course when all is said and done, FileMaker is just a software application and you still have a business to run. Yet for so many, molding the former to help you manage the latter can be an extremely enjoyable chore.

Appendix A

What's New in FileMaker Pro 8.5

Enhancing Your Business Database with FileMaker Pro 8.5

A new version of FileMaker Pro was released in July 2006. FileMaker Pro 8.5 has some excellent new features that can be used to enhance your FileMaker business database. In addition, FileMaker Pro 8.5 has been optimized for universal binary format in order to run at optimum levels on Intel-based Macintosh computers.

Using the New Web Viewer Control

A great new feature that has been added to FileMaker Pro 8.5 is the Web Viewer control. It is now possible to add a dynamic Web Viewer window within a FileMaker layout. The content of the website displayed in the Web Viewer can be manipulated and updated, based on field data for a given record in your business database.

As an example of how to use the Web Viewer control, we can enhance the way that client location maps are displayed in the FMGlass database that is described in Chapter 15. In the original version of FMGlass, the database designer uses a container field to hold a customer location map. The map is copied and pasted from a mapping website. A script called Multimap was used to open a web browser window, using the Open URL script step from within FileMaker. The URL was defined to be the result of the calculation field called View in Multimap. This calculation field includes the Postcode field in its formula.

With FileMaker Pro 8.5, we can enhance the FMGlass solution using the new Web Viewer control facility. We can add a Web Viewer object to the Client layout, which can be automatically defined to display a location map for each client record, based on the contents of the Postcode field. The steps to do this are as follows.

1. Launch the **FMGlass** file with FileMaker Pro 8.5 installed on your computer. We will need layout access to the database. (A copy of the FMGlass file can be downloaded from www.wordware.com/files/fmapps or www.aweconsultancy.com.) Hold down the Shift key (Windows) or the Options key (Mac OS) as the file opens, and type in the Admin account name and password, which are described in Chapter 15.

2. Click on the **Clients** button in the FMGlass menu layout to open the Client layout, and then switch to Layout mode. Click on the new Web Viewer Control button in the Status area, which is located between the Tab Control and Portal buttons and shown in Figure A.1.

Figure A.1:
The Web Viewer
Control button in
the Status area
when in Layout
mode.

3. Move the mouse to the far right side of the Client layout and click and drag a reasonably sized rectangle for a new Web Viewer layout object. When you let go of the mouse button, the Web Viewer Setup dialog box will appear, as displayed in Figure A.2.

The Web Viewer Setup dialog box includes a selection of default websites that can be selected, along with one or more data entry fields specific to the currently selected website. In the example shown in Figure A.2, Google Maps (UK) has been selected. It is possible to control the content of the Google Maps web page using the Address, City, Postal Code, and Country fields. The Web Viewer control can use these fields as part of the Google Maps URL web address. This enables the exact address location of a client, in this case, to be displayed.

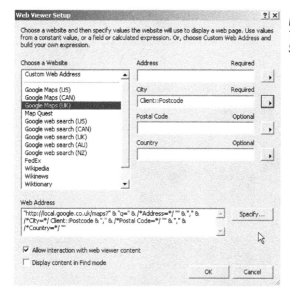

Figure A.2:
The Web Viewer
Setup dialog box.

When the OK button in the Web Viewer Setup dialog box is clicked, the new Web Viewer will be displayed in Layout mode, as shown in Figure A.3. The expression for the URL address is displayed within the Web Viewer layout object.

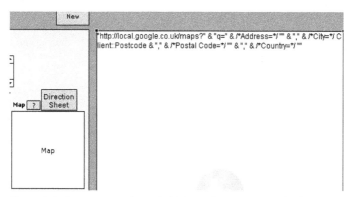

Figure A.3: In Layout mode, a Web Viewer's settings are displayed.

If you switch to Browse mode, and you have an active web connection on your computer, the Web Viewer should display the location of each client, based on the contents of the Postcode field. As you click between records in the database, using the Book icon in the Status area, you should see the contents of the Web Viewer automatically update for the Postcode value in each record. This is shown in Figure A.4.

Figure A.4:
The Web Viewer
in Browse mode.

The Web Viewer layout object can of course be copied and pasted into other layouts. In Figure A.5, the new Google Maps Web Viewer has been copied and pasted into the client's Direction Sheet layout, with the object size set to the same dimensions as the original map container field. This now provides a dynamic client location map to be displayed, based on the contents of the Postcode field. If the client ever moves to a different office or opens a new branch (which can be added to the database as a new client record), the location map will always be accurate and it avoids having to keep copying and pasting static maps from the web into a container field.

Figure A.5:
The Web Viewer
layout object can be
copied and pasted
into the same position
as the original
container field in the
client's Direction
Sheet layout.

Customizing the Web Viewer Further

The new Web Viewer control includes several built-in websites, which are specifically designed to use the information contained within the fields of a FileMaker database. As you become more familiar with it, you might like to add a customized URL address to the Web Viewer for your own business database requirements.

As an example of customizing the Web Viewer, we can add a new shipping tracking feature to one of our own business databases. FileMaker Pro 8.5 already includes the FedEx website in the list of standard web addresses built into the Web Viewer. If you use another company for delivery and dispatch in your business, and your shipping supplier includes an online tracking feature on its website, you can adapt the Web Viewer to interact with its tracking service.

You may already have an Invoice database table that you might wish to add a new field to, called SHIP REF, to record the unique shipping reference given to you by your supplier for one of your orders. A new Web Viewer can be added to a layout to track shipments sent via DHL, for example.

1. In Layout mode, click the **Web Viewer** button and add a new Web Viewer object to your layout.

2. In the Web Viewer Setup dialog box, highlight the **Custom Web Address** option in the Choose a Website panel.

3. Click the button marked **Specify**, next to the Web Address window, to open the Specify Calculation dialog box. In the calculation formula panel, you can type in the URL for the tracking web page, being careful to modify the unique shipping number string within the address for the shipping reference field in your own database solution.

In this example, the DHL tracking URL has been copied from the browser address and pasted into the formula panel of the Specify Calculation dialog window. The field called SHIP REF, which is in the Shipping table of the FileMaker file, has been added to the URL. It is important to enclose the entire URL string within quotation marks for FileMaker to accept the formula as valid, as shown in Figure A.6.

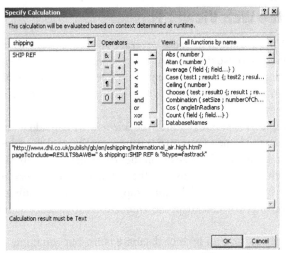

Figure A.6:
The web address for a
DHL website that
includes the SHIP REF
field in the URL.

After you click OK in both the Specify Calculation and Web Viewer Setup dialog boxes, and switch to Browse mode, the resulting Web Viewer control should display a web page similar to Figure A.7.

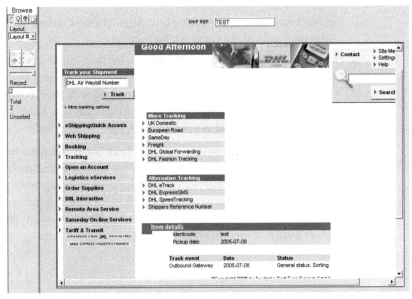

Figure A.7: A shipping tracking web viewer panel that interrogates the DHL website using the contents of the SHIP REF field.

Conclusions

The new Web Viewer is an excellent built-in feature that FileMaker has added to FileMaker Pro 8.5 that enables dynamic web data to be displayed, based on the contents of fields in your business database.

If you are going to enhance the design of your layouts by adding the Web Viewer control, be aware that your colleagues must have a copy of FileMaker Pro 8.5 installed on their computers to make use of the Web Viewer. If a FileMaker file that includes Web Viewer layout objects is opened using FileMaker Pro 8 or 7, the contents of a Web Viewer will not be displayed in Browse mode. If the user switches to Layout mode, an outline of the Web Viewer layout object will be displayed, with the title "<unknown object>," as shown in Figure A.8.

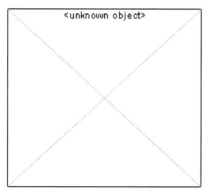

Figure A.8:
When opened with FileMaker Pro 8, a Web Viewer layout object will not work and is displayed with the title "<unknown object>" in Layout mode.

Appendix B

FileMaker Resources

There are few software products that are as actively and enthusiastically supported across the globe as FileMaker.

I would recommend that anyone who is serious about getting into
FileMaker database development, either for their own requirements or to
develop solutions for others, join the FileMaker Solutions Alliance (FSA).
The FSA has over 2,000 members worldwide.

Whether you're an in-house or an independent FileMaker developer,
FSA membership can bring you greater productivity with benefits including
development tools, co-marketing opportunities, and technical support
options. The annual cost of joining the FSA as a Subscriber member, $249
(U.S.) at the time of publication, is about the same as a single FileMaker Pro
license and FSA members receive a copy of FileMaker Pro and FileMaker
Mobile for their own use.

Each of the FileMaker regional offices organize regular meetings for
FSA members. These are a great opportunity for meeting fellow FileMaker
developers in your area, sharing database ideas, and learning new techniques
that can be applied to your own projects. The most important meeting of all is
the annual Developer's Conference, which takes place every August and
attracts over a thousand delegates attending upward of 40 sessions over a
three-day period. More information on DevCon is available at:

http://www.filemaker.com/developers/devcon/

A number of options are available for obtaining help on specific FileMaker
technical issues that are not covered in this book or the manual that ships
with FileMaker Pro. The FileMaker Pro Help system is available by pressing
F1 or choosing **Help>FileMaker Pro Help** when the application is open.

If you have a problem with FileMaker that is not covered in this book or
in the FileMaker Pro Help system, the online, searchable FileMaker Knowledge Base is a great source of reference. You can also get access to FileMaker
technical briefings, downloadable product updates when available, and
registration for your FileMaker product here:

http://www.filemaker.com/support/

If you are based outside North America, you can find more details on FileMaker international websites and regional offices at:

http://www.filemaker.com/company/intl/

A number of websites with associated publications are useful sources for FileMaker tips and tricks:

- *FileMaker Advisor Magazine* — http://www.filemakeradvisor.com/
- FMPug — http://www.fmpug.com/
- FileMaker Developer and Plug-In Directory — http://www.filemaker.com/developers/
- FileMaker small business website — http://www.filemaker.com/ solutions/smallbusiness/

There may also be a FileMaker user group close to you. User groups meet regularly to discuss FileMaker techniques and share ideas and experiences of deploying FileMaker for business applications. Meetings and email discussions are a great opportunity to share ideas and solve database problems. Your regional FileMaker office should be able to pass on the contact details of a user group in your area.

Many of the FileMaker user groups are also registered with FMPug, which has an excellent website that deals with all matters FileMaker.

Appendix C

The FileMaker Challenge

With over 10 million FileMaker units shipped worldwide and nearly 20 years of FileMaker version development, we have yet to come across a business that has not benefited from deploying FileMaker Pro to manage information more effectively.

If you have a business or can think of a business that would not benefit from using FileMaker for data management, contact me and let's discuss your situation. If I can't help you come up with a solution, I will send your example to FileMaker.

I would love to hear from you.

Arthur Evans
AWE Consultancy
211 Piccadilly
London
W1J 9HF
UK

arthur@aweconsultancy.com

Index

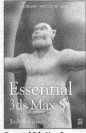